Dr Alan Parkinson is a fo...er teacher, ur......y history lecturer and teacher-trainer. Belfast-.....n, his researc.......ests are wide-ranging, covering areas as div.......s modern Irish.........history, the social history of London, t......na......of political propaga......, the history of schools and their communities and educational research. His publications include *1972 and the Ulster Troubles* (2010), *Friends in High Places: Ulster's Resistance to Irish Home Rule, 1912–14* (2012), and *Charlie Chaplin's South London* (2008). Now retired and living in Devon, he continues to be involved in research projects both in London and Northern Ireland.

ELECTION FEVER

GROUNDBREAKING
ELECTORAL CONTESTS
IN NORTHERN IRELAND

ALAN F. PARKINSON

BLACKSTAFF PRESS
BELFAST

To George, Oliver, Teddy,
Dora and Gwen

Published 2017 by Blackstaff Press
an imprint of Colourpoint Creative Ltd
Colourpoint House, Jubilee Business Park
21 Jubilee Road, Newtownards, BT23 4YH

First Edition
First Impression

A catalogue record for this book is available from the British Library.

Designed by April Sky Design, Newtownards
Typeset by KT Designs, St Helens, England

Printed and bound by CPI Group UK (Ltd), Croydon CR0 4YY

ISBN 978-1-78073-120-9

Contents

Abbreviations

APL	Anti-Partition League
BPA	Belfast Protestant Association
CLP	Commonwealth Labour Party
DULC	Democratic Unionist Loyalist Coalition
DUP	Democratic Unionist Party
ILG	Independent Labour Group
ILP	Irish Labour Party
ILP	Independent Labour Party
INLA	Irish National Liberation Army
IOO	Independent Orange Order
IPF	Imperial Protestant Federation
IPP	Irish Parliamentary Party
IRA	Irish Republican Army
IRSP	Irish Republican Socialist Party
ITUC	Irish Trade Union Congress
LRC	Labour Representation Committee
NDP	National Democratic Party
NICRA	Northern Ireland Civil Rights Association
NILP	Northern Ireland Labour Party
NIWC	Northern Ireland Women's Coalition
OUP	Official Unionist Party (*see also*, UUP)
PBPA	People Before Profit Alliance
PD	People's Democracy
PR	Proportional Representation
PUP	Protestant Unionist Party
PUP	Progressive Unionist Party
RIC	Royal Irish Constabulary
RLP	Republican Labour Party
RUC	Royal Ulster Constabulary
SDLP	Social Democratic and Labour Party
SNP	Scottish National Party
STV	Single Transferable Vote
UDA	Ulster Defence Association
UFF	Ulster Freedom Fighters
UIL	United Irish League
UJWP	Unionist Joint Working Party
UKUP	United Kingdom Unionist Party
UPNI	Unionist Party of Northern Ireland
UUAP	Ulster Unionist Assembly Party
UUC	Ulster Unionist Council
UUP	Ulster Unionist Party (*see also*, OUP)
UUUC	United Ulster Unionist Council
UVF	Ulster Volunteer Force
UWC	Ulster Workers' Council
UYUC	Ulster Young Unionist Council
VULC	Vanguard Unionist Loyalist Coalition
VUPP	Vanguard Unionist Progressive Party

Preface

For many years, I have been fascinated by elections in Northern Ireland and have been increasingly aware – especially from my relatively distant vantage-point in southern England – of the distinctiveness of such contests (both in the types of political parties involved and the issues debated during their campaigns). Much of my previous research has centred around newspaper coverage of political loyalism and politically-related communal conflict, and I decided to undertake a study of several of the most important elections which have taken place in the region over the course of the last century, incorporating the largely contrasting campaign coverage and analysis by unionist and nationalist newspapers.

It is important to stress from the outset that this book does not pretend to be a definitive chronological history of such contests. Indeed, such a task, given the large number of major Stormont and Westminster elections which have taken place during the specified period, would be virtually impossible. However, I do endeavour to provide an overview of the results of all major elections (for Stormont, Westminster and Assembly contests) in an Appendix, and, in an introductory section, I have briefly analysed some of the key characteristics of the region's political culture. This work is however more concerned about giving an insight into the background context of specific elections, the personalities and issues involved, as well as describing the prevailing atmosphere at each contest, mainly through the reports and editorial columns of newspapers reflecting unionist and nationalist opinion (the *Belfast Telegraph* and the *Irish News* respectively).

As stated, rather than tackling this almost impossible task of covering every important election in the region over the course of a century or more, I have instead turned my attention to selecting some of the more significant contests during this long period. It has not been easy to restrict their number to the eight manageable case studies selected here for in-depth analysis. In this decade of anniversaries, when several key events in modern Irish history are being revisited, I have chosen the monumentally important election to the first Belfast Parliament (1921) as one of these case studies. The centenary of this contest – just like the Westminster election which followed the end of international hostilities at the end of 1918 (producing as it did uniquely distinctive results in Ulster, where it was unionists and nationalists who prevailed, rather than Sinn Féin, so dominant in the rest of the island) – is nearly upon us, and fresh analysis of the significance of such contests is timely. Other well-known electoral contests of the twentieth century – such as the "Chapel Gate" Stormont General Election (1949), the "Crossroads" Stormont General Election (1969), and the election to the first Northern Ireland Assembly (1973) – have also been chosen for investigation. Others still have been selected either on account of their uniqueness (such as the Westminster by-election success of a dying hunger striker in 1981 and, five years later, the Westminster by-elections precipitated by mass resignations of unionist representatives), or because they heralded the prospect of potential breakthrough either by parties on the left (such as the threat posed to unionism by the emerging Labour Party at the 1905 Westminster by-election in North Belfast) or by groups associated with Northern Ireland's political extremes (such as the Assembly electoral success of the DUP and Sinn Féin in 2003). The political context of these encounters; the relative positions of the contesting parties; the role played in the campaigns by rival unionist and nationalist newspapers; and the overall significance and legacy of the outcomes of these elections: all of this is outlined in each chapter (these are chronologically organised).

Brief mention must be made of political terminology. I am fully aware that the usage of universally-accepted political terms relating to Northern Ireland is difficult and open to possible misinterpretation. I am also aware of the need to avoid constant repetition of those terms which might be considered acceptable and on occasion have adopted words or phrases (such as 'Ulster' and 'the North') when expressing the respective political aspirations of unionists and nationalists/republicans. Even the term 'Northern Ireland' is not a natural fit for all the contests covered in this book, especially the 1905 North Belfast by-election, although for the sake of convenience this has been adopted in the title. Also, the production phase of this book coincided with the calling of the 2017 Assembly and Westminster elections. Whilst this mitigated against in-depth analysis of the contests, the results and significance of these elections are covered briefly in Appendix 1.

I would like to thank the librarians at the Belfast Central and Linen Hall libraries (especially those in the newspaper section at the former institution), for their help and guidance during the research phase of this project. In addition, I would like to thank staff at the *Belfast Telegraph*, *Irish News*, *Belfast News Letter* and the Public Record Office of Northern Ireland, for facilitating my research and also to the political parties whose statements and manifestos I have referred to in my text.

I am also indebted to several other historians and writers, who have published work related to this study of Northern Ireland elections. I am particularly indebted to Dr Eamon Phoenix for his encouragement and guidance, especially during the initial and final phases of my work. I am grateful to Inez and Ivan Parkinson for forwarding cuttings from local newspapers, especially during the various campaigns between 2015 and 2017. I would also like to thank Malcolm Johnston of Colourpoint Books for expressing interest in this book and, along with editors Susan Feldstein, Michelle Griffin and colleagues, helping it through the production process.

On a personal level, I would like to thank my family for their tolerance and understanding during what has proved to be yet another long-running project. In particular, I would like to thank Janet and Tom for their assistance with a variety of technological issues which baffled this writer, and for their patient proofreading. This book is dedicated to them and to the rest of my family, especially my English grandchildren – George, Oliver, Teddy, Dora and Gwen – in the hope that they might be curious enough to open its pages one day to discover what Papa was actually doing in his study!

Alan F. Parkinson
June 2017

Introduction

"We don't want people to think ..."

Occasionally fiction can appear to be surprisingly more accurate than historical fact. This was certainly the case with Belfast playwright, Sam Thompson's, television play, *Cemented with Love*, which was transmitted by the BBC half a century ago (another satirical, dramatic sketch on the theme of election 'fever' was written and performed in Belfast during the 1960s by local character actor James Young.). Thompson's drama, set in the middle of a bitterly-contested Westminster election campaign, encapsulates several of the characteristics of Northern Irish electioneering at the time, including gerrymandering and voting personation, and captures the typically uncompromising stances of unionist and nationalist politicians, as well as the potentially negative impact of local politics upon family and community life. Thompson, a working-class writer who campaigned unsuccessfully for the Northern Ireland Labour Party (NILP) in South Down at the 1964 Westminster General Election, argued that his play was a parody of "everything that goes on here at election time".[1]

Cemented with Love, which was finally transmitted by the BBC shortly after Thompson's untimely death in 1965, directly attacked the intransigence and shallowness of Northern Ireland's two political "tribes". The play opens in the fictitious northern town of Drumtery, where marching bands herald the arrival of retiring Unionist MP, John B. Kerr, who is hoping to nominate his son William as his successor. The politics of the former, the writer maintains, personify traditional loyalism during the early 1960s. John Kerr told his son:

> We don't want people to think. We want them to vote ... If a sane, sober Orangeman, Protestant or Catholic, started thinking for

himself in this day and age, he'd sooner stay at home than vote for either side.[2]

The son, William Kerr is married to a Catholic as it turns out. He is a moderate and a political visionary, fundamentally opposed to the "no compromise" brand of politics advocated by his father and by his nationalist opponent, Sean O'Bryne. Thompson's play was predictably dismissed as "fiction" by the unionist establishment in Belfast when it first came out. However, it accurately highlighted other peculiarities of northern elections, including the gerrymandering of seats – such as Drumtery, which contained several wards with built-in unionist majorities. Personation was another notorious electoral malpractice in the north, and it too is ridiculed in the play, when a personation "agent", "Nipper" McClure, manages to sell his services to both unionist and nationalist parties. McClure attempts to persuade William Kerr to enlist his help in the forthcoming campaign by pointing out that, "the very corpses in Drumtery, whose names are still on the register, will be voting for you, son, to a man and woman."[3]

Outside observers have often shared Sam Thompson's scepticism about politics in Northern Ireland and have dismissed elections there as being different, almost "alien", compared with those elsewhere in the United Kingdom. They regard such contests as basically encounters between outspoken caricatures of the region's tribalistic, sectarian society, which tend to produce predictable victories for uncompromising political parties.

Yet the evolution of the political system in Northern Ireland is inextricably linked to political change within the rest of the United Kingdom, and, at least in the extension of the franchise and the region's shared participation in national elections, there has been considerable similarity and overlap between the political system centred around the Imperial Parliament at Westminster and local parliaments first established in Belfast nearly a century ago. This part of the introduction looks briefly at the extension of voting rights and changes within the system of voting, and at how major constitutional change and community tension have impacted upon Northern Irish political structures.

Precise information about the nature of nineteenth-century elections in Ireland is difficult to obtain, given the relative dearth of reliable statistics. However, it is clear that a system based on exclusivity rather than democratic involvement prevailed during this time, and indeed well into the twentieth century. Therefore, it was the ownership or renting of land – rather than an acceptance of the principle of equal access to franchise rights – which was the dominant practice. The system was further complicated by the denial of votes to Catholics and of their right to sit in parliament, at least until Catholic Emancipation was conceded in 1829.

Change did eventually come, largely through a series of Representation of the People laws passed between 1832 and 1928. The first piece of legislation extended the vote to many more householders, especially those in the boroughs, whilst further alterations to the Irish franchise system during 1867–8 witnessed a small number of skilled working-class men gaining the vote, as property qualification requirements in Irish boroughs were halved. A more significant extension of the franchise followed in the form of the 1884 Representation of the People Act, which attempted to standardise the voting system across Britain and Ireland, with the vote being conceded to all male householders and lodgers in the Irish counties and to all male householders in boroughs. The next extension of the vote in 1918, following the end of international hostilities, was equally important. This resulted in all adult males (i.e., over the age of 21) receiving the vote, regardless of their property status; the vote was also granted to women over the age of 30, who were either married to ratepayers, or were ratepayers in their own right, but this excluded a large number of spinsters living with their families. In Ireland, the electorate for the Westminster contest in December 1918 rose from 701,475 to 1,936,673.[4] Ten years later, there would be one further major piece of suffrage legislation, with all women being granted the vote on the same terms as men.[5] The electorate went up by nearly a quarter at this point.

The Government of Ireland Act, passed in December 1920, had established a regional parliament in Belfast, which would enjoy considerable devolved powers from Westminster, although it would be ultimately subordinate to the Imperial Parliament in London. The main law-making assembly in Belfast was named the Northern Ireland House of Commons – this initially convened in Belfast's City Hall, followed by a short sojourn at the Presbyterian Assembly College in the city's university area, before a state-of-the-art parliament building at Stormont in east Belfast was opened in 1932. The Assembly was supported by a larger, non-elected Senate: modelled on the House of Lords, this consisted of 126 members, appointed by members of the Commons, sitting for a period of four years. Elections for this new parliament were to be held every five years. It would be composed of 52 MPs,

32 of whom would come from the six counties of Northern Ireland and 16 from the metropolitan boroughs, with the remaining 4 representing Queen's University. (In 1965, this would be ultimately replaced by the creation of new seats in the expanding Greater Belfast districts of Larkfield, Newtownabbey, Lagan Valley and Bangor; the first contests took place in 1969). Additionally, electors could still send representatives to Westminster, though their number was reduced (before Partition, the number of MPs for the nine-county province of Ulster had been 33; this was reduced to 13).

With even the architects of Partition far from convinced that the new parliament would survive the anticipated recommended reduction of its area of jurisdiction by the Boundary Commission, a new, more inclusive system of voting was created aimed at maximising elector choice and involvement. This single transferable vote (STV) method of voting was used for both council elections and for those contests for the new Belfast parliament. It was however abandoned for the local government elections in 1922 and eventually replaced by a pluralist, "first past the post" system for elections to the Belfast parliament in 1929.[6] For the next forty years, the elections to the Northern parliament would be based on contests for 52 single-member constituencies.

In 1972, following the suspension of Stormont, the Northern Irish electorate had to reacquaint itself with the STV voting system for the first Assembly election, in 1973 (see Chapter Five). Although Northern Ireland candidates for Westminster seats would continue to be returned using the traditional system of voting, the STV system would be adopted again for subsequent polls for the Constitutional Convention (1975), European elections, which commenced in 1979, the second Northern Ireland Assembly (1982) and for Assembly elections from 1998 onwards.[7]

⌐

As well as extension of the franchise, other areas of political life in Britain and Ireland underwent considerable reform and change, especially from the late nineteenth century onwards. The Act of Union in 1801 had brought to an end a brief spell of Irish self-government (known as "Grattan's Parliament"), and Irish political representation was transferred to Westminster. However, this did not in itself produce a widening of political access, with tiny electorates choosing candidates from a relatively small number of rural aristocratic families, in an era of open balloting and blatant voter intimidation.

Consequently, the small number of Protestant freeholders who enjoyed the franchise during the first part of the nineteenth century felt pressurised into returning their landlords or their nominees. Yet this did not result in only a minority of Irishmen expressing an interest in political affairs. This period witnessed the populist movements of Daniel O'Connell, agitating initially for Catholic Emancipation (this was granted in 1829), and, during the 1840s, campaigning for repeal of the Act of Union. This latter movement won substantial support from largely disenfranchised rural Catholics in such areas within Ulster as Omagh, Armagh and Monaghan, and provoked low-key sectarian disturbances.

During the last quarter of the nineteenth century, fresh impetus was breathed into Irish politics, with the reforming administrations of William Gladstone. His first administration introduced a fairer distribution of parliamentary divisions and, with the Ballot Act of 1872, established the principle of voting privacy. In Ireland, this reduced the grip which landlords had over their tenant farmers, making the outcome of elections marginally less predictable. As mentioned above, parliamentary boundaries were redrawn, and in Ulster, the 33 allotted seats were divided between those awarded to the nine counties (27 in total) and the boroughs (now six in total, including four in Belfast). Along with this, the total permissible expenses to be incurred by individual candidates was radically curtailed. The most significant change, however, was in the size of the Irish electorate, which tripled following the 1884 Act, with the granting of the vote to agricultural labourers.

The wider question of Ireland's political relationship with Great Britain was subject to considerable scrutiny from Gladstone and subsequent Liberal leaders over a period of some thirty years. The Home Rule question, raised by Gladstone's rapid "conversion" to the cause on the eve of the contest, dominated the 1886 election, resulting in an irreparable split within the ranks of the Liberal Party, and the ultimate fusion of Conservatives and Unionists in Ulster.[8] The 1886 election, like many Victorian and Edwardian contests, was closely fought in Ulster, where deals were struck between Conservatives and Nationalists in constituencies such as Mid- and South Armagh. Of the province's 33 allotted seats, 18 Unionists (including two Liberal Unionists) were returned, compared with 15 Nationalists. The tension surrounding the whole issue of Home Rule and the election itself erupted in large-scale sectarian riots in Belfast.

The threat of Home Rule re-emerged in the early 1890s, when Gladstone's second attempt at introducing a relatively modest measure of Irish devolution was rejected by the House of Lords. Opposition to the proposed legislation in Ulster peaked with a Loyalist Convention and a mass rally attended by 50,000 in Belfast's Botanic Gardens. The election of 1892 followed the declining popularity and rapid demise of Home Rule's leading advocate, Charles Stewart Parnell, and Nationalists experienced mixed fortunes during the elections, with Unionists again winning 18 seats, including Londonderry City and West Belfast.

The early years of the twentieth century witnessed several political developments and events which would have profound repercussions for electors and politicians alike in the north of Ireland. A purpose-built modern party opposing Irish Home Rule, the Unionist Party, was formed in Belfast in 1905 and around this time too, the opportunity of backing the infant Labour Party in the city was rejected by the electorate of North Belfast (see Chapter One). Also during this first decade of the new century, the voice of Irish nationalism was again being heard in Belfast with the election, by a mere 16 votes, of Joe Devlin in West Belfast during the January 1906 Westminster election.[9] At national level, this election proved memorable on account of the return of a Liberal administration, following a spell of thirteen years in the political wilderness. However, Irish Home Rule only became an election issue during the two contests in 1910. The large Liberal majority of 1906 had evaporated and the party was dependent upon the backing of the Irish Parliamentary Party (IPP) – commonly referred to as the Irish Nationalists – led by John Redmond (they numbered some 82 in January and, after the December contest, had increased in size to 84). The nine-county province of Ulster claimed 33 of Ireland's 103 representatives, and these seats were evenly balanced between Nationalists and Unionists (in the January contest, Unionists had 18 members and Nationalists 15, with nationalists gaining a seat in the December contest). Also, a fascinating by-election took place on the eve of World War I. When the Marquis of Hamilton succeeded his father as the Duke of Abercorn in 1913, the seat of Londonderry City became vacant, and an evenly-fought battle between his nominated unionist successor, Lieutenant-Colonel HA Pakenham and the pro-Home Rule Liberal candidate, D.C. Hogg, resulted in a 57-vote victory for the latter (with 2,699 to 2,642 votes).[10] After a twenty-year reprise, the spectre of Home Rule had, therefore, returned to haunt Ulster unionists, and their worst fears were confirmed when the Liberal premier, Herbert Asquith introduced related legislation in the Commons in April 1912. Dependent once again on the backing of Irish nationalists and no longer impeded by the obduracy of the Upper Chamber (the Parliament Act of 1911 had significantly reduced the Lords' powers of delaying or altering proposed legislation), the prospect of an all-Ireland parliament seemed highly likely. Only the tightly-organised resistance movement of Sir Edward Carson, and the support provided by the Conservative Party and large swathes of public opinion in Great Britain, prevented the measure being passed before the outbreak of European hostilities during the summer of 1914.[11]

The post-war election which took place at the end of 1918 promised considerable change across Ireland, where there had been a major transformation in terms of both the size of the electorate and the emergence of a new political climate. In the north, the electorate had nearly trebled, from its pre-war figure of 57,174, to 170,901, with all men now entitled to vote, as well as women over the age of 30 (females now made up 39 per cent of voters in the Greater Belfast area). Politically there had been, of course, seismic happenings in Ireland during World War I, and Sinn Féin achieved political breakthrough in most parts of Ireland following its success in this December contest. However, although the party won 73 seats overall, it fared miserably in Ulster. Despite standing in nine constituencies, republicans failed to have a single representative returned, with Eamon de Valera suffering the ignominy of being comprehensively defeated by Joe Devlin in West Belfast (by 8,882 votes to 3,245), where the incumbent member's campaign promises of tackling wage slavery, unemployment levels and poor housing within the constituency resonated more with voters on the Falls Road than the wider national question being promoted by de Valera. However, despite the success of three Unionist Labour candidates in Belfast seats (in a redistribution of seats, Belfast's share had increased from its pre-war figure of four, to seven), it was the Ulster Unionist Party (UUP) which dominated the election, garnering two-thirds of the vote and winning 23 seats across the province.

⌣

In 1920, British premier David Lloyd George's proposed solution of the "Irish problem" – the Government of Ireland Bill – became law just before Christmas. This measure proposed devolving certain powers to two regional parliaments in Dublin and Belfast, both of which would remain subservient to Westminster. Rejected outright by the vast majority in most parts of Ireland, the new parliamentary arrangements were reluctantly accepted by northern unionists, and the election for the first regional parliament in 1921 resulted in an overwhelming victory for the Unionist Party (see Chapter Two). Although buoyed by their success, Ulster Unionists continued to feel threatened by what they regarded as unstable and hostile neighbours, and also by the belief that Lloyd George's creation of a Boundary Commission, to review ownership of specific border areas, was a back-door mechanism for dispensing with the whole Partition scheme. In 1925, by the time the recommendations of this commission were revealed to be comparatively low-key in their nature, the patterns of parliamentary engagement had already been established. Unionists were convinced of the necessity to maintain power and to remain united in their refusal to accommodate other political groups, reversing the early concessionary offer of proportional representation by the end of the decade. On the other hand, Nationalists also refused to assume the role of a viable opposition in a parliament which they strongly opposed, and decided to pursue a policy of abstentionism towards the end of the 1920s and for part of the following decade. The opportunities to establish normal political dialogue were therefore constrained both by these internal divisions and the perceived threat posed by the government of the Irish Free State. The jurisdiction claims periodically expressed by Dublin, which prompted knee-jerk reactions by two Northern premiers, in calling snap Stormont elections in 1938 and 1949, also adversely affected the chances of normal political debate emerging (the latter election is the subject of Chapter Three).

The long, conservative and politically sterile premiership of Sir Basil Brooke was followed by the more pragmatic and conciliatory approach adopted by his nephew, Terence O'Neill. The latter endeavoured to adopt a more liberal attitude to civil rights issues, but became disillusioned with the opposition from those within the Unionist Party, who were opposed to moderate change; he resigned shortly after the Stormont election in early 1969 (see Chapter Four). The early phase of the modern Troubles witnessed the emergence of new political parties, including those on the right of unionism (the Democratic Unionist Party [DUP], which had its roots in the Protestant Unionist Party [PUP]), the flag-bearers for a group representing the Catholic minority (the Social Democratic and Labour Party [SDLP]), and a party pitching its policies at Northern Ireland's political centre ground (the Alliance Party), as well as the break-up of monolithic unionism and nationalism. The region's own parliament at Stormont was initially suspended and subsequently abolished, and a new legislature, the Northern Ireland Assembly, was briefly established (1973–4), elected under a return to the STV system of proportional representation, which would prove favourable for smaller parties, therefore ensuring a broader sweep of political opinion (see Chapter Five).

For most of the next quarter century, Northern Ireland was governed directly from London, with the electorate expressing its approval or otherwise at Westminster contests.[12] The backdrop of perennial paramilitary violence mitigated against the evolution of a politics of dialogue, instead promoting the obduracy of entrenched positions occupied by right-wing unionism and the SDLP. At the start of the 1980s, the events surrounding the H-Block disputes precipitated the emergence of a political party which had been dormant in the North for many years, Sinn Féin (see Chapter Six). This group had early success in the election for the second Assembly in 1982, and its leader, Gerry Adams, won the Westminster seat of West Belfast the following year. Initially advocating a "ballot box and Armalite" approach, which combined the threat of paramilitary violence and political action, the party enjoyed moderate political success in the decade preceding the ceasefires of the mid-1990s.

⌒

A major change in the region's political landscape took place towards the end of the twentieth century, following the signing of the Good Friday Agreement in 1998, and the electorate's referendum endorsement of the principle of power-sharing. The popularity of Sinn Féin and the DUP within their respective communities increased during this period, though the UUP and SDLP remained the North's most successful parties until the early years of the new century. The first clear-cut signs of political domination by the two parties representing the political extremes in Northern Ireland emerged at the 2003 Assembly election (see Chapter Eight). Since then, the DUP and Sinn Féin have consolidated their support at successive Westminster elections (in 2005 and 2010), and at Assembly contests in 2007 and 2011 – though both parties experienced a slight tailing-off in support at the 2015 Westminster election. The North's political journey, which, against a background of division and violence, had been for so long dominated by one political party, eventually developed into one more associated with political inclusion, although the stated preferences of the electorate continue to reflect a divided community's sectarian fears and prejudices.

⌇

"More of the same"?

For much of the earlier period covered in this study, unionist electoral supremacy was almost guaranteed in Northern political contests. However, despite the unionist landslide victory in the inaugural election to the new Northern parliament in 1921, nationalists would soon enjoy a modicum of electoral success. Although not quite gaining a clear breakthrough in the second contest for the Northern Ireland parliament in 1925, anti-Partitionists still managed to prick the considerable self-confidence of the North's ruling political elite. As with several subsequent contests, the calling of the Election of 1925 was regarded by the Unionist Party's opponents as an unnecessary gesture on the part of unionist leaders, aimed at giving voice to unionist opposition to pending changes being contemplated by the Boundary Commission (this was scheduled to report its findings later that year).

The staunchly unionist *Belfast Telegraph* approved of premier James Craig's decision to call an early election, maintaining it would be: "better for the Government to make the attitude of Ulster on this issue [the border] perfectly clear, and in the most emphatic manner possible, before the Boundary Commission reported, rather than afterwards".[13] Another editorial insisted that people in the fledgling state of Northern Ireland wished to, "preserve our own ideals and our cherished traditions, and we want no other flag but the Union Jack".[14] The *Irish News*, on the other hand, dismissed the decision to call the election, but also applauded the emergent "new organisation" of nationalism spearheaded by Joe Devlin, which was, "now resolved to bring peace and harmony to their ranks".[15] On the eve of the poll, the *Irish News* castigated the introduction, four years earlier, of Partition as "an unnatural expedient", which had merely brought "misery upon all parts of the country".[16]

The rival newspapers concurred in their initial assessments of this 1925 election's outcome, even if their emotional responses were, not surprisingly, very different. The *Belfast Telegraph* conceded that the early results appeared to be "unsatisfactory" – as many as 20 of the 52 successful candidates were from outside the ranks of the Unionist Party, and the government's overall majority had been reduced from 19 to 12. The paper concluded that "many lessons" needed to be learned, including the scale of the electorate's "apathy" (particularly in Belfast and County Antrim), as well as the reasons behind several disappointing results. However, the paper took consolation in the "wonderful" support for the Government party's showing in the border counties, where unionists had displayed, "a more shrewd realisation of the issues at stake than many of the elections in and around Belfast". Despite admitting that results in Belfast had been "disappointing", the *Belfast Telegraph* denied that this indicated "any weakening on the Boundary question in Ulster", and maintained that the crucial outcome of the contest was that, "a Unionist Government [had] once more been returned, thereby ensuring the safety of the Six Counties".[17]

The *Irish News*, on the other hand, believed that the election results had merely confirmed their earlier assessment that James Craig's dissolution of Northern Ireland's first parliament had been "a bad blunder", and had also convinced them that, "the foundations of National Unity [had been] laid on the lines indicated by Mr Devlin and accepted by vast multitudes in the heart of Belfast within the past few weeks".[18] Two days later, another *Irish News* editorial dismissed the Unionist Party's "tame majority", arguing that, "the significance of the reverse [for unionism] must not be minimised, so that careless folk in other countries may be deceived".[19]

⌣

Another characteristic of Northern Ireland elections, especially during the half-century of "Stormont-style" rule, was the all-pervading influence of the constitutional question, which mitigated against the chances of normal political debate being given proper attention. Concern about Northern Ireland's place within the United Kingdom, or about alleged encroachment on its territory by the Irish Free State, dominated the North's parliamentary elections of 1921, 1938 and 1949 in particular. Eamon de Valera had again raised the border question in 1938, calling for a referendum on a new Irish constitution. Reportedly the veteran Northern Irish premier, Lord Craigavon, had come to a snap decision whilst relaxing in bed one morning, to call a Stormont election in response to what he considered de Valera's latest act of "aggression" and imminent Anglo-Irish negotiations in London.[20] Despite the pleas of journals like the *Belfast Telegraph* for unionists to allow Craigavon's Unionist Party candidates to have a "free run" in the election, W.J. Stewart, a "liberal" unionist who was Westminster MP for South Belfast, formed a Progressive Unionist group which was opposed to sectarianism and committed to reducing the high levels of unemployment afflicting the province. The *Belfast Telegraph* was blunt in its condemnation of such an intervention, and warned of the dangers of supporting alternative unionist candidates. A leading article counselled that it was the "imperative duty" of loyalists to "pull together", most notably, "at a juncture when the sacrifice of Ulster is being put in the forefront of the demands of Mr de Valera".[21] Beseeching electors to "leave in abeyance, for the time being, all domestic issues", the paper stressed the need for the North to "show to the world that in her resolutions to be British, Ulster is as resolute as at any time in her history".[22]

Not only did the Progressive Unionists fail to get a candidate elected, but divisions within the nationalist ranks led to a failure to nominate candidates in winnable seats, such as South Armagh and South Down, and anti-Partitionists consequently only managed to return eight representatives to the 52-seat parliament (the Unionist Party had 39 MPs). Two days later, the *Belfast Telegraph* expressed its "profound thankfulness" at the resounding unionist victory and was satisfied that, "Ulster's level-headedness had pulled her through another crisis". However, the *Telegraph* counselled against loyalists being "lulled into insecurity" in the future.[23]

⤿

During the long half-century of Stormont rule, unionist ascendancy was rarely challenged in a serious manner by political parties which supported the union with Great Britain. One of these rare occasions was the Stormont General Election of March 1958, when the pro-union Northern Ireland Labour Party (NILP) dented the self-confidence of the dominant Unionist Party, especially in the Belfast area. With no representatives in the previous parliament, the NILP and other groups opposed to the ruling party were now clearly mounting a serious challenge to unionism. Fifteen parties, including the Protestant Unionist, Republican Labour and Christian Democrat groups, were contesting seats in various parts of the province, presenting a seemingly wide choice to the electorate, and, with over half of the available seats in the chamber not being contested – major unionist figures such as Basil Brooke, Brian Faulkner and Harry West were amongst those returned unopposed – there were a relatively small number of candidates (81) still in the field after the completion of nominations. The *Belfast Telegraph* believed that voters, "had no other choice because of the parlous state of most of the opposition parties and their lack of organisation". This situation, they maintained, was particularly reflected in the "disunity" observable within the ranks of the Nationalist Party, which had "relied too much on emotional appeals" relating to the constitutional position.[24] The *Belfast Telegraph* expressed more sympathy for Labour activists who had made, "a serious attempt to come to terms with the constitutional and domestic issues" and the paper predicted that, "the heavens will not fall if it succeeds in places, now that the Labour Party at Westminster is much more sympathetic to Northern Ireland than it once was".[25] The *Irish News* also commented on the uncontested nature of over half of the parliamentary seats on offer. Noting that the forthcoming election represented little more than "a battle for half a parliament", the *Irish News* compared the nature of the election to those witnessed regularly in eastern Europe. Unionists were, it argued, "returned to power with a monotonous repetition", which failed to provide unionist leaders with "adequate explanation for the return to power of a government [which had] failed in the most pressing of its domestic problems".[26]

⌒

It was this issue – the economic downturn suffered in the region during 1957–8, and its dire social consequences – which prompted significant critical comment in both the nationalist and unionist press at the time. Up to three thousand Belfast shipyard workers were out of work, due to a decline in ship orders and to industrial action, and up to 10 per cent of the Northern Irish workforce was unemployed, at a time when national employment levels exceeded 98 per cent.

The combination of social deprivation precipitated by long-term unemployment, and the apparent reluctance of the unionist administration to ameliorate the suffering of the unemployed and impoverished, especially in areas such as slum clearance, family allowances and the fixing of realistic rent charges, was the subject of analysis by the more questioning *Belfast Telegraph*. The paper's editorials increasingly bore editor John Sayers' qualified stamp of approval for the unionist administration. One leading article pointed out that the government "might do more to make people aware of economic matters, and it might, in this way, promote a better understanding of its difficulties".[27] On the eve of the election, the paper went further, dismissing the view that failing to vote for the Unionist Party meant an individual was being "disloyal". Another editorial praised the merits of voting for the local Labour group, maintaining that it had made, "an honest effort to face the facts of living here", and that there were, "many non-socialists who would like to see some of [that party's] candidates at Stormont."[28]

The *Irish News* was even more strident in its criticism of the unionist government's recent economic record. One headline early in the campaign observed that there were, "48,071 idle in the North", and a subsequent editorial denounced Finance Minister, Terence O'Neill's derogatory references to the southern government's unemployment figures during a television broadcast. The *Irish News* ironically suggested that, in the light of O'Neill's comments, "one would think there [was] no such thing as a workless man in the North". It wryly concluded that, "no bag [was] big enough to hold our unemployment cat".[29]

Both unionist and nationalist journals focused on the changes in voting preferences at this 1958 election. Although describing these as "moderate", the *Belfast Telegraph* admitted that the "outstanding feature" of the declared results was the NILP's success in "gaining four seats at the expense of the Government". The paper's editorial concluded that "bread-and-butter" issues had proved to be "of first importance in these industrial divisions" of Belfast where Labour had enjoyed success, and offered the analysis that such setbacks had been the outcome of "wrong emphases in Unionist policy, unfair aspersions regarding their opponents, and too-exclusive party claims to loyalty and good faith".[30] The *Belfast Telegraph* also referred to panic at such a Labour breakthrough, maintaining that having a small group of Labour parliamentary representatives could make Stormont, "a livelier and healthier debating ground".[31]

Meanwhile, the *Irish News* took some satisfaction in the "shock results for Glengall Street", declaring that the Unionist Party had been "rocked hard on its heels" in Belfast, which, it claimed, was a consequence of "the grave disquiet among former government supporters of the six-county economic situation".[32] The following day, the paper compared the obsession of both loyalists and socialists with the presence of an "army", in the case of the former, in the shape of the IRA (the Irish Republican Army, which had recently been active along the border) and, with the latter, the current "inactivity" of "the workers' army". The socialists, the paper maintained, had exhibited "better judgement". The perspective offered by the *Irish News* differed from the *Belfast Telegraph* in its more optimistic assessment of what appeared to be a poor performance by nationalist candidates (seven had been returned on a total vote of just 36,000), who, the paper stated, had generally "stood up to the battle well".[33]

The ugly nature of civic violence frequently exhibited itself during Northern Ireland's election campaigns, especially those of 1921 and 1973, which will be examined in detail later in this book, and in February 1974, when a series of explosions rocked a wide area of Belfast, resulting in one fatality and three serious injuries, as well as significant damage to numerous buildings. One contest, during which political campaigning directly precipitated a sharp increase in sectarian tension, sparking street disturbances, was the 1964 General Election contest in West Belfast. The Divis Street election offices of Republican Party candidate, Liam McMillan had reportedly displayed an Irish tricolour, thus contravening the 1954 Flags and Emblems Act; the RUC removed the flag on 28 September. This police action had been taken in response to a threat, by a then relatively unknown street preacher, Ian Paisley, to seize the flag, while Unionist Party candidate James Kilfedder demanded that Minister of Home Affairs Brian McConnell "remove the tricolour in Divis Street, which is aimed to provoke and insult the loyalists of Belfast".[34] Despite the threat posed by an estimated crowd of 2,000 republicans, as well as a counter-rally led by Paisley at the nearby City Hall, the police implemented McConnell's order to remove the offending flag, only to see this being replaced by another tricolour.

Serious street violence erupted the following evening, after a further police raid on the Republican Party's office. Liam McMillan wasted no time in despatching a telegram to Labour Party leader, Harold Wilson, condemning the intervention of "armed police using crowbars", who had "smashed" their way into his party's offices "without warning", and asking for his response to "this violence against democracy".[35] Moderate opinion condemned both the decision to authorise the raid on the headquarters of a political party contesting the imminent election, and also the response of that party's supporters. An Ulster Liberal Party spokesman, the Reverend Albert McElroy, suggested that the raid had been "deliberately engineered" by unionists, and that both flags (the tricolour and the Union Jack) were being "prostituted" as "partisan sectarian emblems".[36]

A leading article in the *Belfast Telegraph*, entitled "Ulster's Seamy Side", denounced both the "political blackmail" adopted by loyalist extremists and those who had been responsible for attacking the police in and around Divis Street. The newspaper also called for the "outlawing" of the Republican Party if it "continued to flaunt the state's authority".[37] The paper's editorial maintained that the "guilty men" were those who had participated in an "orgy of blind destruction" the previous evening, and also those in the background who "[did] their damage by the striking of attitudes".[38]

Although the police managed to contain the violence and it had little impact upon the Unionist Party's inevitable domination of the election – James Kilfedder's majority in West Belfast was around 6,000, whilst the Unionist Party won all 12 Northern Ireland seats at Westminster – the incident was significant, both in heralding the arrival on the political scene of the young firebrand, Ian Paisley (Kilfedder publicly thanked him for his intervention), and its reflection of the close links between sectarian passions and electioneering strategies in the city.

❧

The prospect of the election of new legislative bodies in Belfast tended to be accompanied by a cautious optimism about the prospect of political change and compromise. A genuine desire for real change, and a hope that this would be reflected in wider societal progress, was evident in such elections. This was the case with the contests for the first Northern Ireland Assembly in 1973, the Constitutional Convention in 1975 and for the second Assembly, in 1982. The setting up of the second Assembly, which had been implemented as part of Northern Ireland Secretary, Jim Prior's "rolling devolution" scheme, resulted in a number of losses for constitutional nationalism, with Provisional Sinn Féin marking its debut at a Stormont election and gaining five seats and over 10 per cent of all first-preference votes. This Assembly quickly degenerated into a forum ruled by factional disputes and chaos, and direct rule was soon restored to Northern Ireland. By the late 1990s the, albeit tenuous, Peace Process, which had resulted in the Provisional IRA and loyalist ceasefires, had been followed by the signing of the pivotal Good Friday Agreement in 1998. A referendum soon followed in April, producing a clear majority backing (71.1 per cent, and 676,966 votes) for the Belfast Agreement, with fewer than 29 per cent (or 274,879 voters) expressing their opposition. The subsequently proposed Assembly would again be elected by the STV system of proportional representation, with its total complement of 108 MLAs emanating from six member groups of representatives being returned in each of the province's 18 Westminster divisions.

The rival newspapers, in their distinctive manner, welcomed both the Good Friday Agreement and the prospect of a new Assembly. The *Belfast Telegraph*'s editorial, a few days before polling, urged its readers to "turn the page of history [by] voting for the future", and reminded them that those who had expressed their support for the recent Agreement had to "follow through by backing pro-Agreement parties". The newspaper's main message was that voters should reflect more on the long-term prosperity of their children and grandchildren, rather than their personal, short-term political preferences. Describing the election as potentially being "a real turning point" for the region, the paper's editorial continued:

> This election creates an opportunity for Northern Ireland to rule a line under 30 years of violence and begin the healing process. We have lived in the shadow of the gunman and of sectarian attitudes for too long, with disastrous results for our society. Neither terrorism nor bigotry will disappear overnight, but in time they can be marginalised by the democratic process. If politicians are seen to be working together, a new spirit of harmony will pervade the wider community.[39]

The *Irish News* acknowledged that the Assembly election campaign had been a "dull" one, largely on account of the "overkill" factor produced by the recent referendum debate. However, the paper also stressed the importance of maintaining peace, which they argued would be "best achieved by the return of an elected assembly in Northern Ireland, working hand in hand with cross-border bodies and the new British-Irish relationship". The paper also reminded its readership that it was "essential" for voters to exercise their right to the franchise by, "doing so in a way which ensures that pro-Agreement candidates are returned".[40] A previous editorial had denounced the "wrecking" tactics of Ian Paisley's DUP group, but more significantly, the *Irish News* denounced Sinn Féin for its "monumental error" in counselling supporters against backing pro-Agreement unionists, suggesting that such advice actually "reinforced rather than reduced the sectarian nature of politics on this island".[41]

Despite an inevitably low poll (68.7 per cent of those qualified to vote), the results broadly endorsed the verdict of pollsters in the referendum. Anti-Agreement parties won 28 seats which, although reflecting a minority even within the unionist community, still constituted from a Westminster perspective a worryingly large minority of opposition.[42] The UUP (with 28 seats) and the SDLP (with 24) maintained their "top dog" status within their respective communities, but there were also strong performances from the DUP (20 seats) and Sinn Féin (18), whilst the proportional representation voting system had also been kind to the smaller parties, which together returned a sixth of the Assembly's representatives (18 seats).

The *Belfast Telegraph* was bullish in its post-election verdict. Depicting it as "a red-letter day for the people of these islands", the paper claimed that Northern Ireland now found itself "on the threshold of a new era of co-operation". The paper warned however that, although "an opportunity to turn dreams into reality" had been presented, the province's future depended "on whether people are prepared to grasp it".[43] The *Irish News* also combined caution with optimism in its assessment of the Assembly election's outcome. Warning that "the hardest task [was] still to come", the paper took satisfaction in results which had proved to be, "an enormous endorsement" for the "enlightened" party leaders, John Hume and David Trimble, who had "emerged as the leaders of a new nationalism and a new unionism". The editorial's positive tone concluded by pointing out that the dual victory of pro-Agreement parties in referendum and Assembly election meant that they could "now move forward, secure that their faith in the Agreement is shared by the vast majority of their fellow citizens".[44]

Despite the charges of Northern Ireland's failure to embrace political change, it would be churlish to deny significant, more recent, switches amongst voters' preferences, as well as seismic moves in the balance of power wielded by the respective parties. In addition, the nature of electoral debate has also been subject to radical change, as illustrated in the 2015 Westminster election, although these shifts were tempered by the conservative, ultra-religious nature of Northern Irish society. Certainly, there seemed to be a desire on the part of most groups to widen the range of issues for discussion during that campaign. Therefore, rather than restricting debate to the normally infertile pastures of Northern Ireland's constitutional position, new topics generated considerable interest during the month-long campaign. These included the issues of welfare reform and so-called "austerity" measures (strongly opposed by Sinn Féin and the SDLP); increased investment in the province (Ian Paisley Jnr had called for a £1 billion post-election package for the region); improved mental health provision (advocated by the UUP); the reduction of VAT rates on businesses linked to tourism, in order to foster competition with the Irish Republic (put forward by the DUP); and a demand articulated most passionately by those left-of-centre parties for an overhaul of the region's social conservatism (particularly with regard to the issues of gay marriage and abortion).[45] Unbending personal religious convictions meant that leading political figures appeared to disagree with their parties' respective positions on these moral questions – among these were UUP leader, Mike Nesbitt, Alban Maginness of the SDLP, and several other figures in the main parties. However, over the issue of gay marriage, the heat was predominantly on the DUP, especially in the light of the recent resignation of the party's Health Minister, Jim Wells, after he had publicly linked gay relationships to child abuse. One journalist, Fionola Meredith, denounced the "anti-gay mania" amongst the ranks of the province's main party, where "repressed homophobia" would soon prove to be "an election liability, not a rallying call or a badge of Biblical honour".[46]

Notwithstanding this apparent broadening in the subjects for debate, the 2015 contest in Northern Ireland remained peripheral and almost alien in its nature to what was occurring elsewhere in the United Kingdom. Yet newspapers, both in Great Britain and Northern Ireland, agreed on the likelihood of a pivotal role awaiting the DUP's anticipated small group of Westminster MPs, in the likely event of a "hung" parliament. Talk of David Cameron being forced into playing the "Orange card", much in the same way as senior Tory figures of the past (such as Randolph Churchill and Andrew Bonar Law) had done, dominated national background analysis of the contest going on across the Irish Sea. Halfway through the campaign, *The Times* maintained that, "the level of success enjoyed by the DUP will have a considerable impact on the construction of a Conservative-led coalition or alliance".[47] The *Belfast Telegraph*, although not a natural bedfellow of the DUP, was, however, not exactly condemnatory of the party's blatant attempts to "wring concessions out of Westminster". Indeed, the newspaper was more critical of David Cameron for the "very fleeting" amount of time he had spent electioneering in the province, and argued it would be "ironic" if he was to "find himself spending a lot more time in the company of Northern Ireland MPs after the election, having brushed them aside before the poll".[48]

The *Belfast Telegraph* had been even harsher in an editorial a few days beforehand, condemning the absence of Northern Irish political representatives from the leaders' televised debate which had been shown the previous evening. Claiming Northern Irish electors had been "denied a voice in the national debate" by the BBC's refusal to invite the leader of the province's largest party (Peter Robinson of the DUP) to take part, the paper pointed out that local parties had considerably more parliamentary representation than some of the parties which had been invited to participate in the debate. The *Belfast Telegraph* argued that the BBC's refusal to invite Northern Ireland political leaders "defie[d] logic", and the leader went on:

> Northern Ireland politicians – and a fair number of the public – are often accused of being paranoid, but this shambles of a debate could certainly feed into that feeling of coming from a place apart. We are a part of the United Kingdom, yet our politicians are treated as if they were boisterous schoolboys to be shunted out of sight while the grown-ups discuss important matters of state.[49]

The *Irish News* also closely monitored the DUP's plans to exploit a potentially unstable political situation at Westminster. Reporting Peter Robinson's statement that his party would, in the event of a hung parliament, "demand a commission on the Union", the paper reminded its readers that, in the light of the likely electoral success of the Scottish Nationalist Party (SNP), the DUP was, "quite right to be concerned about the future of the Union", and that the "jingoistic unionism" of Peter Robinson's party, which was "based on religious fundamentalism" was "anathema to many secular twenty-first-century Britons".[50]

As noted elsewhere, the results of the 2015 contest delivered a number of shocks, including the narrow victories of a resurgent UUP in South Antrim and Fermanagh & South Tyrone. Unionist pacts in a number of seats – such as the UUP and DUP agreeing not to put up rival candidates in certain constituencies – were primarily responsible for the UUP victories of Danny Kinahan (South Antrim) and former party leader, Tom Elliott (Fermanagh & South Tyrone), as well as the DUP's Nigel Dodds' retention of his North Belfast seat. The other interesting feature of these contests was their acrimonious nature, which was especially evident in the virulent language displayed, particularly by successful DUP candidates in their acceptance speeches. In his North Belfast victory speech, a "furious" Nigel Dodds "blasted" Sinn Féin for its "dirty" battle, whilst his East Belfast colleague, Gavin Robinson delivered a "furious tirade" against his "untrustworthy" Alliance Party predecessor, Naomi Long, describing her spell at Westminster as "five frustrating, long years".[51]

The election had resulted in the return of 2 UUP MPs, with the DUP again collecting 8 seats, the SDLP 3 seats and Sinn Féin 4 seats while independent unionist, Lady Sylvia Hermon retained North Down. On the surface, at least, there were few obvious changes (apart from Sinn Féin losing a seat), but there were other ramifications of these results at both local and national level. As well as the phenomenon of what appeared to be an Ulster Unionist Party revival, press comment turned to apparent electoral apathy on the part of nationalists. The *Irish News* reported that nationalists had "turned away from the polls" and the joint turnout for the SDLP and Sinn Féin had resulted in their "lowest share of the vote since before the ceasefires".[52] The ramifications at national level of Ulster's verdict were perceived to have been of even greater significance, with the pre-election speculation about the DUP being potential power brokers proving to be unfounded, as the party witnessed, "its dream of playing a central role in supporting a minority government – for a handsome price – come to naught, as the Conservatives surged to victory on their own account".[53]

"It's different over there …"

Although the evolution of franchise entitlement, the provision of secret balloting and the removal of electoral irregularities in Northern Ireland followed broadly similar paths to those experienced elsewhere in the United Kingdom, and despite the fact that the region had participated in the same Westminster elections as the rest of Britain throughout this period, Northern Ireland is still regarded as being politically different in several ways to England, Wales or Scotland. Undoubtedly the sheer frequency of elections and the close correlation between religious affiliation and voting preferences are major contributory factors to this prevailing perception. Many external observers have pointed to the unparalleled frequency of election contests in a region where voters "could make a reasonable claim to have had more elected representatives per voter than any place on earth", and where political contests took place in an atmosphere of "ethno-national divisions and sectarian chasm".[54] Despite these differences (which will be discussed in detail later), there are a number of similarities between the political systems in Great Britain and Northern Ireland. For instance, parties in Northern Ireland can also occasionally strike up electoral pacts, such as those agreed by the DUP and UUP for a number of Westminster constituencies during the 2015 contest. Also, tactical voting, especially under the proportional representation voting system now adopted in all other elections in the province, has also been utilised with the basic aim of keeping dreaded opponents out of contention in certain seats – this has also been employed within Northern Irish constituencies at Westminster contests (including the switching in support of many unionists to the SDLP's Joe Hendron in 1992, which ensured the defeat of Gerry Adams in West Belfast). Electors will also display their anger and frustration from time to time with long-serving and normally favoured politicians if they feel let down by them. This was the case with the DUP's Peter Robinson in the 2010 Westminster election when, following recent family-related scandals, he was defeated in East Belfast by the Alliance Party's Naomi Long.

However, these similarities in electoral trends do not disguise the very different nature of Westminster contests fought in Northern Ireland, which are often regarded in Britain as an election within a wider election. The different titles and leanings of political parties in the region, and the more restricted range of issues which tend to be discussed there, are the chief explanation for this impression. However, this is not to deny that contests in Northern Ireland can occasionally warrant some attention in Great Britain, particularly when their outcome might potentially influence the formation of a new administration in London. Thus, as mentioned earlier, the few references in the British media to the 2015 contest in Northern Ireland were largely focused around the possible scenario that the DUP might prove to be the power brokers in a new, David Cameron-led Conservative minority government.

The inevitability of election outcomes was a major characteristic of Northern Irish elections for several decades, a trend which contrasted sharply with the national experience. This stranglehold on political power by one group, the Unionist Party, over both the formation of regional governments at Stormont and in terms of its retention of the majority of Northern Irish seats in Westminster, meant that the surprise factor was more often than not absent in political contests. Another feature of British politics, which is rarely evident in Northern Ireland contests, is the phenomenon of the "floating" voter. Political experts in Britain continue to be fascinated, especially on the eve of major elections, by the likely voting intentions of that relatively small, but potentially decisive group of more flexible voters. By contrast, the electorate in Northern Ireland are more reluctant to exhibit such voting flexibility once in the polling booths. This is, of course, primarily due to the belief that all political contests are, per se, fundamentally about the constitutional issue and as such, constitute a barometer of voters' loyalty, or otherwise, to the British link. An obvious consequence of such "tribalistic" voting patterns has been that elections have been more predictable and, as a whole, less exciting than those elsewhere in Britain, although several electoral campaigns have, despite the relative predictability of their outcomes, nevertheless proved to be highly colourful and often tense affairs.

A further difference between political campaigning in Great Britain and in Northern Ireland has been the type and range of parties which operate in these constituent parts of the United Kingdom. Although informal associations between the three main British political parties and their supposed counterparts in Northern Ireland have been forged (such as electoral backing for Alliance provided by the Liberal Democrats), warranting occasional visits to the province by senior British political figures during election campaigns, there has been little progress in offering the Northern Irish electorate a genuine choice between Conservative and Labour candidates. For too long, the simplistic equation linking unionism and conservatism was propagated and rarely challenged, especially in Britain. Embittered unionists will still point out that it was their so-called Tory "friends", and not their Labour "enemies", who were responsible for loyalism's Armageddon moments, including direct rule in 1972 and the Anglo-Irish Agreement in 1985. Also, the lack of accommodation for left-of-centre Northern Irish voters was a political anomaly, given that the Labour Party, with its long-standing commitment to Irish unity, refused to organise or put up candidates in Northern Ireland, especially during the dark days of political sterility in the region's long conflict. Again, the assertions of Labour Party grandees that Labour was represented in the region in the form of the NILP and SDLP candidates, were disingenuous, given the restricted appeal of the unionist-leaning local Labour group and the nationalist credentials of the SDLP. As a result, Northern Irish electors have been left feeling impotent in the choice of national leaders and governments during general elections.[55] Despite the strong historical bonds between the Conservative Party and mainstream unionism, the need at an early phase of the conflict to adopt a non-partisan approach meant a de-politicisation of the Ulster crisis, and a general acceptance by British parties of the importance of sustaining a non-controversial, bipartisan policy towards Northern Ireland, which would endure throughout the Troubles.

Another key difference between elections in Northern Ireland and elsewhere in the United Kingdom – at least in the cases of local council, parliamentary and European contests – was the use of a different voting system. The practice of the single transferable vote (STV) system of proportional representation, with its benefits of producing enhanced cross-community engagement in the political process, was tried in the North's first local parliamentary election in 1921, and in early local government contests, before the local administration dispensed with the system in 1929 (it was only used once in local government elections, in 1921). Proportional representation was restored in 1973 for elections to the first Northern Irish Assembly, and has been used in subsequent contests for the various Assemblies. It has also been employed in European elections since 1979, in which Northern Ireland has been treated as a single constituency, electing three members to the parliament in Strasbourg.

Electoral contests in Northern Ireland are also associated with a variety of negative phenomena which, whilst not unique to the region, have certainly been more apparent in political battles there. Electoral irregularities which have now been eradicated had blighted the North's political landscape for many decades. These include the gerrymandering of electoral boundaries (especially in the drawing-up of predominantly "one-religion" wards in towns and cities, such as in Londonderry), outdated electoral registers and the commission of personation offences which, although not in themselves constituting problems of epidemic proportions, clearly posed difficulties for local election officials for many years.

Additionally, Catholics were the main victims of an outdated system of voting in council elections, where the franchise was restricted to those paying council rates (although abolished in England in the late 1940s, this restriction would controversially remain in place in Northern Ireland until 1968). This artificial and religiously-skewed creation of local electoral boundaries, as well as the denial of the local council vote to many Catholics, undoubtedly amounted to genuine grievances for the minority, as well as posing a huge barrier to intercommunity progress and dialogue. However, more damaging still was the resulting lack of engagement on the part of Catholics in the life of the Northern Irish state. This was reflected in the abstentionist policy of many nationalist representatives in the early phase of the Stormont parliament. Catholic reluctance to engage fully in what they dismissed as an alien political system led to their increasingly peripheral role in the region's political life, a situation which would not be properly addressed until the momentous political changes brought about by the Good Friday Agreement of 1998.[56]

The degree of intimidation of both voters and candidates in Northern Ireland elections was on a different scale to that encountered in the rest of Britain, as was the frequent recourse to the security forces in order to ensure public safety, particularly on the streets of larger cities like Belfast and Derry, near the climax of political campaigning. Several key elections were contested during prolonged spells of civic violence, and this backdrop of religio-political tension (most notably in the 1921, 1964, 1973 and 1974 elections, as described elsewhere) was certainly peculiar to the region. Incidentally, the presence of violence on the streets did not appear to deter voters from exercising their mandate, and levels of voting were generally high throughout most of the Troubles.[57]

General elections in the North of Ireland are also different, in that there are fewer genuine marginal constituencies there than in other parts of the United Kingdom. In Britain, around 20 per cent of all parliamentary seats are estimated by the parties in possession of them to be vulnerable, and although Northern Ireland has been increasingly liable to potential power shifts between, on the one hand, the UUP and the DUP, and on the other, the SDLP and Sinn Féin, there are fewer instances of political breakthrough on the part of parties representing the "other side" of religiously divided constituencies.

This is not to deny that Northern Ireland has had a number of instances of seats where the results have been far from predictable – with West Belfast, Mid-Ulster and, in particular, Fermanagh & South Tyrone, changing hands on several occasions. For many years, Catholics have constituted a narrow majority of the population in the border constituency of Fermanagh & South Tyrone, though the reluctance of the SDLP and Sinn Féin to forge an electoral pact has resulted in unionists being granted realistic chances of gaining the seat (as was the case in 2015). Fermanagh & South Tyrone, with its finely balanced population, is the best example of a Northern Irish constituency which is prone to close-run electoral contests. These have included the unexpected success of Sinn Féin's Phil Clarke in the 1955 Westminster election (his majority was 261), Anti H-Block candidate, Bobby Sands' spectacular success in a 1981 by-election (see Chapter Seven) and Sinn Féin's Michelle Gildernew's narrow victories over Ulster Unionist, James Cooper in 2001 (her majority was 53) and in 2010 (when her majority was down to 4).

West Belfast has also witnessed closely contested elections, especially before the major demographic changes to the area during the late 1960s and early 1970s, which transformed the constituency from a marginal one, keenly fought over by both nationalists and unionists, into a predominantly Catholic constituency, returning SDLP and, more recently, Sinn Féin representatives (unionists last won the Westminster seat in 1964). One of the closest run battles in this constituency took place in 1906, when nationalist Joe Devlin defeated the sitting unionist member, Captain J.R. Smiley by a mere 16 votes. Another paper-thin majority in West Belfast came in 1951, when veteran Labour representative, Jack Beattie beat Unionist Thomas L. Teevan by just 25 votes. Even when the movement of many thousands of Protestants from within the West Belfast electoral area resulted in a situation favouring nationalist candidates, tactical voting could still spring the occasional surprise, albeit in a division which had been transformed into an apparently safe republican seat – the aforementioned victory of the SDLP's Joe Hendron over Gerry Adams, with a majority was 589, was such an example.

Such close-run contests were not confined to unionist-nationalist battles, and occasionally involved politicians from different factions of unionism, who were contesting safe loyalist seats. Perhaps the closest such contest was in East Belfast during the general election of 1979, when the DUP's Peter Robinson defeated sitting Vanguard Party member, Bill Craig by 64 votes.

Characters All ...

Many Northern political representatives, both at Westminster and in local parliaments like Stormont, have proved to be colourful, fascinating characters. This section looks at a range of interesting politicians, as well as observing the restricted social range, and indeed gender, of those who entered Northern Ireland politics, and also some of the dangers encountered by those who put themselves forward. (Details of more leading Northern Irish parliamentarians can be found in Appendix Two).

For many years, political representatives, especially those sitting in Westminster, tended to emanate predominantly from a uniform social and economic background. Men like Captain Lawrence Orr, Rafton Pounder and Stratton Mills, who represented the Unionist Party at Westminster for many years before the outbreak of the Troubles, appeared to many people to personify privilege. As well as this, it was very much the case that political leadership was provided on an intergenerational basis by men from leading aristocratic, military or business families in the North – most notably, Sir James Craig, Lord Brookeborough, Captain Terence O'Neill and Major James Chichester-Clark. Working-class representatives, although by no means nonexistent, tended to be relatively thin on the ground, largely on account of the inconsistent performances of Labour groups, especially outside the Belfast area. Trade union and Labour figures who did make an impression on Northern politics included William Walker, Jack Beattie, Harry Midgley, and David Bleakley (Walker is considered in more detail in Chapter One and both Beattie and Midgley are given fuller treatment later in this chapter). Occasionally, blue-collar workers were selected to stand in predominantly working-class Belfast constituencies, either as independent unionists like Tommy Henderson (see below), or as those attached, for a while at least, to the Unionist Party. One of the most colourful men in this category was John (Johnny) McQuade, a former World War Two Chindit, a professional boxer and a docker, who represented both the UUP (1965–71) and DUP (1971–2) and served in both Stormont and Westminster parliaments, for the Woodvale and North Belfast constituencies respectively. Not the most articulate of parliamentary performers, McQuade more than compensated for this by his unstinting efforts for his constituents and his feisty presence in parliamentary chambers, especially in the Assembly, from which he was once evicted after a spat with unionist and nationalist rivals.[58]

One major criticism of Northern Irish politicians was that too few of them adopted a "professional" approach to their parliamentary duties. This was partly attributable to the weaknesses of a system, where opposition groups were permanently consigned to such a role, and where many of them, due to a self-inflicted policy of abstentionism, inevitably remained peripheral figures in the local parliament. This was especially the case during the last few years of Stormont in the late 1960s, when the emergence of more polished and business-like political operators, such as Brian Faulkner (see below) and John Hume (see Appendix Two), only seemed to reinforce the impression that there was a pronounced dearth of political talent in the region. Two further categories of parliamentary representatives in the North were the "holy" and the "unholy", who occasionally sat next to one another in the same chamber. In stark contrast with other parts of the United Kingdom and the Irish Republic, Northern Ireland has produced its fair share of "political priests", including the Reverend Godfrey MacManaway, the Reverend Robert Bradford, the Reverend Martin Smyth, the Reverend William McCrea and, the most celebrated of all, the Reverend Ian Paisley (see below). More sinister, shadowy representatives have also been elected to parliament than in other regions in the UK and, at least in the case of the Northern Ireland parliament and Assembly, have actually taken up their seats. These include John Nixon, the alleged leader of "rogue cop" attacks on Catholics during the Belfast Troubles of the early 1920s, who sat in the Northern parliament as an independent unionist. In another bizarre instance, in the early 1920s Cahir Healy, a former internee, sat in the same parliament as Minister for Home Affairs R. Dawson Bates, who had consigned Healy to an indefinite spell on the *Argenta* prison ship. Much more recently, the politicisation of both republican and loyalist paramilitaries during the 1980s and 1990s has resulted in a proliferation of former paramilitary activists who have been transformed into political representatives. These have included Sinn Féin's Gerry Adams, Martin McGuinness and Gerry Kelly, and the Progressive Unionist Party's Assembly representatives, Billy Hutchinson and David Ervine.

With such blurred dividing lines between "men of violence" and "men of politics", it is hardly surprising that some of those in the latter group have been periodically subject to physical attack by men in the former category.

Yet despite strong sectarian tension and the constant danger posed by many politicians' strident political rhetoric and high public profile, there have been relatively few serious assaults on leading politicians. The latter were assigned police protection officers during most of the modern conflict, or else, during its early stages, were permitted to carry their own firearms (Sinn Féin politicians, refusing police protection, were believed to have arranged their own personal security). Whenever attacks were made upon political figures, these generally attracted substantial media coverage, and severe condemnation of the alleged actions of the paramilitary groups suspected of involvement. Such attacks have mainly taken place in Northern Ireland, but several politicians who were especially vociferous in their condemnation of republicanism were targeted by the IRA in Great Britain. These included Unionist MP and former army chief, Sir Henry Wilson, who was shot dead by IRA members in London in 1922 and, much later, Tory critics of republican violence, such as Airey Neave, Shadow Northern Ireland Secretary, and junior minister, Ian Gow: both were both victims of republican car bombs, in 1979 and 1990 respectively. Unionist MPs in the Belfast parliament who have been critical of republican violence were also targets for the IRA over a period spanning close to sixty years. William Twaddell, a unionist MP in the new Northern parliament, was killed by republican gunmen in 1922, whilst the Reverend Robert Bradford – South Belfast's Unionist representative at Westminster – was shot dead in 1981 while conducting a constituency "surgery". Some other leading parliamentary figures were also victims of paramilitary assassination attempts but managed to survive, including Ulster Unionist, John Taylor, who was shot by the Official IRA in 1972, and republican socialist, Bernadette Devlin, shot by loyalists in 1981.

Female parliamentary representation has been even more limited in Northern Ireland than elsewhere in Britain. Yet there have been several individual cases where women have made their mark both in the Northern Irish parliament and at Westminster. Although there were very few female nationalist MPs during the half-century of Stormont rule, there were a handful of representatives from other groups, especially the Unionist Party. Some, like Patricia Ford and Patricia McLaughlin, sat with the Ulster Unionist Party at Westminster: the former served North Down from 1953 until 1955, whilst the latter represented West Belfast from 1955 until 1964. Other female Unionist MPs, who served in the local parliament in Belfast, included Julia McMordie (the widow of William McMordie, a former Belfast mayor and Westminster MP), who was successful in South Belfast in the first election to the Northern Ireland parliament, and Dinah McNabb, who represented Armagh North for nearly a quarter of a century, from 1945 until 1969. Dehra Chichester, another female unionist candidate, was elected to the first parliament and went on to give long and distinguished service in local politics, as well as becoming the first female member of the Northern Ireland Cabinet. Later to become Dame Dehra Parker – and a grandmother of Terence O'Neill – she represented Londonderry in the Northern Ireland House of Commons for close to thirty years, and was also minister of health and local government between 1949 and 1957. The four Queen's University seats were also filled by a number of women, until these seats were abolished in 1965 (the first elections under the new system were held in 1969). Perhaps the best known of these was Sheelagh Murnaghan from the Ulster Liberal Party (ULP), a critic of traditional unionism, who sat in Stormont between 1961 and 1969.[59]

Unquestionably the female representative to make the most immediate and lasting impression in Northern Irish politics and beyond was Bernadette Devlin (later McAliskey), who was elected as an independent Unity MP for Mid-Ulster in a by-election in April 1969. Barely 22 years of age, Devlin, who had made her name in the civil rights protest movement, gained considerable media attention when she was elected as the youngest female member to win a seat at Westminster. Regarded as the voice of the 1960s student protest generation, the left-wing Devlin was initially granted sympathetic treatment by the national and international media. This soon dissipated, however, after she became embroiled in severe street disturbances in Derry in August 1969, and also following her assault on then Home Secretary Reginald Maudling in the House of Commons the day after Bloody Sunday in January 1972. Defeated in the general election of February 1974, Devlin helped to form the Irish Republican Socialist Party (IRSP) later that year, and was to act as a spokesperson for Bobby Sands in the Fermanagh & South Tyrone by-election of 1981 (see Chapter Six).

Another female MP to attract controversy was Iris Robinson, wife of future first minister, Peter Robinson. She represented Strangford both in the Assembly and at Westminster (in the former, from 1998 and in the latter, from 2001), until her resignation in 2010. Her political career was destroyed, following the revelation of an affair with a Belfast teenager.

The last twenty years have witnessed the election of a slightly greater proportion of female representatives than previously, including the return of two Northern Ireland Women's Coalition (NIWC) representatives in the 1998 Assembly, Sinn Féin's Michelle Gildernew in the Fermanagh & South Tyrone constituency (she held the seat between 2001 and 2015), and Naomi Long of the Alliance Party in East Belfast (she defeated Peter Robinson in the 2010 Westminster election before losing her seat to the DUP in 2015). However, Northern Ireland continues to return proportionately fewer female representatives than any other part of the United Kingdom.

Major Political Players

It would be useful to look in a little more detail at eight leading political personalities, covering a range of parties and perspectives, as well as eras, all of whom have, in different ways, made distinctive impressions upon the Northern Irish political scene.[60]

JOSEPH DEVLIN: One of the most influential figures during the first quarter of the twentieth century, Devlin dominated nationalist politics during a crucial period in the North's history. "Wee Joe", as he was known to nationalists and unionists alike, led Catholic agitation for Home Rule in the years preceding World War I, and was the chief advocate of anti-Partitionism throughout the 1920s and early 1930s.

An impressive public speaker, Devlin represented West Belfast both in the new Northern Ireland parliament and at Westminster, where he also represented Fermanagh & South Tyrone. His brand of nationalism often led to disagreements with the local Catholic hierarchy and, although a fiery parliamentary debater, he also led fellow nationalists into a prolonged period of abstention from the Northern Irish legislature. Apart from his underlying conviction of the basic integrity of Irish unity, Devlin's political approach was dominated by a strong sense of the need for social justice and equality. He was also opposed to the physical force strand of nationalism, and his desire to create better relationships with Protestants also led him, particularly in his earlier days, to cooperate with unionist dissidents and socialists in electoral contests.

Despite possessing an acute political brain and maintaining an energetic defence of nationalist issues, Devlin suffered considerable political disappointment during his career. The resistance of Sir Edward Carson's

Ulster Volunteer movement, and the onset of international hostilities in 1914 had resulted in the shelving of Home Rule legislation, and Devlin was a staunch opponent of the Government of Ireland Act (1920), which established Partition. Even the fig leaf of the Boundary Commission was to prove ineffective as far as Catholic aspirations were concerned, and the sense of estrangement and entrapment felt by Northern nationalists grew even more pronounced during Devlin's last years in politics.

Devlin was not however just the authoritative voice of Northern nationalism between 1906 and 1934. A friendly, convivial, "personality" politician, he was also a respected figure across the wider community, and unionist leaders acknowledged his popularity at the time of his death in 1934. He was also prominent in other areas of public life. He served as chairman of the *Irish News* for many years, thereby continuing an association which had begun when he had first worked for the paper; he also enjoyed a long association with the Ancient Order of Hibernians. However, Devlin's public service was not restricted to political and religious spheres, and as a keen benefactor of his less-privileged constituents, he was active in social initiatives such as organising holiday outings for needy city children and mill girls.[61]

JACK BEATTIE: Born into a working-class Presbyterian home in north Belfast, Beattie started his working life in a textile factory, before training to be a blacksmith. He soon got involved in trade union activity, and was a supporter of Home Rule in the pre-1914 period. Beattie was unique in his length of service as an NILP MP, and indeed for many years the cause of socialism was articulated by this large, outspoken thorn in the side of establishment unionism. In a sense, he had two strands to his political career. The first involved his representation of East Belfast in the Belfast parliament, from 1925 until 1949, and his second phase of public service came at Westminster, where he represented West Belfast between 1943 and 1955 (apart from a short period in 1950–1). Jack Beattie was unusual in Northern Irish politics on account of the breadth of support he enjoyed at elections over a period of some 30 years. He had a strong personal vote from people on either side of the sectarian divide, who regarded him as a solid constituency MP. He also enjoyed additional backing from trade unionists, socialists and a small number of nationalists, who were attracted by his abiding conviction in the cause of a united Ireland.

The dark days of economic depression during the 1930s and the increasing problem of unemployment provided Beattie with considerable ammunition with which to tackle the Unionist government at Stormont. Yet the same decade also saw Beattie spending around eight years in the political wilderness, as he was expelled from the NILP for his strong anti-Partitionist stance. An arch-rival of Harry Midgley (see below), he had briefly succeeded Midgley as party leader when the latter defected to the Unionist Party, but Beattie was to leave the NILP shortly afterwards. The latter part of his political career coincided with the landslide victory of the Labour Party in the 1945 election, and for much of this time, Beattie sat as an Irish Labour Party (ILP) representative.

TOMMY HENDERSON: Northern Ireland has benefited over the years from the contributions of a small number of independently-minded, working-class unionist representatives. Undoubtedly the best example of this was former house-painter, Henderson, who served as independent unionist MP for North Belfast and the Shankill area from 1925 until 1953. Largely on account of both his unambiguous backing for the union and his total commitment to his constituents' economic and social needs, Henderson retained the support of his staunchly loyalist constituents for nearly 30 years, despite his strong criticism of the ruling Unionist Party administration. Claiming towards the end of his career that he had refused to make a speech which would "endanger the constitution of Northern Ireland as established by law", Henderson supported draconian government measures against terrorism. However, he was better known at Stormont for his plain-spoken advocacy of labour issues. In an election leaflet around this time, he pointed out to his constituents that he had "always been in sympathy and close touch with the needs and importance of labour", and promised to "continue advocating for better conditions for the workers and a higher standard of living."[62]

Henderson was fundamentally an anti-establishment politician, and nothing gave him more satisfaction than to unsettle the cosy collegiality of the predominantly unionist, middle-class chamber. He was not easily impressed by those in positions of authority. Described by James Kelly, a seasoned Stormont press observer, as the "arch-comedian" of Stormont, Henderson was "a rubicund, talkative little man", who could easily "switch from high-flown oratory to broad comedy, in a twinkling".[63] His chief target was the ever-increasing bureaucracy at Stormont, which he maintained had grown so large that it resembled, "the testicles [sic] of an octopus spread all over the province".[64] Another focus for his censure was none other than the prime minister and adored father figure of loyalism, James Craig. On one occasion, as Craig showed a distinguished party of guests around the parliament buildings, Henderson harangued the flustered prime minister about the inadequate sanitary conditions suffered by residents of the village of Millisle in County Down. The prime minister, Henderson proclaimed, did not care for their predicament, reminding his audience that Craig could "exercise the functions of nature in the lap of luxury"! The verbose Henderson also held the record for the longest speech delivered at Stormont (this was in the region of nine-and-a-half hours). James Kelly witnessed proceedings from the press box at Stormont, and described the speech as one of "wit, invective and broad humour":

> Nobody realised what they were in for, when he was called somewhere around 7.00 p.m., and amidst ironical cheers [he] threw his formidable collection of books and papers on the table and began one of the most hilarious and far-ranging speeches we had ever heard![65]

CAHIR HEALY: Like Devlin, Healy was another leading nationalist who gave long political service to his community. He was also a man of many other interests and talents. Born in County Donegal, Healy was a poet, Irish language revivalist and cultural heritage enthusiast, as well as a politician. He also spent part of his early working life as a journalist, reporting for the *Fermanagh News* during the 1890s; around this time too, he defied convention by marrying a Protestant.

Healy's brand of nationalism, however, differed somewhat from that of Devlin. A member of the early Sinn Féin movement, he was detained on the *Argenta* prison ship during the 1920s Troubles. Yet there was a slow evolution in his political thinking and he grew away from his early associations with physical force nationalism, backing the Anglo-Irish Treaty in 1921 and coming to the conclusion that "Partition had been made almost inevitable by the Easter Rising".[66] Healy was to enjoy a long spell of parliamentary participation, both at Stormont and at Westminster – where his more tolerant views of opponents and capacity to forge friendships across political and religious divides were better suited. His long political career, spread over four decades, was rare in its longevity. However, his final contribution to the life of his beloved Ulster was not a political one. A long-standing interest in celebrating the province's cultural heritage culminated in his campaigning work for a new museum, and once this campaign had proved successful, he lived long enough to become a director of the Ulster Folk and Transport Museum.

HARRY MIDGLEY: Relatively few politicians "cross the floor" of their parliament, and particularly so in Northern Ireland where political transformation can also be associated with a betrayal of one's social and religious community. Perhaps the highest profile case of political conversion was that of Harry Midgley, who started his political life as a trade union activist and labour representative, but finished it as an Ulster Unionist cabinet minister. After leaving school at 14, Midgley had worked as a joiner in the Belfast shipyards and his involvement in socialist politics coincided with the election campaigns of leading trade unionist, William Walker. Midgley often spoke on Walker's behalf on the steps of Belfast's Customs House (known to locals as "Hyde Park Corner"). Wounded in World War I, Midgley later returned to work in the shipyard, where he became prominent both in union and labour circles, gaining over 22,000 votes in a Westminster by-election for West Belfast in December 1923. In 1925, he was elected to the Belfast Council, and in 1933, he won the Stormont seat of Belfast Dock and became NILP leader. However, he was an outspoken critic of the Northern Ireland parliament, which he described as a "deadly" institution, claiming that he (and indeed, many others) could "perform no useful function" there.[67]

Although an active campaigner for improvements in the economic and social conditions experienced by ordinary working-class people, Harry Midgley angered many in his own party by his attempts to gain its support for the constitutional link, and also by his refusal to condemn the sectarian nature of disturbances in his constituency in 1935 – this would cost him his seat in the Stormont election, three years later. Whilst he won the Willowfield seat in East Belfast in a 1941 by-election, the return of his arch-rival, Jack Beattie to the party fold the following year, along with the growing tension between the pro-union and anti-Partition wings of the NILP, resulted in Midgley's decision to leave the party in 1943 to form a new group, the Commonwealth Labour Party (CLP). In April 1943, he was appointed to the war-time Unionist administration (the first non-unionist to be elevated to government office in Northern Ireland), before moving to the Ministry of Labour the following year. Midgley experienced mixed fortunes in the elections which followed the conclusion of international hostilities, retaining his Stormont seat but failing in a bid to be elected to Westminster. The change in emphasis in his election rhetoric – from a basic focus on bread-and-butter issues to a more pronounced pro-union bias – was illustrated in his appeal to electors in South Belfast. Reminding them of his own distinguished military service in World War I, and that of his sons in recently-ended World War II, he made the following promise to his constituents:

> I shall strive with all the power at my command to eradicate from Westminster the evil influence of those who have libelled and misrepresented Ulster to the British people. I hope this way to march with them towards the realisation of a better Britain and a better World, but also [to show] that we are determined to remain an integral part of the United Kingdom and British Empire.[68]

Resigning as CLP leader in 1947, Midgley applied for the Unionist whip, and also joined the Orange Order and other loyalist groups the following year. Now a fully-fledged unionist, he retained Willowfield for his new party in the 1949 Stormont election, and was appointed Minister of Education the following year. There was a rich irony in this, not only on account of his highly unusual political journey, from left-wing politics to a seat at the heart of the unionist establishment, but also in the elevation of an individual with a restricted, elementary school education to such a post. Yet Midgley, who would endure biting attacks from his former Labour colleagues for undergoing a "Churchill-like" political transformation, actually flourished in this role, where he remained until his untimely death in 1957.

BRIAN FAULKNER: Ulster Unionism was frequently rebuked by critics for its dearth of quality leaders, especially since its halcyon period of successful resistance against Irish Home Rule in the years before World War I. Few of its leaders escaped being castigated for possessing "limited vision" or for pursuing "sectarian" policies, and even fewer won the plaudits of their opponents for exercising a professional approach to politics. Despite other weaknesses and his ultimate political failure, Brian Faulkner was such an exception. A small, dapper man, Faulkner was born in County Down and received part of his education in Dublin, which gave him an "all-Ireland" awareness not always shared by his Protestant contemporaries. After a spell working in his father's linen business, he entered Stormont in 1949 as MP for East Down (he would remain its representative until the demise of Stormont), and as the chamber's youngest representative, he was soon considered for a ministerial post. Faulkner went on to acquire a wide range of ministerial experience, including spells at the Ministry of Home Affairs and Ministry of Commerce. It was in the latter post that he made the greatest impression. Combining the business expertise he had gained in his family's textile business with strong personal negotiating skills, he was largely responsible for Northern Ireland's significant economic growth during the 1960s. Faulkner's strength was an ability to "sell" a region which, despite its blackened image, was "proud to be British and [of] leading a productive life". Northern Ireland was, he informed an audience of industrialists and businessmen in Leeds in the mid-1960s, a region where "our farms and factories are as much part of the economic muscle of the country as the mills of Yorkshire", and in its export of products such as linen, whiskey, ships, missiles, optical lenses and oil drills, Ulster was "playing a full part in the economic struggle for prosperity which is vital to every citizen in Britain".[69]

Faulkner's dual appeal – to traditional unionists, he was seen as a hard-liner committed to tackling the threat of republican violence, whilst his eloquent espousal of non-sectarian sentiments made him an attractive spokesman for the Unionist Party's "liberal" wing – resulted in his election in 1971 to party leader and prime minister. He was, however, regarded by his detractors as little more than a political trickster, prone to rapid switches in direction in order to facilitate his personal advancement. He was certainly a political pragmatist, whether it was in playing down his personal association with the Orange Order, or in modifying his initial reluctance to implement some of Terence O'Neill's proposed reforms. Despite this "tricky Dick" image in some quarters, Faulkner condemned religious bigotry and endeavoured to represent the needs of all constituents in his religiously-mixed district. In his memoir, he cited an instance of this fair-mindedness, relating how shortly after his election to Stormont in 1949, he had responded positively to an appeal from a Catholic sports retailer, who required a special licence for the importation of hurling sticks from across the border.[70]

For a politician who had impressed many external observers with his professional approach to politics – one sneering critic suggested that Faulkner was the only Northern Irish politician capable of becoming a junior minister at Westminster – it was surprising that two of his chief decisions as premier ultimately reflected a substantial element of hasty, instinctive political decision-making. His move to introduce internment in August 1971, against the advice of the Tory administration in London, and his immediate response to Edward Heath's ultimatum in March 1972 – a move to sit tight, rather than being seen to do the right thing would have placed the ball firmly in Heath's court, and instead led to an election in the region rather than the immediate introduction of direct rule – resulted in producing a fillip for IRA recruitment and an escalation in their campaign, as well as further disintegration in the ranks of his own Unionist Party. This resulted in a legacy which did not befit a man of such rare political talent.

GERRY FITT: Representing Belfast constituencies at both Stormont and Westminster for over twenty years, Fitt, who had served in the Merchant Navy towards the end of World War II, was elected in 1962 as an Irish Labour MP at Stormont for the Belfast Dock constituency (he was born in the area). Four years later, he won the Westminster seat of West Belfast. Fitt's behind-the-scenes role at Westminster – where he spent countless hours in bars, cafes and meeting rooms, cajoling the large influx of sympathetic Labour representatives into adopting a more questioning approach to the breaking allegations of sectarian discrimination in Northern Ireland – was a crucial, if understated, factor in influencing the policy of Labour administrations, especially when the modern Ulster conflict erupted a few years later.

Fitt was actively involved in the civil rights movement of the late 1960s. He readily adapted to its preferred mode of protest – namely street demonstrations – just as he had taken to the rough-and-tumble of parliamentary debate in London. Fitt was a founder member of the SDLP in 1970 and, as the party's leader and deputy chief executive of the short-lived power-sharing administration in 1974, was the first nationalist to hold such a senior government post. Disagreements over policy direction, as well as some internal backbiting – Fitt and Belfast-based colleagues, like Paddy Devlin, did not espouse the more strident brand of nationalism favoured by leading such SDLP figures as John Hume and Austin Currie – led to his resignation from the party in 1979.

He spent his last years of parliamentary service sitting as an independent socialist, before being defeated by Sinn Féin's Gerry Adams in the Westminster election of 1983. Although he won cross-community backing for his principled denunciation of paramilitary violence, his outspoken attacks on the IRA led to a series of threats to his personal safety and that of his family, culminating in a serious arson attack on his north Belfast home in 1983. He subsequently moved his family to London, and was elevated to the House of Lords later that year.

Central to Fitt's long and colourful political career was his commitment to serve all of his constituents, rather than simply restricting his efforts to gaining plaudits from his own supporters. In a 1966 election leaflet for his contest in West Belfast, bearing the strapline "Win the West with Fitt", he pointed out that he could not be accused of fostering sectarianism. A constituency representative at heart, he claimed that, "from the Falls to Sandy Row, from the Shankill to the Pound Loney, I know West Belfast, and the people know me, as a Labour man they can come to for help in all circumstances".[71] The other key feature of Fitt's political position was his strong opposition to violence, and this was noted by many in tributes following his death in 2005. Dr Sean Brady, the Catholic Archbishop of Armagh, reflected that Fitt had played "a vital role at a critical stage in the search for justice and civil rights in our society", and that as "a courageous opponent of violence", he had always endeavoured to "serve people from all sections of the community at no small sacrifice to himself".[72]

IAN PAISLEY: Undoubtedly the most controversial and enigmatic Northern Irish parliamentarian of the last century was the Reverend Ian Paisley. Born in Armagh and brought up in Ballymena, Paisley was ordained as a minister in 1946 and established the Free Presbyterian Church in east Belfast five years later. Essentially a non-establishment figure, Paisley not only founded his own, breakaway church, but also his own political party, the Democratic Unionist Party (DUP) and, in the 1960s, a newspaper, the *Protestant Telegraph*. He was also prominent in the Independent Orange Order, another breakaway faction – this time from the mainstream Orange Order.

Paisley initially built up a reputation as a street preacher, and was particularly vocal in his denunciation of Catholicism and ecumenicism. During the time of the early civil rights marches by nationalists, his street protests grew increasingly political in their nature, and he served two short jail sentences, the second for blocking one of these protest marches in Armagh in 1968. Ian Paisley was a leading critic of reforming unionist premier, Terence O'Neill, and unsuccessfully challenged him in his Bannside constituency in the 1969 Stormont election (see Chapter Four). This would prove to be the only election defeat in a career which would involve numerous successes at Stormont, Westminster and in European electoral jousts. Paisley would serve as Westminster representative for North Antrim for four decades – from 1970 until his retirement in 2010; he would also sit on various Northern Ireland legislative bodies, including the Assembly (between 1998 and 2011), as well as the European parliament, from 1979 until 2004.

Ian Paisley owed much of his popularity to his unique blend of the rhetoric of religious fundamentalism and an unbending conviction of the veracity of the British connection. Despite being detested by the British political establishment, at least for the greater part of his long spell in politics, the sheer length of his political career was testament to his popularity with grass-roots unionist voters. A highly determined, energetic and charismatic political campaigner, he revelled in his role as an outsider and political underdog. He was an unrivalled orator, who was adept at tailoring his speeches for different audiences. He was also a pragmatist in terms of his driving of party policy, which veered from insistence on United Kingdom integration to supporting the restoration of a Stormont-style parliament, and ultimately, his crucial endorsement of power-sharing with Sinn Féin.

For much of his long parliamentary career, Ian Paisley's name was synonymous with political nihilism, earning him the epithet "Dr No": this was particularly evident in his opposition to the Anglo-Irish Agreement during the latter half of the 1980s (see Chapter Seven). Previously, he had opposed the creation of Northern Ireland's first power-sharing government in 1974, and would be a fierce critic of Unionist Party leader, David Trimble's participation in power-sharing from 1998. As leader of the DUP, he had long renounced the chances of negotiating with Sinn Féin; in one interview, he had claimed he would "never sit down with Gerry Adams", a man, Paisley explained, who would "sit down with the devil".[73]

In a momentous, road-to-Damascus-style conversion, however, he would eventually sit down with Mr Adams' deputy, Martin McGuinness, in a power-sharing administration, in which he, Paisley, became first minister of Northern Ireland (2007–8). In 2011, following internal disputes both within the Free Presbyterian Church and the DUP, Paisley – who had been elevated in 2010 to a seat in the House of Lords, as Lord Bannside – resigned from both his party and the church he had founded. By the time he died in 2014, the man, who for so long had been regarded as a rabble-rouser and sectarian bigot, would be remembered positively by many as a peacemaker and statesman.

Backing One's Tribe?

Apart from predictable differences in the detail afforded to their coverage of Northern Ireland elections, the local press were also more liable than their British counterparts to adopt partisan positions in their interpretation of the unfolding contests. Also, for much of this long period, Northern Irish citizens were less exposed to the views which outsiders held about their political intrigues and squabbles. In an age before the widespread consumption of British newspapers in the region and comprehensive, televised coverage of elections, most Northern Irish voters were largely reliant on the local press for information about politics. Although some Catholics would have regularly consulted Dublin-based journals such as the *Irish Independent* and the *Irish Times*, the majority chose the northern-published *Irish News*. Unionist-leaning electors had more choice in terms of local dailies, with the *Belfast News Letter* (founded as far back as 1764) and the *Northern Whig* providing crucial morning-newspaper services in the region. However, by far the most widely read unionist newspaper was the *Belfast Telegraph*, which was initially printed in the early evening.

For much of the period covered in this study, both the *Irish News* and the *Belfast Telegraph* retained trenchant positions on either side of the North's sectarian divide. Perhaps more so than in the case of their English and Scottish counterparts, these Northern Irish papers were generally unwilling to create too much distance between their own preferred positions and those of the region's political parties. As will be noted in this short section, both the *Belfast Telegraph* and the *Irish News* provided fulsome support to, respectively, unionist and nationalist candidates over the course of many decades. It will also be observed that fundamental changes in the fiercely partisan position of the *Belfast Telegraph* were in evidence from the period just preceding the start of the modern conflict, while a similar loosening of ties with former political bedfellows – albeit on a less striking scale – has been apparent at the *Irish News* in recent years.

The earliest nationalist daily journal in the North was the *Belfast Morning News*, which had been established in 1855. In August 1891, backed by local clergy and leading Catholic businessmen, a new nationalist-leaning newspaper, the *Irish News*, commenced operations and published the

Morning News the following year. The paper's first editor, P.J. Kelly recognised the importance of keeping the bishops, senior clergy, and the rest of the shareholders at the paper on his side, and pursued a traditional, nationalist-leaning approach. The paper's early period coincided with the expansion of the franchise amongst working-class Irish men, and the demise of nationalist leader, Charles Stewart Parnell. The question of Irish Home Rule remained, however, high on the political agenda, especially following the return of a Liberal administration in 1906. Within a decade of its formation, the *Irish News* would warrant rebuke from its prominent backers, the conservative-minded group of senior Catholic clergy, by reason of the close alliance between its new editor, Tim McCarthy, and Joe Devlin's United Irish League. As Eamon Phoenix has noted in his history of the newspaper:

> Under the direction of Devlin and McCarthy's stern tutelage, the paper became undeviating in its support for the official Home Rule Party. However, its markedly sympathetic attitude towards the strikers during the 1907 dock strike and the city's police mutiny of the same year, drew sharp criticism from Bishop Henry's embittered supporters.[74]

The *Irish News* would eventually move away from this early stance of automatically endorsing the party which represented constitutional nationalism. Although the scale of the paper's gradual transition was not on a par with that of the *Belfast Telegraph*'s shift away from being a mere government mouthpiece, the *Irish News* would move away from the cosy relationship which it had enjoyed with Joe Devlin and his political groups. Whilst the paper would remain broadly supportive of many of the policies and political strategies espoused by the SDLP – including the ending of internment, British military excesses, the introduction of power-sharing and the recognition of an "Irish" dimension in any political solution of the Northern Ireland problem – the *Irish News* had to adapt to a changing situation, once that other voice of Irish nationalism, Sinn Féin, finally turned its back on violence. Despite recognising the party's transition into a politically acceptable force, the *Irish News* remained critical of Sinn Féin policies and demands. In its analysis of the 2015 Westminster general election, the paper described the contest as, "one of dashed hopes and unforeseen gains". The agony of the former was shared, it maintained, between the DUP, which had seen its "dream of playing a central role in supporting a minority government ... come to naught", and Sinn Féin, whose hopes that a new Labour administration might have "let them off the welfare reform hook" had also "turned to dust". Acknowledging that the contest had been a good one for the UUP, the paper pointed out that the success of the unionist pact in constituencies such as East Belfast and Fermanagh & South Tyrone, had set a precedent for "similar arrangements in future Westminster elections".[75]

Despite it being "a normally sure-footed electoral machine", Sinn Féin had, according to the *Irish News*, experienced "some stutters in this poll", including the "infamous sectarian headcount leaflet in North Belfast", which had been "a huge misjudgement" and had "damaged" the campaign of its candidate, Gerry Kelly. The editorial was also not slow to criticise the leadership of the SDLP's Alasdair McDonnell, and also pointed out that, "both Sinn Féin and the SDLP should be concerned about the nationalist turnout, which, this time, showed a worrying downturn".[76]

The *Belfast Telegraph*'s origins were in the middle of the controversial 1868 election campaign of independent unionist and Orange Order leader, William Johnston. Johnston's populist brand of street politics – he had, for instance, organised a march from Newtownards to Bangor, County Down the previous summer, which had been attended by around 40,000 people – had resulted in an increased interest in politics being displayed by the wider public. Johnston, who had won one of Belfast's borough seats, had been supported in his campaign by a best-selling broadsheet produced by William and George Baird; two years later, the brothers felt confident enough to start publishing a daily, pro-unionist newspaper, the *Belfast Evening Telegraph*. By the time William's son, Robert, took over in 1886, the paper had developed a reputation as the leading source of loyalist opposition to Home Rule; the *Belfast Telegraph* was to continue in this vein for over seven decades.[77]

It was the appointment in 1953 of a new, "liberal" editor, Jack Sayers, and the *Telegraph*'s 1961 incorporation into the large newspaper group owned by Canadian press baron, Roy Thomson, which would gradually lead to a radical change in the paper's political direction. The timing of this change was also highly significant, as the influence of the press in the 1950s and early 1960s was undoubtedly more widespread and all-pervasive than it would be in the emerging television age. The *Belfast Telegraph* was certainly read by a large proportion of Northern Ireland's citizens at the time – in the early 1960s, its readership exceeded 200,000, compared to an estimated 50,000 in 2015.

Sayers was an eloquent advocate of "constructive" unionism, and even before the reforming premiership of Terence O'Neill, he was expressing, through the paper's editorial columns, the need for Basil Brooke's Unionist Party to do "much rethinking" in the wake of electoral setbacks to the NILP in Belfast in 1958, and called on it to show that it was truly "a party of the centre". Sayers reassured his readers that the election setback for unionism had hopefully reminded the party's political strategists that it was "not 1690, not 1912, nor 1921" but rather "the opening of an era in which Northern Ireland is secure, free, maturing and in search of a fresher mental sustenance".[78]

This 1958 Stormont election had proved to be a watershed moment for the *Belfast Telegraph*, as it was the first time the newspaper had been reticent in backing a unionist government. It quickly "broadened its political and religious views in a way hitherto unimaginable", and this inevitably resulted in strong criticism on its part of the right-wing, veteran prime minister, Lord Brookeborough.[79] Sayers soon found himself more in tune with the conciliatory approach of Brooke's successor, Captain Terence O'Neill, and in his editorials in the early phase of the modern conflict, he sharply rebuked unionist dissenters for resisting political progress. An editorial piece published shortly before Sayers' retirement warned that the removal of O'Neill would "not remove the thousands who see in him the hope of a new era, imbued by a spirit of emancipation". The leading article pointed out that "between those who are already unionist and those who are not, there is the making of a centre party that could be the most significant development that Northern Ireland has yet seen".[80]

Sayers' contributions both to local journalism and to Northern Irish society were considerable. As a result of his pioneering stance at the *Belfast Telegraph*, "liberal unionism was made acceptable, even fashionable, for the first time since 1903". Also, by "adopting an independent line, he broke the stranglehold of Glengall Street [then the headquarters of the UUP] on the media, and revitalised political debate in the province".[81]

The *Belfast Telegraph* continued to be more questioning in its expectations of unionism long after the death of Jack Sayers in 1969. Throughout the long conflict, the paper adopted a stance which appeared to reflect a qualified or provisional unionism, as distinct from its former advocacy of the Unionist Party. This included an unstinting denunciation of terrorism from any quarter, and broad backing for most of the numerous initiatives which emanated from Westminster during the thirty-year period of direct rule.

In the post-conflict era, the *Belfast Telegraph* has continued to articulate the opinions of liberal unionism. This was illustrated recently in its appraisal of the Ulster Unionist Party's success in the 2015 Westminster general election.[82] This unexpected success for a party which had been devoid of representation in the national Parliament for a decade, was described by the paper as a "resurgence". These results, it asserted, showed that the unionist vote was "more fluid than some people had proposed", and the electoral tactic of unionists voting across party lines to support SDLP candidates in Foyle and South Down, in a clear attempt to damage the prospects of Sinn Féin, would "go some way to dispelling the stereotype image of unionism as dour, unbending and unimaginative". Despite these "notable" gains and the Unionist Party's "strong showing", the paper noted that it was "ironic" that the "leverage" of the unionist parties at Westminster would now prove to be "not as strong as they [these parties] might have hoped, due to the excellent polling of Conservatives".[83]

Endnotes

1. M. Megahey, *The Reality of his Fictions – the Dramatic Achievement of Sam Thompson* (Lagan Press, Belfast, 2009), pp. 199

2. *Ibid.* pp. 217–8

3. *Ibid.* pp. 221. There were rumours of over 100 cases of personation in West Belfast during the 1964 Westminster election.

4. J. Bardon, *A History of Ulster* (Blackstaff Press, Belfast, 1992), p. 461

5. The local government franchise was still related to the payment of rates and, despite being abolished in England in 1948, remained controversially in place in Northern Ireland, where those not owning a property, as well as tenants paying rates (nearly a quarter of all adults, most of whom were Catholics) were denied the franchise.

6. Although the removal of the proportional representation voting system was strongly opposed by nationalists, they still performed creditably in the 1929 election, winning 11 seats.

7. Northern Ireland returned three members in a single constituency. *See* S. Elliott, "Voting Systems and Political Parties in Northern Ireland", in *Northern Ireland: Politics and the Constitution*, by B. Hadfield (OUP, Oxford, 1992)

8. It would be the elections of 1910 which would see the practical merging of liberal unionists within the Unionist Party, and another two years before this was formalised. Therefore, the terms "unionist" and "conservative" were interchangeable until well into the Edwardian era.

9. Devlin, who had won the Kilkenny seat four years before, defeated Unionist candidate, Captain J.R. Smiley in a 90 per cent poll, with the nationalist journal, *Northern Star* proclaiming the victory of "the little corporal who has gallantly carried the flag of Liberty and Democracy to success". A.C. Hepburn, *Catholic Belfast and Nationalist Ireland in the Era of Joe Devlin, 1871–1934* (OUP, Oxford, 2008), p. 112

10. The seat remained in Liberal hands, despite Hogg's death in 1914. His successor was Sir J.B. Dougherty. B.M. Walker (ed.), *Parliamentary Election Results in Ireland, 1801–1921* (Irish Royal Academy, Dublin, 1978)

11. A.F. Parkinson, *Friends in High Places – Ulster's Resistance to Irish Home Rule, 1912–14* (Ulster Historical Foundation, Belfast, 2012)

12. The exceptions were the elections to the Constitutional Convention in 1976, to the Northern Ireland Assembly (1982) and the Northern Ireland Forum (1996).

13. *Belfast Telegraph*, 9 March 1925

14. *Belfast Telegraph*, 12 March 1925

15. *Irish News*, 1 April 1925

16. *Irish News*, 2 April 1925

17. *Belfast Telegraph*, 7 April 1925

18. *Irish News*, 7 April 1925

19. *Irish News*, 9 April 1925

20. T. Bowman, *De Valera and the Ulster Question* (OUP, 1982), p. 101

21. *Belfast Telegraph*, 9 February 1938

22. *Ibid.*

23. *Belfast Telegraph*, 11 February 1938. *The Times'* verdict on this election was more sanguine. The paper's stance on events across the Irish Sea was that, "a snap election on an unreal issue" had resulted in unionists gaining a "complete victory". Bardon, *op. cit.*, p. 545

24. *Belfast Telegraph*, 5 March 1958

25. *Belfast Telegraph*, 10 March 1958

26. *Irish News*, 10 March 1958

27. *Belfast Telegraph*, 17 March 1958

28. *Belfast Telegraph*, 19 March 1958

29. *Irish News*, 1 March 1958; 6 March 1958

30. *Belfast Telegraph*, 21 March 1958

31. *Ibid.*

32. *Irish News*, 21 March 1958

33. *Irish News*, 22 March 1958

34. A. Boyd, *Holy War in Belfast*, (Tralee, 1969), p. 179

35. *Irish News*, 30 September 1964

36. *Ibid.*

37. *Belfast Telegraph*, 2 October 1964

38. *Ibid.*

39. *Belfast Telegraph*, 22 June 1998

40. *Irish News*, 24 June 1998

41. *Irish News*, 23 June 1998

42. The London *Independent*, 29 June 1998, described the election as being "historic without being definitive".

43. *Belfast Telegraph*, 27 June 1998

44. *Irish News*, 27 June 1998

45. The DUP's deputy leader and North Belfast candidate, Nigel Dodds also had the question of BBC accountability on his election agenda. In *The Times* (24 April 2015), Dodds argued that the corporation needed to be "cut down to size", and that this could

be achieved by removing the viewer licence fee from a "simply too powerful" BBC.

46. *Belfast Telegraph*, 1 May 2015. An earlier editorial in the paper (28 April) noted how divisive the whole question of gay marriage had been, which "ran contrary to those most vocal on the issue, who suggest the vast majority of people favour same-sex marriage".

47. *The Times*, 13 April 2015

48. *Belfast Telegraph*, 8 May 2015

49. *Belfast Telegraph*, 3 May, 2015

50. *Irish News*, 6 May 2015

51. *Belfast Telegraph*, 8 May 2015; 9 May 2015. Robinson had a 2,597 majority over Long.

52. *Irish News*, 9 May 2015

53. *Ibid.*

54. J. Tonge, from *Sex, Lies and the Ballot Box*, ed. P. Cowley and R. Ford (Biteback, London, 2014), pp. 103–110

55. Although political campaigns in Scotland and Wales also resulted in the participation and success of nationalist parties (especially the SNP in the 2015 election), as well as an undoubted emphasis on local issues, both of these countries retain strong political links with the major British parties, and are therefore not comparable with those in Northern Ireland.

56. The SDLP also opted to use the abstentionist tactic for a spell at the start of the 1970s.

57. Northern Ireland's reputation as a fertile ground for electoral engagement has been dented during the period which has followed the Peace Process, and the region experienced the lowest voter turnout (of any region) in the 2010 Westminster election, and comparatively low polls in several constituencies in the 2015 election.

58. Stories abound about John McQuade's rare speeches at Westminster, where his impenetrable Belfast accent completely flummoxed Hansard recorders, and where he was reported to have read his maiden speech from the back of a cigarette packet!

59. M. McNamara and P. Mooney, *Women in Parliament in Ireland: The Irish Experience, 1918-2000* (Merlin, Dublin, 2000)

60. For fuller biographical details of these and several other leading Northern Irish parliamentarians, see Appendix Two.

61. Devlin's arch-opponent, James Craig insisted that, despite their keen political differences, he had "never entertained anything but admiration for [Devlin's] personal character". S. McMahon, *Wee Joe – the Life of Joseph Devlin* (Brehon Press, Belfast, 2011), p. 223

62. T. Henderson, '1953 Stormont Election Leaflet'; from J.J. Nihill donation collection, Election Manifestos/Material 1942–69, Linen Hall Library, Northern Ireland Political Collection

63. J. Kelly, *Bonfires on the Hillside*, (Fountain Publishing, Belfast,1995), p. 93

64. *Ibid.*, p. 94

65. *Ibid.*, p. 95

66. E. Phoenix, from *Conflicts in the North of Ireland 1900-2000*, eds. A. Parkinson and E. Phoenix (Four Courts Press, Dublin 2010), p. 152

67. G. Walker, *The Politics of Frustration – Harry Midgley and the Failure of the Labour Party in Northern Ireland* (Manchester University Press, 1985), p. 71

68. From Nihill donation collection, *op. cit.*

69. B. Faulkner, *Memoirs of a Statesman* (Littlehampton Book Services, London, 1978), p. 37

70. *Ibid.*, p. 17

71. From Nihill donation collection, *op. cit.*

72. C. Ryder, *Fighting Fitt* (Brehon Press, Belfast, 2006), p. 389

73. The *Independent*, 13 September 2014

74. E. Phoenix (ed.), *A Century of Northern Life – the Irish News and 100 Years of Ulster History, 1890s–1990s* (Ulster Historical Foundation, Belfast, 1994), p. 21

75. *Irish News*, 9 May 2015

76. *Ibid.*

77. M. Brodie, *The Tele – A History of the* Belfast Telegraph (Blackstaff Press, Belfast, 1995)

78. *Belfast Telegraph*, 1 April 1958

79. Brodie, *op. cit.*, p. 126

80. *Belfast Telegraph*, 31 January 1969

81. A. Gailey, *Crying in the Wilderness – Jack Sayers: A Liberal Editor in Ulster 1939–69* (Institute of Irish Studies, Belfast, 1995), pp. 163–4.

82. Danny Kinahan defeated William McCrea to gain South Antrim for the Ulster Unionists, and his former party leader Tom Elliott won in Fermanagh & South Tyrone.

83. *Belfast Telegraph*, 9 May 2015

CHAPTER ONE

A Volatile Cocktail
The North Belfast By-election, 1905

A battle between David and Goliath?

The September 1905 by-election for the North Belfast Westminster seat took place a few months after the formation of the Ulster Unionist Council (UUC), and a similar length of time before the return of the Liberal Party to power, after a gap of some 14 years. These events were not merely matters of chronological coincidence. Rather they represented the beginning of a new political era for Ulster's unionists. The establishment of a more democratic and better organised party structure reflected a more professional approach to politics, and would soon lead to a more considered choice of parliamentary candidates in the period leading up to the crisis over the Third Home Rule Bill. More crucially, this by-election would be the last before the Liberals' electoral success the following year and, especially after the party's change in leadership in 1908, when Herbert Asquith replaced Henry Campbell-Bannerman, would spark a renewed debate over Ireland's political future.

This 1905 contest in North Belfast presented a rare opportunity for those on the political left to break through sectarian barriers in what was then Ireland's most important industrial city. It would also be characterised by an unusual degree of fraternisation between the Belfast Protestant Association (BPA), an ultra-Protestant group which also claimed radical leanings, the Independent Orange Order (IOO), and those campaigning on behalf of North Belfast's Labour candidate, William Walker. Indeed, this fusion of "orange" and "red" in a Belfast election contest spawned an albeit short-lived political movement known as "Walkerism", which married socialist principles with a recognition of the importance of the political union between Britain and Ireland.

Conducted during the last years of an era in which there was a severely limited franchise and when electoral malpractices were rife, the contest also showed the extent to which the local press (particularly the *Belfast Telegraph*) influenced political decision-making in the city during the early part of the twentieth century. This chapter will firstly explore in depth the political context of the time, and then go on to look at the coverage by *Belfast Telegraph* and *Irish News* of the respective candidates' campaigns. The final section will analyse the impact of the election's outcome.

This period – between the demise of Charles Stewart Parnell and the failure of Gladstone's second attempt at Irish Home Rule in 1893, to the return to Westminster of a new Liberal administration in 1906 – was one of relative political calm in Ireland. Whilst the Irish nationalist movement was starting to regroup, the British Conservative administration of Lord Salisbury had largely diverted its attention in Irish affairs to concerns over land and education. This is not to imply that unionists, especially those in Ulster, were complacent about their constitutional security: as has been noted above, a democratically-elected unionist decision-making body, the UUC, was established in Belfast in 1905.

During this period too, the economic differences between the Greater Belfast area and the rest of Ireland continued to be more obvious. Belfast had been awarded city status in 1888, and work had started on its new civic headquarters before the end of the century. This was completed in 1906. The city's industries grew ever more prosperous, especially in the shipyards, linen mills and rope and cigarette factories, as the urban population mushroomed in size.

The new city had a reputation for being a rare bastion of conservatism in Ireland, albeit one with distinctive sectarian hues. This had been evident for many years in municipal and parliamentary elections, where Conservative candidates had generally prevailed. However, by the turn of the twentieth century, Belfast's political landscape had started to shift. Working-class Protestants, whilst still loyal to King and Empire, were increasingly concerned about their jobs, wages and social conditions, particularly as economic depression and unemployment hit several Belfast trades. They were no longer prepared to automatically give their support to electoral candidates from the landlord or aristocratic classes, a trend which was duly acknowledged by unionist strategists, who were increasingly promoting the selection of self-made northern business and professional men as political representatives – men such as Charles and James Craig, William Moore and

William McMordie. The distinctive unease amongst ordinary Protestant voters over the Tory domination of the municipal and parliamentary scene, was evident in quite disparate sections of the Protestant working and lower-middle classes. Criticism of the city's Conservative elite came on the one hand from the anti-Catholic BPA, composed nearly exclusively of working-class men, and on the other, from an emerging group of labour and union activists.

These years therefore witnessed an increase in the popularity of anti-establishment unionism, with pressure groups, parliamentary representatives and polemic writers denouncing Conservative policies in Ireland, as well as the island's Catholic hierarchy. The BPA, formed during the 1890s, was a group which demanded a more inclusive brand of unionism, one which would appeal to the working classes, as well as denouncing the association between nationalism and Catholicism in Irish political life. At a by-election in August 1902, BPA leader, Thomas H. Sloan had replaced another maverick unionist representative, William Johnston, as Westminster MP for South Belfast. Sloan would soon fall out with the leadership of the Orange Order in the city and establish his own Independent Orange Order, which was quickly able to claim a membership of 55 lodges, with nearly half of these in Belfast. The BPA leader's stance blended a unique mixture of sectarian rhetoric with an undisguised empathy with many causes popular with embryonic labour political groups. For instance, Sloan, who had defeated the Conservative candidate C.W. Dunbar-Buller by over 800 votes (3,795 to 2,969) in the by-election, expressed sympathy with issues relating directly to improving the lives of the working classes, such as better housing provision, factory reform, trade union rights; he was also the only Unionist MP to express support for the Miners' Eight-Hour Bill at Westminster.[1]

Sloan and his colleagues were influenced by the political journalism of Lindsay Crawford, a Lisburn-born writer, who was forthright in his denunciation of both the Irish Anglican Church and the Conservatives' alleged policy of "placating Catholic Ireland". In a pamphlet entitled, "The Magheramorne Manifesto", Crawford called for "a patriotic class alliance", and urged the promotion of a progressive social programme. Blaming the Tories for their apparent "obliteration of any Protestant landmark", he lamented the clear "effacing of Protestantism from its programme". Crawford also warned that "although Home Rule [has been] defeated, Rome Rule still survives under the guise of Unionism".[2]

One can understand why many trade unionists and socialists – including the national leaders of the Labour Representation Committee (LRC), the forerunner of the Labour Party – had such high hopes of recruiting numerous members and gaining votes in the Greater Belfast area at this crucial juncture, around the turn of the twentieth century. This was a period when the region's comparatively late industrialisation was nearing its peak, resulting in a considerable industrial workforce spread over a number of key industries. It was also a time when sectarian tension in the North had not been stirred by the question of Home Rule. Obviously both the trade union movement, which had been active in Ireland since the early 1890s, with an Irish Trade Union Congress (ITUC) having been established in 1894, and its political associates in the LRC and later Independent Labour Party (ILP), were tempted by the concentration of workers in Ireland's north-eastern corner, where over 19,000 workers – nearly half of the island's total union membership – belonged to trade unions. As would be seen in the North Belfast by-election of 1905, "the political complexity of the Belfast labour movement emerged as a cocktail of socialism and unionism".[3]

Some of the early national figures in the Labour Party, including Keir Hardie, Ramsay MacDonald and Arthur Henderson, recognised the potential afforded by such a concentration of union members, but were cautious about their degree of involvement in local politics, and this relative uncertainty was reflected in their attitude to both the North Belfast contest and subsequent election contests in Ireland. Historian Terry Cradden has criticised Labour's approach during this period, 1900–1920, as being "superficially consistent but, in reality, full of contradictions". This was because the leadership of the LRC were "by turns either disinterested or exasperated by the intricacies of Irish politics".[4]

The leading figure in Northern Ireland trade union organisation and early labour politics was Belfast-born William Walker, whose parliamentary candidature for Labour in North Belfast was the first recorded in Ireland. He had earned a strong reputation through his trade union activity both at home and in the national organisation of the ILP, of which he was an executive member for four years, and later, in 1911, vice-chairman. He had, during the early 1890s, organised unskilled workers in the Belfast shipyards and, towards the end of that decade, he defended the rights of textile workers during a spell as a Poor Law Guardian. By this time too, he had earned a reputation for his feisty defence of workers' rights, and had been involved in several verbal exchanges on the steps of the city's Customs House with the firebrand Protestant preacher, Arthur Trew. In 1899, Walker was elected leader of the city's Carpenters' and Joiners' Union.

Although a committed trade unionist – his ultimate union accolade was the presidency of the ICTU – Walker recognised the urgent need for working-class political representation. Despite his own role in an industrial dispute involving the Joiners' Union in Belfast around the turn of the twentieth century, he clearly believed that the political route for working-class advancement was preferable to constant threats of strike activity. Speaking in his capacity as president of the ICTU in 1904, he argued:

> Surely it is a better and saner policy to spend £1,000 on the return of a member to the House of Commons, than to spend ten times that amount on a strike which is often not successful[?][5]

This belief led to Walker's election to the city council and his subsequent nomination as Labour's parliamentary candidate. Although his political career would be dominated by defeats – not only was he unsuccessful in the 1905 by-election, but he also failed to be elected in three subsequent Westminster elections – Walker's attempts to offer a viable alternative to Northern voters provided a short-lived boost to local politics.[6] What he offered voters was very different – a distinctive blend of socialism and unionism, which was soon to be called "Walkerism". Arguably his brand of municipal socialism was stronger than his unionism, and his stated support for maintaining the constitutional Union was always less strident than his commitment to improving the economic and social conditions of working men. For Walker, the interests of British and Irish workers were intertwined, with the latter's livelihoods being dependent upon British materials and markets.

During the summer of 1905, the sitting Conservative member for the Westminster seat of North Belfast, Sir James H. Haslett died, and by the end of August that year, the parliamentary division's Conservative Association committee had selected his successor. This was to be the current Lord Mayor of Belfast, Sir Daniel Dixon, whose acceptance speech at Ligoniel Orange Hall prompted "loud applause" from the assembled members.[7] With William Walker's nomination for Labour already in place, it appeared to many observers that the likely battle for the North Belfast seat would take on a "David versus Goliath" quality. On paper at least, Walker appeared to be a rank outsider. Dixon on the other hand was a wealthy ship-owner and timber merchant, who was also a director of the Ulster Rail Company. Many of the North Belfast electors would have been in his employment, and, as noted above, he had additional standing as the city's mayor, a post he had occupied six times.

Yet Sir Daniel Dixon was by no means assured of victory in North Belfast. Unpopular with many workers on account of his intransigent approach to trade union demands – the *Belfast News Letter* actively opposed his candidature on account of his record in this area – the Conservative candidate was also facing allegations of political corruption. These had followed his part in a controversial land deal, which had resulted in the city council purchasing developed land at a grossly inflated price. In addition, Dixon was a poor public speaker, who, on account of his position as the city's mayor, chose to restrict his speaking engagements in the run-up to Election Day. Labour activists in Belfast, as well as several leading party figures in Britain, considered that their candidate, Walker stood a genuine chance of taking the seat. Apart from the perceived weakness of his Tory opponent, there was the fact that a large number of shipyard workers (close to 20 per cent) were out of work at this time; Walker's supporters also knew they could expect a degree of backing from Tom Sloan and the BPA, as well as the Independent Orange Order. There was as well as a small Catholic minority in the constituency who might be attracted to Walker's position. In the light of all of this, many neutral observers acknowledged that the Labour candidate had a chance of making a political breakthrough in the constituency. Finally, for many it appeared to be the right time for socialists to mount a challenge against Tories in Belfast. With Home Rule still on the political back-burner, fewer hard-line electors were more likely to consider new political arguments.

"Alien invaders"
The North Belfast constituency had been a bastion of traditional unionism for many years. Sir James Haslett, who had died on 18 August 1905, had won the seat in a previous by-election nine years previously, following the death of the shipyard magnate, Sir Edward Harland. At a time when all women and a majority of men were still denied the vote, the total electorate in the constituency remained small. Yet the electoral boundaries within the area were some distance apart, stretching from Greencastle to Ligoniel, and embracing many major thoroughfares and districts, such as the Antrim,

Shore, Crumlin and Shankill Roads. Political interest amongst the voters of North Belfast had been high in the recent past, and a large turn-out on polling day, 10 September, was anticipated.

The contest was, as we have seen, to be between a spokesman for LRC, the emerging party which claimed to represent the working man, and the nominee of the Conservative Party, which symbolised older, more traditional values, most especially the formal political links between Britain and Ireland. Hopes of a Labour victory were particularly high, and these were in no small measure due to the belief that the Tory Party was fielding a weak candidate – though this, of course, was not recognised by unionist newspapers such as the *Belfast Telegraph*.

Sir Daniel Dixon's campaign was, to say the least, low-key. During the short, two-week campaign, there appear to have been only a handful of organised meetings held on his behalf, with the Tory candidate preferring to either deliberately absent himself from the gathering (instead issuing a message read out by an aide), or to restrict his vocal contribution to a brief statement about his policies. Dixon insisted this was on account of his mayoral status, and that he was anxious not to damage the office by his overly vociferous involvement in what was likely to prove a bitterly-fought contest.

Some critics, however, concluded that Dixon's reticence at becoming fully embroiled in his own campaign was indicative of an awareness of his limitations as a public speaker. Indeed, historian Austen Morgan has suggested that, "despite his position as first citizen of Belfast, [Dixon was] the proverbial political ass".[8] In his election address, Dixon appears to have made a conscious decision to appeal to those sympathetic to the perilous predicament of the less privileged in the constituency:

> I will support any feasible efforts to solve difficult and pressing problems, [such] as the reform of the Poor Law system, the case of the unemployed, the Housing of the Working Classes, the provision of Old Age Pensions and the peaceful settlement of Trade Disputes. The Workmen's Compensation Act should be improved and extended.[9]

Whilst their candidate's personal contribution to his own campaign seems to have been minimal, the use by Dixon's supporters of distinctively Edwardian electioneering tactics served to enliven Dixon's otherwise low-key campaign. At one meeting, slides were projected with a magic lantern on to gable walls and on to a screen mounted on a horse-drawn van. Meanwhile, one meeting programme depicted "the King, Sir Daniel Dixon, Indian cowboys, the running match, the cycle parade, cycle racing, football celebrations, the great sea serpent and funeral of Japanese standard-bearers".[10]

The *Belfast Telegraph*'s coverage of the election campaign, whilst spasmodic in its nature, was still immensely supportive of the Conservative candidate. This was undoubtedly a vital factor in his ultimate success in a tightly-contested battle, especially given Dixon's lack of popularity with liberal unionists, the *Belfast News Letter*, and with those independently-minded Protestant voters who had become increasingly disenchanted with Tory policies. The *Belfast Telegraph* stressed the Conservative candidate's qualities as a businessman rather than his supposed political acumen, and, on a number of occasions, urged its readers to "vote for Dixon and local employment". Much of the paper's coverage favourably contrasted Dixon's solid standing in municipal politics with the "rowdyism" associated with his opponent, which, it was claimed, had manifested itself at several election meetings. One *Belfast Telegraph* report described the initial meeting in support of Dixon at Clifton Street Orange Hall as a "lively" one, with "Walkerite" supporters positioning themselves towards the back of the venue, where they "tried to drown out speakers". The report noted that these "youths", who were "certainly not voters", were afterwards "treated with contempt" by the bulk of the audience as backers of the Conservative candidate. The paper's editorial cited Dixon's "superiority" over his Labour opponent, highlighting his "close personal associations" with the city as an "employer of labour", and went on to suggest that Dixon would make an "ideal representative" for the North Belfast constituency.[11]

The *Belfast Telegraph* also denounced the "radical invasion" of North Belfast by leading figures in the fledgling British LRC group, and editorials on each of the last three days of the campaign concentrated on this aspect of William Walker's candidature. In the first of these leading articles, the paper pointed out that this high-profile campaigning by such supporters of Walker was taking place in "an intensely loyal constituency", and had been "devised for the specific purpose of informing voters in England and Scotland" of their wider programmes "in view of the probable early advent of a general election".[12] Dismissing the claims of Walker and his supporters that the central issue in the contest was one between "Labour and Capital", the same editorial assured its readers that "the working men of North Belfast will not be made the stepping stones to power of the English Radical Party". Insisting there was "no comparison" between the two candidates, and therefore "no difficulty in deciding between them", the paper reminded its readership that the Conservative nominee sought "no personal aggrandisement" and had "no axe to grind" in his parliamentary candidature, and would consequently not be the "tool of any political party in England".[13]

Another opinion piece in the *Belfast Telegraph* the following day once more deplored the "hostile" and "alien invasion from across the Channel", and its attempt to "hoist the standard of Radicalism and Home Rule in an intensely loyal Ulster constituency".[14] In a final comment on the eve of the contest, the paper's editorial, "A Radical Invasion", accused the Labour campaign group of being "equivocal" and "misrepresentative" in their claims, arguing that a successful William Walker would oppose Home Rule only on account of the question of the "separation of labour" (that is, unionist workers being separated from their trade union colleagues in Great Britain), rather than on "constitutional principle". The paper was especially indignant at Ramsay MacDonald's presence in North Belfast (he was acting as Walker's election agent), dismissing him as a "stranger", who had advocated for Irish Home Rule and the abolition of the House of Lords, as well as adopting a "pro-Boer" stance during the recent war in South Africa. Referring also to the active support within the constituency of other leading LRC figures, such as Keir Hardie and Arthur Henderson, the editorial maintained that "these are the men who are running Radicalism in North Belfast", also pointing out that every Labour parliamentary candidate over the course of the previous decade had backed Home Rule, and condemning this "vigorous effort" on the part of the Left in England to "thrust the issue – the most important Irish question of the day – into the background".[15] The piece concluded that the English Labour contingent would, upon their arrival back in Great Britain after the contest, share a "'deep and honest conviction that the working men of North Belfast are not the fools they took them for".[16]

Central to the thinking of both candidates, and newspapers like the *Belfast Telegraph*, was the fundamental question of the union. Indeed, it was explicitly broached in the election address of the Labour nominee, with Walker emphasising that he was opposed to Home Rule and confirming he was "a unionist in politics". The newspaper queried Walker's commitment to the British link, forecasting that if he was returned to Westminster, he "would vote for Home Rule", and asserted that his campaign team were intent on "subverting the Union".[17] An editorial the following day returned to querying the Labour candidate's sincerity on the union issue. The paper maintained that "both candidates profess unionist interests but with that, the similarity terminates". It argued that the "unionism of the man who is surrounded by Radicals, Socialists and defeated Home Rule candidates cannot, surely, be described as a 'true blue unionism'".[18] Denouncing Walker for his description of the Home Rule question as a "red herring" which had been used by Tories to "obscure the real issue of the election", the *Belfast Telegraph* asserted its conviction that Sir Daniel Dixon would be returned to Westminster in a matter of days. Pointing out that the voters of North Belfast were by no means as "innocent" as the English Labour "muses" believed, the piece went on to argue as follows:

> They [the electors] insist on being represented at Westminster by a man whose Unionism has been tested, tried and not found wanting … Is North Belfast prepared to throw its traditional Unionism in the gutter? We refuse to believe it … it is the duty of every true Loyalist to take off his coat in support of the Unionist candidate.[19]

On the eve of the contest, the *Belfast Telegraph* printed its clearest endorsement of the Conservative Party's candidate. Its editorial, which was entitled, "Nearing the Finish", noted the final "utmost endeavours" being made by both campaign teams, contrasting the "steady and consistent" electoral promises of Sir Daniel Dixon with "a demonstration of Radicalism, which would do credit to the most rabidly socialist constituency in the Midlands of England".[20] Despite Labour's attempts to "hide the cloven hoof of Socialism", the paper asserted that there had been concerted efforts by the Walker team to "blindfold them [working men], and lead them like sheep at the heels of the English Labour and Radical Party", and again questioned the true extent of Walker's support for the British connection, and his creditability as a potential Westminster representative:

> He has not two ideas of his own but is 'deeply interested' in everything that will bring him half-a-dozen votes. Fancy a unionist constituency run by a Labour organisation governed by

Radicals and with a defeated Home Rule candidate for his election agent! Is not that sufficient to ruin him in the eyes of every sane man in the division? He says 'simply nothing' on the Irish issue.[21]

In a final rallying call to voters, the *Belfast Telegraph* expressed its conviction that the electors of the "loyalist stronghold" of North Belfast would refrain from electing a candidate who was "soft" on the question of the British connection. Referring to Sir Daniel Dixon, the paper reminded readers that he was "one of themselves", as well as being "one of the men who has made Belfast what it is as a community and industrial centre". Reducing the contest to a "referendum" on the union, the *Belfast Telegraph* editorial exhorted its readers to "fly the old flag – vote for Dixon!"

The final election meetings took place on 13 September, the eve of Polling Day. Processions representing both sectional interests had "toured the division" and, in stark contrast to subsequent elections, there appeared to be "no ill feeling" at these gatherings. The city's Trades Council organised a workers' demonstration on behalf of the Labour candidate. This started at Carlisle Circus to the north of the city centre and, led by bands and banner-waving tradesmen, proceeded to Comber Place where an open-air meeting was briefly addressed by Walker. At around the same time elsewhere in the constituency, Sir Daniel Dixon appeared at another street gathering, which also "passed off successfully".[22]

Election Day brought favourable weather, and the respective party officials were prepared for a busy day. A close contest was anticipated and a high turn-out was also expected. Thirteen polling stations across the constituency were set to open for twelve hours (from 8.00 a.m. to 8.00 p.m.), to afford workers the opportunity of casting their vote. To prevent any electoral irregularity, ballot boxes were brought to the county courthouse in the constituency, where they warranted a police guard. Apart from the Westminster contest, voters were also asked to nominate a councillor to represent the Woodvale ward on Belfast Council (Sir James Haslett had also performed this role), and the Earl of Shaftesbury was duly elected.

Voting was brisk and just under 2,000 votes were reportedly cast within two hours of the start of polling. This prompted speculation that Sir Daniel Dixon had taken "a substantial lead" of some 300 votes. Both candidates had been out and about in the constituency early in the day to "reassure" their respective supporters, and at the county courthouse, the candidates' campaign teams had utilised a large tent which had been erected close to the courthouse railings – this served as a tally-room for party staff. There was an electric atmosphere around the whole constituency, with hundreds of shipyard workers seen in and about the polling stations; there were also "vehicles of all descriptions, from the humble trap to the lordly motor, flying about bringing voters to the poll."[23]

In its final editorial comment on Election Day, the *Belfast Telegraph* returned to familiar themes, criticising the "Radical invaders", and questioning the personal qualities of the Labour candidate. The former were dismissed as "carpet-baggers and professional politicians", who were simply the "hired soldiers of the English Radical Party". They were men who, "having little to do at present in their own country, have been drafted hither to earn their salaries".[24] Despite its castigation of this external intervention by the LRC, the *Belfast Telegraph* conceded that the numbers of these "invaders" were not as great as had been anticipated, and indeed the British-based Labour officials had been largely restricted to a sideline role during the campaign. This final leading article also endeavoured to place the central issues, at least as far as the journal saw them, into context. Simplifying the election in terms of "a Radical Socialist versus Unionist contest", the newspaper ridiculed the Labour candidate's willingness to please as many sections of the electorate as possible. It suggested that "a more obedient and invertebrate candidate had never been brought before any constituency", and proclaimed that William Walker was "void of any idea he can call his own". Stating with some irony that the Labour candidate "deserved credit for having done what no candidate [had] ever before accomplished", the paper claimed that he had "promised everything asked and swallow[ed] every panacea laid before him". Alluding to Walker's bid to appease both temperance and brewing trade lobbies during the campaign, the editorial berated him for "satisfying at one and the same time an extreme section of temperance reformers and members of 'the trade'".[25]

Finally, reminding its readers of the severe threat posed by Walker's candidature, the newspaper maintained that, "only by every voter doing his duty" would the "Radical and Home Rule invasion of a Ulster Loyalist constituency be defeated", and insisted that "no stone must be left unturned to serve the return of Sir Daniel Dixon at the head of the poll by an overwhelming majority".[26]

"A much maligned man"

Few references were made in the unionist press to William Walker's actual policies, and comment instead tended to focus on his perceived "softness" on the union question. Yet he was advocating major changes, particularly in social and economic policy. These included reforms to the system of land taxation, to railway provision in the North of Ireland and to the working conditions of seamen (a large number of North Belfast's population were dockers or sailors), which he described as being "significant omissions" from the election address of Sir Daniel Dixon. Other areas which were specifically highlighted by the Labour candidate included the system of Poor Law provision, the introduction of state pensions and the controversial issue of temperance reform. In these issues, Walker played on the economic depression and the hardship being suffered by many people around this time, and was particularly forthright in his criticism of Belfast Corporation, which he contended was dominated by "the Unionist landlord party who call themselves unionists".[27] He also played down the national question, maintaining that by electing a representative pledged to maintaining the political union between Britain and Ireland and to improving the position of industrial workers, North Belfast's electorate would be in a better position than if they simply adhered to their allegiances to the one-dimensional Conservative Party. Walker maintained that if electors returned a candidate who was "a unionist, plus a Labour representative, they would be striking the greatest blow that could be struck against the maintenance of Home Rule opposition in England".[28]

Faced with a largely hostile unionist press and a relative dearth of election funds, which necessitated the organisation of several outdoor meetings, William Walker appeared to be a politician fighting a mainly defensive, back-against-the-wall campaign. One early election report noted his speech to an appreciative audience in the constituency's Ohio Street on 31 August, when he promised that he would "rebound" from the hostility and condemnation which was being hurled in his direction and ultimately win the seat. At this meeting, he also pinpointed the weaknesses of his electoral opponent. Quoting from the minutes of Belfast Corporation meetings, which clearly illustrated Sir Daniel Dixon's advocacy of low rates of pay for Corporation workers – the lord mayor was insisting that 16 shillings was a "sufficient" weekly wage for his employees, whereas William Walker demanded a minimum of £1 – the Labour candidate concluded that, "based on his record at the Corporation, Sir Daniel Dixon could not expect to get 100 votes", and that "no one" would vote for the Conservative candidate, "except those who had little time whatsoever for the working man".[29] Further criticism of Dixon's record as mayor came in Walker's denunciation of his opponent's decision to award a large furnishing contract for the new city hall, which was nearing completion, to a Manchester firm, at a time when "the carpenters and joiners were idle in Belfast".[30]

What was so distinctive about this by-election was the involvement in an Irish constituency of several leading members of a new British political party. Apart from Ramsay MacDonald's role as Walker's election agent, both Arthur Henderson and Keir Hardie spoke at his election meetings. Henderson told an audience that, as "a working-man representative from the other side of the water, it affords me great pleasure to stand up in support of my friend".[31] He went on to express his "joy" at the "great change" which was increasingly apparent in the political awareness of British workers, and said that he was confident that Walker would be returned in North Belfast, making it "one of the greatest democratic victories the Labour Party could secure".[32] Speaking in the Shankill district the following evening, Ramsay MacDonald called on his audience to "follow up the example of Woolwich and Barnard Castle, and return a Labour man". Walker's agent also warned those present that a vote for the Conservative candidate would be aiding the interests of "landlordism" in the city, whilst they could remain assured that Walker would "vote every time for the amelioration of the conditions of the poor".[33] Walker also endorsed this notion of a united working-class movement across Britain and Ireland during this "large" gathering in Craven Street. Although this meeting was curtailed due to inclement weather and Walker's imminent departure on an England-bound ferry, the Labour candidate assured supporters that the contest would prove to be a "people's election, and not a party one". His message for English Labour supporters would be that the "electors of North Belfast are going to do their utmost in securing proper labour representation".[34]

This cross-channel influence on the Labour Party's campaign in North Belfast was also evident in posters which were being "extensively posted" across the constituency during the final week of the campaign. This involved the copying of extracts from a manifesto signed by British Labour MPs and trade union officials, calling on the area's working classes to vote for William Walker.[35]

The political tension inevitably rose during the contest's final phase, which also saw the exposure of crucial flaws in the Labour candidate's strategy. Yet just a few days before polling, William Walker's political star appeared to be most in its ascendancy. He had received "a most enthusiastic reception" at a meeting in Fortwilliam Parade, where a loyalist band had made "an ineffectual attempt to interfere". At this gathering, Walker stressed the "unique" nature of the contest, for they were "not appealing to any party sects or religious bigotry, but to all classes of the city".[36]

A few days before polling, the Imperial Protestant Federation (IPF) – a right-wing pressure group with links to the BPA – invited responses from both candidates to a series of controversial, rather crudely conceived questions. The Conservative candidate wisely chose to ignore the request of the IPF for a response to these questions, but Walker, again seeking to counter impressions of being weak on the union question, agreed to engage with this relatively obscure group. In his responses, the Labour candidate asserted his opposition to a Catholic acceding to the throne, or being appointed to the office of Lord Lieutenant of Ireland. He also objected to the establishment of a Catholic university in Ireland, and supported state inspections of convents and monasteries. Walker's opponents maximised this golden opportunity for making political capital, posting copies of the Labour candidate's replies in prominent places within Catholic districts of North Belfast. Liberal unionists, including the editor of the *Northern Whig*, were to the fore in their denunciation of Walker's "sham, narrow-minded bigotry", and even his closest aides were apparently in despair at this clear error of judgement. Writing after he had heard the news of Walker's ill-judged replies, Ramsay MacDonald predicted a defeat in the imminent election:

> I was never more sick of an election than that at North Belfast, and then the religious replies coming at the end of it knocked everything out of me. I am afraid that those answers of his will make it impossible to win the constituency.[37]

In this attempt to woo sectional interests, William Walker had fractured any hopes of appealing to the small but vital contingent of Catholic voters (estimated at around 10 per cent of the total number of electors) and had, in effect, presented the result of the election on a plate to his opponent. This error of judgement was probably due to a desire not to further upset grass-root loyalist elements, rather than proof of some concealed sectarian sentiment – although historian Marianne Elliott has denounced Walker's decision to "place the interests of Protestantism above those of party" as evidence of the ultimate "failure of socialism to surmount Belfast's traditional sectarianism".[38] The Labour candidate privately conceded he had made a mistake, and tried to create a forum to explain these "sensational allegations" by challenging his opponent to debate key issues in the Ulster Hall.[39]

On the eve of the election, a "very large and enthusiastic trade union meeting" was organised by the Belfast Trades and Labour Council. This had the support of a plethora of trade unions, including those representing the city's carpenters, joiners, mill-sawyers, iron-founders, upholsterers, blacksmiths and boiler-makers. A subsequent report noted how, by 6.30 in the evening, "the streets leading to Carlisle Circus began to be thronged with men – obviously workmen after their day's toil – journeying to the rendezvous". Traffic was "somewhat impeded" in neighbouring streets, where trade unionists and accompanying bands had congregated, and soon "the air resounded with the shrilling of the bagpipes, the tooting of the flutes, the rattle of drums and the crash of cymbals".[40] As the North's leading nationalist newspaper, the *Irish News* wrote approvingly of the labour candidate, "a much maligned man", who had "rejoiced loudly at the sight of Catholics and Protestants united in a common cause, the cause of labour". This edition of the paper also described light-hearted banter between the assembling trade unionists and smaller groups of counter-protesting loyalists. A "weird-looking" horse-drawn vehicle, draped in pro-Labour posters – including one bearing the slogan, "Vote for Dixon and Chinese Slavery" – drove past Carlisle Circus, with the *Irish News* noting that the "real Dixon contingent came on sidecars" which drove "light-heartedly into the centre of the crowd".[41]

Although it regarded the contest in North Belfast as fundamentally one between two pro-Union candidates and therefore removed from the immediate interests of their readership, the *Irish News* shared the Labour candidate's opposition to Daniel Dixon, and this was evident in the tone and extent of the paper's election coverage. It had reported the announcement of Dixon's candidature in the constituency in a single paragraph report on 28 August that year; a more substantial report entitled, "North Belfast Representation – Against Home Rule and Devolution", was included in the following day's edition. Once the North Belfast Conservative Association had ratified the decision to nominate Sir Daniel Dixon at a meeting in Clifton Street Orange Hall, the *Irish News* had been barred from attending an informal gathering of the unionist press held afterwards. The Conservative Association's Presiding Officer and former MP for the area, Sir William Ewart, had backed the nomination, although he also conceded that local unionists "would be required to make a good fight to win the election".[42] Sir Daniel Dixon subsequently announced that, to avoid any conflict of interests as the city's Chief Magistrate or Mayor, he would be entering the contest in a private capacity, and would not therefore directly address any political gatherings. He declared himself a strong opponent of the proposed devolution scheme advocated by Lord Dunraven, and stated that, "if any attempt is made to grant Home Rule to Ireland, I will, if elected, do my utmost in Parliament to defeat it".[43]

In the same edition of the *Irish News*, there was more detailed coverage of the formal announcement of Walker's candidature for Labour. A "fair-sized" meeting of Labour Party members in a hall in Dawson Street gave the local man a "cordial" reception. Walker confessed that it would "not be easy" to sustain a campaign, given the party's limited finances. This "handicap" would prevent them from hiring halls for staging meetings, most of which would have to be conducted outdoors. However, he and his party were committed to working towards "lifting the working classes out of the slough of despondency and unenlightenment [sic] into which they had fallen", after "72 years of Liberal and Tory rule". Condemning these parties' joint "legacy of unemployment" and failure to cope with the perennial problem of poverty – he drew his audience's attention to recent claims that there were 12 million people suffering such a predicament across Great Britain and Ireland – Walker called for more stringent land taxes on ground valuations. He reminded his audience that his opponent was against such a proposal, perhaps because Sir Daniel Dixon had "so much land that he is not able to occupy it". Walker added that "not a city in the world would put up with the ground rents we are paying in Belfast".[44]

Whilst the *Irish News* maintained its low-key coverage of the election contest, it reported in copious detail on the opening, on the eve of the election, of a nationalist hall in central Belfast's Donegall Street – the

St Patrick's branch of the United Irish League (UIL). The paper also informed its readers of an imminent meeting of nationalists to be held in west Belfast.[45] A subsequent editorial, "National work in the city", supported these endeavours to develop an effective political organisation devoted to nationalism in the city. Praising Joe Devlin's "well timed and appropriate" remarks at the opening ceremony at St Patrick's Hall, the *Irish News* backed the initiative, pointing out that it was "only through honest political effort and through the agencies which political effort brought into operation, that we can succeed in lifting our country from the impoverishment and desolation to which it has been reduced".[46]

The *Irish News*, although opposed to both Sir Daniel Dixon as a candidate and the party he represented, was, however, not averse to printing his campaign advertisements, publicising details of forthcoming meetings, as well as reproducing the Conservative candidate's election address (the text of which would prove to be particularly significant, given that he was not prepared to give detailed speeches at meetings organised on his behalf). In this address, Dixon claimed he had an "unimpeachable" record as a unionist and, as far as he was concerned, there would be "no compromise" on the union issue. Pledging "firm adherence" to the Conservative administration in London and to its fiscal policy, he went on to make a couple of observations on social issues. His position on the temperance question was considerably more forthright than William Walker's, and, in supporting legislation for banning the opening of public houses on Sundays across Ireland – as well as proposing a further restriction on Saturday opening hours – he deplored the "misery which is being caused by excessive drinking".[47] Dixon also announced his support for recent legislation backing workers who had been injured during the course of their work, and called for the Compensation Acts to be "improved and extended".

Meanwhile, in one of his early election meetings, held in Greencastle on 29 August, Walker told a "well-attended" gathering that he believed there had been irregularities in the selection of the Tory candidate. Pointing out that a number of the members of the select committee had been "in the employ of Sir William Ewart", Walker maintained that "had they failed to attend, they would have been relieved of their positions next morning". Stressing his working-class credentials, Walker denied he was a closet Tory, and called on voters to "send to Parliament the man whose party would assist the people in their adversity".[48]

Whilst the *Irish News* printed Dixon's election address for a second time on 13 September, and included a Conservative Party advert in the following day's edition (under the headline, "Vote early for Dixon today"), the paper's coverage of his campaign remained low-key. Most of its editorial comment focused on the bad feeling between the two "pro-Union" camps, and how this boiled over at official meetings, especially those held by the Conservative Party. One *Irish News* opinion piece described "a spirit of revolt" within the constituency which had "raised its head in North Belfast, and would prove to be one which the erstwhile demigods of the Tory Party would find it hard to lay".[49] The paper reported the "catcalling" of unionist dignitaries, such as Thomas Sinclair and Sir William Ewart, and deplored the "extraordinary" scenes at a Conservative Party meeting in Clifton Street Orange Hall, which had been "besieged" by supporters of William Walker. The audience were "most antagonistic" towards the Tory candidate and "a more disorderly meeting has not been seen in Belfast for many years". The same report condemned the bad language and angry calls from the back of the hall, which were related to denunciations of Dixon's record as a city councillor and mayor. Another interesting feature of this meeting touched upon by the paper was the distribution of hundreds of pro-Labour leaflets, denouncing the use of slavery in the Transvaal. This was a rare case of a contemporary international issue finding itself the focus of election literature in a North of Ireland election contest. Elsewhere in its report, the *Irish News* noted Thomas Sinclair's description of his party's nominee as "a true, tried and tested unionist", who would be a valuable asset at Westminster, especially with the Liberals threatening to introduce Home Rule in a new administration. However, the paper also made it clear that its journalists had no direct interest in this contest:

> We say nothing as to the respective merits of Sir Daniel Dixon and his opponent, Mr William Walker. The occasion is of interest to us only as a demonstration of insurgent democratic feeling. To howl them down and refuse to listen to their speeches is a new development of the democratic attitude of Orangemen towards the men whom they have been taught to consider their superiors in every way. What is this new spirit which impels Orangemen to cry down the men whom they formerly looked upon as their natural leaders?[50]

During the last week of the campaign, the *Irish News* made further references to infighting between the respective election camps. Reporting a meeting in Ballysillan Drill Hall on 5 September, the paper dismissed Dixon's contribution as being "short and, it must be confessed, not a particularly newsworthy one".[51] The report went on to cite instances of "wordy warfare", in the form of "unfriendly interruptions and heckling" from Labour supporters in the audience. Sir Daniel Dixon and his chief backers warned against the election to Westminster of that "veiled supporter of Home Rule", William Walker; the Conservative candidate also briefly attempted to dismiss alleged "misrepresentations" made by his Labour counterpart over his record at Belfast City Council and the low wages he paid his workforce. A few days later, following a further outburst of heckling by Walker's supporters at a Conservative meeting at Castleton Schoolhouse, off the Antrim Road, the *Irish News* again led with reports of "uproar" and "disorder", and criticised the Tory candidate for arranging meetings which had resulted in "scenes of a most disorderly character".[52] At this meeting, a large number of Labour supporters had evaded attempts to bar them from attending, and as the meeting got under way, a pro-Walker Scottish piper even played in the road outside!

The *Irish News* coverage of Election Day was less detailed than that of the unionist press, but the paper too acknowledged the frenzy of anticipation which had been stoked up during the previous fortnight. It reckoned that there had "not for a good many years been an election in Belfast that created such an amount of interest as the contest just concluded in the Northern division".[53] Noting that there had been a couple of arrests for alleged personation offences, the paper's Election Day report described early morning activity at some of the 13 polling stations across the constituency. Observing the frenetic comings and goings at these stations, the paper observed how the supporters of the Conservative Party candidate had "come to his aid with a great number of conveyances, [with] motor cars predominating", and concluded that Dixon had enjoyed "a considerable advantage over his opponent, who had to rely on a few hackney cars".[54] Like its unionist counterparts, the *Irish News* speculated on the relative fortunes of the candidates over the course of the twelve-hour voting period. The paper believed there had been a "strong" unionist vote during the morning, with Labour doing better in the afternoon, and noted that few working-class electors had been seen casting their votes during the early evening.

A "chorus of congratulation"

The results of the North Belfast by-election were formally announced the following day. At this time, barely one in eight adults was believed to have enjoyed the franchise, and the constituency's electoral roll stood at a paltry 10,762. The fact that many working-class men, in particular the unskilled or semi-skilled, were still denied the vote especially disadvantaged the Walker camp. Yet a large number of those who were entitled to do so – 8,453, or some 82 per cent of those on the rolls – actually did turn out on that Thursday, 14 September.

Socialist fears, that William Walker's late, misguided comments on questions relating to Catholicism would scupper his electoral chances, were confirmed by the result. Sir Daniel Dixon's majority of 474 – he gained 4,440 votes to William Walker's 3,966 – was undoubtedly enhanced by the late switching in allegiances of many of the constituency's 1,000-plus Catholic electors to the Conservative camp.

According to the *Belfast Telegraph*, "loud and prolonged cheering" accompanied the announcement of the election's outcome, and the successful candidate, who had been reticent about making "political" speeches during the campaign, briefly addressed his jubilant supporters. Dixon admitted that, three weeks earlier, he had barely anticipated finding himself in his current position, and promised electors "nothing, save that was in my address". He added that this was in contrast with his opponent, who had "promised everything". This remark prompted laughter from the unionist majority in the audience and a protest from William Walker himself, who pronounced that "the time was not right to follow Daniel Dixon's example and make a political speech".[55]

That evening, there were victory celebrations across the constituency and, rather bizarrely, compared with the very different responses which would accompany subsequent election outcomes, supporters of the defeated candidate mingled freely and amicably with those professing support for the victor. A dignified election etiquette was being adhered to, with "no unpleasantness", and both sides "apparently enjoying the display with the best of good feeling". The participation of "Walkerites" in Dixon's victory procession was regarded as symptomatic of the "excellent spirit maintained on both sides from the start" of the contest. [56]

The *Belfast Telegraph* reported that a "chorus of congratulation" was witnessed in "numerous" parts of the constituency, including celebrations in the Crumlin Road, Ligoniel, Duncairn and Greencastle districts, all of which attracted "large crowds". These indulged in "vigorous cheering for the hero of the fight", who expressed his personal gratitude for their support. This "great display of popular enthusiasm" included the lighting of bonfires and the playing of popular loyalist tunes by marching bands. Unsurprisingly perhaps, it was the Shankill area which "excelled" in both its turnout and degree of enthusiasm, and "thousands of interested spectators" congregated into the early hours of Saturday morning to witness "one continual flare of flame", which dominated the skyline from "above Brown Square to West Belfast Orange Hall". The report added incidentally that this provoked "much anxiety" amongst owners of adjoining property in the area.[57]

The *Belfast Telegraph* was triumphalist in its analysis of the Conservatives' election victory. Its editorial, entitled, "No Surrender", argued that, apart from congratulating the new representative, North Belfast's voters also had "cause to congratulate themselves". A defeat for Sir Daniel Dixon, the paper maintained, would have meant that the city would be forced to "hide its diminished hand".[58] While it played down the relatively small majority enjoyed by Dixon, and pronounced that the result was "eminently satisfactory", the newspaper did at least concede that the election had proved to be "one of the most strenuously contested in the annals of Belfast". Dismissing the Radicals' campaign as being merely one where "red flags [had] deceived the real issue", it insisted that the Conservative candidate had refused to indulge in the "mud-slinging" of his Labour opponent, and that after "thirty years of service to the community", he would prove to be a "representative of every section of his constituents".[59]

Interpretation of the election result in British Tory-leaning journals was more measured. The *Morning Post* acknowledged the "comparative success" of William Walker's candidature and suggested that the high level of polling turnout constituted "a disposition among the electors of Belfast to take a rather wider political survey than they have done in the past".[60] However, the paper, with considerable foresight, also predicted that there was "not the least doubt that if the union were in danger, the Protestants of Ulster would set other considerations aside and vote solidly in its defence".[61]

The Labour representative partially excused his defeat on account of the substantially better resources available to his Tory opponent. Claiming that Dixon had benefited from the efforts of over 1,000 paid canvassers, and had sufficient funds to convey potential voters to the polling stations, Walker accused his opponent of employing "corrupt" practices.[62] At the same time, he played down his own advantage of being in the field for longer than the Tories, who had also triumphed despite the inadequacies of their candidate. Additionally, Walker had, publicly at least, failed to acknowledge the foolishness of his decision to respond directly to the loyalist questionnaire which had robbed him of several hundred votes.

The *Irish News'* slant on the election's outcome was radically different from that of its unionist counterparts. In its leader, "The Orange Democracy", the paper focused on the reaction of sections of the British press to the North Belfast result. The left-of-centre *Daily Chronicle* observed that Walker's prediction of victory in a re-run in the constituency at the forthcoming general election was "far from [being] an idle vaunt", and the paper stressed the "division and subdivision into which the Unionist Party has segregated".[63] The *Irish News* itself was more explicit in its assessment of the damage suffered by unionists in the city. Claiming that there was "not a doubt that the way in which the electorate has turned out augurs ill for the future of unionism in Ulster", it suggested that "the leaders of the old-time Orange ascendancy" must recognise this result as being "a forerunner of their final downfall".[64] Summing up the result as "a dwindling almost to nothing" of the Tory majority in the division, the paper's interpretation was of a fundamental change in the voting habits of the loyalist rank and file. "The Orange working man" was now voting "according to his own views", the editorial asserted, maintaining that this represented "the Orange democracy shaking itself from the shackles of the official body". By restructuring itself into "a new and more virile body", the Protestant working- and lower-middle classes had illustrated they had the potential of becoming "a power to be reckoned with in Irish affairs".[65]

⤿

This September 1905 by-election would prove to be the first of three contests in the constituency within an eighteen-month period. Within months of Dixon's success, and indeed before he had assumed his seat at Westminster, a general election was declared. Three of the Belfast's four unionist representatives would face bruising encounters with strong opponents. As well as Walker standing again in North Belfast, Joe Devlin contested West Belfast and Tom Sloan defended his South Belfast seat. Promising cooperation with men like

Sloan and Walker if they were elected, Devlin and his associates forged an unofficial election "alliance" involving socialists, nationalists and working-class loyalists.

Sir Daniel Dixon, adopting a more serious approach this time, stood down as mayor of Belfast before the election, and managed to gain an additional 467 votes (4,907 in total). However, despite polling an additional 650 votes himself (now 4,616), William Walker was again defeated, this time by a majority of 291. Tom Sloan was returned in South Belfast, and in West Belfast, Joe Devlin beat Captain J.R. Smiley by a mere 16 votes (4,138 to 4,122) to compound unionist woes.

Another by-election was called in North Belfast in April 1907, after Sir Daniel Dixon's death, and this time Walker had to be persuaded to represent Labour once more in the constituency. On this occasion, he had to face a new, more sophisticated political opponent, Sir George Clark, who gained a comfortable majority of 1,827: Walker's vote dropped by 422 to 4,194, compared with the victor's poll of 6,021.

Labour was damaged by the subsequent Dock Strike in the city led by James Larkin, and within three years, unionist vulnerability appeared to vanish, as the spectre of Home Rule once again appeared on the horizon. By the time of the general election of January 1910, unionists were once again in the driving seat, in Belfast at least, winning three of the city's four seats. William Walker remained active in Labour politics, debating socialism and Irish unity with the likes of James Connolly, who resided in the city for a period before World War I. In these discussions, Walker called on nationalists to abandon their calls for Irish unification, and instead to embrace the task of consolidating links with the British labour movement. In 1912, he was appointed a Poor Law Commissioner in Belfast and gradually retreated from the political scene.

❧

The 1905 North Belfast by-election provides a fascinating insight into the nature of political campaigning over a century ago, and also illustrates the intensity of public interest in political contests despite the disenfranchisement of the majority of the population. We have seen the contrasting political coverage provided by the main newspapers within the respective Catholic and Protestant communities. The *Irish News*, despite its stance of detachment from the parties contesting the seat, was clearly fervently opposed to the candidature of the Conservative Party's Sir Daniel Dixon, and mildly sympathetic to that of William Walker. The *Belfast Telegraph*, on the other hand, offered unconditional support to Dixon and, despite having a significant number of Protestant working-class readers who would have been sympathetic to the Labour cause, the paper strongly counselled against returning a Protestant candidate who combined nominal support of the union with a profound sympathy for working-class sectional interests.

Sir Daniel Dixon was one of the last old-style unionist candidates to be elected to Westminster, as a growing number of representatives, committed to a more professional and modern approach to the job, emerged on the political scene. The relative success of independent unionists like Thomas Sloan, and the genuine threat posed by Labour's William Walker, ensured that the unionist leadership would grow to respect grass-roots loyalist concerns – until, that is, the renewed threat of Irish unity, the proliferation in the number of Unionist Clubs and the ultimate formation of the Ulster Volunteer Force (UVF) all but obliterated the promise of a "liberal" unionist approach. For Belfast's infant Labour Party, Walker's by-election campaign marked its first serious challenge against the forces of conservatism and, on account of the imminent Home Rule legislation, it probably represented the last occasion for nearly half a century when the labour movement would enjoy a serious chance of making a significant political breakthrough.

In the new political climate which emerged later that decade, Walker's "combination of reformist socialism and unionism" would be doomed, as such pro-Labour and pro-Union groups crumbled as a result of "increasing pressure from a rejuvenated Unionist Party, and mounting tension on the Home Rule front".[66]

Endnotes

1. The BPA's role would be assumed by the Unionist Clubs during the Home Rule crisis on the eve of World War I, but the group would be revived during the Troubles at the start of the 1920s, when many of its members were involved in sectarian clashes with Catholics in Belfast.

2. J. Bardon, *A History of Ulster* (Blackstaff Press, Belfast, 1992), p. 416

3. R. Rees, *Ireland 1905–25, Volume One* (Colourpoint Books, Newtownards, 1998), p. 126

4. T. Cradden, "Labour in Britain and the NILP, 1900–70", in *The Northern Ireland Question in British Politics*, eds. P. Catterall and S. McDougall (Palgrave Macmillan, Basingstoke, 1996)

5. W. Walker, from J. Gray, *City in Revolt – James Larkin & the Belfast Dock Strike of 1907* (Blackstaff Press, Belfast, 1985), p. 27

6. William Walker would also be defeated in Leith at the first general election of 1910.

7. *Belfast Telegraph*, 1 September 1905

8. A. Morgan, *Labour and Partition – the Belfast Working Class, 1905–23* (Pluto Press, London, 1991), p. 71

9. *Ibid*, pp. 71–2

10. *Northern Whig*, 7 September 1905

11. *Belfast Telegraph*, 2 September 1905. Incidentally, Dixon did not attend this meeting, and a representative read out a statement on his behalf.

12. *Belfast Telegraph*, 7 September 1905

13. *Ibid.*

14. *Belfast Telegraph*, 8 September 1905

15. *Belfast Telegraph*, 9 September 1905

16. *Ibid.*

17. *Belfast Telegraph*, 2 September 1905

18. *Belfast Telegraph*, 8 September 1905

19. *Ibid.*

20. *Belfast Telegraph*, 13 September 1905

21. *Ibid.*

22. *Ibid.*

23. *Belfast Telegraph*, 14 September 1905

24. *Ibid.*

25. *Ibid.*

26. *Ibid.*

27. W. Walker, in H. Patterson, *Class Conflict and Sectarianism – the Protestant Working Class and the Belfast Labour Movement, 1868–1920* (Blackstaff Press, Belfast, 1980), p. 54

28. *Northern Whig*, 7 September 1905

29. *Irish News*, 1 September 1905

30. *Ibid.*

31. *Ibid.*

32. *Ibid.*

33. *Irish News*, 2 September 1905

34. *Ibid.*

35. *Irish News*, 5 September 1905. Labour's election rivals also distributed posters calling on "loyal men" not to vote for William Walker.

36. *Irish News*, 6 September 1905

37. Morgan, *op. cit.*, p. 75

38. M. Elliott, *The Catholics of Ulster – A History* (Allen Lane, London, 2000), p. 331

39. *Irish News*, 8 September 1905

40. *Irish News*, 14 September 1905

41. *Ibid.*

42. *Irish News*, 29 August 1905

43. *Ibid.*

44. W. Walker, in *Irish News*, 29 August 1905

45. *Irish News*, 9 September 1905
46. *Irish News*, 11 September 1905
47. *Irish News*, 30 August 1905
48. *Ibid.*
49. *Irish News*, 2 September 1905
50. *Ibid.*
51. *Irish News*, 6 September 1905
52. *Irish News*, 12 September 1905
53. *Irish News*, 15 September 1905
54. *Ibid.*
55. *Belfast Telegraph*, 15 September 1905
56. *Belfast Telegraph*, 16 September 1905
57. *Ibid.* A flute band also entertained a crowd which had gathered outside Sir Daniel Dixon's Holywood residence. The latter placed a "thank you" note in the *Irish News* on 16 September, describing it a "high honour" to "represent North Belfast in the Imperial Parliament".
58. *Belfast Telegraph*, 15 September 1905
59. *Ibid.*
60. *Morning Post*, quoted in the *Belfast Telegraph*, 16 September 1905
61. *Ibid.*
62. Morgan, *op. cit.*, p. 76
63. *Daily Chronicle*, quoted in *Irish News*, 18 September 1905
64. *Irish News*, 18 September 1905
65. *Ibid.*
66. Rees, *op. cit.*, p. 128

CHAPTER TWO

The "Partition" Election
Elections to the First Northern Ireland Parliament, 1921

"Shipyard Confetti"

The "Partition" election of May 1921 was unique, in that it resulted in the return of the first parliamentary representatives for Northern Ireland's new legislative body, and with that, the implementation of major constitutional change for Ireland. It was memorable too for taking place in an atmosphere of fierce sectarian conflict, and against a backdrop of widespread violence across the whole country, including most significantly, sectarian rioting, shootings and bombings in the Greater Belfast area. This section will provide a brief explanation of the causes and nature of the sectarian violence which was ravaging Belfast at the time of the elections, as well as an outline of the provisions of the Government of Ireland Act, 1920, which had led to the creation of Northern Ireland and its new parliament.

Several distinct, but overlapping and concurrent, factors combined to ignite widespread sectarian disturbances in Belfast during the summer of 1920. On 12 July that year, Sir Edward Carson had returned to Ulster to address the main Orange demonstration in Belfast. In his speech, he threatened that, in the event of the British government "failing to protect us from the machinations of Sinn Féin", loyalists would proceed to "take the matter into our own hands".[1] Although parliament was at the start of its summer recess, Lloyd George's Irish legislation – unpopular for different reasons with both sections of the northern community – was proceeding through the House, and was destined to become law before Christmas. The assassination of a senior Royal Irish Constabulary (RIC) officer in Cork, just a few days after Carson's Orange Day speech, had only served to compound the rising sectarian tension. Colonel Gerald Smyth, the Ulster-born divisional police commander for Munster and a fierce critic of republicanism, was shot in Cork city. The final spark which would ignite conflagration of violence in

Belfast occurred on 21 July.[2] A shipyard protest meeting organised by hard-line Belfast Protestant Association (BPA) members took place at Queen's Island during the workers' lunch break. Protesting against IRA violence in the rest of Ireland and demanding the expulsion of "non-loyal" workers, a large and angry crowd of several thousand forced their way into the premises of Harland and Wolff. There they systematically attacked Catholic workers, hurling "shipyard confetti", before chasing them from their place of work.[3] Similar intimidatory tactics were adopted at other major industrial sites and factories that afternoon. When the loyalist workforce made their way homewards that evening, large groups of angry, dispelled Catholics attacked them as they approached the nationalist enclave of Short Strand. Within a couple of days, street disturbances and shootings had spread across the city of Belfast.

The sectarian disturbances which erupted on Belfast's streets in the summer of 1920 were to endure for another two years and persisted into the run-up and beyond the course of the 1921 elections to the new Northern Ireland parliament. The main feature of this violence was its intense and intermittent nature, with the bloodiest period occurring early in 1922, just over six months after the elections.[4]

By this time, both sides had greater access to more powerful weaponry, and sniping attacks were particularly deadly, given the city's densely-packed side-streets. Republicans targeted police officers, politicians and ordinary Protestants in numerous shooting attacks, whilst loyalist gangs and groups of "rogue cops" inflicted even greater suffering upon the city's Catholic population. The IRA also coordinated many bombing attacks, especially on workers' trams and at industrial or commercial premises.[5]

Street rioting – especially in interface areas, where an enclave of one religious minority bordered on a district with a majority of people of the "other" religious persuasion – was particularly vicious, and normally spontaneous in its nature (attacks tended to be in "revenge" for recently conducted outrages). A disproportionate number of victims were Catholics – they represented nearly two-thirds of the total number of casualties, approximately double their proportion within the overall population – a circumstance which has prompted some to suggest that these disturbances constituted a "pogrom". However, this is to ignore the fact that the violence was far from one-sided, as well as the lack of evidence that the new state was culpable of orchestrating such an organised campaign of "ethnic cleansing".[6] What was happening on the streets of the northern capital might be better described as an "unholy war". What is certain is that the sectarian disturbances and tension which were ongoing in the city during the middle of 1921 provided a far from ideal atmosphere for the conducting of the region's most crucial election in living memory.

A heavier-than-usual security presence in Belfast around the time of the election and also in the period leading up to a Royal visit a few weeks later, did however result in a scaling-down of the violence during this month-long period of political campaigning and constitutional change. Despite this, at least seven people lost their lives in May, including a senior police officer, who was shot in west Belfast on 7 May, and a harbour constable, who was killed at York Docks three days later.[7]

The Better Government of Ireland Bill – David Lloyd George's proposed solution to the Irish problem – formally passed its final reading in the House of Lords on 23 December 1920. The measure, which was contemptuously described by its nationalist opponents as the "Partition Bill", had experienced a long and contentious passage through both Houses.

Lloyd George, anxious to alleviate a long-festering sore for British politicians, genuinely believed he had found a compromise which would, to some degree at least, satisfy all sides. In his estimation, the extensive local powers bestowed by the measure would relieve his administration of the day-to-day responsibility for governing the region, which would in turn be popular with the British public, who had become increasingly impatient with the ever-prevailing stalemate in Anglo-Irish relations. Nationalists had been offered their own administration in Dublin, and Lloyd George believed that they would be more prepared to accept the existence of a Belfast legislative assembly than a separate northern entity exempted from the legislation. In addition, Lloyd George estimated that Ulster Unionists would acknowledge the value of what had been offered, even though it would necessitate an alteration in their longstanding political mindset. After all, northern unionists had vehemently opposed the establishment of an Irish administration – admittedly, one based in Dublin – during negotiations on the proposed Home Rule legislation on the eve of World War I.

Several of the features of the Third Home Rule Bill could in fact be found in the new legislation now being proposed. Many functions currently deployed by Westminster – including responsibility for law and order, local government, agriculture and industry, and education and local trade –

were to become the responsibility of the Belfast administration. This new entity would, however, be allotted subordinate status to the Westminster Parliament, which would continue to have custody over "exempted" areas of governance, including the Crown, foreign policy, external trade, taxation and the armed services. There were still contentious issues to be addressed, though – such as the definition of the exact areas to be under the jurisdiction of both Irish Free State and Northern Ireland governments (a question not in fact to be resolved until 1925) – and these remained areas of concern for Ulster unionists.

Both communities expressed considerable interest in the events unfolding at Westminster during the run-up to Christmas 1920, but fortunately this escalation in political tension was not reflected in an increase in sectarian disturbances on Belfast's streets. The United Irish League (UIL) leader, Joe Devlin expressed the fears of "abandonment" felt by northern nationalists. Speaking in a debate at Westminster, he maintained that there were around 340,000 Catholics, who would shortly be "at the mercy of the Protestant majority in the North of Ireland". He asked:

> What will we get when they [unionists] are clothed with the authority of government, when they have cast round them the Imperial garb: what mercy, what pity, much less justice or liberty, will be conceded to us then?[8]

The *Irish News* was also sceptical about the prospects for their readers of the imminent New Year. An editorial on Christmas Eve questioned if "a more ghastly Christmas gift" had ever been "thrust on our nation".[9]

Northern unionists were of course considerably more upbeat in their reflections on the parliamentary measure. Unionism's public responses to the legislation were generally ones citing "duty", "obligation" and "compromise", though unquestionably they privately noted, in a less altruistic fashion, that these political and constitutional changes would also bolster their own position. The *Belfast Telegraph* recorded its "relief" and "thankfulness" that the right of unionists for "separate treatment" and to be "arbiters of her [Ulster's] political testimony" were "now recognised in fact and by Act of Parliament".[10]

The new Northern Ireland parliament was to be a bicameral legislature, based on the Westminster model, and would consist of an elected body and a Senate, or Upper House. The first elections for the new regional Assembly would take place under the single transferable voting system of proportional representation. Voting for the 52 places in the Northern parliament was scheduled to take place on Empire Day – 24 May 1921.

"Loyalty against disloyalty"

Unionist newspapers supported the region's political establishment, in their endeavours to assuage the fears of grass-roots supporters regarding the uncharted waters to be navigated as a consequence of the imminent self-government proposals, and in backing the integrity of recently appointed party leader, Sir James Craig.[11] Encouraging readers to "make the best" of the terms of the Better Government of Ireland Act, and to stand firmly behind Craig and his official Unionist candidates, a *Belfast Telegraph* leading article, published on the day electoral candidates were to be nominated, reminded them that the election for the new parliament constituted "a landmark in the history of Ireland". Warning unionists that their Sinn Féin opponents in the south "want us not because they love us, but because they wish to get control of the North and its wealth and industries", the paper stressed that the powers soon to be wielded by the new legislative body in Belfast were "by no means parochial", since "almost every matter touching the daily life of the community" was about to come "under the jurisdiction of the Northern Parliament". The editorial ended with a reminder to readers that the basic issues in the election were those of "loyalty against disloyalty" and of "a Republic or the British Empire".[12]

Confidence amongst the loyalist ranks because of the strength of their numbers and their communal cohesion was tempered, however, by the realisation that northern unionists were, for the first time, standing alone in an important political contest. The week before Nomination Day, a public information notice featuring County Antrim Unionist candidates admitted that Ulster loyalists could "no longer count upon the support of members returned to constituencies in Great Britain, or rely upon their help in counteracting the voting strength of our opponents in Parliament".[13] However, far from being daunted by this prospect, the County Antrim candidates urged voters to grasp the opportunity of taking on "the whole responsibility for the internal government of our Province".[14]

Unionist unity rested upon the integrity and dependability of their new leader. In one of his earliest campaign speeches, Craig had asked his

Bangor audience to imagine surviving a stormy voyage before approaching a welcoming harbour.[15] Craig's creditability as a trustworthy leader was soon tested however, when news broke that he had visited Eamon de Valera in Dublin on 5 May. Loyalist opinion-makers reassured their audience "not to be alarmed" by such an excursion into "enemy" territory, with the *Belfast Telegraph* pointing out that Craig had "committed himself to nothing", and had made "no offer of anything".[16] Within days, Craig personally dismissed any fears that his resolve was weakening. Addressing a loyalist gathering in Belfast's Ulster Hall on 10 May, he promised "never [to] bow the knee to treachery or allow a whisper of 'Republic' to enter my thoughts".[17]

Loyalist electoral fears owed less to the political challenge posed by Sinn Féin or Devlin's nationalist group, and rather more to a dread of apathy and weakening in loyalist unity, especially given the alternative option of three socialist candidates standing in constituencies within Belfast's industrial heartlands. The role of the unionist press during the long election campaign was of pivotal importance in ensuring that both apathy and internal divisions were avoided. Constant reminders of the crucial importance and the key issues at stake in this election were clearly outlined in the pages of papers like the *Belfast Telegraph*. In the contest's earliest phase, the paper maintained that there was a stark choice for Ulster's voters: that between "the British Empire and loyalty on the one hand, [and] separation and disloyalty on the other".[18] Fear of the unknown was another concern which had to be tackled early on in the campaign by unionist propagandists. The complexities of a new voting system and the initial confusion precipitated by their political leaders' calls to back a system of self-government which, on the surface at least, closely resembled that which they had so vehemently opposed less than a decade before, were addressed efficiently by unionists at an early stage. A policy of zero tolerance in relation to the trio of socialist candidates in Belfast was also adopted (see below). The *Belfast Telegraph* and other unionist-leaning newspapers constantly warned against political indifference within the Protestant community, pointing out that a satisfactory turnout would only be achieved by "a united rally of all Loyalists voting for all the official candidates".[19]

Election "fever" was particularly evident in the working-class quarters of loyalist Belfast. Whilst the middle classes appeared to be more concerned about "clothing themselves in white and board[ing] the trams that take them to the cricket-grounds and tennis courts", many loyalist workers were prepared to devote their more limited leisure hours to participating in demonstrations and meetings arranged to arouse support for the unionist candidates.[20]

Several election meetings were held in the Greater Belfast area – these combined the emotional fervour engendered by Orange songs and cultural symbolism with the more topical appeal of election slogans and catchphrases. One such demonstration, on Saturday, 7 May, set off from the traditional Orange vantage point of Carlisle Circus to the north of Belfast's centre. A cacophony of sound, stemming from brass, flute and Lambeg drum-led bands which accompanied long ranks of Orangemen (mostly working men, including many with recent war service), drew an admiring audience of mainly women and children. Eventually, three large banners were unfurled, on which were emblazoned the names of the Unionist Party candidates for North Belfast, together with hearty exhortations such as "Vote for Union, Home and Empire!", and "Ex-soldiers – don't betray your colleagues who shed their blood!". The march proceeded down side-streets and along the Shankill Road, before winding its way back to Clifton Street and Peter's Hill. The onset of steady rain could "damp neither bands nor enthusiasm, and the police presence determined that there would be no untoward incidents".[21]

Although a combination of alert policing and good fortune mitigated against widespread rioting and heavy casualties during the election campaign, one unionist demonstration in East Belfast, a few days before the conclusion of the contest, resulted in tragic loss of life. On 18 May, a large loyalist parade, involving the Orange Order, ex-servicemen and several bands, marched through Belfast's centre on its way to the Oval football grounds in the east of the city.[22] Orangemen on a "feeder" parade, which had started in the Shankill area, were fired on as they made their way to the city centre, and a young marcher was fatally wounded. Rumours of this shooting soon spread amongst the ranks of marchers, and there was considerable anger in their ranks as the parade arrived at the Oval. Shots were reportedly fired in the air, as the marchers passed the nationalist Short Strand district on the edge of the Newtownards Road, but serious disturbances flared up after the meeting dispersed, a couple of hours later. Many of the participants had heeded the advice of their party leader and march organisers, returning to the city centre via the Albert Bridge Road. However, a significant minority chose instead to return down the Newtownards Road, walking past the Short Strand. Gunfire was directed into the nationalist quarter, and an ex-soldier,

John Smyth, from nearby Seaforde Street, was fatally wounded.[23]

Unionist newspapers, like their nationalist counterparts, proved to be unofficial party election journals in the period leading up to Election Day on 24 May. The *Belfast Telegraph* advertised forthcoming election meetings both in Belfast and across the full range of Northern constituencies, reported the speeches of leading unionist candidates, and provided advice on the new system of voting. On 13 May, the paper gave details of a loyalist meeting involving the four Unionist candidates for South Belfast scheduled to take place at St John's Church Hall, Newtownbreda. Alongside this was notification of a meeting of County Down Unionists – which would include an address by the party leader, one of the candidates in Down – at the Newtownards Guildhall the following evening. Announcements of further meetings both in Belfast and in rural constituencies across the province were made in the paper throughout the campaign. These included a meeting of Tyrone and Fermanagh candidates on 14 May; a County Derry rally in Magherafelt on 17 May; and a meeting of North Belfast Unionists held at Clifton Street Orange Hall on 20 May.[24]

With the introduction of a new proportional representation system of voting – the first of its kind to be operated in Britain – advice on how to cast one's vote was clearly required, as was the need to ensure that those who qualified for a second "property" vote were fully aware of their entitlement. Illustrations of the PR voting system were provided in the *Belfast Telegraph*'s 18 May edition, under the headline, "The Ulster Parliament – how the citizens should vote". Apart from practical advice on how to mark candidates in order of preference on the voting slips, there was a strong reminder of the individual voter's "duty" and responsibility on polling day, with the paper telling its readers that "every man and woman who has a vote should go to the poll, and exercise the franchise in a spirit of serious responsibility, and with the knowledge that to some extent each vote will make or mar the vote of Ulster".[25] Less than a week later, the paper printed a last-minute reminder to the business section of their readership that many of them had the right to a commercial premises vote in a neighbouring constituency, as well as their normal residential franchise. It stated that such entitlements were "not generally known", and urged those in such a fortunate position to "exercise their rights".[26]

Unionist-leaning newspapers were, on the whole, dismissive of their nationalist opponents, whose campaign apparently warranted relatively little coverage in the unionist press. If anything, more attention was paid to criticising "bored and weak-kneed British Unionists" and political opponents in southern Ireland.[27] As far as the latter were concerned, Sinn Féin's "clean sweep" at the uncontested election for the Dublin parliament was regarded as a threat to the stability of the new northern administration, while also highlighting the contrast between the "democratic", keenly-fought contest in the north, and the "undemocratic", uncontested nature of the election in the rest of Ireland.[28]

More attention was paid in the unionist press to the threat posed by the three Labour candidates standing in Belfast constituencies. Although the unionist establishment had endeavoured to ensure that no independent candidates would stand and risk compromising loyalist voting strength, three independent Labour candidates – James Baird, John Hanna and Harry Midgley – had been nominated in Belfast constituencies. A major blow to the chances of these socialist candidates came on the evening of 16 May, when their election meeting at the Ulster Hall was hijacked by a considerably larger group of loyalists – many of them believed to have arrived directly from their work in the shipyard – who then promptly took over the building to stage their own impromptu meeting. The *Belfast Telegraph*'s headline spelled out that the "historic Ulster Hall [had been] held by Islandmen", and that the "Red Faction [had been] excluded".[29]

No further socialist rallies were held after this blatant act of intimidation, and the Labour candidates felt obliged to place notices in the local press, outlining their political position. One of these notices stated that, "owing to the conduct of those politically opposed to us, we are compelled to cancel meetings announced in the press".[30] Thus, spontaneous grass-roots action had resulted in the virtual removal of a key threat facing Unionist Party strategists, namely that of widening divisions within the Protestant working class. Yet the distasteful nature of such tactics could not be camouflaged, and was seized upon by unionism's opponents. The *Irish News* deplored the "barring of free speech", and went on to castigate the tactic adopted by their opponents:

> The leaders of the July and September Pogroms, which have had such woeful and truly disastrous consequences for Belfast, were pressed into the service again, and those who cared to hear what the Labour candidates had to say were driven forth with violence,

so that the Hall might respond to the senseless shibboleths of faction once again.[31]

Loyalist politicians and journalists joined forces on the eve of the election in urging a maximum loyalist turnout at the polling booths. Both the "old" and "new" leaders of Ulster Unionism, Edward Carson and James Craig, were to the fore in demanding a large unionist vote across the Province. The former, speaking at a loyalist rally in Belfast's Assembly Hall, pleaded with his audience to, "Vote! Vote! Vote!", pointing out that Ulster had to be "saved from the tyranny of the assassin!"[32] His successor also appealed to Ulster voters to "do your duty" for "a sacred cause", which was eminently "worthy of every sacrifice". Beseeching them to, "rally round me, so that I may shatter your enemies and their hopes of a Republican flag", Craig reminded his followers that "the eyes of our friends throughout the Empire are upon us", and that they should be seen as being as "determined, as they [are] to uphold the cause of loyalty".[33]

The *Belfast Telegraph* also took full advantage of "a final word" to the Ulster electorate, maintaining that "a clearer line had never been presented". Reminding readers that the choice the following day was "between the British Empire and a Republic", and "the sweets of liberty" or "the tyranny of gunmen", it remained upbeat in its expectations of the contest's likely outcome. It forecast "a good working majority" for Craig, and praised the "magnificent solidarity" of Ulster's loyalists throughout the campaign, reflected, it maintained, in the absence of independent candidates. Pointing out that the elections had "no terrors for loyal men and women", the paper insisted that the "real issue" facing electors was "the British connection – to be or not to be". Opponents and supporters alike were reminded that Ulster "did not ask for this Parliament"; and the paper stressed that "no combination of Sinn Féiners, Nationalists, Bolsheviks and Socialists will take it from her".[34]

"National suicide"

Despite their unequivocal opposition to a Belfast-based administration, both Joe Devlin's nationalist group, the UIL, and Sinn Féin opted to contest the northern elections as an opportunity to test the barometer of public support for such constitutional change. The morale of nationalists had been boosted by their success in municipal elections earlier in 1921, when they had gained control of Tyrone council for the first time, as well as retaining power in County Fermanagh. Circumstances clearly had changed from those prevailing in Ireland during the general election which followed the end of international hostilities towards the end of 1918, when the nationalist voice had been virtually drowned out in Sinn Féin's electoral tsunami. As one historian pointed out, this coming together in 1921 was mainly due to a shared opposition of Partition and a common sense of optimism over the new system of voting, making it easier for the two parties to agree than had been the case three years before.[35]

Sinn Féin had greater available resources than the ailing UIL, and many of the party's big names threw their support behind its northern campaign, with several opting to stand in Northern Ireland constituencies – these included Arthur Griffith in Fermanagh & South Tyrone, Michael Collins in Armagh and Eamon de Valera in County Down. Although divisions between these nationalist and republican groups would soon become evident, the influence of the Catholic Church and a genuine desire amongst its community to unite forces against the greater threat posed by Partition, meant that both the UIL and Sinn Féin were looking for a compromise a few weeks before the start of the electoral campaign.

Following a meeting between de Valera and Devlin, a pact for the May elections was agreed on St Patrick's Day, and formalised on 6 April. This highlighted not only their joint rejection of the Partition principle but also their shared focus on self-determination, and a commitment (though this was more emphatically stated by Sinn Féin) to abstain from the business of the new Belfast parliament. The benefits of such an agreement were plain for all to see. The new voting system required candidates to be listed in order of preference, and the pact signatories agreed to encourage their supporters to cast their second preference votes to other anti-Partition groups. Both parties also agreed to putting forward a specified number of candidates in constituencies across Northern Ireland (Sinn Féin ended up fielding 20 candidates, compared to the UIL's 13).

At the start of the election contest, one republican candidate in Belfast expressed his concerns over the danger likely to be faced by Catholic ex-residents of areas which had suffered considerable population dispersal as a result of widespread intimidation during the previous summer. Speaking at a Belfast Corporation council meeting early in May, Councillor Archie Savage observed that, "many people who had been driven out of districts would have to go back ... to record their votes": this, he believed, was "not a reasonable thing to ask them to do".[36] The difficulty in disseminating public information about republican meetings and the likelihood that such candidates were restricted in their movements (on account of their involvement in the IRA) meant that Sinn Féin was not able to mount an organised programme of meetings on a par with those put forward by their Unionist and Nationalist rivals.

St Mary's Hall in central Belfast was a popular meeting place for nationalists and republicans, and Savage was one republican candidate to speak there during the campaign.[37] Another Sinn Féin candidate, Sean MacEntee, spoke at an open-air meeting in the nationalist district of Smithfield on 22 May, where he described the concept of Partition – which involved the "cutting of a country in two in order to unite the people" – as a "paradox".[38] Some other leading Sinn Féin figures also addressed hastily-convened meetings in nationalist districts and towns. These included Michael Collins, Frank Aiken, who spoke in Armagh on the night prior to the election, and Eamon de Valera, who crossed the new, tightly-policed border on a couple of occasions, reportedly speaking in west Belfast as well as in his County Down constituency. De Valera's addresses were markedly more combative than those of his nationalist opponents. He implored his audience to "cast your vote for nothing less than the legitimation of the Republic for Ireland against Empire, for freedom against slavery, for right and justice against force and wrong, here and everywhere!"[39]

If anything, the Irish News was even more of a mouthpiece for the UIL than the Belfast Telegraph was for Craig's Unionist Party. Indeed, as noted previously, both Joe Devlin and T.J. Campbell had previously worked for the newspaper.[40] Its dismissal of Partition and the election promises of the likely prime minister of the new Northern Ireland, Sir James Craig, was unequivocal. In an editorial at the start of the campaign, Craig was described by the paper as the "new chief of Reaction", and was heavily criticised both for his defence of Partition and his party's election manifesto, which the Irish News maintained was devoid of "a trace, or suggestion, of a definite policy or programme".[41] The paper was also quick to suggest the possibility of division amongst unionist ranks in the wake of Craig's meeting with de Valera in Dublin. Referring to unionist hard-liner, William Twaddell's denunciation of the appointment of a "papist" viceroy, and to widespread concern [in the ranks] over the party leader's secret trip south, the Irish News mischievously suggested that "no one is exactly in a position to contradict a constant rumour that Councillor Twaddell is preparing a hostile reception for [Craig] when he comes back".[42]

Within the first full week of the election contest, the *Irish News* published a series of rebuttals of Partition and the proposed northern parliament. On 4 May, its editorial, "The Fight Before Us", contemptuously forecast that the parliament of the six northern counties would prove to be "a bankrupt institution from the day of its birth", and described the "inoperable" system of Partition as "indefensible on any ground that would appeal to the reasonable common sense or ordinary patriotism of any section of the Irish people".[43] A few days later, the paper focused on what it perceived as a lack of logic and morality behind the proposed constitutional changes, as was apparent in its leader, "The Case against Partition":

> No camouflage can completely hide the grim reality. There is no thoughtful man – Nationalist or Sinn Féiner, Southern Unionist or Ulster Covenanter – who does not realise in his inner consciousness that the setting up of a legislative divorce between the six counties and the 26 is fraught with evil, alike to the North East corner, and to the rest of the country.[44]

During the early stages of the contest, the *Irish News* also published the key parts of the UIL manifesto. At the centre of text lay the party's, and indeed the newspaper's, contempt for the principle of Partition. The manifesto claimed that Partition would mean "National Suicide", arguing that its concept was "as unnatural as it is unnational", and that the whole idea was "not an act of national peace and reconciliation, but a trick of English politicians."[45] The same edition of the paper reported on the start of the nationalist campaign, noting the "stirring" UIL meetings which had taken place in Belfast and other parts of the province, as well as the "local spirit of Nationhood [which was] strong and undaunted".[46] Within a few days of this came a report that the nationalist campaign had entered the "active stage in the North East of Ireland", with "big" meetings taking place in Belfast – including gatherings in Oldpark, Ardoyne and Oxford Street in the centre of the city – and in Armagh. At this early stage of the contest, the optimism of the *Irish News* regarding the election's outcome probably exceeded the private expectations of Joe Devlin and his colleagues. An editorial trumpeted that there was, "a probability amounting to a certainty, of killing Partition if all the people who dread or abhor it assert and exercise their right to vote".[47]

Two of the most important meetings of the UIL campaign occurred during its second full week in north Antrim and west Belfast. Devlin's "personal energy and enthusiasm", exhibited to the full during the previous week at meetings in County Antrim towns and villages – including Larne, Randalstown, Money Pass, Carnlough, Cushendall and Cushendun – had boosted morale at local level, as well as producing "a virile nationalist organisation working day and night for the triumphant return of Mr Devlin", according to the *Irish News*.[48] The central thrust of Devlin's "fighting speech" in the County Antrim coastal town of Ballycastle on 17 May was the unethical and undemocratic nature of the proposed constitutional changes, and a plea for reconciliation between Catholics and Protestants:

> The days of the landlord class have gone, the days of the sweater have gone, [and] the day of the people has come. I have come here not only to fight County Antrim upon the platform of a united Ireland from the centre to the sea, but under the noble dispensation of rallying Catholic and Protestant together ... for the love of humanity and high Christian principles.[49]

Within a couple of days of his "mini" tour of County Antrim, Devlin had returned to Belfast, where he made further hard-hitting, eloquent speeches against his unionist opponents and their defence of Partition, including at an open-air meeting in Mill Street off the Falls Road, which attracted a crowd of several thousand. Praising the "excellent muster" in the nationalist quarter, the *Irish News* reported Devlin's rousing speech in considerable detail. Dismissing the Act which had created the new Parliament as an "English dodge", initiated simply to, "raise a banner between North and South", Devlin warned that it would "create a permanent division, where there ought to be unity."[50]

Particularly as the election campaign entered its final phase, Catholic voters were directly targeted, not just by politicians but also by newspaper editors and journalists, who offered practical advice on the new system of voting and electoral arrangements, and the hierarchy of the Catholic Church. The latter, and especially Dr Joseph MacRory, the Bishop of Down and Connor, had for some time been critical of the potential repercussions of Lloyd George's legislation. Bishop MacRory dismissed the Act as "a mockery, not only of Ireland's claims, but of all justice and fair play".[51] On the eve of the contest, the Bishop went a step further, suggesting that there might be longer term ramifications such as Catholic apathy and division. He asserted that "the character of your children's education and with it, perhaps, their eternal welfare", might depend upon the election result.[52]

The *Irish News*, like its unionist counterparts, advised its readers on how to maximise their votes in the new electoral system, and also listed in its columns the names of anti-Partition candidates.[53] The paper also endeavoured to reassure those Catholic electors who had been displaced during the previous year's sectarian disturbances, urging them to be proactive by ensuring their names were on the electoral rolls and also by casting their votes in their "home" districts. A public announcement was duly placed in the *Irish News* on 11 May, urging "all nationalists who have changed their addresses since July 1920" to "call at the Nationalist Election offices in West, East, North and South Belfast."[54]

The *Irish News* also kept its readership updated on the progress of UIL meetings across the North during the final week of the contest, including reports of what had taken place in Lurgan, Derry and Newry. Final meetings were held across Ulster on Sunday, 22 May, but "the greatest of all was Belfast's Final Rally at the Celtic Park". Here, all the city's nationalist candidates – Joseph Devlin, T.J. Campbell, Frank Harkin, R. Byrne and Bernard McCoy – addressed a large and enthusiastic audience. Rejecting the prospect of being "driven like sheep into a Carson compound", Devlin pleaded with the Protestant electorate to realise that their best interests lay, "not in the perpetuation of ancient hatred and fratricidal strife, but in that union of men and women marching together in the soldier army of democratic progress".[55]

The *Irish News* was wary about adopting an overly pessimistic attitude to the contest's likely outcome, and earlier in the campaign had attempted to assure its readers that the new proportional representation voting system constituted "a probability, amounting to a certainty, of killing Partition, if all the people who dread and abhor it assert and exercise their right to vote".[56] Like its unionist counterpart, the *Belfast Telegraph*, the *Irish News* put its columns to best use on 23 and 24 May, to remind readers of their responsibilities and what would really be at stake on Election Day. Keen to encourage a high turnout of its readers, on the eve of the election, the paper urged "Irish men and women" to, "rise up early tomorrow morning in Belfast, and throughout the land from Fairhead to Kilkeel, and to the farthest corner of Fermanagh, to go to the polling booths, at all costs to vote the policy of Partition out of existence".That day's editorial did not minimise the personal dangers involved in exercising one's right to vote, but stressed the enormous responsibility facing individual voters. It maintained that, "whoever shrinks from inconvenience, unpleasantness, or actual peril, is unworthy of the sacrifices made and the sufferings endured by the men who fought and died for Ireland".[57] On the morning of the election itself, the exhortation from the *Irish News* was again one of "duty" and a call for electors to "vote against Partition and the destruction of Ireland".[58]

Election Day and its Aftermath

Election "fever" was at its peak on Election Day, 24 May, and particularly in Belfast.[59] Unionist newspaper, the *Belfast News Letter*, postulated that, "never at any period within the recollection of the present generation has there been such a profusion of flags, or such a wonderful manifestation of patriotic feeling."[60] Certainly the turnout at the election stations, especially within the Greater Belfast area, was unique in its scale, with a reported poll in excess of 90 per cent in several constituencies. The *Daily Telegraph*, a sympathetic pro-unionist paper, noted that, in loyalist districts, "crowds ... long queues of voters ... were waiting for the polling booths to open". Outside the voting centres there was a frenzy of political activity, as "decorated motors with the loyalist colours flashed to and fro in great numbers".[61] Although voting was also brisk in solidly nationalist areas such as the Falls Road, it would predictably be in religiously mixed districts that the political "temperature" was at its highest.

Whilst widespread violence was avoided, largely on account of heavy security presence, several instances of intimidation and violence did occur. Newspapers on both sides acknowledged such outbursts, though they vehemently disagreed on their significance and who was culpable. For nationalist papers like the *Irish News*, the "organised tyranny" of loyalist groups had provided the most enduring image of Election Day. "Disgraceful" scenes of "brutal violence and gross intimidation" were reported in several parts of the city.[62] Instances of nationalists being stoned in taxis and railway carriages, as they ventured back to their former areas to register their votes, as well as menacing groups of shipyard workers "loitering" outside polling stations were reported in the *Irish News*. The worst intimidation was in east Belfast, particularly on the Newtownards Road which borders the nationalist district of Short Strand. The paper claimed that "thousands of Catholic voters were forcibly and brutally prevented from exercising the franchise", and that what had occurred constituted "a mockery of a free election."[63]

Unionist politicians and journalists disputed the degree of the intimidation being reported, pointing out that the emphatic support for the unionist candidates at the polls was the real story of the elections. The *Belfast News Letter* suggested that "no degree of misrepresentation or abuse about imaginary intimidation and terrorism" could "minimise or explain away the significance of such a sweeping victory".[64] The *Belfast Telegraph*, indeed, maintained that, given the prevailing "high pitch of popular excitement", such relatively low-scale intimidation was "inevitable", but concluded that it was "a matter for thankfulness" that the elections had passed off "so quietly".[65] It also focused on the "unambiguous results" of the contest. During the period when the cumbersome task of vote-counting was being conducted, the paper was pleased to speculate that "a glorious unionist victory" was imminent. For this paper, "the loyal democracy of Ulster [had] given its answer to the murder campaign, the boycott campaign, the attempt to drive the Union Jack from these shores".[66]

It was not just loyalists who contested the nature and degree of the intimidation. Assistant Undersecretary Sir Ernest Clark, a leading British civil servant, reported that any coercion of this kind had little effect on unionism's emphatic victory and that, in any case, both sides had engaged in minor electoral malpractices and personation. Though arguably guilty of fence-sitting and the trite dismissal of the intimidation of hundreds of voters in several areas of Belfast, it would be wrong to conclude that the result of this election was primarily the product of foul play on the part of the authorities. Eamon Phoenix, a leading commentator on Northern nationalism, has concluded that intimidation, "probably did not have any marked effect on the overall results of the contest".[67]

The unionist press were jubilant at both the "extremely gratifying" loyalist successes in the election, as well as the poor performance of nationalists and republicans. The *Belfast Telegraph* asserted that the projected final outcome pointed to "an even greater unionist victory than was looked for", and that the unionist candidates had "effectively pricked the anti-Partition bubble", and shown that Ulster voters "value the British connection more dearly than anything else in this world".[68] Subsequent leading articles gloated at the election failure of their opponents. The following day's editorial, drafted at a time when over half of the results had been confirmed, was entitled, "The Sinn Féin Rout", and, after identifying loyalist "solidarity" as the crucial factor behind the result, proceeded to castigate the other side. Nationalists and republicans were, the paper affirmed, "overwhelmed at the severity of their defeat, and allegations of letting each other down are already being hurled to and fro".[69] With final results confirmed, the next day's leading article lauded the "glorious" result for Craig's candidates, one which constituted a "100 per cent victory" for unionism. Referring to the abstentionist policy likely to be adopted by the small group of successful anti-Partition candidates, the editorial reassured readers that "their abstention will not have the effect of paralysing the Parliament in Belfast, which will be functioning shortly".[70]

The initial response of the *Irish News* to the overwhelming unionist success was dismissive. Repudiating the idea that a "parliament" had been established to represent barely a sixth of Ireland's area, the paper maintained that the "qualified support" from the populace of that small corner of Ireland and the election of a regional government, "possessing neither policy nor programme, and inspired by no higher ideal than unreasoning and groundless antipathy" to the rest of Ireland, did not "indicate an institution [which was] destined to endure".[71] Bizarrely, the paper was also to declare two days later that "the outstanding feature" of the results had been "the triumphant return" of Joe Devlin in both West Belfast and County Antrim.[72] The following day, the *Irish News* clearly felt it was at last time to directly address the poor electoral performances of the parties representing Catholic voters. Blaming "stale and ineffective" party organisation and disharmony between the two respective political groups, the paper's editorial hinted at a more serious analysis of internal shortcomings to follow.[73] This belated political realism on the part of the North's leading nationalist newspaper was long overdue, since throughout the election campaign the *Irish News* had consistently been guilty of an unjustified sense of optimism.[74] Such a tendency towards bullish overconfidence was, by no means confined to the nationalist press, however.

Given the inevitable delay in the counting of votes under the new franchise system, post-election excitement and anticipation, if anything, eclipsed that of most previous contests. Party members were encamped for a long time at polling stations, at which "all [was] bustle and activity".[75] Most of the results were known within two days, by which time a pattern of widespread unionist success – even greater than party officials had dreamed of – was emerging. Over two-thirds of the votes cast – 582,464 in total – went to unionist candidates, with anti-Partitionists gaining 165,293 votes (32.3 per cent of the overall poll). The Unionists had nominated 40 candidates across Northern Ireland, and every one of these was returned.[76] The remaining 12 places in the new legislature were evenly divided between the UIL and Sinn Féin, representing a disappointing return for the comparatively large anti-Partitionist vote – Joe Devlin had forecast 15 to 20 nationalists and republicans being returned. The Unionist Party had clearly benefited from the absence of independent unionist candidates, and James Craig, the new prime minister of Northern Ireland, was assured of a sizeable parliamentary majority (28 seats). Yet, under closer analysis, this success was a qualified one. Close to a third of the electorate had expressed their rejection of the establishment of the new state, with the majority of pollsters in one county, Fermanagh, opposing Partition. As well as this, ominously, the more extreme of the anti-Partition groups, Sinn Féin, had polled considerably more votes than their nationalist opponents.[77] In addition, the quality of new unionist representation was far from impressive, with only a small number of liberal unionists securing posts in a new regional administration, which was dominated by older, more traditional unionists.[78] As a result of the self-imposed absence of leading nationalists and republicans, the new assembly would inevitably lack the cut-and-thrust exchanges of other democratic chambers.

The results were particularly disappointing for the UIL, although the party, and the *Irish News*, tried to deflect attention away from their performance, and concentrate instead on the personal success of their leader. However, even the return of Devlin in two separate constituencies did not constitute a major triumph, with the UIL leader only managing seventh place in the County Antrim contest, where he polled 9,560 votes. His showing in West Belfast, where he gained over 10,000 votes, finishing in fourth place, was of course more impressive. Despite staging fewer meetings, leading members of Sinn Féin, including Eamon de Valera and Michael Collins, proved to be more successful. Collins, who was returned in Armagh, polled 12,656 votes.[79] Overall, however, Sinn Féin was disappointed at having only capturing 6 seats, a relatively low number and at failing to have any of its 5 candidates elected in Belfast.

Both the *Belfast Telegraph* and *Irish News* gave generous space to the respective celebrations of the victorious electoral candidates. Victory parades for successful candidates were held in several constituencies, including in Ballymacarrett in East Belfast on 26 May, and in Larne and South Belfast the following evening.[80] In South Belfast, the four successful unionist representatives – Thomas Moles, R.M. Pollock, Crawford McCullough and Julia McMordie (wife of a former mayor of Belfast) – were driven on a lorry bedecked in loyalist colours along the Stranmillis Road, and across the King's Bridge to the Ballynafeigh Orange Hall on the Ormeau Road, where speeches were delivered.[81] A similar victory parade was staged for Joe Devlin in the west of the city that night. Described in the *Irish News* as "a wonderful night", there was a large crowd lining the Falls Road, and many green and gold flags were waved, as the ebullient Devlin was cheered by spectators from open windows along the length of the Falls. Devlin delivered an upbeat speech to his followers. He declared:

> Belfast has never been false to Ireland. She was never truer than she was today. We will go on defending the right; fighting for our principles, promising peace with honesty and ultimately succeeding in the great lifework for which we have laboured in common – the freedom of our country and the happiness of our people.[82]

Within a month, the new parliament was formally opened by King George V. Despite the reticence of his advisers, the monarch made a fleeting visit to declare the new institution open in Belfast's City Hall. Attitudes to both the royal trip and the new parliament were predictably polarised. With the continuing occurrence of sectarian shootings, as well as a series of incidents which saw Catholics being expelled from predominantly loyalist areas, tensions across the city were almost palpable.

The *Irish News* had little enthusiasm for the imminent arrival of the King. Referring to an estimated 150 Catholic families who had allegedly been driven from their homes, the paper asserted that if Belfast "today is to be a beflagged city, it is also a besmirched one" and that for the suffering families, the day would "pass as one more day of suffering and anxiety".[83]

The following day, the *Belfast Telegraph* enthused that the King's visit had "struck a chord in the hearts of his loyal citizens".[84] Another *Belfast Telegraph* editorial two days later turned its attention to the future the citizens of Northern Ireland were facing. Ulster was, the paper suggested, "turning her face eagerly and hopefully towards the dawn"; a new Northern administration could be trusted to "accord the same rights and privileges, as its duty, to all classes and creeds".[85]

The King's party sailed up Belfast Lough during the mid-morning of 21 June. The royals and their entourage were protected by a huge blanket of security on land and at sea, and they enjoyed a rousing reception, both as they broached the shoreline and after they disembarked at the docks in Belfast.[86] The highlight of the King's four-hour stay was his opening of the new parliament. In a momentous speech of reconciliation and hope for the future, undoubtedly drafted by David Lloyd George and his advisers, King George V made an emotional appeal to the people of Northern Ireland:

> I speak from a full heart when my coming to Ireland today may prove to be the first step towards the end of strife among her people, whatever their race or creed. In that hope I appeal to all Irishmen to pause, to stretch out the hand of forbearance and conciliation; to forgive and forget, and to join in making for the land they love a new era of peace, contentment and goodwill.[87]

By early evening, the royal party was back on board the royal yacht, after what loyalists proclaimed "a great day". Writing in her diary, the wife of Northern Ireland's new premier recorded that "the King and Queen [had] the most wonderful reception, the decorations everywhere are extremely well done and even the little side streets, that they [would] never be within miles of, are draped with bunting and flags".[88] Above all, those responsible for organising the visit were relieved at the enthusiastic and peaceful reception afforded to the royals.

Yet the maintenance of heavy security during both the election campaign and the King's visit could not last for ever, and violence soon returned to the region. A train carrying over 100 soldiers, who had formed part of the massive protection unit for the royal party was attacked in County Armagh, close to the new Irish border. Four soldiers, two civilians and over eighty horses perished in the blast near Bessbrook. High levels of violence would soon return to plague the citizens of Belfast, peaking during the first half of 1922.

However, optimism among unionist opinion-makers was high in relation to the future possibilities afforded by the new Assembly in Belfast. Shortly after its inauguration, the *Belfast Telegraph* maintained:

> Ulster turns her face eagerly and hopefully towards the dawn. She knows that the future is in her own hands. She means to shape that future to noble ends and the achievement of a happy destiny. To all classes and creeds, the Government will accord the same rights and privileges, as is its duty. It will, in return, expect from all classes and creeds obedience to the laws and a due regard for those rights of safety of property and person which are common to all.[89]

On the surface at least, this Partition Election had proved to be a resounding success for James Craig and the Ulster Unionist Party. Indeed, the degree of support for unionism in May 1921 had exceeded their already high expectations of success, and resulted in communal reassurance that there would be no return to the pre-war days of constitutional uncertainty. However, as Eamon Phoenix has pointed out, the election also, "registered the antipathy of the sizeable politico-religious minority to any form of Partition".[90]

The existing political divisions between the two sections of the Northern community were exacerbated by the violence across Ireland in the immediate post-war years, and the tone was set for subsequent decades of electioneering, where contests like this Partition Election of 1921 would be marked by party and personal rancour, accusations of electoral malpractice, high poll turnouts and a sharply divided electorate, unwilling to switch their allegiances to parties representing the "other side".

Endnotes

1. A.F. Parkinson, *Belfast's Unholy War – the Troubles of the 1920s* (Four Courts Press, Dublin, 2004), p. 26
2. This was the first day back at work for many thousands of Belfast workers, following the Twelfth of July holiday.
3. This consisted of sharp pieces of steel, iron nuts and bolts.
4. About half of the conflict's estimated 500 fatal incidents occurred during the first half of that year, including the Weaver Street bombing and the shooting of several members of the McMahon family in North Belfast.
5. As well as the large loss of life and many thousands of injuries, over £3 million worth of commercial damage was reported.

6. This is a central theme of the author's book, *Belfast's Unholy War*, *op. cit.*

7. See note 63 below for an account of violence during the election campaign.

8. Joseph Devlin, from Parkinson, *op. cit.*, pp. 100–101

9. *Irish News*, 24 December 1920

10. *Belfast Telegraph*, 22 December 1920

11. James Craig, who had earned a reputation for his organisational ability during Edward Carson's leadership of the Unionist Party during the pre-war campaign against Irish Home Rule, would remain prime minister until his death in 1940 (see Appendix Two). Craig had been appointed party leader on 4 February after Carson had declined the opportunity to lead the party the previous month.

12. *Belfast Telegraph*, 13 May 1921

13. *Belfast Telegraph*, 6 May 1921

14. *Ibid.*

15. *Belfast Telegraph*, 5 May 1921

16. *Belfast Telegraph*, 6 May 1921

17. James Craig in *Irish News*, 11 May 1921

18. *Belfast Telegraph*, 2 May 1921

19. *Belfast Telegraph*, 13 May 1921. James Craig also wrote to the *Belfast Telegraph* on 3 May, beseeching his supporters to, "close on their ranks and apply themselves with their characteristic energy and determination to the founding of a parliament which will be worthy of their community".

20. W. Ewart, "A Journey to Ireland", 1921, from P. Craig (ed.), *The Belfast Anthology* (Blackstaff Press, Belfast, 1999), p.198

21. *Ibid.*

22. James Craig was the main speaker at this meeting, which took place in the grounds of Glentoran Football Club.

23. The *Belfast Telegraph*, 19 May 1921, described the incident as, "an unprovoked attack on bands".

24. James Craig spoke at the latter meeting and also at several others during the campaign, including one in Banbridge in early May, when he advocated "tolerance" and "fair play" towards political opponents.

25. *Belfast Telegraph*, 18 May 1921

26. *Belfast Telegraph*, 23 May 1921

27. *Northern Whig*, 4 May 1921

28. *Belfast Telegraph*, 14 May 1921. The newspaper's report sneered at how "many (128) of the representatives [of the southern parliament] are at present in jail or interned in Ballykinlar".

29. *Belfast Telegraph*, 17 May 1921. James Craig, in London at the time, despatched a telegram with the unequivocal message, "Well done big and wee yards": J. Bardon, A *History of Ulster* (Blackstaff Press, Belfast, 1992), p. 480

30. *Belfast Telegraph*, 18 May 1921. However, socialist candidates still placed advertisements in the local press during the run-up to Election Day.

31. *Irish News*, 17 May 1921

32. *Belfast Telegraph*, 24 May 1921

33. James Craig, from P. Buckland, *James Craig* (Gill and Company, Dublin, 1979), p 59

34. *Belfast Telegraph*, 23 May 1921. Other public announcements in the columns of this edition of the paper urged loyalists to "do your duty" and to "show the world that

Ulster stands now as it always stood, for Loyalty, Liberty and Progress".

35. A.C. Hepburn, *Catholic Belfast and Nationalist Ireland in the Era of Joe Devlin 1871–1934* (OUP, Oxford, 2008)

36. *Irish News*, 3 May 1921. When he asked colleagues where polling stations would be situated, a fellow councillor recommended the cemetery! Quoted in J. McDermott, *Northern Divisions – the Old IRA and the Belfast Pogroms*, 1920–2 (Beyond the Pale, Belfast, 2001), p. 80

37. Parkinson, *op. cit.*, p. 79. A pipe band played nationalist tunes at this meeting.

38. *Irish News*, 23 May 1921

39. In *Weekly Northern Whig*, 7 May 1921. My father, John Parkinson, recalled de Valera speaking "on spare ground" at Hamill Street near Christ Church to the west of Belfast city centre, and how RIC personnel stood at the back of an excited crowd, "watching his every move like a hawk": Parkinson, *op. cit.*, p. 336

40. Devlin was a reporter, whilst Campbell served for a period as the paper's editor.

41. *Irish News*, 28 April 1921

42. *Irish News*, 4 May 1921; 5 May 1921. The viceroy was Lord Edmund FitzAlan.

43. *Irish News*, 4 May 1921

44. *Irish News*, 7 May 1921. Two days later, another editorial dismissed the argument that the Better Government of Ireland Act would produce peace in Ireland. It urged readers to ignore the "political dupe" of the legislation's architects, suggesting that "neither peace nor the liberty which heralds and leads to peace can come of Partition".

45. *Irish News*, 7 May 1921

46. *Ibid.*

47. *Irish News*, 9 May 1921

48. *Irish News*, 11 May 1921

49. Joseph Devlin in *Irish News*, 9 May 1921

50. *Irish News*, 13 May 1921

51. *Irish News*, 7 February 1921

52. Parkinson, *op. cit.*, p. 121

53. *Irish News*, 19 May 1921; 14 May 1921 editions respectively

54. *Irish News*, 11 May 1921

55. *Irish News*, 23 May 1921

56. *Irish News*, 19 May 1921

57. *Irish News*, 23 May 1921

58. *Irish News*, 24 May 1921

59. The election had been arranged by James Craig to fall on the same day as that most patriotic of occasions at the time, Empire Day.

60. *Belfast News Letter*, 24 May 1921

61. *Daily Telegraph*, 25 May 1921

62. *Irish News*, 2 May 1921. A liberal-leaning newspaper, The *Manchester Guardian*, 25 May 1921, concluded that it would be, "hard to find even in the corrupt history of Irish politics an election less corrupt as that for the Northern Parliament".

63. *Irish News*, 27 May 1921. In his autobiography, *Fifty Years of Ulster, 1890–1940* (Irish News Ltd, Belfast, 1941) p. 108, T.J. Campbell, UIL candidate in East Belfast, recalled escorting an elderly, bloodstained voter to an empty police barracks at Mountpottinger, and being stopped by a British soldier who, pointing at the sad figure of the old man, told him, "We think, Sir, that you people over here are all mad!"

64. *Belfast News Letter*, 27 May 1921

65. *Belfast Telegraph*, 25 May 1921

66. *Ibid.*

67. E. Phoenix, *Northern Nationalism: Nationalist Politics, Partition and the Catholic Minority in Northern Ireland, 1890–1940* (Ulster Historical Foundation, Belfast, 1994), p. 130

68. *Belfast Telegraph*, 26 May 1921

69. *Belfast Telegraph*, 27 May 1921

70. *Belfast Telegraph*, 28 May 1921

71. *Irish News*, 25 May 1921

72. *Irish News*, 27 May 1921

73. *Irish News*, 28 May 1921. References were also made to disturbances between nationalists and republicans during the latter stage of the election campaign in Belfast's Short Strand district.

74. Phoenix, *op. cit.*, p. 131. Much of the obvious dismay at the outcome stemmed from the ill-founded euphoria of the local nationalist press in advance of the elections.

75. *Belfast Telegraph*, 25 May 1921. The reference was to counting the votes cast in North and West Belfast constituencies which took place at the Ulster Hall.

76. Some, like Julia McMordie, the widow of former Belfast mayor and Unionist MP, Robert James McMordie, were returned on relatively low mandates (in McMordie's case, 2,372 votes).

77. Sinn Féin polled 104,716 votes (20.5 per cent of the total votes cast), compared to the UIL's vote-haul of 60,577 (16.8 per cent of total poll): Phoenix, *op. cit.*, p. 129.

78. They included Sir Richard Dawson Bates, who was returned in Belfast (he received 10,026 votes). A leading figure in the anti-Home Rule movement of 1912–14, Bates was appointed minister of home affairs and proved to be a controversial figure in this post.

79. S. Elliott, *Northern Ireland Parliamentary Elections, 1921–72* (Chicago, 1973)

80. Three Unionist candidates were returned in East Belfast, where, apart from R.D. Bates, Captain Dixon (8,849 votes) and Thompson Donald (6,856 votes) were also successful.

81. Moles received an astonishing personal mandate of 17,248, more than double the number of votes gained by any other candidate in this seat.

82. B. Follis, *A State Under Siege: The Establishment of Northern Ireland, 1920–5* (Clarendon Press, 1995), p. 57

83. *Irish News*, 21 June 1921

84. *Belfast Telegraph*, 22 June 1921

85. *Ibid.*

86. One eye witness, Robert Preston, recalled staying overnight in Bangor in order to see the royal yacht proceeding up Belfast Lough, before catching a tram into the city. Once there, he managed to watch the royal procession from the first floor of the factory where his father worked: Parkinson, *op. cit.*, p. 131.

87. H.M. Hyde, *Carson* (Constable, 1987), p.458

88. Parkinson, *op. cit.*, p. 131–2

89. *Belfast Telegraph*, 24 June 1921

90. Phoenix, *op. cit.*, p. 130

CHAPTER THREE

The "Chapel Gate" Election
The Stormont General Election, 1949

"Throwing dust in to the eyes of the Irish people"

U nquestionably one of the most bitterly-fought contests in the history of Stormont general elections was the "Chapel Gate" Election of February 1949. This had been precipitated by the unprecedented actions of politicians south of the border, who had just declared their intentions of forming a Republic and leaving the Commonwealth, as well as their renewed territorial interest in the north-eastern corner of the island. The scale of this intervention (not to mention the practical, cross-party support provided by southern politicians for northern nationalists), the fury which this provoked amongst the unionist community within Northern Ireland, and the constitutional response of the British administration at Westminster – all of these factors meant that this election would be arguably the most multi-faceted contest in the region's history.

In theory, Northern Ireland unionists might have anticipated a warm reception from the British authorities in the months which followed the conclusion of hostilities in Europe. The region had played its full part in the national war effort. Although national security issues had mitigated against the introduction of conscription in Northern Ireland, many thousands of local men – Catholic and Protestant – had volunteered for war service; Belfast had suffered a deadly blitz in 1941; and the region's strategically important geographical position had been crucial in the Allies' naval war against Germany (the enemy submarine fleet ultimately surrendered on Lough Foyle in 1945). All this had been in sharp contrast with Éire's neutral stance, during a global conflict fundamentally between the forces of democracy and those of fascism. Northern Ireland's war contribution had, in the words of historian George Boyce, "placed Unionist Ulster in an unusually favourable position with all sections of British opinion".[1]

Yet unionists could not afford to be complacent when mundane political debate replaced the daily, "fight-for-survival" mentality which had dominated the war years. Indeed, they soon realised that there was a triple-pronged threat to the security of their commercial interests and treasured constitutional position within the United Kingdom. Nationalist opposition in Northern Ireland, for so long prone to negative, abstentionist tactics, had adopted a strategy of more active participation in the affairs of the newly-elected parliaments at Westminster and Stormont in 1945. By the late 1940s, the newly-formed Anti-Partition League (APL) had implemented tighter party organisation, and had adopted a more coherent, articulate presentation of minority grievances and aspirations. Unionists were also wary of the threat posed by left-leaning political groups, both within Northern Ireland and in Great Britain. Mirroring the swing to Labour at Westminster in the 1945 election, the NILP won four seats and amassed over 113,000 votes in the Stormont election later that year. The return, by a large majority, of a Labour administration promising considerable social and political reform, as well as the existence of a pressure group, the Friends of Ireland, expressing the support of a considerable number of Labour MPs for a united Ireland, meant that, for many, the province's post-1925 sense of security was now "by no means a foregone conclusion".[2] Most ominous of all for unionists in this post-war period was an upsurge in nationalist feeling within the south of Ireland, specifically in the desire to unite the island, as well as to formally reject the last vestiges of imperial power. This combination of factors had the consequence, therefore, of increasing tension within Northern Ireland's unionist community. Paradoxically, however, this would culminate in a strengthening of their bargaining position.

It was the developments south of the border around this time which caused most vexation amongst Northern loyalists. Inside an eighteen-month period, towards the end of the 1940s, the Irish government announced a proposed policy aimed at dismantling Partition and removing Éire from the Commonwealth, as well as providing political and financial support for the election campaign of nationalists in Northern Ireland. This strategy would ultimately backfire on both the Irish administration and on other southern political parties, and lead to a cementing of the unionists' constitutional position.

Further pressure from the south would ultimately result in Sir Basil Brooke calling an election in Northern Ireland. During a visit to North

America in the late summer of 1948, Irish Prime Minister John A. Costello announced that he considered himself to be premier of all of Ireland, and that he intended to reopen the debate on Partition. Linking this question to the wider one of Ireland's participation in any imminent international alliance, Costello made it clear that a fundamental rethinking of Ireland's relationships, with both its cross-border neighbour and the rest of the United Kingdom, was at the top of his agenda.

Costello's speech predictably provoked a wave of anger in the unionist press, where he was condemned for "condoning Éire's neutrality in the recent war", and for "offering Washington a pretext for urging the British Government to bring pressure to bear upon Ulster". Nearly two weeks later, noting the Irish prime minister's intention to repeal Ireland's External Relations Act (1936) and initiate moves to withdraw his country from the Commonwealth, the same newspaper returned to the attack. The *Belfast News Letter* maintained that these speeches by the Irish premier indicated, "the yawning gulf that separates Ulster from Éire, and the futility of his [Costello's] hopes of bridging it by means of threat, bribe or indirect pressure".[3] Costello enjoyed cross-bench consensus for his stance in the Irish parliament, and also in wider Irish society, with opposition leader, Eamon de Valera once again proving to be an outspoken advocate of destroying Partition, and of removing the final formal link between Ireland and Britain. Indeed, the Fianna Fáil leader was to return to this theme during the run-up to the eventual election in the North, when he addressed a 20,000 crowd in Birmingham. There, he defended the chapel collection (see below), which was "designed to bring home to as wide a public as possible the injustice of Partition". De Valera also condemned the timing and rationale behind Northern Irish prime minister, Basil Brooke's decision to call the election:

> We know perfectly well that this election is going to be made the excuse for maintaining Partition. The same thing happened in 1938. The prime minister rushed on the election, simply for the purpose of throwing dust in the eyes of the Irish people.[4]

By the end of 1948, John Costello's Republic of Ireland Bill became law in the Dáil, and a few months later he formally removed Éire from the Commonwealth. These decisions by the Dublin government forced British Prime Minister Clement Attlee to clarify his position on Northern Ireland.

Introducing his Ireland Bill towards the end of 1948, Attlee acknowledged that Northern Ireland, on account of its war contribution, should be "rewarded" with a constitutional guarantee. Historian George Boyce has observed that this "British anger at the pre-emptive nature of Irish departure from the Commonwealth, and concern for Northern Ireland's strategic importance enabled the Ulster unionists to press home their advantage at last".[5]

The strident approach adopted by the south's political class was to provoke another counterattack by their northern opponents. Sir Basil Brooke's decision to call an election was therefore a direct response to Dublin's latest legislation and its decision to leave the Commonwealth, and in a sense, the northern premier regarded such a political contest as a referendum on the whole question of Partition. As noted above, unionists had initially been guarded about the prospect of a Labour administration, which had been elected by a huge majority. However, despite this early sense of caution and the concern over unionists' constitutional security, Brooke enjoyed the ready, and increasingly sympathetic, ear of British Prime Minister Clement Attlee. Between the end of 1948 and start of 1949, Brooke had a number of face-to-face meetings with his British counterpart. In November 1948, the two men had met at Chequers Court, where Brooke was given an assurance that Northern Ireland's constitutional position would be "safeguarded" by Attlee's government. Two months later, the Northern Ireland premier had two further encounters with Attlee, as pressure from the Costello administration in Dublin mounted.[6] On 11 January 1949, following the first meeting in Downing Street, the Belfast Telegraph recorded that "Ulster's position [would be put] before the British Cabinet tomorrow", and that, following the prime ministerial discussions a few days previously, legislation on Northern Ireland was "imminent".[7] Just over a week later, another meeting between the two leaders took place, and within forty-eight hours of his return to Northern Ireland, Brooke had announced the election. He briefed his Cabinet on 19 January, and the Belfast Telegraph forecast that unionists' imminent election strategy would be based on the premise that a "strong Unionist Party [was] the best safeguard for the future".[8]

Brooke had been unequivocal in his denunciation of Costello's intentions, demanding that Attlee should take a resolute stand against the Dublin administration. Maintaining that Attlee's delay in implementing the Republic of Ireland legislation had been deliberate and provocative to unionists in the North, Brooke insisted that the "current uneasiness" in that area had been "deliberately fostered by the speeches of responsible statesmen in Éire", concluding that:

> The position has now been reached when our people require some assurance that the Imperial Government are alive to the dangers which may threaten Northern Ireland. They look to you and your colleagues to take steps to allay any anxiety in the matter, and to let it be known without equivocation that your Government will not tolerate continuance of the policy of threats and incitement directed at this part of the United Kingdom.[9]

Whilst unionist press criticism of Clement Attlee's approach to the impending crisis in Northern Ireland lacked the venom which characterised their dismissive treatment of southern politicians like John Costello and Eamon de Valera, the perceived reticence of the British premier to openly rebuke his counterpart in Éire deeply irritated many loyalists. During the election campaign, in response to southern politicians' organisation of fundraising for northern nationalist groups and their nomination of "observers", with the brief of uncovering electoral irregularities in the conduct and systems deployed by northern officials, the loyalist press was far from happy with Attlee for both his reluctance to admonish Dublin-based politicians for their interventions, and also for his apparent unease over allegations of intimidation conveyed personally to him by northern Labour election candidates. A report in the *Belfast Telegraph*, under the title, "Attlee is doing nothing on Éire election interference", noted how the British premier had told his parliamentary colleagues that "no useful purpose would be served" in registering such a complaint.[10] A subsequent post-election editorial, referring to this southern political intervention, asked whether the "present offensive" from Dublin was to "continue without any action by the British Government", and labelled Attlee's earlier parliamentary response as "unsatisfactory".[11]

Also around this time, the *Irish News* noted the British leader's distinction between the actions of a party in government and a cross-party political grouping, such as the Irish all-party group, the Mansion House Committee, which Atlee described as "a collection of individuals in various parties (and) not a government".[12] The paper was far from impressed with Brooke's meetings with the British prime minister, arguing that such face-to-face encounters marginalised the role of the Northern Irish parliament. In a leading article published the previous month, "Parliament left out", the *Irish News* contended:

> Unionists who are demanding new safeguards for their Parliament, whose existence they feel is never out of jeopardy, may ask themselves, what are its uses when their own prime minister carries on negotiations with the leader of the British Government, without consulting it about the nature of these discussions ...[13]

Other leading figures in the British Labour movement lent their sympathy and support to Northern Ireland's unionists during this anxious period of impending constitutional change. These included Deputy Labour Party Leader Herbert Morrison, who was forthright in his backing of the Partition principle during the Ireland Bill's second reading in the Commons. A few years previously, Morrison had also assured his Cabinet colleagues that Sir Basil Brooke was "most reasonable and cooperative", and that the Unionist Party was "by no means wholly a Conservative Party". His conclusion in a memorandum to the Cabinet was that there was "no need to worry about the constitutional issue".[14] Foreign Office Minister Ernest Bevin, who had met his Irish counterpart, Sean MacBride in London on 9 May 1949, expressed a warmth for Ulster's loyalists which had been absent in his party's previous and, indeed, subsequent statements on Northern Ireland. Bevin said afterwards:

> Many people in this country, and many people in the present Government, are in broad sympathy with the idea of a united Ireland. But we cannot ignore the history of the last 40 years. Northern Ireland has stood in with us when the South was neutral. Without the help of the North, Hitler would unquestionably have won the submarine war, and the United Kingdom would have been defeated ... Until the majority of the Northerners are persuaded that it is in their interest to join the South, the British people will oblige us to give them guarantees that they will not be coerced.[15]

The successful passage of the Ireland Bill, which became law in May 1949, represented the "culmination of a sustained period of trust and close cooperation" between the Labour government and Brooke's Belfast administration.[16] The new legislation proved to be memorable mainly because of its constitutional guarantee for unionists. Bringing to a closure the uncertainty and anxiety engendered by the terms of the Government of Ireland Act, 1920 (and in particular, its Boundary Commission clause), the Ireland Act provided northern unionists with a substantial degree of leverage for numerous future discussions on their region's political future. The vital "guarantee" clause read:

> It is hereby declared that Northern Ireland remains part of His Majesty's Dominions and of the United Kingdom, and it is hereby affirmed that in no event will Northern Ireland or any part thereof cease to be part of His Majesty's Dominions and of the United Kingdom without the consent of the parliament of Northern Ireland.[17]

Chapel Collections

Sir Basil Brooke's announcement of the election on 18 January had been anticipated by many in the province. Parliament was prorogued on 20 January, with the closure of nominations being scheduled for 31 January, and Election Day pencilled in for 10 February (the new parliament was to be called on 1 March). Early speculation focused on the likely make-up of the new parliament. The composition of the Stormont parliament which had been elected in 1945 was 35 unionists (two of these were independents), 10 nationalists, 4 Labour representatives, 1 Socialist-republican and 2 independents. Speaking at a function in Belfast on 20 January, Brooke justified his decision to call for a new mandate, which, he insisted, was necessary in order to obtain clarification on the electorate's attitudes to Northern Ireland's constitutional status. He told his audience: "We are a determined people in Ulster, and we are determined not to cast loose those historic and economic links which bind Northern Ireland to the rest of the United Kingdom."[18]

Although Brooke's critics were not surprised by his decision, they were far from convinced about the rationale for staging such a contest, as well as being unhappy with its timing. The *Irish News* reported the claim of Anti-Partition League leader and Mourne parliamentary candidate, James McSparran, that the election was a "ruse", designed in order to "get a fresh lease of power for the existing Government, against whom the tide of opposition [is] flowing at the present time".[19] The paper returned to this theme two days later, when its leading article suggested that the election was being held on "the pretext that the repeal of the External Relations Act has in some way imperilled the future of 'Ulster'", and maintained that the contest represented "a bare-faced dodge to give a new term of office to a Government faced with rapidly-growing opposition to measures which it has recently passed or which it is sponsoring".[20]

The *Belfast Telegraph*, on the other hand, applauded the timing of the election which, scheduled for 10 February, would prove to be "well in advance of the declaration of an Éire Republic". The election would, the paper believed, constitute a "referendum on the British constitution", and it reminded its readers that "the most effective reply from here to Éire's decision and to the threats of pressure will be a solid vote for unionism".[21] Stressing the importance of "strength" and "unity" amongst the unionist section of the electorate, the paper suggested that the public was "entitled to know where the various parties stand in regard to the Border question, which is of vital and intimate concern to every class".[22]

In the days following the announcement of the election, newspaper coverage centred round the early preparations of the leading parties. The *Irish News* reported that the various "party machines, which have been geared up to a high state of preparedness, have already been set in motion, and there is evidence of much pre-campaign activity amongst all the parties". However, it also noted the obvious advantages enjoyed by the Unionist Party, where the "majority" of candidates had "already been selected", whereas, "many of the standard-bearers for the other parties have not yet been announced".[23]

A few days into the election campaign, the major story was the calling, in central Dublin, of a cross-party meeting, at which southern parties put aside political differences, to step up the pressure on Basil Brooke's Northern administration. Picking up on the upsurge in nationalist fervour which had accompanied Éire's decision to form a Republic, and fearful of British intentions to offer Northern unionists a constitutional guarantee, Irish premier John Costello had called a public meeting of all parties in the 26 counties, as well as a small number of northern nationalists, to be held in Dublin's Mansion House on 27 January 1949. The more specific purpose of this gathering was to raise revenue for Anti-Partitionist candidates campaigning at the imminent Stormont election. Additionally, a new Anti-Partition body – the Mansion House Committee – was established to oversee the collection of funds designed to assist the campaigns of these nationalists. The main effort of this fundraising drive was to be a collection outside churches in Éire the following Sunday (this was repeated on the following Sunday, the final one before the contest). In a post-meeting statement, the Mansion House Committee declared that "the candidates in the forthcoming election who stand for the unity of Ireland deserve the support of the united Irish nation".[24] The *Irish News*, the north's leading nationalist newspaper, heralded the creation of this "national fund to aid [a] united Ireland", and the following day would remind its readers that, "preparations for [the] Anti-Partition fund [were being] collected in the 26 counties tomorrow", and that "all parties [were] cooperating".[25]

Unionist reaction to the breaking news of the events south of the border was, initially at least, surprisingly low-key. Although northern Protestants were undoubtedly enraged by what most of them regarded as a blatant intrusion into their affairs, it would be the subsequent interventions by southern politicians which resulted in the most vitriolic unionist responses. The *Belfast Telegraph* dismissed these southern attempts to raise funds for northern nationalists as "the chapel gate collections".[26] The paper's coverage of the first round of church collections, however, was detailed. The following day's edition noted that collections had taken place outside churches of all denominations, and that the fund organisers were "well-satisfied with the results so far". Reportedly the largest contribution in the Dublin area came from the north-eastern part of the city, with the Donnybrook district "heading the parish contributions, with over £300".[27] Photographs of the church collections were featured in the *Belfast Telegraph* the following day, under a caption noting that "scenes like these were enacted outside Roman Catholic chapels through the length and breadth of Éire on Sunday, when collections were taken to furnish funds and support Anti-Partitionist candidates in the Northern Ireland election". The running total for the Anti-Partition Fund was estimated at being in excess of £20,000.[28]

A few days later, the *Belfast Telegraph* reported on the case of an Anglican rector, Canon Walter Simpson, who was allegedly threatened after complaining about an Anti-Partition collection taking place outside his church in Dublin.[29] Newspaper interest in the second church collection on 6 February was on a smaller scale, especially as this coincided with the northern campaign nearing its climax – though the newspaper reported that the total collection for the Anti-Partition Fund had reached £46,000.[30]

Whilst the organisation of the Anti-Partition Fund in the South undoubtedly assisted the financing of the northern nationalists' campaign, its overall contribution to their cause was probably a negative one. Although the large amount of generated funds would enable nationalists to contest an unprecedented 17 seats (including in a number of "safe" unionist constituencies, such as Lisnaskea and south Londonderry), many Catholics were at the very least indifferent to such a move, especially as southern-based politicians had scarcely involved themselves in northern election campaigns for a quarter of a century. More crucially, it would be the indirect impact which the Chapel Gate collections (and other instances of southern intervention into northern affairs) had, in rejuvenating the unionist campaign, which would constitute the main legacy of the initiative. The location chosen for the collection of funds especially irritated Ulster Protestants, who saw a clear link between fundraising for Anti-Partitionist groups in the north and the Catholic Church, which, they believed, continued to dominate much of Irish life.

"King or Republic?"

Party candidates were required to submit their nomination papers on 31 January at seven designated centres across Northern Ireland. The most striking feature of the final election line-up was the sharp increase in the number of contested seats – which was an unprecedented total of 32, out of a total of 52 Stormont seats (this included 4 university seats). This was largely due to the greater profile of nationalist candidates, especially in rural constituencies. The *Irish News* headline on the day following the nomination of candidates declared: "17 Anti-Partition candidates nominated – 2 returned unopposed".[31] Unionists were contesting all of these seats, and apart from the Anti-Partitionist candidates, there were 9 from the NILP, 3 independent Labour candidates, 1 independent Unionist, and 1 Communist Party candidate (the latter was standing against Lord Glentoran and a Labour candidate in Bloomfield, which was the scene of the only three-party clash). There were still, however, 20 constituencies where single candidates would be returned unopposed, including Mid- and West Down, Ards (all safe unionist seats) and 6 in Belfast.

Each of these 57 candidates was allocated a fuel allowance of 250 gallons of petrol, amounting to a total of some 18,750 gallons (though, as noted later, nationalist candidates would enjoy a distinct advantage over their opponents, on account of the Anti-Partition fundraising in the south). In an atmosphere where dissident or independent unionist candidates would inevitably endure hostility over the possible splitting of the loyalist vote, only one independent unionist stood in the election, and as a consequence of this, as well as republican apathy, six "walkovers" were recorded in Belfast. The *Belfast Telegraph* argued it was "significant" that, despite the "definite Nationalist tendencies of some of the left-wing candidates, not a single Anti-Partitionist as such was nominated in Belfast".[32]

The City Hall was again the hub for considerable Nomination Day activity, as a mainly loyalist crowd gathered outside Belfast's grand municipal headquarters or loitered along its spacious, winding corridors. One reporter observed how the "usual number of semi-hysterical women [were] mobbing their candidates", and how "uniformed police and detectives kept a close watch inside and outside the building".[33]

The main thrust of the APL attack would come in rural, and particularly border areas, including a "triple contest" in Fermanagh, which involved Sir Basil Brooke and Cahir Healy in defence of their seats. The prime minister issued a Nomination Day "good luck" message to Unionist Party candidates, and, "given the gravity of the situation", urged unionist voters to remember the "necessity for playing their part on polling day." For Brooke, the issue was a simple one, of "King or Republic". The prime minister also exhorted Ulster loyalists to demonstrate that "we are King's men".[34]

True to form, the rival newspapers interpreted the ramifications of the nomination pairings quite differently. The *Belfast Telegraph* commented that unionists were "early in the field" in constituencies such as South Armagh and Mid-Tyrone, where nationalists were being "challenged on their own grounds", whilst the *Irish News* maintained that Nomination Day had proved to be one of "keen disappointment" for unionists.[35] Suggesting that unionists would be stretched by having to defend particular constituencies, the *Irish News* went on to implore nationalist-minded supporters to back their nominated candidates. The editorial argued:

> It would have heightened the pride of the Ascendancy group, could they have shown that they had sufficient numbers returned unopposed to form an Administration … It is for Nationally-

minded voters ... to support their standard-bearers, not only in
the strongholds of Irish unity but in those other divisions where
their candidates are fighting against still heavier odds, in order
to prove that the Unionists are not, as they think, the lords and
masters of Ulster.[36]

Even a few days before Basil Brooke had announced the election, a *Belfast
Telegraph* editorial called for "Strength through Unity". The paper asserted
that such a contest "cannot be far distant", and reminded voters of their "duty"
and need to "realise plainly the fundamental issue involved". Reminding
its readers of the "coming proclamation of an Irish Republic", the paper
described the "fresh threat" to Northern Ireland's constitutional position,
which would ensure that the imminent election would unquestionably prove
to be the "most important" one since the establishment of the state in 1921.
The editorial ended by pleading "for all men and women, who value their
citizenship and the benefits of the British connection, to rally round Sir Basil
Brooke and his team".[37]

Less than a week later, the election had been formally declared, and the
Belfast Telegraph returned to this theme of the election being the "most
critical in the history of the Province".[38] A photograph in this edition of the
paper showed Sir Basil Brooke addressing the Unionist Council's standing
committee in Glengall Street. In the party's manifesto, published a few
days later, Brooke's message to electors was succinct. He declared that "our
country is in danger", and that "today we fight to defend our very existence
and the heritage of our Ulster children". Brooke's final call to his supporters
was a familiar one: "No Surrender! We are King's Men!"[39]

Despite the scarcity of election meetings and an incomplete list of
nominated candidates (especially those from opposition parties), less than
three weeks before polling day, the *Belfast Telegraph* was determined to paint
a picture of "feverish activity" amongst the parties.[40] The paper, probably
accurately, maintained that the Unionist Party had established "a good
lead, with most of their candidates selected and local organisations alerted".
In addition to this, local printers were being "inundated with election
addresses, ballot papers and placards, and halls are rapidly being booked up
for meetings".[41]

The first reports on the unionists' election campaign only featured in
the local press less than two weeks before voters actually went to the polls.

Unionist Party candidates spoke at several venues, both in Belfast and in rural areas, towards the end of January. The candidate for Ards, Morris May, addressed meetings in Portaferry and Greyabbey on 27 January, and there were rallies in east Down addressed by Harry Midgley and unionism's rising star, Brian Faulkner. There were also several unionist meetings in Belfast around this time. The Grand Master of the Grand Orange Lodge of Ireland, J.M. Andrews, addressed a gathering of Orange Order members in Clifton Street Orange Hall in north Belfast, where he claimed the key issue in the election was clear – that of "Empire or Republic" – whilst the Ulster Young Unionist Council (UYUC) staged a rally at Strandtown in east Belfast.[42]

Just after the Mansion House meeting in Dublin, Northern Ireland Minister for Home Affairs, Edmund Warnock, addressed an audience at the Unionist Party headquarters in Glengall Street, who were coming to terms with the breaking news from Dublin. Warnock did not mince his words, condemning the "intrusion" of the Dublin representatives, and warning them that "when strangers – foreigners at that – begin to interfere, then, like the Apprentice Boys of old, we close the gates".[43] The cabinet minister dismissed the significance of the southern intervention, arguing that the initiative had "damned the chances of the opposition before the election even starts". This "interference" would simply "ensure a unity and solidarity amongst Loyalists, such as not been seen in Ulster for 30 years", Warnock assured his audience.[44] There were further parades and meetings in districts like Pottinger in the east of the city, and at Duncairn, in its north. UUC President, Lord Glentoran led a torch parade in the former area, calling for "a solid front against intruders".[45]

This plea to "unofficial" and "independent" unionists, to refrain from contesting seats which might result in a split in the loyalist vote and possible nationalist gains, was frequently expressed in the days leading up to the deadline for the submission of nomination papers, and at least one "unofficial" candidate withdrew (in the Ards constituency). Northern Ireland Health Minister, William Grant, a seven-times victor in the Duncairn seat originally won by Sir Edward Carson, addressed a unionist gathering in the constituency which he had represented at Stormont for many years – and here, as in Oldpark, where four loyalist bands played in a parade backing William Morgan, another unionist candidate in North Belfast – the "No Surrender" message rang out loud and clear.[46]

The main target for condemnation in the leader columns of the unionist press during this election campaign was the southern administration, as well as other politicians in Éire who had lent their support to the Mansion House group. The *Belfast Telegraph*'s label for those southern politicians who had intervened in the debate over the North's constitutional future was that of "meddlers", and this was a constant feature of editorial comment. Following the publication of the Unionist Party's manifesto on 25 January, the *Belfast Telegraph*'s "Voice of Ulster" editorial explained the party's rationale in calling for a mandate, as well as supporting a successful campaign outcome. The paper argued:

> Against the consequences of Éire leaving the British Commonwealth, Sir Basil Brooke and his Government are seeking safeguards for the people of this province, and now they seek endorsement for their action ... Continuing pressure is the tactic which has been practised for years, and it is certain to remain the policy of Northern Ireland's political opponents.[47]

Two days later, the paper returned to its denunciation of southern "meddlers". This editorial suggested that, "knowledge of the North and the feelings of its people" were as "limited as ever in Dublin", if the advocates of southern interventionism believed their action would increase "mutual understanding". Indeed, the paper asserted, it was likely to have "the very opposite effect".[48] Nearly a week later, another *Belfast Telegraph* leading article, "Call off the Meddlers", condemned the disingenuous stance adopted by southern politicians, and also demanded a reciprocal intervention on the part of the British prime minister. Reminding its readers that the Éire electorate had been "given no chance to say whether or not they wished to remain in the Commonwealth", the paper asked if it would be "fair" for the Northern Ireland electorate to be "told [that] they had no right to hold an election". The editorial concluded, by declaring that it would be "interesting to hear what Mr Attlee has to say about intervention by Éire into Northern Ireland's affairs".[49]

Not only were the loyalist press enraged by the announcement of the Chapel Gate collections, but they also condemned the decision of Irish Minister of External Affairs, Sean MacBride to appoint four southern "observers" to oversee the conducting of the final stage of the northern election. The *Belfast Telegraph* again dismissed the "active" intervention of the south's political class, including "this piece of propaganda" (the appointment of the "observers"), which reflected "a lower degree of intelligence in Éire than any one even dared to credit their political leaders with before".[50] Suggesting that many Catholic voters would agree that this latest development represented "an impertinence and an affront to their ordinary intelligence", the editorial blamed the southern intervention for "importing" into the northern election campaign "a bitterness of word and emotion that can do no good to anyone, and [will] present the result on a plate to their opponents".[51]

Although most of its venom was released on southern political leaders, the unionist press also turned its ire on perceived "enemies" within the North and also on unsympathetic British newspapers. The *Manchester Guardian* fell into the latter category, on account of its temerity in concurring with the prevailing nationalist sentiment that the Northern Ireland election had been "rushed on a stale register, and that there [was] no reason why it should not have been held on the new register in April".[52] Whilst conceding that a rotation in the control of government – something which was not even on the North's political horizon – was a good thing for a democracy, the *Belfast Telegraph* proceeded to describe Basil Brooke's decision to call an election as "perfectly defensible in [its] timing". The editorial censored instead the leader of the Irish administration, for the way in which he had "rushed through his Republic", which could "scarcely be cited as an exemplary way in which to bring about a constitutional change".[53]

Nationalists too, unsurprisingly perhaps, came in for rebuke from the unionist press, although, on account of the level of abuse being hurled at the southern "meddlers", this was more low-key than usual. One editorial, a few days before the election, made a far from favourable comparison between unionism's old foe, Joseph Devlin – whom "everyone liked, despite strong religious differences" – and the Anti-Partition League's leader, James McSparran, whom they accused of reverting to simplistic, emotive, "green" rhetoric. An example of this was his claim that "the Ulster Tories have drowned all such issues" (social and economic ones) in "bucketfuls of Boyne water". The piece, published in the *Belfast Telegraph*, went on as follows:

> Is that the best that a King's Counsel, who is a candidate in
> Mourne, can do to put up to intelligent people? Campaigning in
> Mourne, he prophesises that Sir Basil Brooke's tactical success will

be a strategic defeat. Well, we shall see. Certainly, if he imagines that allegiance to the King and regional pride are opposed to the good of Ireland, the record of history is against him, and it is not surprising that Nationalism is a spent force.[54]

The last week of the campaign saw an escalation in the activities of all parties, especially the Unionists. A photograph of a motorcycle despatch rider leaving Glengall Street headquarters with posters and other material, bound for outlying districts, was featured in the *Belfast Telegraph*'s edition of 2 February. The previous day, a torchlight parade had been held in support of Morris May, the party's candidate in Ards, and that evening, Harry Midgley addressed street gatherings in Cherryvale Street and Woodstock Road in east Belfast, where he challenged Clement Attlee to denounce the southern intervention into Northern Ireland affairs. The following day, the Northern Ireland premier spoke at a midnight rally in support of Brian Faulkner, his party's candidate in east Down, and there were other reports in the *Belfast Telegraph* on the respective campaigns of Edmond Warnock in Belfast's St Anne's division, Maynard Sinclair in the city's Cromac constituency, and Lord Glentoran in Belfast's Bloomfield division.[55] A few days later, the paper announced the start of the campaign's "last lap", with all the parties "working at high pressure to complete their plans".[56] The following day, the paper reassured its readership that the Unionist Party was "standing firm in a barrage of propaganda from the Dublin press and Radio Éireann".[57]

Loyalists would also have appreciated the additional boost to their campaign of the arrival in Belfast of members of the Carson family. Sir Edward Carson's son, himself a Westminster MP, accompanied by Lady Carson (Sir Edward's widow), took to a handful of election platforms, including one in his father's old Duncairn constituency. Here in particular, the son of the Unionist Party's former leader received a "great ovation" after speaking on behalf of Unionist candidate, William Grant. Lady Carson also spoke at a meeting in Bloomfield, in support of indisposed Unionist candidate, Lord Glentoran.

An interesting insight into the election rituals of this time is provided in an election report appearing in the *Belfast Telegraph*. In this piece, reporters described the "good luck" gifts symbolically donated to unionist candidates during the final stage of their campaigns. Major J. Maynard Sinclair, standing in Belfast's Cromac division, addressed street gatherings in McClure Street,

Cromwell Road and Agincourt Avenue, and was presented with "numerous black cats, as well as a magnificent shillelagh inscribed, 'Good luck, Sinclair, 1949'". Another unionist candidate, Dr Sam Rodgers, standing in East Belfast's Pottinger constituency, was pictured "pressing the flesh" of some of his constituents, including "a Navy man who sails to China tonight". This same gentleman was snapped in Fraser Street, holding up his baby (appropriately named Edward Carson), in whose lap lay "a lucky horseshoe", which was duly handed over to Rodgers. The report concluded:

> At the junction of Pitt Street and Fox Street, the gift was a New Testament; at the corner of Convention Street, a blackthorn walking stick. The Doctor was given a lucky "black cat" in Cuba Street by a little kilted girl, who was marched up to him by the skirl of her father's bagpipes![58]

For a party leader not generally regarded as energetic, Sir Basil Brooke sustained a high profile for most of the campaign and, despite missing a speaking engagement due to illness, he addressed numerous meetings, both in his Fermanagh constituency and across the province (on one day alone, he spoke at four meetings in Belfast). Just after the election had been announced, the *Belfast Telegraph* published a feature article on Brooke, "Ulster's Man of the Hour", in which the paper's correspondent described the premier's "non-stop round of duty".[59]

Like many other major unionist campaigns previously, the climax of this one was to be an event programmed to take place at the Ulster Hall, two days before polling. A "rush for Ulster Hall tickets", including passes for 25 "representatives of the world's press", was noted in the *Belfast Telegraph* on the day of the rally; the following evening's report of the meeting described the "stirring" rally, again attended by members of the Carson family and featuring Sir Basil Brooke's "March with Me" call to his supporters.[60] The paper recounted how "every vantage point in the historic building was occupied", whilst outside in Bedford Street, "thousands of men and women stood for several hours in the cold February air, listening to rousing, relayed election addresses." Speaking to his excited followers, the prime minister drew upon the familiar and trusted rhetoric of his predecessors:

> I ask you to cross the Boyne ... with me as your leader, and to fight for the same cause as King William fought for in days gone by ...

My friends, my soldiers, march with me. Your battle-cry is "No Surrender". We are the King's Men![61]

The *Belfast Telegraph* had sustained its enthusiastic support for Brooke and the Unionist Party during the election campaign's final week. Apart from a continued denunciation of the southern "meddlers" and northern nationalist politicians, the paper warned of the danger of conceding ground to Labour candidates in urban areas, and reminded readers of their electoral "duty". Slogans at the foot of election report pages – such as, "Unity with Britain depends on Unity in Ulster" – helped to reinforce this message of holding firm and staying together amongst the majority community.[62] During the days leading up to polling, the paper's editorial columns also returned to familiar messages. Observing that the "political temperature" was "higher than at any time since the Ulster Covenant", it once again castigated southern "interference" in the political affairs of another country, which was deeply "resented" by northerners. In suggesting that such an intervention "smack[ed] of the Sudetenland", the paper drew parallels between these moves on the part of the south and the annexation strategy of the Nazis during the run-up to war in the late 1930s. Readers were reminded that unionism was "a good cause", and loyalists were urged to follow the example of Sir Basil Brooke, who had "chosen the high ground in this election", and to "stick to the high ground, leaving Mr MacBride to forage from glen to glen."[63]

Less than 48 hours before voting commenced, the *Belfast Telegraph* warned against the economic damage which would occur if the electorate followed the advice of John Costello and Sean MacBride. The latter had promised such benefits as cheaper tobacco and alcohol if the North joined forces with the south in a new Republic, but the newspaper counselled against the broader economic consequences which would accompany such constitutional change. Its editorial argued that, "cut off from Britain, the industries of the North would wither and die", and that voters' livelihoods would "depend on the choice you make on Thursday."[64] A final pre-election editorial described the campaign which had just concluded as being "short and bitter", and advised the individual reader to "make this election a matter of his or her intimate concern".[65] Again denouncing the "indefensible" action of southern political leaders for "interfering actively" in the contest, the paper's opinion piece, "The Will of the People", described the imminent vote as representing "a plebiscite on the British connection, and all that it means in [terms of] spiritual and material values". Stressing the urgent need for "as big a majority as possible" on polling day, the *Belfast Telegraph* maintained that Sir Basil Brooke and his new administration would "not fail, and their policy will serve all classes and creeds better than those [sic] of their opponents".[66]

"The tyranny of the Unionist Party"

The *Irish News* meanwhile condemned the rationale behind the calling of the election, suggesting that it was simply a "stunt" being pulled because unionists had once again believed Northern Ireland to be in "danger". Éire's announcement, that it was planning to declare itself a Republic, which would leave the Commonwealth, had provided Sir Basil Brooke with the chance to "paint the Orange lily", and a further "opportunity of sounding the tocsin and telling his followers they must vote for him or perish".[67] The election call was also flawed, it contended, not least because of developments south of the border. Dismissing unionist claims that their decision to announce the contest represented "a tactical victory", the paper suggested that loyalist "feelings of triumph" had quickly been "dissipated" and that they were left feeling "badly shaken", in the wake of the "dramatic demonstration of unity" which had been evident at the Mansion House conference in Dublin. The paper highlighted this "determination of the Irish people to give every possible help to the Anti-Partition cause and its candidates."[68] As well as criticising unionist hastiness and misplaced optimism, it lambasted the very essence of the North's political and civic society, which had been underpinned by draconian Special Powers legislation, and had resulted in "a Six-Counties police state".[69] Other attacks on the province's political infrastructure and electoral system targeted its "gerrymandered constituencies", and a "stale" current electoral register. The *Irish News* also declared the decision to pre-empt a contest "a bare-faced political dodge", which had been designed to bring about "a new term of office to [a] Government faced with rapidly growing opposition to its policies".[70]

Midway through the election campaign, the *Irish News* renewed its attack on what the paper saw as the undemocratic nature of government in the region – specifically the fact that there had been no changes in the composition of government over a period of some 30 years since the creation of Northern Ireland. Condemning Brooke and his administration for merely paying "lip service" to the idea of creating a genuinely democratic government benefiting all its people, the *Irish News* suggested that a comparison with the Soviet Union was apt:

> When the Kremlin arranges an election in any country under its control, it knows the result beforehand. When a "call to the country" is made in the Six Counties, the result is also known beforehand.[71]

The *Irish News* not only articulated the doubts and grievances of the Northern minority, both in regard to this election and the proposed policies of the likely new unionist administration – it also shared the cynicism of sympathetic British press observers. Reproducing a detailed report by William Connor, a *Daily Mirror* reporter, the *Irish News* attempted to reassure its readers that sympathy for northern Catholics extended beyond Irish shores. In his article, "Drums along the Border", Connor described the election as "a religious war", which had been "inspired by hatred [and was] nourished by bigotry". He forecast that the contest would "reach its foregone conclusion, sustained by bitterness".[72] Concluding that the election "battle" had been won about 25 years ago, when the election boundaries were drawn up, or perhaps even 400 years earlier at the time of the Reformation, William Connor and the *Daily Mirror* reminded their British readership that "these mockeries of democracy" were not occurring in "some remote foreign dictatorship, but just across the narrow channel of the Irish Sea".[73]

Nationalist-leaning journalists were dismissive about the assertions outlined by unionists in their election manifesto, which was published on 24 January. Deflecting Sir Basil Brooke's claim that "our country is in danger", the *Irish News* proclaimed that such a document was mere "melodrama", and that "the Ascendancy Party are men without a country".[74] The paper's editorial queried the nature of such "danger", maintaining it had been due to the record of government rather than the constitutional issue. Reminding readers that 37,000 people remained jobless, the leading article went on:

> The plain people know to their bitter experience what a source of danger his Government is to their welfare. They are, in the eyes of Stormont, mere creatures in the queue, docketed, rationed and labelled, offering many social ills. Hopes held out that these ills will be uprooted are not fulfilled.[75]

In the early stages of the election campaign, an *Irish News* editorial observed that unionist representatives were "advocating that more of their nominees should enter the field against Nationalist candidates". Sarcastically alluding to the "gerrymandered" voting system in the province, which had resulted in "one Unionist vote equalling 20 more Nationalist votes", the paper suggested that the Ulster Unionist Party should "adopt two or three candidates for every constituency". By doing this, unionists "could not make the election a greater farce than it is".[76]

As the campaign progressed, the *Irish News* turned its attention to unionists' irate response to southern engagement in the North's contest, as well as loyalists' notions of "Irishness". Referring to unionist claims, that southerners had been "poking their noses into Northern affairs", the paper reminded its critics that Sir Edward Carson – still "hailed by Brooke as a prophet" – actually "came from the 26 Counties, and was by the same token a foreigner".[77] In a subsequent editorial, the same paper dismissed Brooke's recent claim that he was "a good Irishman", who was only interested in the "happiness and prosperity" of his region's populace. Referring again to the large number of unemployed in Northern Ireland, the *Irish News* argued that Brooke's "No Surrender" slogan was intended to distract the minds of his supporters from domestic issues, such as unemployment and lack of housing. The paper's concluding comment was more overtly controversial in terms of its political stance, in pointing out that the prime minister "ought to know that there is no good Irishman who does not believe in the unity of his country".[78]

❧

Although widespread rioting and communal violence was averted, this election did witness the clearest incidence of the intimidation of candidates – especially those representing left-wing groups – since the 1921 elections that preceded the opening of Northern Ireland's parliament. The long-serving Labour representative, Jack Beattie, who was also an independent Labour MP for West Belfast at Westminster, was a particular target for loyalist intimidatory tactics. Beattie, standing once more in the Pottinger constituency he had represented since 1925, endeavoured to separate the constitutional question from the Brooke administration's domestic policies. He claimed that the election did not constitute "a genuine attempt to secure a mandate for or against Partition", but was instead "rushed" on account of the Brooke government's "fear that growing unemployment ... would swing the balance against them if they delayed too long."[79]

Though not candidates they would normally endorse, the *Irish News* did give considerable coverage to Labour candidates' disrupted campaigns, both in Belfast and County Antrim. The paper's front-page story reported the stoning incidents which interrupted Jack Beattie's meeting in his constituency on 1 February, and how "howling unionist mobs (over 2,000 strong) ... hurled bricks, oranges and other missiles" during the sitting member's initial campaign meeting in east Belfast's Templemore Avenue. At this loyalist counter-demonstration, which was backed by a flute band, many people "screamed derisive taunts at Mr Beattie while he was speaking, and at intervals broke into raucous singing of party songs, including 'Derry's Walls' and 'The Sash', punctuating their behaviour with shouts of 'Lundy!'".[80] Beattie, who had wisely donned a steel helmet before speaking, curtailed his street address, and later that evening despatched a telegram to prime minister Clement Attlee, which included the following text:

> Stoned by official unionist mobs and denied the right of free speech in my election campaign tonight. Armed Stormont police took no action. My agent protested and was arrested. As Imperial member, I request at once a stop to these Fascist mobs and a guarantee of free speech in these elections, by sending official observers from the British Labour Government. Wholescale intimidation evident.[81]

Postponing a number of street meetings, Beattie and his supporters swiftly produced and distributed leaflets in his Pottinger constituency. Beattie condemned the "organised mobs of outsiders", denouncing the intimidatory tactics of these "hooligans" and urging his constituents to "resist this interference with the right of free speech in Pottinger, by working and voting so as to ensure my return for the constituency which I have faithfully represented for the past 24 years".[82] The response of Jack Beattie's unionist opponent, Dr Sam Rodgers, was one of derision. Describing the Labour candidate's decision to send a telegram to Downing Street as "a strange thing" for "a big six-footer like him, to go to a wee man like Mr Attlee to seek protection", Rodgers added that Beattie should "do his crying to

Mr Costello, the man he really supports".[83] Within days, Jack Beattie returned to Westminster, where he briefed many Labour MPs and the home secretary who, he reported, were "horrified" at the recent events in Belfast.[84] Towards the end of the election, Beattie complained that "the tyranny of the Unionist Party is worse than that of the Hitler regime".[85]

Although his high profile in local politics meant that Jack Beattie bore the brunt of intimidation by extreme loyalists, he was by no means the sole Labour-leaning candidate to have his election campaign severely disrupted. Newspaper reports, particularly those in the *Irish News*, informed readers that several Labour candidates – including Beattie, James Donnelly (also standing as an independent Labour candidate in Belfast's Cromac division) and William Gregg (standing for Labour in Antrim) – postponed a number of scheduled meetings on account of intimidation or actual violence. Hugh Downey, the Labour candidate in Belfast's Dock constituency, was hit by stones whilst speaking at an open-air meeting in the Nelson Street area on 11 February, and the *Irish News* condemned the "scenes of hooliganism" at both the meetings of Beattie and Downey that evening.[86] James Donnelly experienced similar abuse at a meeting on the Ormeau Road that evening, and would also complain in a telegram sent later to the British prime minister. At least one Labour candidate had to receive hospital treatment for injuries received during attacks at campaign meetings. Antrim candidate, John Gregg had been addressing a small but sympathetic crowd in the town's square on 2 February, when a mob of angry unionist counter-demonstrators (estimated at being over 1,000 strong) attacked the candidate's car and removed amplifiers. Gregg's English-born agent, a Mr A. Johnston, was thrown to the ground after calls of, "We don't want Englishmen here!", and an "orange barrage" (a range of missiles) was thrown at the platform party, resulting in the instant abandonment of the meeting.[87]

Labour candidates were not alone in suffering disruption to their campaigns. Reports also appeared in the nationalist press of APL candidates being intimidated or assaulted at meetings outside Belfast. On 8 February, J.B. Agnew, the South Derry nationalist candidate, was attacked in Magherafelt, when a variety of missiles, ranging from stones, bottles and items of scrap iron to rotten eggs, were thrown at the platform. Just after the conclusion of his campaign, Agnew was interviewed at length in the *Irish News*. He complained that he and his campaign team had been "denied freedom of speech at Garvagh and Magherafelt, thanks to organised Unionist mobs who paraded with bands".[88] On Election Day itself, after visiting a polling station at Innisrush, Agnew was "ambushed just outside the village by unionist supporters hidden behind hedges on each side of the road".[89] Bricks and stones were then hurled at the van and Agnew's driver needed hospital treatment for his injuries.

The *Irish News* highlighted such cases of intimidation, arguing that "not since the first General Election for Stormont [sic] have acts of intimidation been so prevalent as during the contests in Belfast on Thursday".[90] In condemning this election interference by extreme loyalist elements, the paper took some satisfaction in the response of outsiders to such intimidation. Noting the statement of the British prime minister the previous day – "I have had news of quite a number of incidents in Northern Ireland, which show the elections there are not conducted on quite the same lines as ... over here" – the *Irish News* declared that "now people at home and abroad know more than ever before of the evils which the Stormont Government has created".[91]

The scale of the intimidation and street violence meant that even the *Belfast Telegraph* felt obliged to comment on these unsavoury incidents which had occurred in loyalist districts and, although not directly acknowledging unionists' responsibility for the attacks, stressed the need to avoid more trouble. The paper acknowledged the rising political temperature which had "not been so high since the days of the Ulster Covenant", and wrote of its "duty" to "appeal to all parties to counsel their spokesmen and supporters to behave with dignity and restraint, [and] to avoid any tactics which provoke disturbances".[92]

The nationalist campaign was not given much coverage in the unionist press, but regular updates on the selection of nationalist candidates were provided in the columns of the *Irish News*. Among the paper's front-page headlines on 26 January were: "Anti-Partitionists to fight Brooke's seat"; "Conventions in many areas today"; "Election preparations speed up".[93] The nomination of APL candidates, Cahir Healy in South Fermanagh (which he had represented for 24 years), and Philip McCarron, who was opposing the prime minister in Lisnaskea, were announced in the *Irish News*; the following day, the paper reported four further nominations of APL candidates. One of these was sitting nationalist member for Mourne and Chair of the Anti-Partition League, James McSparran, who suggested there was "abundant evidence to indicate that the Nationalist-minded people of this traditionally anti-Partition division will give their utmost support to retain their control of it".[94] The paper informed its readers that "preparations continue[d]" for the selection of APL candidates, with National Conventions due to be held in Omagh that evening, and in Newry and Carrickmore the following day.[95] A few days later, the *Irish News* noted the "intensification" of the nationalists' campaign, with more anti-Partitionists than ever contesting unionist-held seats.

Early APL election meetings, including those addressed by James McSparran in Mourne, and Cahir Healy and William Blake in Fermanagh, were, as the *Irish News* reported, "characterised by big attendances and the greatest enthusiasm". The chances of nationalist contenders were pondered over by the paper's political correspondents. The "main interest" for nationalists in the forthcoming election would be focused on the border counties of Fermanagh and Tyrone, and also on Derry city, where the Anti-Partitionist candidates were "conducting the greatest fight for many years in the gerrymandered areas".[96] These journalists were convinced that there was "every prospect of a very heavy Anti-Partitionist poll" in constituencies contested by candidates, "pledged to the unification of the country". The "big gathering" at St Mary's Hall in the County Down seaside town of Newcastle, was addressed by James McSparran, who was defending a 2,240 majority. The APL leader's speech warranted comprehensive coverage in the *Irish News'* columns. The Mourne MP claimed that the election had been called on "a purely artificial issue", and maintained the Brooke administration had kept the date of the contest secret, in order to gain an electoral advantage, especially in the organisation of transport, hall-booking and the printing of election posters and literature. This amounted, McSparran argued, to "a most disgusting exhibition of characteristic Tory tactics, and they ought to be ashamed of the whole business, if they had any shame".[97]

During the last week of the campaign, the *Irish News* printed extracts from the APL's manifesto. These included the nationalists' claim that the contest represented "a grotesque travesty of democratic practice and fair play", which made "a mockery of the Reform Act and Ballot Acts".[98] The APL also suggested that the "outstanding issue in Irish politics today" was whether the will of barely two-thirds of people in just six of the island's thirty-two counties could "defy the will of the nation". The manifesto asked how "such a claim would be received by any self-respecting nation of the world." In an editorial, the *Irish News* backed the claims made in the APL manifesto, which had "exposed the fallacies of the unionist position".[99]

The paper also updated its readers on the progress of nationalist candidates in several rural constituencies, as their campaign neared its climax. "Much enthusiasm" was evident at Joseph Connellan's meeting in Newry, where earlier a loudspeaker van had "paraded" through the town, advertising that evening's event. At this meeting, a pipe band marched through the town, headed by a "monster" tricolour. The Margaret Street square was "packed to capacity, and the huge gathering overflowed into Hill Street and other adjoining thoroughfares".[100]

Further morale-boosting nationalist meetings were held in Fermanagh and Derry. Speaking at a meeting in County Fermanagh, Cahir Healy informed his audience that tax rates in the North were double those of the south, and that, despite the prime minister representing the county for many years, it remained the "worst-housed area in these islands".[101] Edward (Ned) McGrady, the APL candidate in East Down, was one of several APL speakers to condemn their main political opponents. McGrady claimed that unionists again had "no policy", except their "old cry that Ulster was in danger", and he appealed to traditional unionist voters "not to be bluffed any longer" by "a Government of landlords and reactionaries".[102] There was also "intense activity" in the South Armagh districts, and on 4 February, James McSparran addressed an estimated 3,000-strong audience in St Patrick's Hall, Downpatrick. The APL leader's message was unequivocal in its defence of Irish unity:

> It is to the advantage of me, of Ireland, as well as of England, that this nation should be united and free. It is not merely to the material advantage of the country, but to her spiritual advantage that she should be united.[103]

The nationalist message was also voiced at a range of venues outside Belfast. These included Bessbrook, where loyalists snatched a tricolour from an election worker's car; Derrygonnelly, where William Blake addressed "a great rally", at which there were "blazing torches and bands playing rousing airs"; Enniskillen; Lisnaskea (at this meeting of 8 February, Cahir Healy was praised by the *Irish News* for orchestrating, "a tremendous demonstration of national demonstration"); Castlewellan; Newry, on 6 February; and Omagh, where an address by APL candidate R.H. O'Connor was given on 9 February.[104]

In the final days of the contest, the *Irish News* switched its attention to assessing the effectiveness of the APL campaign which had just ended, and focused on gauging the chances of success for their candidates. A "resounding victory" was predicted for James McSparran in Mourne, who had set "a fine example" for other nationalist candidates by the "meticulous attention to detail" which he and his support staff had demonstrated during their campaign.[105] The paper's editorial and news columns also drew attention to the possibility of collusion between the leaders of cross-community organisations and the Unionist Party, and the mendacious nature of that party's policies and claims. In relation to this, the *Irish News* highlighted the participation of J.M. Wadsworth, the president of the Ulster Farmers' Union, at a unionist rally in Iveagh.[106] The paper also dismissed the monotonous tone of the unionist campaign where, "speakers continue to chant the Border bogey chorus, with variations, hoping as in the past, by appealing to the emotions of the people, to obscure vital issues".[107] A subsequent editorial also claimed that, despite his party enjoying the "advantage of months of preparation for the election", Sir Basil Brooke had actually "lost the war on propaganda."[108]

"Victory in Royal terms"

By the time Election Day dawned on 10 February, interest in the outcome had peaked and there was a genuine air of excitement across the province. Bookmakers, as ever, cast a cautious eye over the contest's likely results, with odds of 6–4 being offered for an increased government majority, and similar favourable odds being offered for the return of 35 Unionist representatives. The *Belfast Telegraph* claimed that it too was making "election history" on a day most journalistic pundits had proclaimed would have considerable historical importance for the region. With a main headline that read, "Round the Polling stations by Radio Van", the paper proudly informed its readers that it was, for the first time, covering polling at various centres across Belfast with the aid of its own radio unit – with journalists relaying their stories through to the newspaper offices from the van. The newspaper also contained photographs of scenes at busy polling stations in Belfast and County Armagh. At Harding Memorial Primary School in East Belfast's Cregagh district, UUP candidate, Harry Midgley was pictured alongside a six-year-old boy whose name had bizarrely appeared on the electoral register. Although young Francis Turtle, of Loopland Gardens, was not permitted to cast his vote, this story – along with another photographic account of a 98-year-old woman casting her vote for the unionist candidate in Lurgan – added a "human interest" angle to the paper's election coverage.[109]

The *Belfast Telegraph*'s prediction, that Ulster's majority community would resist polling day apathy, was confirmed on 10 February. The paper's main headline that evening – beneath a photograph of the iconic Edward Carson statue at Stormont – was emphatic: "Ulster gives her answer – early signs of one of the heaviest polls". The paper maintained that its reporters were aware of people "coming in to vote unionist, who had not voted for many years", and declared that there was "no doubt" about the key issue at stake. Its editorial anticipated a definitive election outcome, and expressed confidence that the British authorities would "accept the answer of the polls as an indication of the people's will".[110] The paper also published a sympathetic report from that morning's *Daily Mail*, which had forecast that unionists would "win hands down". In this report, entitled, "Carson's soul goes marching on", the *Daily Mail* had declared that the election result was "conceded before the poll opens", and concluded that "Britain would find it hard to cast away a people who seem willing to go to the stake rather than desert the British flag".[111]

That day's early-morning edition of the *Irish News* reminded its readers to take proof of their identity to the polling stations, and was reasonably upbeat about the chances of their favoured APL candidates. Under the headline, "Voting will be strong against those who disown their country", the paper referred to the radio message of the APL's main spokesman, James McSparran, on Radio Éireann and the BBC Overseas Service, and reminded its readers that nationalist candidates were in direct opposition to 15 unionists in over half of the contested seats. McSparran's last-minute broadcast appeal was an optimistic one, aimed at a much wider audience than those preparing to go to the poll in Northern Ireland, as he claimed:

> The General Election in the Six Counties has given the cause of Anti-Partition by far its greatest impetus since the Government of Northern Ireland was established over a quarter of a century ago. It has reawakened the spirit of nationality in the heart of every Irishman throughout the world-wide empire of the Irish race. Through the glare of publicity which it has directed upon

the incontrovertible justice of the cause of Irish unity, it has accomplished more in one month than the propaganda of Anti-Partitionists in 20 years.[112]

The *Irish News* also reported on high turnouts in specific nationalist-leaning areas (including a purported 90 per cent poll in Newry), and on incidents of intimidation or violence in a range of districts. These incidents included a mass fight in a mill at Sion Mills in County Derry, which had erupted over the display of a loyalist placard, a brick being thrown at an APL van in Portglenone in County Antrim (an election worker required hospital treatment), and an attack on a Labour Party office in Belfast's Oldpark area.[113]

Both leading newspapers vividly described the atmosphere and mounting excitement in town and country constituencies on Election Day. In a report on the border constituencies of Fermanagh and Tyrone, where eight unionists and eight nationalists were directly opposed, the *Belfast Telegraph* maintained that the respective party workers "soon showed they are the cockpit of the election". The paper highlighted a rare APL advantage over their unionist rivals – namely their easier access to fuel, which was especially important in rural constituencies. The report continued:

Fleets of cars were being sent out by both parties from early morning to bring in the voters. The Unionist agents made no complaint of availability of transport, but it was seen that fleets of Éire cars were being used by the Nationalists. Crossing the Border with full tanks, they were busy all day and, when necessary, went back for more petrol paid by the Anti-Partition Fund.[114]

The *Belfast Telegraph*'s description of frenetic Election Day activity noted that "placarded cars were also seen in droves" around Belfast, where the "only difficulty for unionists was the shortage of the official allocation of fuel". The paper's report referred to the Unionist Party's headquarters as "the Clapham Junction of the city's unionist transport system" while a photograph of a busload of Fermanagh-bound unionists, "off to vote in the Battle of the Border", was also included in this edition of the paper.[115] The *Irish News* also described the transport arrangements and polling activities of nationalist election workers the previous day. Observing how "hundreds" of motor vehicles had crossed the border at various points between Donegal and the northern counties of Tyrone, Fermanagh and Derry, the paper informed its readers that volunteer drivers were "busy throughout the day conveying voters to booths, particularly in rural districts".[116]

At 79.3 per cent of the total electorate, the turnout on polling day represented a significant increase on the corresponding election four years before (this had been 70.2 per cent). There was certainly a sharp rise in the number of people declaring their support for the Unionist Party, with the total of 234,202 representing 55,440 more than the 1945 figure. However, nationalists had also turned out in force, with 106,459 electors siding with the APL candidates. The big loser was the NILP, which lost its three parliamentary seats in Belfast (Dock, Pottinger and Oldpark), and saw its vote more than halved – from 66,053 to 26,831. Nationalists, with an increased share of the votes cast (now 27.2 per cent of the total), would be the sole representatives sitting on the opposition benches in the new parliament, with 11 of their 17 candidates having been elected (the best result for nationalists since Partition). Unionists were euphoric with the performances of their candidates, especially in terms of those gains from Labour in Belfast, which the Belfast Telegraph described as "striking".[117] The Unionist Party now had 37 representatives in the 52-seat parliament – an increased majority of 4 – and they had managed to garner 62.7 per cent of all votes cast, representing an increase of over 12 per cent since 1945.

Whilst the big news story in the unionist press on the day following the election was the death of Lord Londonderry, the Belfast Telegraph acknowledged the early successes of Sir Milne Barbour in South Antrim, Lord Glentoran in Bloomfield (where he gained a 12,000 majority), the victories of J.C. Cole in Dock and Lt. Col. S.H. Hall-Thompson's win in Clifton, and, importantly, the first election victory in a long political career for Brian Faulkner in East Down (his majority was 2,652). Referring to the Unionist Party's win in Dock, the Belfast Telegraph claimed that loyalists had "mustered 95 per cent of their strength" in the constituency, which had resulted in the Labour candidate being "thrown out".[118] Ignoring the widespread intimidation of Labour candidates by loyalists in the run-up to the poll, the paper instead chose to denounce the "unpleasantness" at the count in Derry city, where the controversial unionist candidate, Reverend Godfrey MacManaway was returned. The paper's evening editorial had a headline which would become more synonymous with subsequent election contests. In its "Ulster says No" leader, the paper predicted that a "sweeping unionist victory" was "likely" after the government's gain of seats from Labour in Belfast. The paper was in triumphant mood:

> Ulster has once again told the world that it stands for the King and British Commonwealth. The General Election results today give an overwhelming rejection to inclusion in the Irish Republic. Everywhere the Unionist vote has broken records, and Sir Basil Brooke is assured of an increased majority in the House of Commons. In Belfast, Labour was in danger of being completely wiped out.[119]

Its jubilation continued the following day, when all the results had been declared. The paper described the Unionist Party's result as a "victory in royal terms", the proportions of which had "surprised everybody". In an attempt to explain the demise of the Labour groups, the paper's editorial suggested that, contrary to its opponents' enunciations on the subject, the border question was "a bread-and-butter issue", which actually "affected housing, clothing, shelter, work, pensions, not to mention freedom of thought."[120] Within a couple of days, the *Belfast Telegraph* turned its attention towards the criticism emanating from its nationalist counterpart. Condemning the response of the *Irish News* to the election result, the *Belfast Telegraph* dismissed the attempts of the "vanquished" to "represent that they have not had a fair deal", and denounced their "resort to fresh allegations, studiously prepared in advance of the result."[121]

The *Irish News*' interpretation of the election outcome was, naturally enough, radically different to that of the *Belfast Telegraph*. Its front-page headline on the day after the election announced the "Record Vote against the Partition of Ireland", and, whilst conceding a unionist win was "a foregone conclusion", the paper returned to its one of its perennial themes, castigating the region's "corrupt" political system, manifested in its "gerrymandering" and "obsolete register".[122] The paper's main report in the following day's edition was a detailed piece on how gerrymandering had operated in practice during this election, with its spotlight on the "glaring" case of Fermanagh. The constituencies in this border county represented "a barefaced case of gerrymander", it maintained, and stressed that the unionists standing there had gained two seats with a combined vote of 13,895, compared to the solitary seat won by nationalists who had amassed a poll of 15,582 votes. Noting unionist "displeasure" at the "strong nationalist poll", the paper reminded its readers that all seats previously held by nationalists had been retained, and that Anti-Partitionist voters had "come out in strength" to back their candidates. Examples of this were the large majority enjoyed by Malachi Conlon in South Armagh (7,503) and Cahir Healy's return in Fermanagh, with a majority of 4,084. In its editorial on 12 February, the *Irish News* celebrated the "double victory" in County Down of APL candidates James McSparran (for Mourne) and E.K. McGrady (in East Down), and praised nationalist electors across the province, concluding that they had "good reason to be proud of the vote they polled against the Border", and that nationalists in general had "a magnificent achievement to their credit".[123]

In its post-election editorial columns, the *Irish News* also condemned the phenomenon of intimidation, which had been evident throughout the campaign. Declaring that the Unionist Party's eagerness to let the world know about Ulster's "loyalty" had instead led to "the exposure throughout the nations of the earth of the fraud and mockery perpetuated in the sacred name of democracy in this 'Imperial Province'". The *Irish News* suggested that, in practice, the election's outcome had been "a strategic defeat" for Brooke and the Unionist establishment.[124]

The political repercussions of the "Chapel Gate" election were profound for most parties in the short term. For nationalists, the "relative success" of the APL in the contest proved to be illusory, as the infrequent attendance and participation of APL representatives – along with the apparent lack of a clear political strategy on the part of the chief opposition party in the Stormont parliament – resulted in them "losing ground" in local politics.[125] This failure to mount a credible opposition to the governing Unionist Party would not be rectified until the formation of another party, some twenty years later – the SDLP – which would represent a broader range of opposition groups. In the short term however, the APL's modest success resulted in a short-lived political resurgence for republican groups in the mid-1950s.

The election also saw a sharp decline in support for the NILP in the Greater Belfast area, and despite the party's belated acceptance of the constitutional status quo in Northern Ireland on the eve of the election, the NILP, as well as the independent socialist candidates, were clearly unable to surmount the huge barrier of the constitutional question. An improving economic climate, largely the outcome of new, relatively generous welfare benefits, also undoubtedly made their stance seem less immediately relevant in the public's perception. However, nearly a decade later, the Labour Party was to experience a revival in its fortunes in Belfast, when it put up a creditable performance in the Stormont General Election of 1958.

For unionists, the 1949 election had resulted in a solidification of the Partition arrangement first established a quarter of a century before, and these groups felt undoubted relief that their constitutional future, so uncertain since the Government of Ireland Act of 1920 had established the State, was now distinctly more secure. Yet this sense of security was far from being unassailable. In their euphoric response both to their electoral success at the start of 1949 and to the constitutional guarantee contained in the Ireland Act which was passed six months later, unionists failed to spot that such a guarantee was "largely as permanent as their devolved parliament".[126] A resulting false sense of confidence on their part meant that Brooke's new administration would miss an opportunity to consolidate their position, by broadening the base of their popular support through the gradual implementation of a programme of social reform and equality. Their failure to do this would kill off any hope of cross-community support for a unionist administration, and would result in the emergence, nearly 20 years later, of a street protest movement, aimed at overturning the inequality of their system.

The 1949 election had been the product of external circumstances, rather than the response to a demand for change from within Northern Irish society. These external factors were the Éire government's move to form a Republic and its declared intention to leave the Commonwealth, as well as British prime minister Clement Attlee's resolution to effectively "reward" Northern Ireland for its war contribution. Just as Lloyd George had been determined to "solve" the Irish question at the end of one global conflict, so Britain's post-World War II premier was set on achieving a definitive settlement of the Irish question. In doing so, Attlee stressed that it had been the Irish government – and not, as claimed by John Costello, the British administration – which had "tightened the ligature around the body of Ireland".[127] In Attlee's Ireland Act, undoubtedly the most important clause was Clause 1 (b), which read:

Parliament hereby declares that Northern Ireland remains part of His Majesty's Dominions and of the United Kingdom, and affirms that in no event will Northern Ireland or any part thereof cease to be part of His Majesty's Dominions and of the United Kingdom, without the consent of the Parliament of Northern Ireland.[128]

What made the "Chapel Gate" election truly different from other Northern elections was the degree of southern intervention which had both precipitated and influenced the contest. In practical terms however, the decision of the south's political elite to directly embroil themselves in Northern Ireland politics generally backfired, not only enabling unionists to record a resounding success at the polls, but also resulting in the postponement of any chance of substantial political reform in the province for another two decades. The involvement of the Éire government in the affairs of the Stormont administration was the impetus behind a strong unionist campaign, leading also to a withdrawal of the threat posed by independent unionist and socialist candidates; far from enhancing the chances of creating a parliament with a broader range of interests, the resulting opposition representation was, for the first time since Partition, exclusively nationalist (at 11 MPs, the APL comprised just over 20 per cent of the chamber).

While the election was undeniably "a direct response to the Republic of Ireland Act" which had been passed in December 1948, it would also evolve into "a classic confrontation between Nationalism and traditional Unionism". Historian Dennis Kennedy has suggested there was a certain degree of "appropriate irony" surrounding this "rejuvenated Anti-Partitionism and a precipitated act by a Dublin Government" and its outcome, a "legislative guarantee for the Unionists", which meant that, "not for the first time, Irish nationalism had proved unionism's greatest supporter".[129] At the same time, this election was, however, far from being a loyalist whitewash of its chief opponents, the nationalists, whose vote actually increased.

What the "Chapel Gate" election had clearly demonstrated was that normal political debate and interaction would continue to falter in Northern Ireland, as long as perceived constitutional ambiguities remained such a force within the region's political culture.

Endnotes

1. G. Boyce, *The Irish Question and British Politics 1868–1996* (Palgrave Macmillan, 1996), p. 98

2. P. Buckland, *A History of Northern Ireland* (Gill and Macmillan, Dublin, 1981), p. 84. At least 35 Labour MPs were members of the Friends of Ireland group.

3. *Belfast News Letter*, 28 August 1948; 7 September 1948

4. *Irish News*, 31 January 1949

5. Boyce, *op. cit.*, p. 101

6. The *Belfast Telegraph*'s headline on 18 January 1949 read, "Sir Basil Brooke guest at Number 10 for second time in a fortnight".

7. *Belfast Telegraph*, 11 January 1949

8. *Belfast Telegraph*, 19 January 1949

9. R. Rees, *Labour and the Northern Ireland Problem 1945–51* (Irish Academic Press, Dublin, 2009), pp. 132–3. Brooke had also requested the withdrawal of the right to vote for Irish citizens living in Britain: *Irish News*, 21 January 1949

10. *Belfast Telegraph*, 8 February 1949

11. *Belfast Telegraph*, 14 February 1949

12. *Irish News*, 11 February 1949

13. *Irish News*, 19 January 1949

14. Boyce, *op. cit.*, p. 99

15. Rees, *op. cit.*, p. 138

16. *Ibid.*, p. 133

17. Boyce, *op. cit.*, p. 101

18. *Irish News*, 21 January 1949

19. *Irish News*, 19 January 1949

20. *Irish News*, 21 January 1949. An Agricultural Bill was unpopular with Ulster farmers, and there was also opposition to the proposed introduction of the National Insurance scheme.

21. *Belfast Telegraph*, 20 January 1949

22. *Ibid.*

23. *Irish News*, 22 January 1949

24. *Irish News*, 28 January 1949

25. *Irish News*, 29 January 1949

26. *Belfast Telegraph*, 31 January 1949

27. *Ibid.*

28. *Belfast Telegraph*, 1 February 1949

29. *Belfast Telegraph*, 4 February 1949

30. *Belfast Telegraph*, 7 February 1949

31. *Irish News*, 2 February 1949

32. *Belfast Telegraph*, 31 January 1949

33. *Irish News*, 1 February 1949. There were calls of "Lundy" as Labour candidates, including Jack Beattie and James Morrow, arrived to leave in their nomination papers.

34. *Belfast Telegraph*, 31 January 1949

35. *Belfast Telegraph*, 31 January 1949, and *Irish News*, 1 February 1949.

36. *Irish News*, 1 February 1949

37. *Belfast Telegraph*, 14 January 1949

38. *Belfast Telegraph*, 20 January 1949

39. *Irish News*, 25 January 1949

40. *Belfast Telegraph*, 21 January 1949

41. *Ibid*.

42. *Belfast Telegraph*, 28 January 1949

43. *Belfast Telegraph*, 30 January 1949

44. *Ibid*.

45. *Ibid*.

46. *Belfast Telegraph*, 31 January 1949

47. *Belfast Telegraph*, 25 January 1949

48. *Belfast Telegraph*, 27 January 1949

49. *Belfast Telegraph*, 2 February 1949

50. *Belfast Telegraph*, 31 January 1949

51. *Ibid*.

52. *Manchester Guardian*, quoted in *Belfast Telegraph*, 22 January 1949

53. *Belfast Telegraph*, 22 January 1949

54. *Belfast Telegraph*, 7 February 1949

55. *Belfast Telegraph*, 4 February 1949

56. *Belfast Telegraph*, 7 February 1949

57. *Belfast Telegraph*, 8 February 1949

58. *Ibid*.

59. *Belfast Telegraph*, 21 January 1949

60. *Belfast Telegraph*, 8 February 1949; 9 February 1949

61. *Belfast Telegraph*, 9 February 1949

62. *Belfast Telegraph*, 28 January 1949

63. *Belfast Telegraph*, 3 February 1949

64. *Belfast Telegraph*, 8 February 1949

65. *Belfast Telegraph*, 9 February 1949

66. *Ibid*. In the same edition, a large drawing of the Ulster Unionist leader featured the slogan, "Ulster expects every man to do his duty tomorrow".

67. *Irish News*, 22 January 1949

68. *Irish News*, 29 January 1949

69. *Irish News*, 31 January 1949. The paper was expressing the fears of many of its readers, concerned about the state's powers to arrest and intern people without trial.

70. *Irish News*, 21 January 1949

71. *Irish News*, 3 February 1949

72. *Daily Mirror* (11 February 1949), quoted in *Irish News*, 12 February 1949

73. *Ibid*.

74. *Irish News*, 25 January 1949

75. *Ibid*.

76. *Irish News*, 29 January 1949

77. *Irish News*, 2 February 1949

78. *Irish News*, 7 February 1949

79. *Irish News*, 2 February 1949

80. *Ibid*.

81. *Irish News*, 8 February 1949
82. From J.J. Nihill donation collection, Election Manifestos/Material 1942–69, Linen Hall Library, Northern Ireland Political Collection.
83. Bardon, *op. cit.*, p. 601
84. *Irish News*, 5 February 1949
85. *Irish News*, 9 February 1949
86. *Irish News*, 2 February 1949
87. These "oranges" contained concealed razor blades. *Irish News*, 4 February 1949
88. *Irish News*, 12 February 1949
89. *Ibid.*
90. *Ibid.*
91. *Irish News*, 9 February 1949
92. *Belfast Telegraph*, 4 February 1949
93. *Irish News*, 26 January 1949
94. *Irish News*, 27 January 1949
95. *Irish News*, 25 January 1949
96. *Irish News*, 31 January 1949
97. *Ibid.*
98. *Irish News*, 8 February 1949
99. *Ibid.*
100. *Irish News*, 3 February 1949
101. *Irish News*, 4 February 1949
102. McGrady from J.J. Nihill donation collection, *op. cit.*
103. *Irish News*, 5 February 1949. Despite this unambiguous demand for Irish unity, McSparran appeared unaware of the irony in a subsequent claim in the same speech, when he talked about how the "old bogey" of Northern Ireland being "in danger" had been "brought to the surface again".
104. *Irish News*, 7 February 1949; 9 February 1949
105. *Irish News*, 9 February 1949
106. *Irish News*, 8 February 1949
107. *Ibid.*
108. *Irish News*, 9 February 1969
109. *Belfast Telegraph*, 10 February 1949
110. *Ibid.*
111. *Daily Mail*, quoted in *Belfast Telegraph*, 10 February 1949
112. *Irish News*, 10 February 1949
113. Another Labour candidate was threatened in south Belfast's loyalist Sandy Row district. *Irish News*, 11 February 1949
114. *Belfast Telegraph*, 10 February 1949
115. *Ibid.*
116. *Irish News*, 11 February 1949
117. *Belfast Telegraph*, 12 February 1949
118. *Belfast Telegraph*, 11 February, 1949. A photograph in this edition of the paper showed the victorious Hall-Thompson standing alongside his oldest and youngest supporters (98 and 6 years old respectively) at a polling station in his constituency.
119. *Ibid.*

120. *Belfast Telegraph*, 12 February 1949

121. *Belfast Telegraph*, 14 February 1949

122. *Irish News*, 11 February 1949

123. *Ibid.*

124. *Ibid.* Brooke's own Lisnaskea majority over nationalist John Carron was far from convincing (1,420).

125. Rees, *op. cit.*, p. 140

126. *Ibid.*

127. Boyce, *op. cit.*, p. 102

128. Buckland, *op. cit.*, pp. 88–9

129. D. Kennedy, *'The Widening Gulf – Northern Attitudes to the Independent Irish State 1919–49'*, (Blackstaff Press, Belfast, 1988) p. 239

CHAPTER FOUR

The "Crossroads" Election
The Stormont General Election, 1969

Times, they are a-changing!

The "Crossroads" election of February 1969, which was ostensibly called to bolster support for the besieged Unionist Party leader and prime minister, Terence O'Neill, ultimately resulted in further party division, and also witnessed changing fortunes for opposition groups and political leaders. It would be the last realistic opportunity for a divided society to sanction a programme of reform and to build cross-community trust in a comparatively progressive political leader, before the onslaught of a sustained paramilitary campaign would make such hopes impossible. The contest also saw the emergence of new political personalities and parties, many of whom would soon play a major part in reshaping the region's political landscape.

During the late 1960s, a desire for political change had been very much in the air across Europe, when "revolutions" – albeit of different kinds – were experienced in cities like Paris and Prague. Within Northern Ireland too, there had been an increase in community tension from the mid-1960s, which manifested itself, for example, in 1966, when minor disturbances broke out in Belfast following republican commemorations of the fiftieth anniversary of Dublin's Easter Rising. February 1967 had seen the formation of the Northern Ireland Civil Rights Association (NICRA), an amalgam of various radical, nationalist and republican representatives, who were primarily calling for a more equitable distribution of jobs and housing across the religious divide. This organisation quickly gained substantial support, particularly within the Catholic minority community, and in the last quarter of the following year, began staging protest marches. It would be the street clashes between civil rights protestors and the RUC, which broke out after NICRA leaders ignored the late banning of a march on 5 October 1968, which would catapult the region into the national, and indeed international, consciousness. The weekend of violence which ensued would result in close to ninety people (including eleven police officers) receiving mainly minor injuries.

In the aftermath, external observers – including the Cameron Commission, which had been established to report on the violence in Derry – largely focused on the "ill-coordinated and ill-conducted" response of the police. The next few months would see a number of other civil rights marches, increasingly dominated by hard-line activists of the radical People's Democracy (PD) group, and along with these came counter-protests organised by Reverend Ian Paisley's Protestant Unionist Party (PUP).[1] This led to confusion and further division within unionist ranks on how to contain a worsening political and security situation.

During the latter half of the 1960s, there had also been change in the nature of leadership provided by the Unionist Party. Although the party leader and prime minister, Captain Terence O'Neill, had come from the same aristocratic background as his predecessor – and uncle – Sir Basil Brooke, his proposed policy of reform was very different from the policies advocated by the unionist leaders of the past. O'Neill, a former Etonian and Irish Guards officer, had been Stormont MP for Bannside since 1946, and had served as minister of home affairs and finance minister, before becoming party leader and prime minister in 1963. However, despite his unprecedented, "fraternal" meetings with southern leaders, Sean Lemass and Jack Lynch (in 1965 and 1967 respectively), to discuss ways of improving economic cooperation between the two administrations as well as with his elaborate and sustained attempts to widen the appeal of his party within the Catholic community, Terence O'Neill's limited personal charm and poor presentational skills mitigated against his party making significant inroads with this potentially new source of electoral support.

However, Terence O'Neill's courting of Catholic opinion was genuine and sustained, and not restricted to photoshoots of visits to senior clergy or the handing out of prizes at schools. His administration had started to address minority grievances during the latter part of the 1960s, and on 22 November 1968, he announced a five-point reform programme, which directly addressed many of the grievances articulated by the leaders of the civil rights movement. These measures, which had won broad backing from a majority of party representatives, included: fairer, more transparent allocation of council housing, based on a points system; the creation of an ombudsman post to aid the impartial investigation of grievances; a review of the Special Powers Act; the abolition of the company vote in local elections; and other reforms within the sphere of local government, including the replacement of the Londonderry Corporation with a more broadly-based Development Commission.

Whilst these reforms were dismissed by opponents as being too modest, they did represent a substantial shift in the thinking of the unionist leadership and contrasted sharply with the ultra-conservatism favoured by O'Neill's predecessors, Basil Brooke, John Andrews and James Craig. Indeed, on the surface at least, it might seem surprising that Terence O'Neill's reforming premiership would soon be so fatally wounded. After all, these proposed reforms directly addressed many of the complaints voiced by representatives of the Catholic minority, and had been supported by a majority of Unionist Party members.[2]

However, quite simply, Terence O'Neill was the wrong messenger to deliver the right message. It was his insipid leadership style which would prove to be the crucial factor in his ultimate failure. On the one hand, his inability to convince his rank-and-file supporters that his approach was "the correct one to safeguard the Union" would make his internal position untenable; on the other, nationalist scepticism over his genuine willingness, or capacity, to deliver these reforms and the "new Ulster" which he promised, meant progress was unlikely.[3] In the "Crossroads" election of February 1969, it would be O'Neill's "gesture politics", and his tendency to "plunge into the politics of public relations with little thought about the actual Ulster public", which resulted in his failure to harness sufficient backing.[4]

Faced with the conflicting demands of internal party back-biting over his perceived leniency to Catholic voices of opposition, and ever more critical calls from civil rights groups for meaningful reform, O'Neill felt obliged to speak directly to Northern Ireland's people about the crucial and urgent issues confronting them. In a broadcast transmitted on 9 December 1968, the beleaguered premier suggested that the region was at a "crossroads" in its history. He reminded those listening that he had "tried to heal some of the deep divisions in our community" for over five years, and went on to denounce his unionist critics, who merely "talk of independence", and represented little more than a version of "Protestant Sinn Féin". O'Neill then pointed out that unionism "armed with justice" would have "a stronger cause than unionism armed merely with strength". However, it was in the closing part of his speech that the premier was most explicit with his listeners, as he asked them:

> What kind of Ulster do you want? A happy respected Province, in good standing with the rest of the United Kingdom? Or a place continually torn apart by riots and demonstrations, and regarded by the rest of the United Kingdom as a political outcast?[5]

Reaction to O'Neill's key speech was generally positive, and for a short while at least, he appeared to have stolen a march on his critics. Within days of the broadcast, he sacked his increasingly outspoken Minister for Home Affairs, William Craig, and on 12 December, he obtained a strong expression of support from his parliamentary colleagues, with 29 MPs in favour of him continuing to lead the party and, although there were four abstentions, nobody directly opposed his leadership. He was also backed by some surprising sources, including the leader of the Irish Catholic Church, Cardinal William Conway, and Nationalist Party leader, Eddie McAteer.

The *Belfast Telegraph*, which had been a firm advocate of O'Neill's "reconciliation" brand of politics, launched a petition expressing support for the prime minister on 10 December. The front page of that day's edition (and also the next day's leading article) encouraged readers to sign and return pro-O'Neill coupons enclosed within the paper. These coupons read: "I approve of Captain O'Neill's broadcast, and support his efforts to heal the division in our community".[6] The paper received a substantial endorsement for its campaign, and close to 150,000 signed coupons were received during the period leading up to Christmas.

On the first day of 1969 however, O'Neill's cautious optimism was quickly shattered. Just prior to this, the left-wing PD group, which had increasingly been to the fore at organised civil rights rallies, announced its intention of staging a march from Belfast to Derry, starting on New Year's Day. On the third day of this protest march, the contingent of seventy-strong marchers were attacked at Burntollet Bridge in County Derry by a considerably larger group of loyalists, marshalled by Major Ronald Bunting, a leading figure in the PUP. Bernadette Devlin, soon to be elected to Westminster, was on the march that day and later recalled that, "the attackers were beating marchers into the ditches and across the ditches into the river". She conceded that "a few policemen were at least trying to stop us from being killed", but maintained that most of the others were "quite delighted that we were getting what, in their terms, we deserved".[7]

Television coverage and news reports of the Burntollet attack, after which thirteen people required hospital treatment, were broadcast around the world. The damage to O'Neill's administration increased as, later that evening, violence also erupted in Londonderry shortly after the arrival in the city of the fatigued and bruised marchers. The PD leaders were criticised for proceeding with the march and, the day after the Burntollet incident, the prime minister proclaimed that, "enough is enough", and that the people of Northern Ireland had "heard sufficient for now about civil rights [but] let us hear a little about civic responsibility".[8]

However, the events of 4 January were to have a significance well beyond the relatively minor scale of the violence committed that day in County Derry. Catholic hostility to the state was hardened by the police's slowness to react at Burntollet, and the march marked "the pivotal point at which the Troubles changed from being primarily about civil rights to the more ancient disputes concerning religious and national identities".[9] Civil rights protestors were far from finished with expressing their frustration, and another parade in Newry the following week also ended in violence.

At the same time he had to contend with this mounting Catholic dissatisfaction and outpouring of grievances, O'Neill had also to face growing discontent and indeed anger within the ranks of his own party. In stark contrast with the cross-class cohesion evident within Edward Carson's Unionist Party during the Home Rule crisis of 1912–14, now grass-roots disquiet over the civil rights street protests and, more especially, O'Neill's leadership, escalated, as the crisis deepened.[10] The perception held by working-class Protestants, that the ruling class which continued to lead unionism was betraying their interests, became ever more entrenched, largely due to O'Neill's confrontational approach to dissident loyalists.

Senior members of the administration publicly expressed their concerns about the prime minister, and two prominent ministers, Brian Faulkner and William Morgan, resigned towards the end of January. Around this time also, several dissident members of the Ulster Unionist parliamentary group (UUP) issued a joint statement, calling for a change in the party's leadership. While maintaining that they supported the "progressive" policies of O'Neill's administration, these representatives described the party disharmony as being of "grave proportions", and something which could only be addressed by a change at the top of the organisation. [11] At a meeting in a Portadown hotel on 3 February 1969, twelve of these Stormont representatives – including Faulkner, Morgan and the recently-dismissed Home Affairs Minister, William Craig – called for the removal of the prime minister.

This show of defiance by a significant section of the parliamentary party at a meeting soon to be dubbed the "Portadown Parliament", provoked an instant response from Terence O'Neill. Dismissing the rebels' claims that their disquiet was primarily related to his leadership of the party, rather than the wider issue of ongoing reform, the prime minister announced that he was calling a general election on 24 February. O'Neill and his cabinet colleagues rationalised that the very public denunciation of his party stewardship meant that this bickering could no longer be resolved internally, but necessitated the formal backing of the wider electorate. This conclusion was in turn dismissed by one of the Portadown dissidents, Captain Austin Ardill, who rebuked O'Neill for instigating an electoral contest in which "no one knows the issues at stake", when in reality what was occurring was merely "a family dispute", which represented "a matter to be sorted out behind closed doors".[12]

The decision that evening of 3 February to call for an election was far from being a complete surprise, with the *Belfast Telegraph* forecasting a couple of days beforehand that O'Neill would "shortly seek to have his leadership endorsed at an early general election". The paper was upbeat about such a scenario, reminding readers that the pro-O'Neill "support movement" was "building up throughout the country".[13] Yet many other observers felt that the prime minister's immediate reaction to threats made at the "Portadown Parliament" constituted a knee-jerk response to the speeches and actions of a minority of his parliamentary colleagues.

"At one another's throats"?
As noted above, rumours of a likely electoral contest became more persistent at the start of February. The *Irish News* headline on 3 February – "O'Neill rebels are now on the defensive – Premier will call the election tune" – forecast the imminent announcement of the contest; the accompanying front-page report noted that support for the premier had been "pouring in" over recent days.[14] The rival newspapers concurred in their backing of O'Neill's decision, although in the case of the *Irish News*, its backing was more qualified. The *Belfast Telegraph* forecast that O'Neill would triumph, and that the likely

outcome of the contest would be "a new-look Stormont".[15] Although the *Irish News* suggested that the premier was taking a "gamble", its editorial asked, "how else is he to defeat the dissidents in his Party and revive the body of Unionism, now lying inert in the gutter?"[16] The paper also expressed a degree of grudging praise for the leader of the beleaguered administration:

> However partisan Government by O'Neill has been, it has shown some groping towards an altered and more humane approach; and that this is preferred to government by a Right-Wing Unionist group, infused by the hatred and bigotries of Protestant extremism.[17]

In an interview with the *Belfast Telegraph* on 5 February, Terence O'Neill provided his own explanation for calling the election. Pointing out that it was "a time of great difficulty" for his administration, he stressed that "important decisions" had to be taken, which would "shape the future of Northern Ireland as a whole". Focusing on his belief that his internal opponents were really motivated by their opposition of his policies, rather than his leadership, the prime minister declared that the contest was required to provide him with "a clear vote of confidence to carry on with our moderate and progressive policies".[18]

His opponents within the party lambasted their leader for calling an unnecessary election at a time when strong government was needed to stem the swelling tide of street confrontation. On 6 February, speaking to a large audience in Derry, the recently-dismissed minister for home affairs, William Craig, expressed his "sadness and anxiety" that he and his colleagues had been "placed in a dangerous situation by the reckless act of a panicking Government".[19] While unionist hard-liners focused on what they believed were the weak leadership qualities displayed by O'Neill, the prime minister's supporters stressed that the choice for Ulster's voters would be one between "maturing politics, or going back to square one".[20] For the traditional wing of the party, the unity of the organisation was of paramount importance, whilst "liberal" unionists sought to use the contest to obtain a mandate for the prime minister and his politics of modernity. Little wonder that the stated intention of the contest – at least, that of the pro-government faction of unionism – of appealing to Catholics for their political backing, would prove to be a failure.

Yet this election would be, theoretically at least, very different from previous contests in Northern Ireland's history. As the *Belfast Telegraph* noted a few days into the campaign, the Catholic population was, for the first time, "faced with a divided rather than [a] monolithic Unionist Party", and that section of the community now had "a real opportunity to participate in deciding the shape it [the next Unionist government] will take".[21]

Another unusual aspect of the 1969 general election was the confusion amongst voters over the contest's intended purpose. This theme was a constant feature of *Irish News* editorials. At an early stage in the campaign, the paper suggested that this contest had provoked "the greatest confusion ever known since Partition created the Six Counties", and depicted O'Neill's decision to call it as his "ultimate throw". It argued that the "lack of basic differences" between the two main strands of unionism (apart from the clearly obvious ones over the leadership question) made the contest "unrealistic", and that "no amount [sic] of platitudes can make it anything else". The paper also speculated that the election's likely outcome – the return of Terence O'Neill's "dissident colleagues to Stormont … with hardly a casualty" – would "leave us as we were, except that Mr O'Neill will have a bloc of dissident Unionist MPs sniffing at his heels".[22]

This exasperated response from nationalist commentators about the calling of the election was not publicly expressed by unionist media pundits, especially those in the *Belfast Telegraph* – which remained, to all intents and purposes, the mouthpiece of O'Neillism. The *Irish News* was also more likely to depict the contest as a bitter internal feud. A leading article, early in the campaign, predicted that unionists would soon be "at one another's throats" in a petty squabble which would largely bypass nationalist voters. The paper complained that the election would restrict itself to solving the unionist leadership question, by its "emphasis on personalities, and not policies". The paper described the election as a "unionist internecine struggle", and argued that the contest would only be of "marginal importance" for the nationalist community.[23]

On account of this central focus on the question of unionist leadership, there was inevitably speculation over the selection of candidates, especially those to be announced by the Unionist Party. The *Belfast Telegraph* heralded the "widespread challenge" to O'Neill's opponents in several constituencies, with "the emergence of O'Neill men in force" in seats such as St Anne's and Willowfield in Belfast, Larne, and in North Derry.[24] A week later, the same paper announced the "return unopposed of five members of [the] Government" and reported on the unique feature of "miniature elections" in several unionist associations.[25] At such meetings, those sitting Unionist MPs who opposed O'Neill found themselves fighting bitter, and often personal, battles against alternative pro-O'Neill candidates, frequently nominated at the last moment. There were further unpleasant and negative soundings emerging from Unionist Party constituency selection meetings. At one of these in South Down, the non-selection of a leading Catholic member of the party drew attention to its supposed commitment to broadening its appeal. Louis Boyle – brother of civil rights activist, Kevin Boyle – was rejected as a candidate, and his non-selection prompted the *Irish News* headline the following day: "Glengall Street spurns hand of Catholic Unionist – wooing of moderates fails its first real test".[26]

A few days before the final nomination of candidates was announced, the *Irish News* optimistically declared that "all Stormont seats" were to be contested for "the first time in 40 years".[27] In reality, only 7 of Stormont's 52 seats were to be uncontested, including 5 held by pro-O'Neill administration members.[28] Nomination Day, on 13 February, witnessed a "record" number of parliamentary candidates – 119 from an estimated 13 different parties or groups – a situation which the *Irish News* described as "the multi-coloured battle of the hustings".[29] In what was declared as a "bonus for democracy", several safe unionist seats were to witness election contests for the first time in over twenty years. However, the *Irish News* issued a word of warning about this enhanced degree of electoral choice. In an editorial entitled "No dearth of candidates", the paper admitted that "the battleground had been widened", but lamented that "all sorts of people have got into the act, declaring in favour of one side or the other", and that this had "confused the situation, until it becomes almost impossible to see the wood for the trees".[30]

Apart from the considerable interest in the Unionist Party's official and unofficial candidates – in the end, 42 Unionist candidates, comprised of 27 pro-O'Neill and 10 opposing the prime minister, would be selected – there was a high degree of interest in the emergence of candidates from other, relatively new, political groups. The PUP fielded 6 candidates in Belfast and in various parts of Ulster, highlighted by the candidacy of its leader, Ian Paisley in the prime minister's Bannside seat, and the PD announced it would field up to 12 candidates, including several youthful hopefuls such as Bernadette Devlin and Michael Farrell.

Both of the rival newspapers had an important role to play during the electoral contest. From its beginnings, over a century before, the *Belfast Telegraph* had been a staunchly unionist newspaper. However, the "wind of change swept through the *Telegraph*" after the appointment of Jack Sayers as editor in the mid-1950s. The paper, which had a daily circulation estimated at over 220,000 in 1968, soon "broadened its political and religious views, in a way hitherto unimaginable", and perhaps inevitably, this led to open criticism of the long-serving premier, Lord Brookeborough.[31] Sayers soon found himself more in tune with the conciliatory approach of Brooke's successor, Captain Terence O'Neill, and his editorials at the start of the conflict sharply rebuked unionist dissenters for resisting political progress. In an October 1968 leading article, Sayers, who would step down from the editorship shortly before his death in 1969, had stressed the importance of good community relations and equal opportunities in housing and employment. In this article, he warned traditional loyalists:

> Unionists, who think that some of these things can be given but not others, are misguided; the possibility that some councils may prove to have Roman Catholic majorities cannot stand in the way of the proposition that the fairer the treatment of the minority, and the greater the general prosperity, the more the religious distinction in politics will disappear, and the longer Stormont is likely to survive.[32]

Unsurprisingly then, the *Belfast Telegraph*'s support for the policies and leadership of O'Neill was a constant feature in its coverage of the election campaign. Apart from its organisation of pro-O'Neill pledges in the period following the premier's "Crossroads" broadcast in December 1968, and its orchestration of fundraising for the pro-O'Neill campaign – it announced on 12 February that over £2,000 had been raised, proclaiming that "many thousands of people in Northern Ireland are now backing their desire for a moderate Government with hard-earned cash" – the paper's choice of front-page stories, supportive and optimistic editorials, and letters' pages brimming with pro-O'Neill correspondence from readers, all contributed significantly to the premier's cause.[33]

From the start of the contest, the *Belfast Telegraph* warned its readers against apathy in the forthcoming poll. A "viewpoint" editorial on 7 February stressed that, "the strength of the anti-O'Neill vote must be tested in every constituency, if we are not to return to square one on 24 February".[34] The paper also left few readers in any doubt about both the rationale behind calling the election, and its potential significance. On the day that the Unionist Party launched its manifesto, an aptly-titled editorial, "Into the New Age", agreed with the document's claim that Ulster was still at the "crossroads". Describing the manifesto as representing "a new platform for official Unionism at the beginning of an election campaign, with a broad appeal being made for the first time to Roman Catholic voters", the leader elaborated:

> The election is to decide whether it goes forward under an enlightened leadership or turns aside. The way ahead is towards a single society. The other way is to perpetuate the old enmities and in so doing to court the risk of new unrest and disorder. The declaration of principle is historic. Never before has the Unionist Party so addressed itself to the whole population.[35]

The *Belfast Telegraph*'s support for the pressurised leader of the Unionist Party was unambiguous. A week after the election had been declared, the paper surmised that the anticipated nominations of unionist candidates would produce a pro-O'Neill majority in parliament, though it conceded that the party's future was "on a knife-edge". Criticising the prime minister's internal opponents, the newspaper pointed out that "forceful" leaders who were prepared to "modernise an old and crusty party" were "rare", and that for a party in "transition", it was necessary to "have a leader with the courage of his convictions".[36]

A regular theme of comment from the paper during the election campaign was the perceived need for change, acknowledged both within and outside the province. Referring to a British opinion poll, which indicated a clear majority of respondents in favour of O'Neill's reforms and for the extension of the local government franchise, the *Belfast Telegraph* reminded its readers that it was on "the basic goodwill of the British people that our future prosperity ultimately depends". Stressing the need for voters to fully appreciate the importance of British public opinion, the paper pointed out that, "the image we tried to present for so long has not stood up to close scrutiny and the need for something more than a facelift must be apparent."[37] Three days later, the paper turned its attention to the seismic changes which it believed had started to occur in local society. Highlighting the results of a Marplan poll conducted for the *Belfast Telegraph*, which indicated a clear majority of support for O'Neill and his policies – estimated at around 68 per cent of the total electorate – the paper's editorial claimed that wider society, as well as the region's political establishment, was in full support of the besieged prime minister. The editorial maintained:

> Civil rights, if they have done nothing else, have brought Northern Ireland to a political watershed, one at which all the questions overhanging the evolution of our regional self-government are being put to the proof ... In this process, many of the basic instincts of the race are being revived. Only this can account for the influence that the Churches, people of the highest education and standing, and so many of the young with their ideas untrammelled are bringing to bear.[38]

The *Belfast Telegraph* used more column inches to denounce Unionist Party opponents of the prime minister than it did in criticising the policies of the numerous opposition parties and groups which were also contesting the election. One favourite target for the paper's condemnation was former prime minister, Lord Brookeborough, who had attacked his successor's leadership a couple of times during the campaign. One editorial criticised Brookeborough and other "traditionalists" in the party for refusing to accept that, "the life they knew well, will never be the same again". It went on to remind those sceptical of the prime minister's leadership style and approach that, "the real background to the election" lay in their "refusal to face [that] Unionism is in course of the most profound reform in its history".[39] The following day's leader was even more personal in its criticism of the veteran politician. The newspaper "deplored" the intervention of the former premier, who, it insisted, was "trying to stigmatise the Catholic community as disloyal and unco-operative". Occurring in the middle of an election "so critically concerned with Northern Ireland's peaceful evolution", the peer's statements were "sadly out of keeping with his reputation as a statesman".[40]

Brookeborough was not the only Unionist Party establishment figure to be reproached in the *Belfast Telegraph*'s leader columns. Shortly before the attacks on the former premier, the paper had seized the moral high ground in its rebuke of former Health and Social Services Minister William Morgan's emotional attack on the prime minister. Morgan had denounced his party leader for "leading a wicked campaign" in his promotion of unofficial candidates who had promised to back his position as party leader at the expense of those anti-O'Neill candidates selected by their constituency associations, and for "vilifying decent men", who had dared to criticise the premier. Central to Morgan's blunt statement was his reference to O'Neill's strong connections to "belted earls and feudal dukes", the significance of which was ignored by the *Belfast Telegraph*, though not the *Irish News*. Instead the former emphasised the party's "short-sighted management in the past", and declared that the party's "present dilemma" had been inevitable since 1921.[41] Unfortunately by ignoring the reference to O'Neill's social standing, the paper had missed an opportunity to analyse Morgan's thesis that these class divisions within the Unionist Party had resulted in the prime minister being isolated and out of touch with most of the electorate.

As the election campaign neared its climax, the *Belfast Telegraph* expressed its optimism and confidence, and not only in the ultimate success of the premier's policies, but also in their moral justification. Three days before polling, the paper maintained:

> The proof of what he [O'Neill] has done is seen as much outside as inside the party ranks. A dam of public opinion has broken. Never before have so many Protestants and Catholics stood up and said that they have had enough of narrow and petty politics. Never have so many written to the *Telegraph* to say what they think, with their own names and addresses.[42]

Throughout the campaign, the *Belfast Telegraph* informed readers at regular intervals of a supposed "swing" to the prime minister's camp. Determined to offset potential apathy amongst voters bemused by internal bickerings and the bitter street rhetoric of several of the candidates, the paper was at pains to portray an atmosphere of busy campaigning, as the election approached its final stage. One report noted the impact of inclement weather on the contest, describing "the battle for votes" which was being "fought on the doorsteps in Arctic-like conditions".[43] On the last full day of campaigning, the paper expressed its conviction that O'Neill was "virtually certain" of increasing the support for his leadership and its "Monday's

Child" editorial urged the new, incoming administration not only to pursue the path of reform started by O'Neill, but also to "lead the development of thought, most of all among those unionists who are in danger of being left behind".[44] The *Belfast Telegraph*'s "Election Day" edition returned to these themes of the effect of the weather and apathy upon likely voting patterns. The paper's headline read "Crossroads Poll in the rain – electorate respond to O'Neill's appeal for massive turnout". Noting the premier's description of the election as "our day of destiny", the *Belfast Telegraph* observed how voters at polling stations across Northern Ireland were "braving intermittent downpours" and "streaming in to register the verdict of the ballot-box".[45]

A central feature of *Irish News* coverage of the election was the ongoing "internecine feud" within unionism.[46] In particular, the paper reported fiery speeches by O'Neill's opponents, including William Craig, Lord Brookeborough and William Morgan, as well as O'Neill's condemnation of his critics. Noting the irony of the application of the term "rebels" to that supposedly most "loyal" of political groupings, the Unionist Party, the *Irish News* dismissed unionism's "facade of unity" in the past, before going on to describe the "inner conflicts" being experienced within contemporary unionism. The editorial sardonically observed that, "only Gilbert and Sullivan could do justice to the farce of it all".[47] This was a reference to the illogical position which unionism now found itself, conducting an election campaign where "unofficial" candidates were being supported by a party leader determined to resist those "official", constituency-backed, candidates opposed to his leadership.

On the eve of the election, Craig had attacked O'Neill's "presidential" style of government, and also his subsequent decision not to support constituency-backed dissident unionists.[48] O'Neill also denounced "rebels" like Craig in a number of strong personal attacks. In one critique of Albert Anderson, an O'Neill opponent and the official candidate in Londonderry, the premier suggested that this candidate was guilty of "adopting liberal attitudes in public and reactionary ones in private".[49] O'Neill also maintained that Craig had been culpable of a number of "blunders" whilst he had been the home affairs minister, including his decision to ban a civil rights march in Derry the previous October, and the delivery of a succession of "inflammatory speeches".[50]

However, it would be the interventions of former prime minister, Lord Brookeborough, which would dominate *Irish News* coverage of unionism's inner turmoil. Noting Brookeborough's claim that the election had been "unnecessary", the *Irish News* considered the "struggles within unionism" in an accompanying editorial. In the piece, which commented upon the many "conflicting voices and warring factions" within the unionist family, the paper argued:

> The Unionist electorate must be woefully confused by the presence of dissidents, "rebel" moderate and immoderate backers of O'Neill, turbulent ex-Ministers who are now casting themselves in the role of "progressives". One thing is clear. Unionism is involved in a struggle within itself and, in a sense, its problems are only now opening up.[51]

The following day's *Irish News* editorial suggested that the arguments over who should lead the Unionist Party had managed to drown out mention of the usual loyalist scare stories of a united Ireland. It noted that the "same old tired arguments" about the "necessity" of unionism, as well as "the Border bogies and IRA scares" had been "quietly relegated", and that the "legitimacy" of O'Neill to lead his party was now "the theme of election speeches".[52]

Another area of discontent within unionism which was given considerably more prominence in the columns of the *Irish News* than in the unionist press, was the "building up" of a "class consciousness" within the Protestant community.[53] Referring to the speech of O'Neill critic, William Morgan, in which the ex-minister had appeared to denounce the privileges enjoyed by the prime minister's family and their close connections with "belted earls and feudal dukes", the *Irish News* suggested that the former minister's words might "cause some soul-searching amongst the faithful", many of whom had been "chivvied into voting Unionist and remain[ing] steadfast to it, simply because it stands for Protestantism and security".[54]

"What kind of Ulster do you want?"

It was well over a week into the already brief election campaign, before the Unionist Party unveiled its manifesto to Northern Ireland's one million-strong electorate. This had the unmistakeable stamp of O'Neillism in its strong moral tone and, although theoretically representing the views of all the party, including the election candidates, several critics of O'Neill's leadership (including Brian Faulkner) would soon articulate their own views in "personal" manifestos. Additionally, the ten dissident Unionist MPs had agreed upon the issuing of a "rebel" alternative to O'Neill's manifesto, which stressed "party unity, strong and stable government", and placed "democratic policies for all" at the end of its list of priorities.[55]

The official, six-page party manifesto, "What kind of Ulster do you want?" informed electors that the forthcoming contest would be "no ordinary election", with its outcome determining "the kind of country this will be". The manifesto was a declaration of principles upon which future party governance would be based. The Unionist Party committed itself to a "full recognition" of "the obligations and rights of all citizens", and expected from every voter, "a proper sense of responsibility and wholehearted participation in the life of the state". The manifesto expressed its commitment to "heal those divisions in our community which have so far prevented Northern Ireland from fulfilling its best hopes", and insisted that a future unionist administration's policies would be "designed to ensure that all Ulster citizens continue to enjoy the benefits of the British connection, not just in high standards of service but in high standards of tolerance, fairness and justice". The document concluded by stating, "this is the sort of Ulster *we* want", assuring the voter that "in this crucial election you can make sure in Ulster it is a reality".[56]

The "admirable sentiments" expressed in the party manifesto, and the "genuine" attempt of O'Neill to steer his party down a "different road" were also acknowledged by nationalist opinion-makers. However, the *Irish News* also suggested that O'Neill's endeavours to make his party "break the habits of a lifetime", would be a journey too far. The paper described the manifesto as "a last despairing counsel to unionists to stop pushing the minority around" before it proved to be "too late". The editorial concluded:

> We admire, but do not share his [O'Neill's] optimism ... The manifesto could be the First Book for the education of the Party. As a teacher, Mr O'Neill has a long road ahead of him.[57]

Although there would be considerable interest in both the wider debate fuelled by such "What kind of Ulster do you want?" rhetoric, and the participation of a host of new parliamentary candidates, it was inevitably the premier's personal battle in his Bannside seat which attracted most media attention. This had been O'Neill's constituency for 20 years and for the first time, the sitting MP had to face opposition from two very different challengers. One was Michael Farrell, a young People's Democracy activist, who was expected to test O'Neill's ability to attract minority votes. The other was the leader of the fledgling loyalist group, the Protestant Unionist Party (PUP). Reverend Ian Paisley, soon to become a major force in Northern Irish politics, had already emerged as a well-known figure, albeit one whose street protests had resulted in him becoming a source of ridicule. He had recently been released on bail from prison, following a sentence related to his involvement in a demonstration in Armagh.

Standing in Bannside would represent a career landmark for the politically inexperienced Paisley. This contest would be the PUP leader's first foray into mainstream political campaigning. His candidacy was fundamentally based on his opposition to the reformist and conciliatory tendencies of O'Neill, a man whose aristocratic aloofness contrasted sharply with Paisley's populist style. The PUP leader believed that his head-to-head constituency challenge against a premier, whom he had accused of being "soft" on key issues of concern for Protestants – such as further concessions to Catholics and the border question – would result not only in a personal defeat for the premier but also for his wider brand of politics. Paisley was not the sole standard-bearer for the Protestant Unionists. A small team of five colleagues were standing in constituencies both in Belfast and in staunchly loyalist rural seats – John Wylie in North Antrim, William Beattie in South Antrim, Charlie Poots in Iveagh, Major Ronald Bunting in Belfast Victoria, and William Spence in Belfast's Bloomfield division.

The PUP had few actual policies but it was certain about what it opposed. In an election interview with the *Belfast Telegraph*, the party's leader was asked what sort of Ulster he desired. In his response, Paisley denounced the leader of the Unionist Party, Harold Wilson, the British prime minister and the media, amongst others. He argued:

> Protestant Unionists want an Ulster that is not plunged into an election on an outdated register in order to solve the problem of who should lead the Unionist Party. We want an Ulster where, instead of being pressurised by a corrupt press, television and radio, the people will be free to elect their parliamentary representatives without being blackmailed by Mr Harold Wilson or any other Westminster politician.[58]

Unlike most other parliamentary candidates, Paisley did not restrict his electioneering to the confines of his own constituency, appearing on platforms and at street meetings in a variety of locations. On a wintry Saturday afternoon in early February, he addressed a three-thousand-strong crowd in Lisburn, and towards the end of the campaign, on 20 February, he led a five-mile parade in Belfast. However, in contrast to his main rival in Bannside, Paisley also sustained a high-profile presence in his own constituency. On 17 February, he received an "enthusiastic reception" at a packed meeting in Ballymoney, where he criticised O'Neill for arranging a meeting at Stormont with the "Republican murderer", Sean Lemass.[59] This was one of several stinging assaults on the prime minister, who, Paisley alleged, had broken his promise not to meet the Irish Republic's premier until the south had renounced its constitutional claims on the north. He also argued that the Northern Ireland premier had a three-point plan to "destroy" Northern Ireland, commencing with a bid to break up the Unionist Party. This, Ian Paisley forecast, would be followed by the creation of a coalition with nationalists and, following pressure from Harold Wilson, would end in a united Ireland.[60]

Ian Paisley's election campaign was a colourful one, he and his entourage drawing large crowds and creating a carnival atmosphere, as they arrived in rural towns and villages. Those who attended would march behind loyalist bands and "a forest of Union Jacks", before being addressed by the Protestant Unionist leader, "a towering figure, sporting an Ulster Protestant Volunteer sash, a white raincoat and a Russian Cossack hat".[61] At this early stage in Paisley's political career, his reputation as a showman and colourful personality was a major factor in his ability to attract large crowds. His fiery cocktail of the vitriolic denunciation of political opponents and gospel rhetoric, along with his street oratory and penchant for humorous one-liners and put-downs of political opponents, proved to be popular with his audiences. At one meeting, held in freezing weather, for example, Paisley, referring to O'Neill, declared that "nobody but a snowman could call an election at this time of the year", and then reminded his audience, "what happens to a snowman when the heat is on!"[62]

The unique combination of religious fundamentalism and no-compromise political rhetoric, which was to become Paisley's hallmark, was evident in this first election campaign. In an election card, entitled "For God and Ulster – vote Protestant Unionist", the PUP leader insisted that O'Neill had, "now succeeded in doing what the IRA [had] failed to do – break up the Unionist Party". While reminding potential voters that he had been temporarily released from prison to contest the election, Paisley insisted that his "only crime" had been "loyalty".[63] Max Hastings, who was covering the election for a national newspaper as a young journalist at the time, stressed the "politics of the fairground" dimension of Paisley's Bannside campaign. He wrote:

> It rattled the very bones of Ulster Protestantism. Fife and drum band, [the] Shankill Road Young Conquerors, followed Ian Paisley most nights. Muffled in an overcoat and fur hat, sash across his massive chest, Paisley careered from housing estate to meeting hall, from village square round the little streets, proclaiming the salvation of Protestantism with that fantastic voice and superb showmanship.[64]

Although its own coverage of Paisley's Bannside campaign was relatively muted, compared with its treatment of O'Neill's wider campaign, the *Belfast Telegraph*'s final campaign report, alongside a photograph of the Protestant Unionist leader canvassing in his constituency, declared that, "the eyes of the world [were] on Bannside".[65]

In contrast with Paisley's exuberant, barnstorming campaign, O'Neill's defence of his parliamentary seat was more sedate and low-key. Perhaps fearing counter-demonstrations from his street politician rivals, O'Neill chose not to speak at public meetings in his constituency, adopting instead a "light touch" of daytime canvassing in a few towns and villages during the last week of the campaign. Max Hastings recalled how O'Neill's "amblings around the Bannside in the snow left spectators bemused and sceptical", and compared the prime minister's "lonely trudges by day" with Paisley's colourful evening parades, in which he "brought the fair to town". Hastings and a few other external observers felt that the public's response to the candidates' campaigning in the constituency predicated the fact that the premier was in "deep trouble".[66] When O'Neill did make reference to his own contest in the Bannside, he too resorted to personal criticism of his chief opponent, labelling Ian Paisley a political "dinosaur", and describing the Protestant Unionist leader and his supporters as "a collection of Canutes, trying to hold back the tide of the twentieth century".[67]

Most of O'Neill's time during the contest was taken up with conducting press conferences at Unionist Party headquarters in Belfast's Glengall Street, and supporting pro-O'Neill candidates in their own constituency contests. At these appearances, he raised a number of issues, including what he believed to be the real objections of his party's critics, and he was the first Northern Ireland premier to appeal directly to Catholics for their support at the polls (see below). One of his attempts to support pro-O'Neill candidates in Belfast caused considerable controversy and a backlash from local residents. Media coverage of O'Neill chatting to a resident of the predominantly Catholic Jamaica Street in the Oldpark area of north Belfast, was subsequently condemned by over 130 local householders, who organised a petition that claimed his visit had cast "a slur on the self-respect of the members of the community".[68]

Political campaigning did not really suit O'Neill's personality, and he was much happier delivering a mix of political and moral homilies in comfortable television studios. Addressing the electorate three days before polling, he appealed to the province's "silent majority" for their support. He asked his audience to "trust, accept and respect" one another, and to "put our old religious divisions aside to work together for the good of the country". The prime minister ended his broadcast by offering voters a stark electoral choice:

> We are asking you to give us a mandate for all we have been doing to make Ulster a better place to live in … This has been called the Crossroads Election, and indeed it is. We can go forward into a bright future within the United Kingdom as a united people. Or we can sink back into the bog of religious differences. It is with confidence in your common sense that I place the future of our country in your hands.[69]

For the first time since the inception of the state, a unionist leader and prime minister was directly courting the support of the Catholic population. Given the party's historical reticence in fostering political inclusion within the province, it was barely surprising that nationalist opinion was sceptical about O'Neill's appeal to Catholic electors. Referring to the minority casting a "cynical eye" on such a move, the *Irish News* pointed out that it was being asked, "with some impertinence, to vote for Unionist candidates, so that

Mr O'Neill can get on with his task of reform and the development of his progressive policies".[70]

This was a theme to which the *Irish News* returned in subsequent editorials. In the following day's leading article, "In search of our votes", the paper reminded unionists that Catholics would "choose candidates without interference from anybody", and, referring to rumours that O'Neill was preparing to contact the leader of the Catholic Church in Ireland, Cardinal Conway, in order for the latter to persuade his co-religionists to seriously consider the prime minister's request for electoral support, the *Irish News* warned:

> These last-minute attempts to secure the influence of the Church in favour of Unionism will, we hope, be treated with the same contempt which Unionism has shown in the past to any overtures from the Catholic minority for justice and equality ... The Catholic voter will not be deceived when Unionism tries to make light of its past [and] asks for his vote.[71]

Although the *Irish News* was unambiguous in its warnings against Catholics providing electoral support for O'Neill's Unionist Party candidates in their moment of crisis, there were signs that not every nationalist candidate opposed these overtures from the O'Neill camp. The *Belfast Telegraph* reported the West Tyrone Nationalist Party candidate, Roderick O'Connor's claim that his party's manifesto had actually provided "a clear hint to Catholics to support pro-O'Neill candidates, where the central battle is between pro- and anti-O'Neill forces."[72]

By the time Election Day dawned, the focus of the *Irish News* had returned to the need for opposition unity, rather than further denunciation of O'Neill's pleas for support from the Catholic electorate. Urging voters to take full advantage of "the greatest opportunity since the State was formed to return a viable opposition", the paper's editorial reminded readers about unsettled matters, including universal local government suffrage and the repeal of the Special Powers Act. Referring to the "new factor of zest from the Civil Rights campaign", the *Irish News* leader was optimistic in its tone. Without specifying which opposition faction to vote for, the paper's editorial demanded the return of "a bigger opposition", which would help, "prepare the ground for the gradual diminution of unionist power".[73]

This election was not only memorable on account of its exposition of the huge cracks existing within unionism at the time. It also served to highlight the ongoing changes within opposition politics in the North, which were largely attributable to the recent emergence of the civil rights movement. At the start of the campaign, the *Belfast Telegraph* noted Austin Currie's advocacy of an Opposition which would be "demonstrably left of centre, as well as Anti-Partitionist", and surmised that "a new Nationalism is emerging".[74] Towards the end of the contest, the *Belfast Telegraph* returned to the prospects of opposition parties in the election, forecasting that, in general, they would perform "rather badly". Describing the Nationalist Party as being in a state of "fragmentation", the paper predicted "serious internal problems in the future" for the group.[75] The following day's leading article warned that unionists should be wary of the dilemma facing Opposition parties, as internal divisions were not confined to their political opponents. The newspaper's editorial maintained that, "the changing state of Nationalism" was, in itself, "remarkable", and that "in the wake of civil rights", it was also "providential". The paper suggested that if the "stauncher" unionists were "waiting for another signal before they too take a step forward, this [was] it."[76]

Growing differences in nationalist-minded parties soon manifested themselves in the proliferation of opposition candidates putting themselves forward. The day after the small PD group announced that it was putting up 12 candidates, the *Irish News* expressed its dissatisfaction at the lack of unity within Anti-Partition groups. In a leading article entitled, "Why not a united opposition?", the paper fumed:

> When Unionism is in such disarray, it is a sad, pitiable exhibition of lack of political sense to see so many candidates, who are fundamentally opposed to the Unionist Party, fighting one another in this election. Although the picture may change radically on nomination day, opposition groups seem bent on an exercise which may yield them paltry results after polling day.[77]

The paper also referred to the "tragic spectacle" of three civil rights campaigners – Eddie McAteer, John Hume and Eamonn McCann – standing in direct opposition to one another in the Foyle constituency of Londonderry, and the further contests between other civil rights campaigners, such as

Ivan Cooper and Paddy O'Hanlon (up against Tom Gormley in Mid-Derry and Eddie Richardson in South Armagh respectively). The *Irish News* and other nationalist-leaning newspapers were undoubtedly concerned that these additional candidates were likely to split the opposition vote in their constituencies, and perhaps hand seats over to their unionist opponents. Although internecine squabbling amongst nationalists was not, publicly at least, on the same scale as that exhibited almost daily by their unionist opponents, internal infighting did occur from time to time. John Hume, for example, made a number of thinly-veiled attacks on the lack of direction shown by Eddie McAteer's Nationalist Party in recent years, and told a Creggan audience that the forthcoming election was, "a fight for survival in the North West".[78]

As the election contest neared its conclusion, the *Irish News* made a final call for nationalist unity, though the tone of its leading article suggested it was not over-optimistic that this would actually materialise. Maintaining that public opinion had been "sounding for straightforward fights between Unionists and non-Unionists", the paper conceded that time had "all but run out", and made a final plea for "no diffusion of votes on polling day".[79]

Like the traditional wing of the Unionist Party, the Nationalist Party was increasingly accused of being stale, outdated and ultra-conservative in its vision of the future. The party's role as champion of the North's Catholic minority had been under threat since the emergence of the civil rights movement. A number of nationalists, including party leader, Eddie McAteer, in post since 1964, had been active in civil rights agitation since 1967, but McAteer and senior colleagues appeared to be vague and uncertain in their responses to challenges posed by the street protest movement. For instance, McAteer and his party's small group of five parliamentary representatives, as well as most of the party's core support, were reluctant to embrace the more radical tendencies of younger civil rights leaders, like John Hume and of their own party representative, Austin Currie, whose proposal of non-violent civil disobedience in certain areas had been overruled by the party at a conference towards the end of 1968. When McAteer had publicly sided with Terence O'Neill in his decision to ban street parades until the New Year, he was also believed by many Catholics to have been backing the wrong horse, and it was a move which backfired after the RUC's failure to adequately protect marchers at Burntollet in the early days of 1969. The Nationalist Party was also culpable of failing to show disapproval of what many feared was the confrontational nature of civil rights street protests, and this was to cost the party many middle-class Catholic votes in February 1969.

The smaller National Democratic Party (NDP) – a breakaway group from the Nationalist Party which operated mainly in the Belfast area during the late 1960s – put up 7 candidates in the election and criticised the Unionist Party for its 'hollow moderation'. Its five-page manifesto, "The Real Choice", insisted that, rather than solving the "irrelevance" of internal unionist disputes, the contest should be about "the quest for a truly just society". Pledging the group's determination to bring about "opposition unity" in the north, the manifesto castigated unionist administrations past and present:

> Our concern is not variation in sectarian or private government. It is the houses, the jobs and the wages of the people; it is the unemployed and underprivileged. What has the present government done for them? Little or nothing … Their deplorable unconcern in the past gives little confidence for the future.[80]

Several NDP candidates castigated the recent performance of O'Neill's administration and the sincerity of its professed reforming zeal. Tom Sherry, standing in Belfast's Larkfield constituency, told an audience in Andersonstown that their opponents were really just "old Unionists in new wrapping". Meanwhile, in a fiercely-fought contest in East Down, Eddie McGrady chastised Unionists' failure to bring economic prosperity to "a Cinderella constituency for too long" – his chief opponent, Brian Faulkner, had been the minister primarily responsible for bringing considerable industrial investment to other parts of Northern Ireland earlier in the decade.[81]

McAteer, meanwhile, also dismissed the likelihood of the "new" Unionist Party attracting substantial Catholic voters at the expense of his party. In an interview with the *Belfast Telegraph*, he reasoned:

> Words without actions make no lasting impressions, and so far the role of fair play is not really established. I would hope that all parties would try to recruit from both sides of this religious fence. Against this background, the answer is not yet.[82]

Despite a stuttering campaign, and the apparent inability of the party to make inroads on the Unionist parliamentary group's own internal difficulties, the Nationalist Party remained upbeat on polling day. Their final message to the electorate was that, "a stronger, experienced and united opposition" was essential to take on the anticipated new Unionist administration, and that they were "in the vanguard of providing such opposition".[83]

The decision of several leading figures in the civil rights movement to stand as candidates in the election was regarded by many as an inevitable outcome of their increasingly pronounced public profile. Although they came from a range of political backgrounds, some bearing mainly "green" rather than "red" credentials, most were aware of the shortcomings of existing opposition parties and indeed, the following year, many would join together in a newly constituted opposition party of their own, the Social Democratic and Labour Party (SDLP).[84] Buoyed by a largely sympathetic response to their street campaign, civil rights candidates believed that the time was right to offer a new brand of opposition politics in Northern Ireland, and one which was not restricted to national identity or religious persuasion. Their decision to stand, especially that of John Hume in Foyle, did however provoke some local murmurs of discontent and even disbelief. Following the announcement of his decision to put his name forward for the Foyle seat, Hume issued a statement explaining his motives in standing as an independent candidate in the North's "most important" election since Partition. Denouncing the concept of "Catholic unity" – which, his critics maintained, his candidacy had damaged – Hume argued:

> There are those who say that with the Unionist Party torn apart, this is a wonderful opportunity for the opposition to unite. To think this is to misunderstand completely what has happened in the past four months. Those who speak of Opposition unity mean, in fact, Catholic unity. Surely the lesson of 50 years is that Catholic unity is the quickest way to unite the Unionist Party, for one has fed upon the other. What we need, in fact, is political unity against Unionism and Conservatism, and an end to sectarianism. At a time when the Protestant conscience is clearly tearing itself apart to decide what way it should go, it would be criminal ... were the Catholic community to do likewise.[85]

The left-wing group, the PD, had come to the fore during the recent period of civil rights agitation, especially after their organisation of the Belfast–Derry march the previous month. The group's 12 candidates were fighting mainly uncontested seats or opposing high-profile unionist candidates. Their campaign was a heady mixture of unequivocal denunciation of what they saw as the Unionist Party's class-based politics and a Marxist social programme, including the establishment of community farms, workers' control of local factories and a mass public-housing programme. One PD candidate, Eddie Wiegleb, claimed that 93 per cent of residents in his Belfast Cromac constituency did not possess bathrooms in their homes. In a sarcastic reference to the Unionist Party's trade missions in Great Britain and overseas, the PD candidate suggested that, "civic weeks [were] no substitute for civil rights".[86]

Early in the campaign, one of the PD's best-known figures, Michael Farrell, declared that for his group the "real issue" would be "the choice between civil rights and social justice on the one hand, and reactionary unionism on the other". The Bannside candidate rejected the notion that Terence O'Neill's reforming policies were attractive to Catholics, claiming that there was "little difference" between the "urbane and polished brand [of the unionism] of Captain O'Neill [and] the crude and vulgar one of Mr Paisley", as the "end result is the same".[87] Farrell and his colleagues warranted a fair degree of coverage in nationalist papers like the *Irish News*. Most of this concerned the high-profile contests involving PD candidates – Michael Farrell against Terence O'Neill and Ian Paisley in Bannside, and Bernadette Devlin's battle against the minister of agriculture and future premier, Major Chichester-Clark in South Derry – with many reports concentrating on the group's "youthful candidates". One profile on Devlin described her as "a quietly-spoken 21-year-old from Cookstown".[88] The article emphasised that this would be the first contest to be held in South Derry since 1949, and noted Devlin's offer to debate the key issues with Chichester-Clark, in order for him to "put his policies to the people". As in the case of Bannside, this seat epitomised the People's Democracy's desire to confront "Big House" Unionism head-on, and Devlin poked fun at the sitting member's low profile in his constituency, where, she claimed, "many people have told me they wouldn't know him if they saw him." The report on Devlin laid emphasis upon her "deep-felt dedication and determination", and proposed that her "youthful, calcuated vigour" was an "essential element of the [civil rights] movement that has matured and hardened rapidly".[89]

Labour groups and candidates of one shade or another – the Northern Ireland Labour Party (NILP), Republican Labour Party (RLP) or Independent Labour Group (ILG) – stood in several constituencies, especially in Belfast and Derry. The election promised to be a stiff test for the struggling NILP. Although in the recent past, Belfast had proved to be a profitable hunting-ground for left-wing candidates, the party had lost two of its four Stormont seats in the 1965 election, and it was feared that this representation would be even further reduced. The emergence of radical street politicians from the ranks of the civil rights movement, and the upsurge of support within working-class Protestant districts for populist unionist groups like Ian Paisley's PUP, mitigated against Labour consolidating its position at Stormont, and the *Belfast Telegraph* accurately suggested that its election prospects were "dull".[90]

However, many Labour candidates were positive about their prospects for the contest, with one of them, Norman Thompson, suggesting that the split in Unionist ranks in his Belfast Clifton constituency had provided "a wonderful chance for this constituency to return an Opposition member".[91] Like nationalist groups, the party was critical of the Unionist Party's record in government. Its election pamphlet, "Unionist Ulster or British Ulster?" argued that the recent breakdown in law and order had constituted "symptoms of sickness, not the sickness itself", and maintained that reforms to date were "no more than sticking a plaster over the symptoms", which would "not cure the disease".[92] For those Labour candidates with more pronounced nationalist credentials, denunciation of the Unionist Party was even more strident. Paddy Devlin, standing in the Belfast Falls constituency, told his election workers that "not until the Unionist Party lies in ruins can a united community be built in Northern Ireland". For Devlin, the Unionist Party had, by "cunning manipulation", succeeded in "dividing this community into Protestant and Catholic, whereas the true division is between the haves and the have-nots".[93]

The NILP fought a determined campaign, even canvassing on Election Day itself on the streets leading to the Belfast shipyard.[94] In its polling day address to voters, the party turned again to more traditional socialist issues. Its candidates maintained it had been the "only party to offer a social programme, including the provision of houses and jobs" during the contest, and argued that "a strong Labour Party in Parliament is the only way to

175

vote for a peaceful, democratic Ulster".[95]

Republican Labour candidates also had high expectations of success in a number of Belfast constituencies. Party leader, Gerry Fitt's main emphasis was on rejecting the offers being made to Catholic voters by O'Neill and the reformist wing of the Unionist Party. Fitt was sceptical about O'Neill's reforming claims, and criticised the Unionist Party for, "pretending to be something which it is not".[96] The following day, Fitt pleaded with an audience of constituents in Belfast Dock – which was likely to record the first result to be declared in the election in a few days' time – to let their answer to O'Neill "ring out loud and clear", and to ensure that, "whatever happens elsewhere, the working class of this area steadfastly cling to the Connolly idealism".[97] On Election Day, the party leader returned to his main electoral target, the forces of unionism. He reminded voters that "the Unionist leopard cannot change its spots, and one brand of unionism is just as dangerous as the other".[98]

"The most confusing election"[99]

The results of this general election – the last one to be staged for returning members to a parliament at Stormont – were contradictory and indeterminate. The Unionist Party leader and prime minister would see a decline in the number of parliamentary colleagues declaring themselves opposed to his leadership (from 14 to 12), and the pro-O'Neill vote was comfortably ahead of the anti-O'Neill camp. Yet the abiding image of the election would be the rejoicing of the narrowly-beaten candidate, Ian Paisley, in O'Neill's Bannside constituency. Beyond this, the general consensus was that the contest had provided no clear mandate for a continuation of reform, and certainly little evidence that Catholics had changed their voting habits and were now actually voting for moderate unionist candidates. The turnout was high, although at 71.9 per cent across the province, not as good as had been expected in some quarters, and indeed, as had been hoped by supporters of the prime minister.

In terms of seats, three-quarters of the new Northern Ireland House of Commons (39 seats) would be members of the Unionist Party (an increase of two seats on the 1965 contest), with 27 of these backing the prime minister and 12 opposing him.[100] Despite Ian Paisley's fine showing in Bannside, the PUP failed to win a seat and there was a high-profile Unionist Party casualty, William Morgan, who was defeated by pro-O'Neill candidate, Major Robert

Lloyd Hall-Thompson in Belfast Clifton. There were also sweeping changes in the composition of the opposition benches. The Nationalist Party retained 6 seats but lost 3 to independent civil rights candidates. Labour groups returned 4 candidates in Belfast constituencies. These were equally shared between Republican Labour and the NILP which, however, lost 2 sitting MPs.

In terms of the votes cast, pro-O'Neill candidates had garnered over 246,000 votes (44 per cent of the total poll), whilst anti-O'Neill candidates gained 96,000 votes (over 17 per cent of the poll). The election also proved to be a turning-point for the opposition parties. Although the main beneficiaries, in terms of parliamentary seats, were the mainstream political groups, the fringe parties, which had emerged on account of the recent disturbances – most notably the PD and PUP – performed creditably, winning 23,645 and 20,991 votes respectively.[101] Taken as a whole, the 1969 election's essential feature was an undoubted weakening in the position of traditional parties on either side of the constitutional issue, and, during the following decade, further seismic changes within unionism and nationalism would take place.

The election has been described as "sounding the death knell for nationalism", and the traditional party of opposition to unionism was clearly in abject disarray by the end of this contest.[102] Three sitting nationalist members, including party leader, Eddie McAteer in Derry's Foyle constituency, lost their seats to independents and political newcomers from the ranks of the civil rights movement, and the party only narrowly retained South Down, where Michael Keogh defeated a PD opponent. Indeed, of all 15 Nationalist candidates, only James O'Reilly, in the Mourne constituency, actually increased his share of the vote. Many Catholic voters appeared to have agreed with John Hume's pre-election assessment that the Nationalist Party had seemed pleased with the status quo in the North, and had failed to mount a direct challenge to unionism in the years before the emergence of civil rights agitation. Hume's victory by a clear margin in Foyle epitomised the transformation occurring within opposition politics. His majority over Eddie McAteer was 3,653, and within a year John Hume would be one of the central figures behind the formation of a new political party, the SDLP, which, theoretically at least, would unite Labour and nationalist groups in their continuing opposition to unionism.

Nationalist opinion-makers were, despite the obvious shortfalls of existing opposition groups in the North, somewhat taken aback by the election outcome, which necessitated a speedy reassessment of the options of opposition groups. For such a long time the mouthpiece of constitutional nationalism, the *Irish News*, began to question whether a party restricting itself to "green", or constitutional, issues offered the best long-term bet for Catholic voters. The paper announced that "moves for [a] unified opposition" at Stormont were a "distinct possibility", and that the emergence of the civil rights movement constituted "a new big factor" in the North's political future. The editorial suggested that the recent election had indicated the electorate's "longing for a vigorous and viable alternative to traditional splintered groups who differed little on basic issues", and forecast that a more promising political future beckoned for the Catholic minority in Northern Ireland.[103] Indeed, Austin Currie, who retained his seat in East Tyrone, wrote later that the new parliament was a "more interesting" place to be working in, where the "presence of so many MPs identified with civil rights meant that there was a link between parliamentary and extra-parliamentary activity". The emergence of a "cohesive and effective" opposition at Stormont within two years of the contest was, as Currie suggested, the direct outcome of the recent splintering within opposition groups, and the mixed fortunes of parties like the Nationalist Party, Republican Labour and the NILP at the "Crossroads" election.[104]

Unsurprisingly, interpretations of the potential repercussions for both Terence O'Neill and wider unionism differed in the region's press. The *Belfast Telegraph*, whilst expressing its disappointment at the voting patterns in certain constituencies (most especially in Bannside), retained its optimism for the future, as well as its faith in the beleaguered prime minister. The day after the election, the paper's headline read, "O'Neill calls Cabinet to discuss verdict", and the accompanying piece reassured its readers that the premier was "ready to fight on, despite the return of backbench opponents". Rather more cautiously in the wake of the declared results, the paper observed that the contest had "not failed to provide proof of another advance in Northern Ireland's political education".[105] The following day's edition reinforced the message that O'Neill should stay on and proceed with his policy of reform and "progress". The piece warned readers that nothing would be "more symptomatic of disaster or injurious to Ulster's reputation, than the deliberate overthrow of a Government, all the Ministers of which have only three days ago been given the unquestionable confidence of the electorate".[106]

Other commentators pointed to the high turnout at the polls – particularly given the prolonged spell of inclement weather – and the highest poll for unionist candidates in modern times. Well over double the number of electors had sided with O'Neill candidates than with those unionists opposing his leadership, particularly in urban areas – and most notably in Belfast, where pro-O'Neill candidates had polled over 17,000 more votes than anti-O'Neill unionists, meaning that backing for the premier was only slightly down on what O'Neill "loyalists" had been anticipating.

However, there could be no disguising the fact that O'Neill's gamble, in appealing directly for the first time to Catholics to support his party, had backfired and there could be no denial that his personal result was highly embarrassing and damaging for the Unionist Party leader. The cross-voting that O'Neill had anticipated clearly had not occurred, as voting patterns in the main remained along the usual sectarian lines. As the election results started to emerge, the *Irish News* headline read: "Premier's prestige takes a nosedive in Bannside". The paper went on to inform readers that, with the "return of most unionist rebels", the "power struggle" within the party was "likely to continue in the new Parliament".[107] With all the results known, the following day's edition of the *Irish News* claimed that the election "still has not solved Mr O'Neill's inner party problem", and that he had "failed to destroy the power and influence of his right wing".[108] For, although the prime minister had retained his Bannside seat, it was a pyrrhic victory, as he had scraped through with only a 1,414 majority over Ian Paisley.[109]

With O'Neill pointedly boycotting the results ceremony, the scenes of jubilation at the count in Ballymoney were hijacked by the supporters of the defeated challenger. A beaming Ian Paisley was given an ovation by a large, triumphant crowd, as he told international journalists and TV crews from around the globe that his result was "a magnificent vote", and announced he was going home "a proud man". More tellingly, Paisley took the opportunity to release his venom on the victor again, describing the prime minister as "despised, discredited and disturbed".[110] This election had proved to be a moral victory for yet another emerging political force. Within a year, Paisley would see the departure of his political nemesis, O'Neill, and his own election to both Stormont and Westminster. Even the *Belfast Telegraph* could not disguise its degree of disappointment in the premier's personal vote. Stressing the less depressing, province-wide result for the O'Neill wing of unionism, the paper described the poll in Bannside as "the harshest of ironies", and asked of local electors, "where [was] the Antrim men's noted hard-headedness, when so many were taken in by the partisan beating of the Paisley drums?"[111]

Once he had digested the bitter disappointment and shame at his personal result in Bannside and his apparent failure to attract sufficient compensatory Catholic votes to offset the ebbing away of traditional unionist support, O'Neill would turn his attention to the formation of a new cabinet and the resumption of his reform programme. At the end of February, the Unionist parliamentary group reelected O'Neill as its leader by an overwhelming majority, though a dissident group of ten MPs deliberately refused to register their votes. This vote of confidence in O'Neill's leadership was deceptive however and, as the weeks passed by, the worsening security situation and political manoeuvring elsewhere in the party combined to make his position extremely tenuous. O'Neill himself conceded in a parliamentary speech the week after the announcement of the election results that the way ahead for the party's liberal wing would not be "all plain sailing". However, he reminded the house that they had "made promises to the people of Ulster", which he felt "committed to keep". The premier went on to claim that "the stark choice" between an "Ulster united for prosperity", and one "divided for disaster" had to be made by Stormont's recently elected representatives.[112]

Civilian disturbances following a civil rights march in Lurgan and also in Belfast, along with further political setbacks in April, would finally persuade O'Neill to make a speedy but relatively dignified exit from office. On 17 April 1969, Bernadette Devlin beat off a unionist challenge in the Westminster constituency of Mid-Ulster to become the youngest female MP in British parliamentary history. Within days, two bombing incidents – inaccurately reported as being the work of republicans – at an electricity substation in east Belfast and at a reservoir outside the city, was instantly interpreted by many as further evidence of the province spiralling out of control. In between these explosions in greater Belfast, O'Neill's "one man, one vote" local government franchise changes were narrowly approved by his parliamentary group (28 to 22), though a leading member of the cabinet, O'Neill's cousin, James Chichester-Clark, resigned over the timing of the proposed measure. This was regarded by some as a leadership move by Chichester-Clark, and indeed he would soon succeed O'Neill as prime minister.[113] A narrow vote of confidence in O'Neill's leadership (338 to 263) was eventually forthcoming from the party's governing body, the UUC, but his mind was already made up, and he resigned as prime minister on 28 April. In his final TV broadcast the following day, O'Neill pleaded with his followers "not to be dismayed", as their mission had been "morally right, politically right, right for our country and all who seek to live in peace within it". He ended his address with appropriately prophetic words:

> I have tried to break the chains of ancient hatreds. I have been unable to realise during my period of office all that I have sought to achieve. Whether now it can be achieved in my lifetime, I do not know. But one day these things will be, and must be, achieved.[114]

One of the chief features of the "Crossroads" election was its confusion. Apart from a lack of clarity about why the election was called and the basic bemusement felt by electors as they prepared to cast their votes, there was also an uncertainty about how to interpret the contest's results. Additionally, differing opinions on the causes of O'Neill's demise – whether he fell from power on account of personality weaknesses, or because of the public's reticence about his reform policy – continue to generate debate. There has also been a degree of reassessment of the election's true significance, given that Stormont, and indeed the Unionist Party, were to struggle on for another three years.

Yet a certain degree of clarity can be gleaned if one probes behind this apparent confusion. Certainly, the results were ambiguous, with O'Neill soon resigning, despite witnessing an increase in the number of new backbenchers supporting his policies. However, this should not disguise the fact that, as confirmed by his own embarrassing result in Bannside, O'Neill's premiership was in deep trouble, given the ever-widening schism within unionism and, despite the initial warm words of support, the prime minister's patent inability to siphon off Catholic votes from the Nationalist Party and other opposition groups. Historian Graham Walker has suggested, with some justification, that O'Neill was "incongruously cavalier at the vital moment, and he placed on the line his party's future, as well as his own, with apparent insouciance."[115] Not only does Walker condemn O'Neill for a seemingly hasty decision in calling the election, but he also contends that its outcome, "far from clearing the air", actually resulted in an "increasing in the mood of forbearing in Northern Ireland society."[116]

Yet despite his apparent haste in calling an election and his ill-tempered exchanges with party opponents during the campaign, it is likely that O'Neill's administration would have soon found itself in even deeper trouble if he had not confronted this opposition from within his own party. Although he might have bought some valuable time in which to woo more support from the Catholic community and persuade his own critics that he was indeed the right man to lead his party, Terence O'Neill was ultimately the wrong person to take on such a Herculean task and such a tightrope walk of political diplomacy. Despite the eloquence of his TV broadcasts and their common-sense messages, his Achilles heel was an inability to connect with the electorate, and his profound disdain for the murky world of political infighting which was needed to unite a party in danger of internal combustion. And O'Neill himself was in no doubt that he was right in calling the election as he made clear when addressing the Northern Irish people in his final TV broadcast in April 1969:

> A few short weeks ago, you, the people of Ulster, went to the polls. I called that Election to afford you the chance to break out of the mould of sectarian politics, once and for all. In many places, old fears, old prejudices and old loyalties were too strong. Yet I am not amongst those who say that the Election served no useful purpose. For it did allow me, with my loyal colleagues, to proclaim a new Declaration of Principles which now binds every Unionist returned to Parliament. It commits the Party, in honour and conscience, not merely to do nothing to enlarge the divisions of our community, but to work positively to end them ... There IS no other course![117]

In a society, where the prospect of an election producing major political change had traditionally been remote, the uncertain and cliffhanger nature of the 1969 contest was considered unusual. Its political legacy was profound. On the one hand, it led directly to the resignation of Terence O'Neill, and proved to be a watershed in the fortunes of the Unionist Party, leading to the dismantling of unionists' political hegemony and the demise of a previously monolithic party. The election also reflected similar division between the traditional party for voicing Catholic grievances, the Nationalist Party, and its results ensured that opposition politics would also start down a different political road in the near future. The election saw the emergence of two political leaders, John Hume and Ian Paisley, who would reflect these sweeping changes within nationalism and unionism, and who would themselves have a radical impact upon transforming the North's political landscape over the next 30 years.[118]

Although the 1969 contest would fail to provide a clear outcome, O'Neill's imminent resignation would lead to further turmoil both within his party and in wider Northern Irish society. The breakdown of monolithic unionism and the worsening security situation in the province were inevitable after O'Neill's departure. However these would ultimately engender a mood of compromise which would, to a degree, be apparent in the Assembly election of 1973, and the short-lived power-sharing exercise of 1974.

Endnotes

1. T. Hennessey, *The Origins of the Troubles* (Gill & Macmillan, Dublin, 2005), p. 142
2. Even those standing on an anti-O'Neill ticket had accepted his November reform package.
3. J. Harbinson, *The Ulster Unionist Party 1882–1973* (Blackstaff Press, Belfast, 1973), p. 165
4. P. Bew and H. Patterson, *The British State and the Ulster Crisis from Wilson to Thatcher* (Verso Books, London, 1985), p. 16
5. *Belfast Telegraph*, 10 December 1968
6. *Ibid.*
7. B. Devlin, *The Price of my Soul* (Macmillan, London, 1969), pp. 139–140
8. T. O'Neill, from J. Bardon, *A History of Ulster*, (Blackstaff Press, Belfast, 1992), p. 661
9. P. Bew and G. Gillespie, *Northern Ireland: A Chronology of the Troubles, 1968–93* (Gill & Macmillan, Dublin, 1993), p, 12
10. A. Parkinson, *Friends in High Places: Ulster's Resistance to Irish Home Rule, 1912–14* (Ulster Historical Foundation, Belfast, 2012)
11. Hennessey, *op. cit.*, p. 191
12. *Ibid.*
13. *Belfast Telegraph*, 1 February 1969
14. *Irish News*, 3 February 1969
15. *Belfast Telegraph*, 4 February 1969
16. *Irish News*, 4 February 1969
17. *Ibid.*
18. *Belfast Telegraph*, 5 February 1969
19. William Craig, from *Belfast Telegraph*, 7 February 1969
20. Tom Caldwell, a pro-O'Neill candidate in Belfast's Bloomfield constituency, from *Belfast Telegraph*, 7 February 1969
21. *Belfast Telegraph*, 7 February 1969
22. *Irish News*, 6 February 1969
23. *Irish News*, 4 February 1969
24. *Belfast Telegraph*, 6 February 1969

25. *Belfast Telegraph*, 13 February 1969

26. *Irish News*, 12 February 1969

27. *Irish News*, 10 February 1969

28. This low number of uncontested seats contrasted sharply with the figure for the previous election in 1965 (23 seats).

29. *Irish News*, 10 February 1969

30. *Irish News*, 14 February, 1969

31. M. Brodie, *The Tele: A History of the Belfast Telegraph*, (Blackstaff Press, Belfast, 1995), p. 39

32. *Belfast Telegraph*, 29 October 1968

33. *Belfast Telegraph* (12 February 1969). In the 10 February edition, a full page of letters was printed, under the headline, "Why we must back O'Neill".

34. *Belfast Telegraph*, 7 February 1969

35. *Belfast Telegraph*, 14 February 1969

36. *Belfast Telegraph*, 11 February 1969

37. *Belfast Telegraph*, 10 February 1969

38. *Belfast Telegraph*, 13 February 1969

39. *Belfast Telegraph*, 18 February 1969

40. *Belfast Telegraph*, 19 February 1969

41. *Belfast Telegraph*, 17 February 1969

42. *Belfast Telegraph*, 21 February 1969

43. *Belfast Telegraph*, 19 February 1969

44. *Belfast Telegraph*, 22 February 1969

45. *Belfast Telegraph*, 24 February 1969

46. *Irish News*, 10 February 1969

47. *Irish News*, 13 February 1969

48. *Irish News*, 4 February 1969

49. *Belfast Telegraph*, 18 February 1969

50. *Irish News*, 15 February 1969

51. *Irish News*, 18 February 1969

52. *Irish News*, 19 February 1969

53. *Irish News*, 18 February 1969

54. *Ibid.*

55. *Belfast Telegraph*, 15; 21 February 1969.

56. Ulster Unionist Party manifesto, "What kind of Ulster do you want?": Linen Hall Library, Northern Ireland Political Collection, P1208

57. *Irish News*, 15 February 1969

58. *Belfast Telegraph*, 21 February 1969

59. *Irish News*, 18 February 1969

60. Hennessey, *op. cit.*, p. 192

61. E Moloney and A. Pollak, *Paisley*, (Poolbeg, Dublin, 1986), p. 174

62. B. McIvor, *Hope Deferred: Experiences of an Irish Unionist* (Blackstaff Press, Belfast, 1998), p. 45

63. From Nihill donation collection, Linen Hall Library, Northern Ireland Political Collection

64. M. Hastings, *Ulster 1969: The Fight for Civil Rights in Northern Ireland* (Gollancz, London, 1969), pp. 97–8

65. *Belfast Telegraph*, 22 February 1969

66. Hastings, *op. cit.*, pp. 97–8

67. T. O'Neill, *Belfast Telegraph*, 12 February 1969

68. *Irish News*, 22 February 1969

69. T. O'Neill, *Ulster at the Crossroads* (Faber & Faber, London, 1969), p. 66–7

70. *Irish News*, 19 February 1969

71. *Irish News*, 20 February 1969

72. *Belfast Telegraph*, 19 February 1969. It was the dismissive response of another Nationalist Party candidate, James O'Reilly, in the Mourne constituency, condemning Captain O'Neill's, "temerity to seek Catholic voters", which earned the headlines in the *Irish News* edition of 20 February.

73. *Irish News*, 24 February 1969

74. *Belfast Telegraph*, 8 February 1969

75. *Belfast Telegraph*, 20 February 1969

76. *Belfast Telegraph*, 21 February 1969

77. *Irish News*, 10 February 1969

78. *Irish News*, 18 February 1969. In an election statement, Hume claimed that "the wind of change" circulating throughout the North had been "created by the people of Derry", and asked electors to "stand shoulder with me to carry this change into the political arena". From J.J. Nihill donation collection, Linen Hall Library, Northern Ireland Political Collection.

79. *Irish News*, 21 February 1969

80. NDP Manifesto, "The Real Choice", Linen Hall Library, Northern Ireland Political Collection, P1765

81. *Irish News*, 18 February 1969; 20 February 1969

82. *Belfast Telegraph*, 18 February 1969

83. *Irish News*, 24 February 1969

84. Those standing on independent tickets, like John Hume, Ivan Cooper and Paddy O'Hanlon, later joined forces with republican Labour representatives like Gerry Fitt, Labour Party members such as Paddy Devlin, and radical members of the Nationalist Party like Austin Currie, in the new Social Democratic and Labour Party (SDLP).

85. John Hume, *Irish News*, 11 February 1969

86. *Irish News*, 15 February 1969

87. *Irish News*, 11 February 1969

88. *Irish News*, 22 February 1969. Bernadette Devlin would soon be elected as Westminster MP for Mid-Ulster, and until the election of Mairi Black of the SNP in 2015, she was the youngest female MP in British history.

89. *Irish News*, 22 February 1969

90. *Belfast Telegraph*, 20 February 1969

91. *Irish News*, 18 February 1969

92. *Irish News*, 5 February 1969

93. *Ibid.*

94. A photograph of NILP election workers "wooing yard men at the eleventh hour", was featured in the *Belfast Telegraph* on 24 February 1969.

95. *Irish News*, 24 February 1969

96. *Irish News*, 19 February, 1969

97. *Irish News*, 20 February 1969

98. *Irish News*, 24 February 1969. There were other candidates and groups representing forces on the left. The veteran Liberal politician, Sheelagh Murnaghan, was correctly predicted as being "unlikely to retain" her North Down seat: *Belfast Telegraph*, 20 February 1969.

99. Bardon, *op. cit.*, p. 663

100. Two further unionists were undecided about the leadership, and three of the pro-O'Neill MPs had stood as "unofficial" candidates.

101. For a detailed account of the election results, see W. D. Flackes and S. Elliott, *Northern Ireland: A Political Directory, 1969–88* (Blackstaff Press, Belfast, 1989).

102. E. Staunton, *The Nationalists of Northern Ireland, 1918–73* (Columba Press, Dublin, 2001), p. 256

103. *Irish News*, 26 February 1969

104. A. Currie, *All Hell will Break Loose* (O'Brien Press, Dublin, 2004), pp. 121–2

105. *Belfast Telegraph*, 25 February 1969

106. *Belfast Telegraph*, 26 February 1969

107. *Irish News*, 25 February 1969

108. *Irish News*, 26 February 1969

109. Terence O'Neill obtained 7,745 votes; Ian Paisley, 6,331; and Michael Farrell (the PD candidate), 2,300.

110. Moloney and Pollak, *op. cit.*, p. 174

111. *Belfast Telegraph*, 26 February 1969

112. O'Neill, *op. cit.*, p. 75.

113. James Chichester-Clark narrowly defeated Brian Faulkner (by 17 votes to 16) in a contest for the party leadership on 1 May 1969.

114. O'Neill, in Bardon, *op. cit.*, p. 664

115. G. Walker, *A History of the Ulster Unionist Party: Protest, Pragmatism and Pessimism* (Manchester University Press, 2004), p. 170

116. *Ibid.*, p. 172

117. O'Neill, *op. cit.*, p. 200

118. John Hume would later be awarded the Nobel Peace Prize for his contribution to the Northern Irish peace process, and Ian Paisley (for whom this would be the first and only defeat in over 20 regional, national and European election contests) would eventually become first minister in a power-sharing administration which included leaders of Sinn Féin.

CHAPTER FIVE

Hopes of a Breakthrough
The First Assembly Election, 1973

Difficult times

The elections to the first Northern Ireland Assembly, held in June 1973, occurred at a time of deep intercommunal uncertainty, political division and widespread violence. The first real test for a plethora of political parties which had been established at the start of the decade, these Assembly elections spelled the death knell for traditional Ulster electioneering, which had previously been dominated by the monolithic machines of the Unionist and Nationalist parties. Set against a backdrop where brutal sectarian assassination (including that of prominent nationalist representative, Paddy Wilson) and terrorist bombings were rife, the election was also different, both in terms of the nature of the legislature for which membership was being contested, and the manner in which electors would cast their all-important votes. Additionally, it represented the first attempt by a British government to establish a broader-based, "community" style of administration in the North, and in this sense, the calling of the election was based on a substantial measure of optimism, as well as a conviction that it would ultimately see the voices of moderation prevail over the sterile views of the parties of no-compromise and violence.

As observed at the end of the previous chapter, there had been considerable political and societal change within Northern Ireland since the "Crossroads" election of February 1969. Despite his nominal victory, Terence O'Neill felt disillusioned by the result of the contest, and quit office within weeks of the electorate's verdict. His cousin, Major James Chichester-Clark, succeeded him and continued to push through a number of liberal measures, but he too was overwhelmed by political strangulation by both the ranks of his own party and by an irate Catholic minority whose appetite had merely been whetted by the carrot of relatively mild political reform. Chichester-Clark had presided over the party during the Stormont and Westminster elections of the early summer of 1970. These had, in the main, failed to produce significant change in the composition of Northern representation, although they had seen the arrival of Ian Paisley at both parliaments. Meanwhile, street violence and civil disturbances had escalated in the province, and the IRA had emerged from the shadows towards the end of 1970.

When Chichester-Clark resigned from office in March 1971, his party chose a successor who, they believed, was capable of uniting them, and who at the same time would be able to successfully smooth over an increasingly troubled relationship with the London government. Despite his considerable political accomplishments, this successor, Brian Faulkner was taking on a virtually impossible task. As the political gap between the various parties (not to mention the factions within these groups) grew wider, so the military campaign of the Provisional IRA was intensifying. During the summer of 1971, Faulkner, who had built up a reputation as a no-nonsense unionist hard-liner on security issues, took the draconian – and ultimately fatal – step of introducing internment. This might have placated sections of his own party, but it was at the expense of further alienating moderate Catholic opinion, and soon led to an increase in IRA membership and activity. Faulkner also failed to paper over the cracks in his own party, one which had for so long seemed impervious to external political threat or danger. As his party colleagues continued to agonise over his policy direction – from their perspective, he was failing to cope with the terror threat, whilst at the same time being guilty of attempting to appease the Catholic minority with previously unthinkable concessions – other political groups began to emerge and pose new challenges to unionism's once impregnable grip over Northern Ireland's political life.

Nationalist and Republican Labour representatives had put aside their differences in 1970 to form the Social Democratic and Labour Party (SDLP) determined to bring about Irish unity by constitutional methods. The SDLP's strident stance on the IRA's campaign of violence, and its willingness to step up pressure on the Faulkner administration, won it early and considerable support from moderate Catholics. Other political parties and groups also emerged at the start of the decade. The Alliance Party, a pro-Union, moderate party directly appealing for support among Catholics and Protestants, was established in 1970, whilst on the unionist side, two new groups had maximised the divisions within mainstream unionism. Ian Paisley's PUP widened its appeal by transforming itself into becoming the Democratic Unionist Party (DUP) in 1971, whilst the Vanguard Unionist Progressive Party (VUPP) was officially launched two years later, on the eve of the Assembly election (the right-wing Vanguard movement had been formed at the start of 1972, and had quickly won considerable popular support in working-class Protestant areas). As if all this internal political pressure and community tension was not enough to contend with, Brian Faulkner had also to cope with increasing admonishment from a critical Conservative administration led by Edward Heath.

Following the fatal shooting of fourteen Catholics in Derry on 30 January 1972, in an incident which would become known as "Bloody Sunday", it was merely a matter of time before Heath introduced a major new initiative on Northern Ireland. The British prime minister later recalled that he and his colleagues had been "sick of [their] responsibility [for Northern Ireland] without having [any] power" over security issues and knew that it was essential for his administration to "take control of the situation" immediately. Believing that the region was "on the threshold of complete anarchy", Heath decided to "remove Stormont's control over its law and order policy".[1] Part of his rationale was a conviction that handing back Stormont's powers to London would result in the British government regaining the initiative over an increasingly rampant Provisional Irish Republican movement – later, Heath also wrote that at this time he had been contemplating introducing direct rule for over a year.

Whilst, as a result of his March 1972 intervention, Heath initially gained a reputation for not being afraid to take decisive, if unpopular, action in Northern Ireland, the fortunes of the other main protagonist in the talks preceding Stormont's suspension rapidly deteriorated. Faulkner, the ultimate professional and pragmatic politician, was uncharacteristically guilty of poor judgement, in failing to anticipate Heath's proposals, and in then responding impulsively to the announcement. Indeed, there might well have been a different outcome if Faulkner, instead of offering his own resignation and that of his government, had simply left the talks, since this would have forced Heath to call an election in Northern Ireland. However, the Northern Irish premier, who later admitted that, on hearing Heath's pronouncement, he had been left "shaken and horrified" and feeling "completely betrayed", resigned on 23 March 1972.[2]

Unionists were virtually alone in their condemnation of the Westminster intervention, which the *Irish News* described as representing "an indictment of unionist rule" for the last half-century.[3] Vanguard organised a two-day strike which harnessed considerable support, with the culmination of the action being a protest march to Stormont. A rather sheepish Faulkner addressed the large loyalist crowd from the parliament's balcony, and attempted to reassure his disgruntled audience:

> My friends ... we have tremendous power. Our power is the power
> of our numbers; our power is the justice of our cause; our power
> is the responsibility of our conduct. Let us show the world that, so
> far as we are concerned, violence and intimidation are out. British
> we are, and British we remain![4]

The legacy of Heath's suspension of Stormont was considerable, representing the single most significant political watershed of the Ulster conflict, as it helped to define the attitudes and responses of the various Northern Ireland parties to political settlement in the years to come. Part of this apparent refinement in British understanding of the conflict was an acceptance by all national parties that the ideal replacement for Northern Ireland's parliament would be a cross-community, power-sharing legislature and executive. It was to this scenario which the Heath administration now turned its attention.

Direct rule was always regarded as a stop-gap, and Heath's government instantly probed for ways by which many of the powers of government might be restored to Belfast. The weeks and months which followed the introduction of direct rule therefore produced a series of discussions involving Northern Ireland's first Secretary of State, William Whitelaw, and a range of officials from most (but not all) of the region's political parties. Whitelaw hosted a meeting of Northern Irish political leaders at Darlington in September 1972, but the SDLP and DUP refused to attend and little progress was made. The Conservative government then endeavoured to collate a series of proposals for a speedy return of devolved powers to Belfast. A discussion paper, "The Future of Northern Ireland", published at the end of October 1972, was designed to make explicit the government's position, as well as stimulating debate amongst local political groups. Ideas for discussion included the acceptance of the North's position within the United Kingdom, a shared recognition of the existence of an "Irish" dimension, the involvement of representatives from both communities in the day-to-day running of any

Belfast administration and a commitment to full civil rights for all.

The full scale of the Tory administration's shift in approach to the whole question of governance of the region was made more apparent in the March 1973 publication of the government's White Paper, "Northern Ireland Constitutional Proposals". In this, the Conservative government's conviction was made explicit, that any Belfast-based executive could "no longer be solely based upon any single party, if that party draws its support and its elected representatives virtually entirely from only one section of a divided community".[5] The chief proposals of this White Paper formed the nucleus of the Northern Ireland Constitution Act, which became law a few months later. This legislation formally abolished the Stormont parliament, and set out a series of proposals for restoring autonomy to a new legislature in Belfast. A governing Executive, consisting of representatives from a range of parties across the whole of Northern Irish society, would be responsible to a 78-member Assembly (which would be elected by proportional representation). In terms of its reduced legislative powers, the new administration would represent a stark contrast to the old Stormont – for example, both the Executive and Assembly would have no control over the army or police. Another crucially different feature of this Assembly would be the establishment of a committee system, which would take responsibility for the various areas of government, with each governmental head required to act as chair of a committee. The composition of the committee would be determined by the balance of the various parties' strength in the Assembly, with each of the committee chairmen comprising the Executive. Other innovations included periodic plebiscites, and the creation of institutions to facilitate cooperation with the Irish Republic.

Although the new Assembly and Executive were criticised for their relative lack of powers and low level of responsibility (especially with regard to dealing directly with terrorist-related violence), the proposed changes constituted "a dramatic change from the bad old days of Stormont, when Unionists ruled supreme without interference from either Dublin or Westminster".[6] These changes received a mixed response from Northern Ireland's electorate. Republicans rejected outright the package of constitutional reforms, whilst the SDLP welcomed William Whitelaw's proposals. Unionists were again divided, with the DUP, Vanguard, the Orange Order and loyalist paramilitary groups like the Ulster Defence Association (UDA) opposing it.[7] Brian Faulkner declared that unionists would "neither reject it totally, nor do we accept it totally."[8] In a bid to assuage unionist fears of a "sell-out", which had been accentuated by the imposition of direct rule, a referendum was held in March 1973, asking voters if they desired to remain within the United Kingdom. Although a resounding 98 per cent of those who cast their votes expressed a desire to retain the British link, a larger number than usual of the electorate – 43 per cent – stayed away from the polling booths.

A "trial run" for the Assembly elections was held a month beforehand, on 30 May 1973. The council election which took place that day represented a "first" on several counts. It was the first local election in six years, and the first contest of any kind since 1970. More significantly, it was the first election for nearly half a century to be held under the proportional representation system of voting, and it also provided an initial opportunity for a plethora of fledgling political parties (including the SDLP, DUP, VUPP, Alliance and Republican Clubs) to gauge the extent of their popularity with voters.

The overall turnout for this "trial" May election was in excess of 68 per cent, higher than normal for a local election, and the contest's overall outcome offered some encouragement to a British administration which was attempting to outflank extremists in the province. The SDLP won 83 council seats and the party polled well in many districts, but middle-of-the-road parties fared less well, with the NILP gaining just 4 seats, and the Alliance Party, 63 elected councillors. Although unionists of different shades won some 303 of the 526 available council seats, nearly a quarter of these were claimed by unionists opposed to the more moderate leadership of Brian Faulkner (the UUP won 233 seats).

There was however little opportunity for celebration or reflection for political strategists in the North at this point, especially as the election to the new Assembly was scheduled to take place within four weeks. Electors would be expected to adapt to a system of voting which had not been used in parliamentary elections since 1929, and would have to select candidates from a wider range of parties than in the past. The prizes for successful candidates were seats in a newly-constituted, 78-member legislature (which would still be based at Stormont in east Belfast). The election bandwagons of the major parties, which had already seen action in the recent council elections, would soon pick up momentum for what was regarded by many to be a crucial contest for representation in Northern Ireland's first Assembly, on 28 June 1973.

Party lines

It was hardly a secret that Heath, Whitelaw and the Conservative government were longing for a victory of the "moderates" – in other words, those parties supporting their White Paper, and particularly those groups denouncing the partisan politics of the past. Hopes were therefore high for the fortunes of the relatively new Alliance Party – which was fielding 35 candidates, nearly as many as the Unionist Party – and the NILP.[9] The latter's manifesto, "Peace through Partnership and on to Prosperity", implored electors to join in "raising our politics to a new level" and to "start to give generously to one another". Challenging voters to reject the "improved versions of the old Unionism and Nationalism" which would be on offer, and instead opt for the "truly radical lead" of Northern Ireland Labour, the NILP insisted it represented "a real alternative". Stressing its support for a White Paper which offered the "possibility of a just peace", the party described power-sharing and the appointment of an executive as a "Ministry of all the Talents", and maintained that, "in place of fear offered by so many of our politicians, Labour offers peace through partnership and on to prosperity as being the only real alternative".[10]

The early days of the campaign were taken up with the various parties drafting their manifestos and preparing to hand in their nomination papers. Whilst the SDLP took longer to name their candidates, many unionist challengers had thrown their hats into the ring within hours of nomination opening, on 5 June. That evening's *Belfast Telegraph* contained photographs of UUP leader, Brian Faulkner and Vanguard chief, Bill Craig handing in their nominations. An anticipated 180 candidates were expected to contest the 78 available seats, with several constituencies offering a range of political alternatives, especially East Belfast, where 23 candidates (16 of them representing unionist parties) were contesting 6 seats in the constituency. The *Belfast Telegraph* announced the start of nominations as "the big fight for power", and predicted that "the most formidable struggle" would be between the UUP (with an estimated 50 candidates) and the Craig–Paisley Loyalist Coalition (with an estimated 45), which constituted "the most powerful election challenge the Unionist Party has faced".[11]

The Unionist Party's manifesto, "Peace, Order and Good Government", was to win as many headlines for the party's insistence that Assembly candidates should endorse its principles by signing a pledge, as for the document's actual content. Backing the manifesto and its chief architect, party leader, Faulkner, was for many the "key issue" in the forthcoming contest. The *Belfast Telegraph* described the "crucial leadership battle inside and outside" the Unionist Party and, whilst admitting Faulkner was "the man in the driving seat", it pointed out that his position was "by no means secure", on account of the fact that, "a number of official unionist candidates are opposed or unsympathetic to him".[12] Additionally, he had to contend with the threat posed by the estimated 45 nominees from the Loyalist Coalition, who would "appeal to the same section of the electorate" and consequently, "so much [would] depend on the pre-election pledge which Mr Faulkner is putting to all unionist candidates".[13] In fact, the emphasis on Faulkner's "pledge" helped to divert attention from the dearth of new policies in the party's twenty-four-page document. The key issue identified was a predictable one – the need to maintain the union, which remained, "fundamental to the preservation of civil and religious liberties and to the future prosperity of Ulster". The party promised to take "whatever steps are necessary to defend this position", reminding voters that the Unionist Party differed from other groups in that its candidates actually "support the Union", rather than "merely accept[ing] it in a tepid and equivocal manner".[14]

The Unionist Party manifesto was much less effusive in its responses to the British government's White Paper, stressing that its election candidates would "not be prepared to participate in government with those whose primary objective [was] to break the union with Great Britain". Another major theme of the manifesto was the party's stated desire to work for "the widest possible devolution of power to the new Ulster legislature and executive". In its bullish final remarks, the document announced that its candidates would approach the future, "confident in the good sense and goodwill of the Ulster people", and endorsed their capacity to "develop and mould the new structures into the kind of Government and Parliament which Northern Ireland needs".[15] The *Belfast Telegraph* joined forces with the *Irish News* and other journals in condemning the Unionist Party's muted endorsement of the White Paper, and denounced the "double-talk" and "evasion" which dominated the pages of the party's manifesto. The once staunch backer of Ulster Unionism now denounced its leader for "sidestepping the issue" of executive power-sharing with Catholic representatives, and stressed the need for a swift "clearing of the air".[16]

The election statements of the other main unionist parties were not as detailed as that of the Unionist Party's manifesto, but were more explicit in their proposals for the future. According to the *Belfast Telegraph*'s political reporter, John Wallace, the VUPP's "Power for the People" plan advocated a federal arrangement for Ulster's future governance, and would be criticised for its "grandiose schemes", which included the introduction of a new constitution and the restoration of a Northern Ireland government. Vanguard's "very hypothetical" document depicted "an Ulster busy at work and relaxing by playing golf and fishing".[17] He suggested that the "big if" for the Northern Irish electorate was "whether the British would under any circumstances negotiate with Mr Craig and Mr Paisley, either to give them back the Parliament they want, or accept the Vanguard alternative of a federal arrangement".[18]

Meanwhile the DUP's four-page manifesto described the forthcoming contest as the region's "Destiny Day" and declared that the "hour [was] grave" for a province which had been "brought to its present horrifying condition" by the "disastrous appeasement policies pursued by the Unionist Party at Stormont, and now by the Westminster government". The DUP insisted that these policies had "given the IRA subversives the needed momentum, by establishing beyond dispute the disastrous principle – Republican violence pays!"[19] The manifesto's concluding statement summed up the election as being one about "law and order and a proper Northern Ireland within the United Kingdom", and blamed the leadership of the Unionist Party for refusing to participate in a united loyalist condemnation of the White Paper. The manifesto ended with the following statement:

> The IRA must be defeated, the voices of the law-abiding people of Northern Ireland *must* be heard and heeded by the British Government, and real and proper democratic institutions for Northern Ireland within the Union must be established. To accomplish this task, the UDUP is dedicated. Service ever – Surrender Never![20]

The SDLP's manifesto was not published until a week after the unveiling of its unionist counterpart. The document was predictably more effusive in its backing of the Conservatives' White Paper. Committing the party to the considerable task of "building a new North and a new Ireland", the SDLP pledged itself to bring into life an operational Council of Ireland, helping to end internment, producing an amnesty for "political" prisoners, and helping to create a new police force. Underlining the necessity of having a system of government which would be "seen to be fair and just to all", the SDLP played down the short-term significance of their ultimate goal of Irish unity, maintaining they did "not seek instant unity as the ultimate solution", because they "recognised the many problems standing in the way: political, social and economic."[21]

An interesting aspect of SDLP policy was its commitment to a new "labour-intensive" system of economic growth, as distinct from one created solely from the profits made by "capital-intensive" industries. The party pledged itself to achieving "a more balanced development of industry by type, size and regional distribution".[22] Appeals were made to both political opponents in Northern Ireland and in Great Britain, and to the Protestant section of the North's community. The manifesto insisted that the "honest and blunt truth" was that "the only way now to end internment" was through forging "a political settlement". Referring to Ulster loyalists, the party appealed to "our fellow citizens, to drop the defensive mentality that has stultified their political thinking for so long, and to recognise these steps are the only reasonable way forward for the people of Ireland, North and South".[23] The SDLP's election document was strongly endorsed by the North's leading nationalist newspaper. The *Irish News* argued that the recently-published manifesto was just "what we have come to expect of SDLP policy strategy", praising its "practical and intelligent nature".[24]

Editorial Comment

For once the rival unionist and nationalist newspapers were in broad agreement over their support for the proposed British initiative of shared community government. In the case of the *Belfast Telegraph*, this backing of power-sharing also involved an obvious awareness of the broader question of reciprocity over the union itself. Following the intervention of leading Labour frontbencher, Jim Callaghan – who had warned that Britain could not financially "bleed for ever" over Ulster – the *Belfast Telegraph* pointed out that the union had to be "a two-way affair", which necessarily involved "obligations on both sides". Callaghan had referred to statistics which fully encapsulated the scale of Britain's commitment to the region – over £200 million of investment, and the presence on the streets of more than 15,000 troops – and the *Belfast Telegraph* stressed that such a statement was merely what "everyone in their heart of hearts should know". This, the leading article pointed out, meant that if Northern Ireland continued to "reject one reasonable solution after another, and opts for confrontation rather than reconciliation, Britain [could not] play referee forever".[25] This attempt by the *Belfast Telegraph* to counsel its readers to seriously contemplate the ramifications of rejecting power-sharing was accompanied by the paper's wholesome backing for the creation of a cross-community government. In an earlier editorial, it had referred to the news that Derry City Council, which had just elected its first nationalist mayor, had agreed to elect a unionist deputy. The paper backed this gesture of goodwill, declaring that "Ulster's future as a governable province must depend on such a system, at every level".[26] However, the paper had also some foreboding news for its readers. Unionists had failed to return a similarly generous gesture in Armagh, where they "took all the meagre spoils", and the rival parties had failed to break "deadlock" in Enniskillen. The paper suggested that "generosity [would] reap its own rewards in the only terms worth having – harmony and stability".[27] The *Irish News* combined an approach of espousing support for the White Paper and the new Assembly, with warnings that nationalists would not tolerate unionist prevarication on the question of power-sharing, and that the imminent contest constituted Northern Ireland's "last hope".

In an editorial published relatively early in the campaign, the *Irish News* had attacked "armchair moderates", for not turning out to vote in the recent council elections, and called on them to "rise up in their numbers and vote for those candidates who, collectively, can give a measure of reality and relevance to the new Assembly". The leading article went on to suggest that the new legislative body could "provide for radical reconstruction, and it should be given a chance to work".[28] Warning that the new legislature would need "men of wider vision" than the unionists – who had, they maintained, displayed little of this quality during their half century of Stormont rule, the paper concluded that "an anti-Unionist voice at the seat of power is now not only possible but highly necessary if we are to move forward."[29]

A fortnight later, another editorial in the *Irish News*, entitled "A test of belief", described the forthcoming contest as a "judgement day", not only for the province but also for the career of Secretary of State, William Whitelaw. Expressing sympathy for the sentiment which had recently been expressed by James Callaghan, the paper predicted that "the result of this fight for political power could well influence the British people's attitude to the whole 'Ulster' imbroglio".[30] Referring to the genial Whitelaw, the editorial warned that, in the event of a large loyalist vote for "unreason", the "hopeful smile will quickly disappear from Mr Whitelaw's face", and that an alternative route to solving the North's political problems would have to be pursued. Urging the Ulster secretary to impress upon the "extremists on the Unionist side" that, if they chose to reject the chance to share political power with representatives of the SDLP, he and his government would "have to think in another direction".[31]

For the first time in their respective histories, both the *Belfast Telegraph* and *Irish News* were critical, albeit to varying degrees, of the leader of the Unionist Party during an election campaign, and vocal regarding their respective concerns over the direction into which unionism appeared to be lurching. In an editorial entitled, "Election tactics", the *Belfast Telegraph* dismissed the Unionist Party's manifesto as being "substantially the same as the blueprint issued before Darlington, ignoring the implications of the Green and White Papers". Suggesting that both the Unionist Party and SDLP had failed in their obligations to impress upon the public that this was "to all intents and purposes, the last chance election for Northern Ireland", the paper also forecast that an outcome which did not lead to an agreement would merely lead to "more and more direct rule, or radical disengagement by Westminster".[32] The same editorial turned its wrath on the Unionist Party leader for failing to remind the electorate about this "last chance" nature of the contest, and also for his disparaging remarks about the moderate Alliance Party, which might "make good copy, but is [this] sensible politics in Ulster's crisis situation?"[33]

The *Belfast Telegraph* returned to its assault on Faulkner on the eve of the election, which they were now labelling "Spaghetti Junction", on account of the confusion caused by a multitude of political vehicles appearing to steer in different directions. Again offering its backing to those candidates who were "determined to make the Assembly work", the paper's leading article accused the former Unionist prime minister, a man renowned for his political dexterity, of not being totally candid in his remarks, on account of his desire to maintain party solidarity. Faulkner's "equivocal" position on power-sharing was highlighted by the paper, which pointed out that this new system of government would not be restricted to the inclusion of "token" non-unionist representatives from other political parties sympathetic to the maintenance of the union, or even senior unelected figures from the Catholic community, but that in order to be "meaningful at all times", it was essential to have "an elected representative from the Roman Catholic population".[34]

The *Irish News* also noted the Unionist Party leader's reputation for political trickery, but focussed primarily on the plight of Faulkner and mainstream unionism. Early on in the campaign, an editorial suggested that Faulkner "must be counting his troubles", which included the serious threat posed by the nomination of over 40 candidates from the DUP–VUPP coalition, who were "determined to square up to the former prime minister". In addition, Faulkner was being forced to "fend off the challenge of erstwhile supporters".[35] During the latter stage of the contest, the *Irish News* joined forces with the *Belfast Telegraph* in criticising the Unionist Party leader for his jibes at the SDLP (the "new wreckers of the Assembly") and Alliance (the "I-buy-anything" party). Maintaining that Faulkner was in fact facing "a tough challenge" from both parties, the *Irish News* despaired of the reaction of "thoughtful" electors to such verbal assaults from a unionist leader, who also "skirts skilfully over the issue of power-sharing". This, the paper maintained, was however the issue which Faulkner needed to devote his attention to in the remaining days of his campaign. The editorial argued:

> Unless the principle of power-sharing with no matter who is elected to the Assembly is fully established by Mr Faulkner, the Assembly will be doomed before it has got underway ... It is the very eagerness with which Mr Faulkner castigates not only his other unionist opponents but the anti-unionist parties, which puts a strain on the belief of all those opposed to unionism in the sincerity of Mr Faulkner's utterances.[36]

In a number of its editorials, the *Irish News* also attacked the wider unionist threat. Referring to dissidents within the Unionist Party, the paper suggested that such opponents of the party leader would likely restrain their "fierce opposition" to Faulkner in order to "receive the benedictions of Glengall Street on their candidatures".[37] Acknowledging the "strength of right-wing Unionism", both within and outside the Unionist Party, the paper warned that it could lead to a "road to further crisis", as loyalist refusal to compromise would clearly not result in a change of British policy. The paper added that the fact there would be "no return to the old Unionism" appeared to have "escaped too many of the Unionist Party's opponents".[38] Three days later, another *Irish News* editorial predicted that "the ganging-up of the

Unionist hard-liners" indicated that "unionism's once most loyal supporters [were] prepared to go to any limit in the assertion of their tribal rights, which they manifestly fear will count for little in the Assembly".[39]

On Election Day itself, the *Irish News* returned to its condemnation of loyalist dissidents, describing them as "wreckers", not least for their back-handed assistance to the under-pressure Unionist Party leader. The paper maintained that Faulkner's opponents had actually managed to present him with "a reason and an opportunity to don the mask of moderation and to laud the idea of the Assembly, where once he spoke of it with contempt".[40]

Unionist parties were not the only groups to be criticised by the *Belfast Telegraph*. A series of leading articles attacked the SDLP for its policies and its election campaign, especially in certain parts of the province. In an editorial entitled, "Danger course?", published on 14 June, the paper maintained that the SDLP's "negotiating terms" were "almost as stiff as those of the right-wing wreckers". Dismissing several of the party's "controversial" proposals, including the complete removal of internment, the introduction of an amnesty for "political" offenders, the abolition of flags and emblems legislation and the reorganisation of the RUC, the editorial argued that the SDLP manifesto offered "a bleak prospect for agreement on difficult and complex issues".[41] The following week, the *Belfast Telegraph* resumed its attack on the SDLP, this time directing its ire at local activists. Referring to the party's proclaimed commitment to "building a new North", an opinion piece pointed out that in Mid-Ulster the party was "urging its supporters to vote for an abstentionist and [to] ignore all pro-Union candidates". Castigating the party's "destructively negative" tactics in the constituency, the paper fumed that "the only winners will be the wreckers".[42]

As the contest neared its conclusion, the *Belfast Telegraph* reflected upon what the party offered electors. Cutting to the chase, the paper's assessment was that, "for all its protestations about being non-sectarian, it remains a Catholic-based party", whose campaign tactics had proved "open to question in several areas", and were "not calculated to win the degree of trust from its opponents [which was] needed to build a new North".[43]

Not surprisingly, the *Irish News'* assessment of the SDLP's proposals for change as well as its election campaign differed radically from that of the *Belfast Telegraph*. Declaring that the party were, "offering themselves as the only effective opponents of Faulkner's Unionism", the *Irish News* also expressed optimism both in terms of the election's final outcome and its hopes for the new Assembly. Despite the "limited" powers of the latter, the new legislature would "provide the machinery for an interim political settlement, leading to the long-term one of ultimate reunion".[44] As the province anxiously awaited – with "a great holding of breaths" – announcement of the electorate's verdict, the *Irish News* predicted that local politics were "certain to be transformed". Notwithstanding the paper's "reservations" about the Assembly – particularly in regard to its capacity to deliver all of the content of the White Paper – the new Assembly would, it declared, have the potential for creating "radical reconstruction" and "should be given every chance to work". Referring specifically to the Catholic section of the North's community, the paper reflected that those who had been "denied their rights and justice are no longer resigned", and asserted that this forgotten group of society would "hold the Assembly, and those who are to compose it, to account if they are not immediately forthcoming".[45]

Other political groups came in for unfavourable analysis, even if this was not on the scale of that directed at the perceived "wreckers" and the broad "negativity" of the leading parties. The *Irish News* mocked the Alliance Party for its attempts to "evangelise us with the good news that it can provide us with an alternative to the sterile sectarian political stances of the past". The editorial reminded its readers of the party's "boasts" that it had "bridged the sectarian divide", but also pointed out that it would be the electorate's responses, and not the reassurances of political groups, which would prove if this merely constituted a "vain boast". The paper also speculated on whether the "nationally-minded voter" would be "willing to adjust to a party that is, in essence, all for the British connection".[46]

Security incidents, which were major news stories during the period of electioneering, were also the subject of political comment. This included analysis of the impact of violence upon the campaign, especially major incidents like the Coleraine and Omagh car bombs, and the shooting of politician Paddy Wilson (see below). Another focus for the media was the imminence of groundbreaking political and constitutional change. With the formal abolition of Stormont, the role of governor – the monarch's representative in Northern Ireland – had become obsolete, and the *Belfast Telegraph* observed that the departure of the last governor, Lord Grey, had "marked the end of a period of history", but also pointed out that the election later that week would provide "a unique opportunity – if properly grasped – for a new beginning for Northern Ireland and all its people".[47] Discussing the findings of a Westminster working-party group that same day, the *Irish News* once again drew attention to a perennial nationalist gripe, namely employment discrimination. The newspaper welcomed the findings of the Westminster group's report, maintaining it "pointed the way to a happier future", and that the document's recommendations "must be speedily implemented".[48]

Yet Another New Beginning?

The hopes of moderate-thinking people for the Assembly election were high, given the outcome of the council contest a few weeks earlier. One newspaper post-mortem analysis of this local election noted the "interesting and quite encouraging showing" of both the SDLP and Alliance Party, and those in government were also cautiously optimistic about the chances of other forces for moderation, including Brian Faulkner's Unionist Party and the NILP.[49] For the electorate, this contest promised hopes of yet another "new beginning", but on this occasion, there was a genuine belief that something "different" was swirling around in the political air. Not only were electors being asked to nominate representatives for a new legislature, but they would also cast their preferences utilising a "new" system of voting (or to be more accurate, one which had not been employed for nearly 45 years). Additionally, for the first time in a major contest, a number of political parties, formed after the start of the conflict, were now standing in the political ring, asking for the endorsement of electors in this vital contest. This sense of political freshness – a new parliament, a new voting system and new political parties – combined with the fact that this would be the first major election to be fought since the full onslaught of sectarian violence four years before, meant that the significance of this Assembly contest would undoubtedly resonate with Northern Irish voters.

The campaigns of both republican and loyalist paramilitaries were in full flow by the early summer of 1973, and the strong likelihood of violent encounters provoked by rising political passions was fully appreciated by military chiefs, who ensured that security levels were high throughout the four-week campaign. The threat of violence meant the implementation of restrictions to the various parties' election activities, especially in venturing into "unfriendly" territory and in staging open-air meetings, particularly in sensitive, "interface" districts. Although cars and lorries displaying posters and flags, as well as broadcasting candidates' loudhailer messages, remained common features of this contest, they were restricted to "safe" districts. Therefore, candidates addressed supporters in Orange halls, church rooms and social clubs, and targeted wider audiences through carefully-crafted press statements and broadcast interviews or debates. Television news bulletins and newspaper campaign reports kept an engaged Ulster electorate fully informed about party positions, and if there was any ambiguity, this would be swiftly dispelled by the inclusion of party advertisements in popular papers such as the *Belfast Telegraph* and *Irish News*. Even groups which were not standing for election got in on the act. For instance, an advertisement in the *Irish News* on the eve of the election from "Cage 7 internees" in Long Kesh implored nationalists to refrain from casting their votes. The advertisement read: "End internment – spoil your vote – vote for a lasting peace – spoil your vote!"[50]

The universal acceptance of the importance of the occasion on 28 June was not the only factor indicating a very high turnout. Summer elections, especially those occurring during spells of warm weather and on the eve of the start of the school holidays and the traditional annual Twelfth of July holiday, usually produced higher than usual turnouts. This trend also pleased government officials, anxious about ensuring as broad a spectrum of electors as possible entered the polling booths.

Unionism was, if anything, even more divided going into the Assembly election campaign than it had been during the "Crossroads" contest four years earlier. Opposing loyalist political parties were fielding more candidates across Northern Ireland than the once omnipotent Unionist Party (now also known as the Official Unionist Party), which was having problems persuading their own candidates to commit to a pledge backing the White Paper and party manifesto. Early on in the campaign, the *Irish News* pointed out that the former prime minister was "well aware" that he would not lead the majority group in the new Assembly. With a minimum of 40 representatives needed to claim a majority in the new parliamentary body, the Unionist Party only had 43 official nominees, "up to a quarter" of whom were against Faulkner's position on the White Paper. Faulkner was also facing "a powerful challenge" from the Loyalist Coalition headed by Craig and Paisley, and "lesser threats from almost a dozen other hues of Orange campaigners", which would culminate in a situation where there was, "no possibility of an overall majority of the Official Unionists".[51]

Confusion over the standing of unionist candidates and their degree of support for the White Paper was to prevail throughout the campaign.

Towards its close, the *Belfast Telegraph*'s John Wallace maintained the Unionist Party's officials had to urgently "sort out the 'who-is-unionist-and-who-isn't' row".[52] This chaotic state of affairs was hardly helped by a series of mixed messages coming from the heart of the party's organisation. Glengall Street, the party's headquarters at the time, refused to endorse a number of candidates who had been proposed and backed at local level, including five of the eight people nominated by the South Antrim Unionist Association.[53] A front-page story in the *Belfast Telegraph* on 8 June reported that unionist candidates opposing the White Paper had been given "a surprise assurance" that they would not be "disowned" by the party. The *Belfast Telegraph* reported that, following a meeting with disgruntled unionist nominees (including John Taylor and Harry West) in Portadown the previous evening, the Reverend Martin Smyth, the UUC's vice president, had confirmed that such dissidents had the "full backing" of his colleagues. However in a separate statement in the same paper, the party's leader insisted there would be "no party support for any candidate who didn't back the manifesto". The *Belfast Telegraph* argued that such internal chaos was "certain to produce another major row in the party", as the dozen candidates involved were "declining to sign the undertaking requested by the leader, Mr Brian Faulkner, to support party policy".[54]

Just as was the case with Terence O'Neill four years before, much of the media's interest in the election concentrated upon the difficulties being experienced by the Unionist Party leader, Brian Faulkner. It was certainly a frenetic campaign for Faulkner, who later recollected that it had been "hectic and more hard-fought than any I could remember". His message to electors in his South Down constituency was that he would "cooperate in the Assembly with all those who are prepared to make the new institutions of government effective".[55]

Faulkner's campaign was not restricted to meetings or walkabouts in his own constituency. He delivered several key addresses in various parts of the province, as well as appearing in several television and radio interviews and leading press conferences at Glengall Street. As someone who clearly relished the cut and thrust of robust electioneering, Faulkner soaked up the personal criticism and venom which was hurled in his direction by impassioned opponents, but more than countered such attacks with his own stinging invective. Referring to a forthcoming meeting involving the British premier, Edward Heath and his Irish counterpart, William Cosgrave, Faulkner urged voters to send "a united team" to the Assembly, as anything else would lead to Heath and Cosgrave, "assuming that we don't care". The Unionist Party leader maintained that, "if a team of wreckers and saboteurs goes to the Assembly, they will write us off as people who have renounced their British citizenship".[56] The following week, Faulkner directed his wrath at opponents outside his own party. Speaking in Downpatrick, he denounced the recent attacks on the security forces in Belfast by loyalist paramilitaries. It was known that Vanguard had a close association with the paramilitary UDA, and so, referring to the Vanguard–DUP coalition of "sinister bedfellows", Faulkner argued that there were "bloodstains on their joint election platforms". To vote for either party was, the Unionist Party leader maintained, tantamount to "voting for all of them".[57] Over a week later, Faulkner returned to this message of counselling supporters against casting their lower-preference votes for candidates from the Loyalist Coalition. Speaking at Dromore, he argued:

> One of the greatest dangers of polling day would be for ordinary unionist voters to be deceived into thinking that those groups, posing as "breakaway unionist parties", are really not all that much different from Official Unionists, and that, under proportional representation, they are worth a few votes further down the preference list. Nothing could be further from the truth … If you want a strong Unionist Party, not only for the present but for the future, do not vote even in low preference for parties which claim to be unionist but are, in fact, a threat to unionism.[58]

The Unionist Party leader was also condemnatory of other political parties, although the tone of his rebuke tended to be more ironical than impassioned. Speaking in Donaghadee, Faulkner drew his audience's attention to "a lot of fancy political outfits on display up and down the country". He attacked the non-confrontational and supposedly passive image of the Alliance Party, dismissing its members as making up a "party of acceptance", which assured the British government to "tell us what you want us to do and we will do it."[59] Faulkner also defended Ulster Unionists from the "slanderous" attacks levelled at them from political opponents and media agencies, which had been growing in their intensity since 1969. He insisted that his party had "no need to don the sackcloth and ashes" for an alleged "fifty years of misrule", and urged his colleagues to "go out and nail this malicious slander and go for what has been achieved in five decades".[60]

Senior Ulster Unionist colleagues were broadly supportive of Faulkner and his qualified support of the White Paper, and attempted to relieve the pressure on their leader by insisting that the top priority for the Northern Ireland people had to be the eradication of terrorism. Former Stormont minister, Roy Bradford, standing in East Belfast, maintained that the "prospects of political advancement" were dependent upon "the success of the security forces in stamping out terrorism", adding that this was the "first priority" of both Protestant and Catholic sections of the population.[61] Veteran unionist politician, William Morgan, standing in North Belfast, was one of relatively few unionists who placed social issues to the forefront of his election programme. The former Stormont cabinet minister called for "a determined clear-up of houses", which had been "left vacant because of the Troubles".[62] Cecil Walker, his fellow unionist candidate in North Belfast, was highly vocal in his denunciation of political rivals, including the Alliance Party, which he accused of spreading "sweet nonsense" in its party literature, and he also dismissed another key new party, the DUP, for its "tawdry" election manifesto.[63] A few days later, Walker deflected the claims of the SDLP's Paddy Devlin, who had poked fun at the Unionist Party's "fragmented" nature. Walker insisted that Devlin and other critics would soon discover that "the alleged fragments will have cut deeply into those who would strive to play politics with our lives". In the same speech, he insisted there was "no room" in the election for "power-sharing politics", and that he was "not prepared to participate in Government with those whose primary objective is to break the union with Great Britain".[64]

Although some unionists sceptical of Faulkner's brand of "moderate" unionism could be found within the ranks of his own party, the majority of hard-line unionists had either defected to Paisley's DUP which had been formed two years before, or had joined the recently politicised Vanguard movement. Both parties, the DUP and the new VUPP, had joined together in an unlikely coalition, with the parties' respective election titles being the Democratic Unionist Loyalist Coalition (DULC) and the Vanguard Unionist Loyalist Coalition (VULC). The former group, fielding 17 candidates, had a recent history of fierce rivalry with Bill Craig's Vanguard movement, especially over its close links with loyalist paramilitaries and its espousal of Ulster nationalism. Indeed, the DUP had recently found itself in the shadow of Vanguard, which had earned significant levels of support among

Ulster loyalists in the months either side of the suspension of Stormont. The DUP had pursued a policy of integration which contrasted sharply with Vanguard's proposals for independence, although there was some common ground between the two parties in their respective calls for the restoration of a Stormont-style parliament.

As would be the case with many subsequent election campaigns, Ian Paisley's party was clearer about what it opposed than what it was actually advocating, and the familiar bogeys of treacherous unionist leaders, vicious IRA terrorists, weak-kneed British politicians and interfering Irish political leaders predictably dominated candidates' election statements and party literature. An illustration of this was Paisley's fiery denunciation of the news that the Irish prime minister was meeting Heath in London the following week. Paisley warned that, "if Mr Cosgrave sticks his nose into the affairs of the Northern Ireland Assembly, it will be a broken, bloody nose he will get back".[65] This nihilistic, opposition-focused brand of electioneering would remain a DUP trademark for many years to come, and the party still appeared to many to be little more than a vehicle for the personal outpourings of its controversial party leader. The widespread lack of understanding of DUP policy direction was however not solely attributable to the party's own shortcomings. Their campaign was afforded scant coverage in the local press, especially in the columns of the *Belfast Telegraph*, with which Paisley had a long-running dispute. Consequently, there were few reports on the party's election campaign, though the DUP retained high hopes of gaining seats in some Belfast constituencies (including East Belfast, where Paisley's wife, Eileen was standing), as well as faring well in its heartlands of North and South Antrim.

For its political baptism, Vanguard fielded a substantial number of candidates (27 in total), and was confident of victory in several constituencies, including North Antrim (where its leader Bill Craig was in direct opposition to Ian Paisley), Fermanagh & South Tyrone, where Ernest Baird was amongst the favourites to be elected, and in Londonderry, where local loyalist activist, Glen Barr was endeavouring to put pressure on the SDLP's John Hume). Craig's assurance to electors was that he would endeavour to "restore strong, democratic and realistic government" to Northern Ireland – something, he maintained, Brian Faulkner and the Unionist Party had recently failed to deliver; he also pledged to "provide bold, honest leadership", which would prove to be "worthy of the trust and confidence of the Ulster people".[66] Ernest

Baird, another Vanguard candidate hopeful of being elected, denounced the "totally discredited" party led by Faulkner, which had "given away the Parliament of Northern Ireland which they were pledged to maintain".[67] Several Vanguard candidates had defected from the Unionist Party and such criticism of their former colleagues was especially biting. Marvin Gowdy, standing in South Belfast, referred to his "long service" to the Unionist Party, but admitted that he now regarded "the gyrations of the leadership of the so-called 'Official' Unionists with deep regret and suspicion".[68]

Many of the "hate" figures of Vanguard propaganda were shared by the DUP. Harold Wilson, the Labour Party leader, had sparked considerable fury amongst loyalist ranks the previous year, when he had raised the prospect of a united Ireland within a specified time frame, and more recently William Whitelaw had ill-advisedly returned to this scenario. In a statement, which probably had the opposite effect of what he had intended – namely to reassure Ulster's Protestant community – Whitelaw had dismissed any prospect of Irish unification within the following decade. Vanguard candidate Jim Rodgers suggested that this was all the more reason for unionist-leaning electors to return to the new Assembly "a majority opposed to the White Paper", and that "anything less" would result in "a united Ireland by 1985".[69] Other themes of Vanguard candidates' election speeches and statements included their denials of being "wreckers", and the fundamental need to adopt a strong law and order policy (something which had been strongly advocated by Vanguard since its inception).

An independent member of the Loyalist Coalition, Hugh Smyth (standing in West Belfast), maintained it was not dissident loyalists but rather pro-Faulknerites backing the White Paper who were "the real wreckers" and he pledged to "renegotiate the White Paper to get terms acceptable to the majority of people who wish to remain in the United Kingdom".[70] Stanley Morgan, a Vanguard candidate in South Belfast, suggested that direct rule had "failed to maintain law and order", and declared that the role of Brian Faulkner and the Unionist Party in allowing this to happen had only consolidated his opposition to them. Morgan also referred to the recent bomb "outrage" in Coleraine as well as "the destruction of my business premises in an IRA bomb attack in [Belfast's] Donegall Street", and argued that "those who would call upon us to support the White Paper are betraying our Ulster heritage".[71]

As mentioned earlier, hopes were high for those "moderate" parties that were supportive of the Heath administration's White Paper. Chief among these was the SDLP, contesting a major election for the first time. The party fielded a strong team of candidates – many of whom had earned their reputations during the recent period of civil rights agitation – and were hopeful of success in a range of constituencies across the North. Senior party figures, such as John Hume (in Londonderry), Gerry Fitt (in North Belfast) and Austin Currie (in Fermanagh & South Tyrone) were all positive about the party's chances. Inside the first few days of the campaign, Fitt argued that he was providing his North Belfast electors with, "a clear choice between the various brands of Unionism and a real, radical alternative".[72]

Yet even in this early phase of the SDLP's development, strains were apparent between the "red" strand of the party (epitomised by Gerry Fitt) and its "green" element (associated more with the likes of John Hume). Owen Adams, standing in East Belfast, was unequivocal in his demands for Irish unification. Stating his party's intention to "restrict and eventually eliminate British influence in Irish political life", Adams declared that there was "no substitute for self-determination", and reiterated the SDLP's intention to use the Assembly to "create a legislature with the machinery of government that reflects the aspirations and respects the traditions of all the people".[73]

Other SDLP candidates turned their sights on their political opponents. A handful of Irish nationalists had decided to stand in the contest and Michael Canavan, one of three SDLP nominees in Londonderry, denounced their intervention, suggesting it was at "risk [of] forfeiting credit for its years of service."[74] There was a series of SDLP attacks on the Alliance Party, which was, like themselves, backing the British government's White Paper. Ben Caraher, standing in South Belfast, described Alliance as a "middle-class unionist party", which was "obsessed with religious tags" and seemed unable to "raise itself above the level of sectarian accusations".[75] On the eve of the election, Paddy O'Donoghue, standing in South Down, questioned the party's honesty over its position on the constitutional question. He claimed that the Alliance Party had, in its early phase, "pretended to take no firm line on the constitutional link", but that, "as always, Alliance wanted it both ways".[76] The Loyalist Coalition also came in for a barrage of criticism from the SDLP's election contenders. Austin Currie, speaking in support of North Antrim SDLP candidates, attacked the "myth" that the "wreckers" and the "irresponsibles" were all on the "non-unionist side", and suggested such a misconception was being "dispelled by the actions of Craig, Paisley, the

UDA and others, and can be exploded entirely in the weeks and months to come".[77]

The enthusiasm and optimism of the SDLP as a new party helps to makes sense of its desire to challenge unionist supremacy in the largely uncharted waters of constituencies like North Antrim. Two of its candidates, John O'Hagan and John Turnly, were making "a determined assault on the hold exercised over the area by parties representative of the various shades of unionism". Party campaigners had been active across the constituency and the SDLP was confident of producing "a large turnout of voters" who, "sickened by years of Unionist misrule and records of sectarianism and religious division", would help to return two SDLP representatives.[78] Turnly was an interesting choice of candidate for the SDLP in this predominantly Protestant constituency. He insisted that being born a Protestant did "not mean that you cannot be Irish", and asked for the chance to "bridge that divide, in the best traditions of Wolfe Tone, Robert Emmet and Charles Stewart Parnell".[79]

Continuing to provide the backing it had offered to other nationalist-leaning parties for so many years, the *Irish News* maintained its practical and moral support for the SDLP cause. As mentioned elsewhere, its editorial comment flagged up the shortcomings of its unionist rivals, and generally backed the policies proposed by the SDLP. The paper also gave copious coverage to party advertisements – including one under the title, "Vote SDLP – a new North" – as well as warning against the dangers of voter apathy, informing readers about the new voting system, and keeping them apprised of the choice of SDLP candidates on offer (by reproducing a map of the province on which the photos of the candidates were displayed in the relevant constituencies).[80]

Meanwhile, the NILP, despite its disappointing showing in the May council elections, was hopeful that many unionists, disaffected by internal divisions over the direction of the Unionist Party and especially by its prevarication over the White Paper, would seriously contemplate switching their allegiances to them. The party's East Belfast candidate and former Stormont Minister, David Bleakley, told a party meeting on 3 June that an Assembly without the experience and presence of figures from the Trade Union movement would constitute a "farce", but also stressed that positive change was on its way. Arguing that many electors were starting to realise the "danger signals" transmitted by the local council results, Bleakley pronounced that the "avalanche" of recent support for his group reflected a desire for Labour voters to "return to their traditional base for the more important Assembly results".[81]

Other Labour nominees, including the Reverend John Stewart, who was standing in North Belfast, maintained that the forthcoming election represented a "search for new leadership", involving those candidates who exhibited "ability, integrity, honesty, and most of all ... goodwill", who would be able to "engender hope in the hearts of all people".[82] The chief targets for Labour censure were Vanguard, with whom the NILP was in direct competition for the sizeable working-class Protestant vote. A number of official party statements referred to the "nasty smell of fascism in the air", with the clear implication that Vanguard was the alleged guilty party. Towards the end of the campaign, Labour's representation declared that fascism "must be strenuously fought in the ballot box".[83] Another reference to Vanguard's far-right tendencies had been made by David Bleakley a few days before, following Bill Craig's lighting of a William Whitelaw effigy on a bonfire in Portadown. Bleakley condemned the Vanguard leader and his supporters, calling them "torch-bearers for UDI [a unilateral declaration of independence]", who had clearly "taken leave of their senses".[84] This strong denunciation of Vanguard also provoked an internal feud within the NILP's own ranks. Another Labour candidate standing in Belfast, Billy Boyd, appeared to defend the actions of the UDA in Portadown, as well as criticising both the interventions of the British Labour Party and the "sermonising of people like David Bleakley". Bob Johnson, a Labour nominee in South Antrim, also offered counsel to his party colleagues – although in this case, his focus was on the dangers of restricting the party's appeal to the Protestant section of the community. Johnson warned of the electoral dangers of the NILP "presenting ourselves as imitations of the Unionist and Alliance parties".[85]

The main standard-bearer for moderation was the Alliance Party, which was clearly enjoying growing cross-community support, particularly in middle-class areas mainly around Greater Belfast. Dismissed by its opponents for the class-based nature of its appeal, the party was hoping to benefit from the support of another category of voter – young, recently enfranchised electors. Oliver Napier, standing for the Alliance Party in East Belfast, forecast that he would "score" with the "young married couples", who in particular were "sick of the old sectarian politics", and who "longed for a society for their children which [would be] free of bigotry".[86]

Most of the large number of Alliance candidates were appealing to electors to consider breaking the voting habits of a lifetime, by choosing a fresh alternative on 28 June. The party's nominee for South Belfast, Michael O'Shea, suggested that people were unknowingly voting for "division, disorder and death" by "simply voting for their traditional party". He warned that such voters would have "no grounds for complaint, if the final insane curtain is running down on Northern Ireland amid sad scenes of violence, which could make 800 deaths and thousands of grievous injuries seem like children's play-acting".[87] Unlike most of its political opponents, the Alliance Party was not averse to issuing dire warnings about the possible scenario if the centre ground in Northern Irish politics were to remain small after the contest. Phelim O'Neill, who had defected from the Unionist Party over a year before, told a Belfast news conference held for the launch of his new party's manifesto, that such a pessimistic scenario would result in a growth in the demand for British withdrawal. O'Neill gloomily predicted that, "if Alliance does badly, I fear for the future of this Province".[88]

Alliance's main appeal for several thousands of less partisan voters was its commitment to the White Paper, which one of its candidates, Liam McCallum, maintained, actually reflected "in principle the suggestion put forward by the Alliance representatives at Darlington, and [which] naturally has our support".[89] The party also benefited from its publicity being reproduced at regular intervals in the *Belfast Telegraph*. One advertisement towards the end of the campaign advised electors that voting for a "Protestant" or "Catholic" party would only "help to build up the barriers of distrust", and declared that the new Assembly "needs Alliance in strength".[90]

A variety of other political groups were fielding candidates in this first Assembly election, though hopes for their success were relatively modest. Two Liberal candidates were standing on pro-White Paper tickets, and one of these, Berkley Farr in South Down, queried the desire for "peace" expressed by the majority of people in both sections of the community. Farr suggested that what they really meant when requesting "peace" was "merely unconditional surrender by the other side", and that, as a consequence, they were "prepared to turn a blind eye to the violence used by their own tribal fanatics".[91]

The Republican Clubs group was fielding 10 candidates in the contest. This party, set up as the political wing of the Official IRA which had disbanded in

1970, was campaigning on a class-based, non-sectarian programme. Seamus Lynch, standing in North Belfast, claimed he had received "considerable correspondence from many Protestant workers", eager to learn more about his party's social and economic policies; he went on to suggest that this proved the capability of his party to "destroy sectarianism".[92] In a subsequent statement, Lynch pointed out that his group was the only one composed in the main of working-class people and asserted that all of these other parties were "prepared to do a deal with the corrupt system". His party was "only interested in the welfare of the Irish working class and, as followers of James Connolly, we put that before everything else".[93] Some of the political rhetoric employed by Republican Club nominees would however have deterred many of the Protestant voters they were endeavouring to entice into their ranks. The party's candidate in West Belfast, Sean O'Hare, whilst distancing his group from the "tribal warfare" of the pro-Union parties, also pronounced that Britain was "our enemy" and that his party was prepared to "go straight at their political throats" – sentiments which would not have been obvious vote-winners on the nearby Shankill Road.[94]

The severely weakened Nationalist Party was making what would prove to be its last stand at a Northern Ireland election. A major plank of its policy was a demand for an immediate end to internment, which one of its candidates, James O'Reilly in South Down, claimed was the key issue in the contest. Party leader, Eddie McAteer, lambasted by the SDLP for standing again in Derry, also stressed the fundamental importance of this issue, and pointed to the "terrible connection" between internment and the current level of violence. McAteer "made no apology for putting this in the foremost of my election thoughts", because he realised that there would be "matching violence, for so long as the violence of internment continues in any form".[95] Many Catholic voters would have been alerted to a statement smuggled out of Long Kesh three days before the election, and duly published in the *Irish News*. Entitled, "Remember the pledge to the men behind the wire", the statement from the republican prisoners in Long Kesh pleaded with Catholic electors to abstain from voting. It went on:

> In their quest for personal power, it seems they [those standing for election] are prepared to sacrifice those presently interned … a vote for any candidate in the election is primarily a vote for Whitelaw and British policy here.[96]

A series of constituency "focus" reports provided *Belfast Telegraph* readers with a multi-dimensional picture of the highly varied electoral mood across Northern Ireland in the run-up to the election. During the first half of the campaign, there was a sense of apathy and election fatigue in several constituencies. William Simpson reported from the "deserted Antrim hills" between Cushendall and Ballycastle, which was "a part of the country where you find more sheep on the road than vehicles". There, 18 candidates were, in theory at least, contesting the 7 seats up for grabs, but with a fortnight to go to polling day, "a stranger could still be unaware such an event was pending", in a vast area where there were "few election posters" on display, and where in coastal resorts like Portrush and Ballycastle, there appeared to be more concern about the "lack of tourists" visiting the area than interest in the issues of the imminent election.[97] Two days later, Jim Davis's election report, "Bag of dolly mixtures in South Down", also had the theme of "studied apathy" regarding the contest. As with the following day's campaign report from Mid-Ulster, the main contributory factor to the contest's slow-burning nature was identified as the recent council elections, which had "exhausted all voting energy". Meanwhile Mid-Ulster was, of course, synonymous with tightly-fought and dramatic contests in the past, and the constituency was certainly "unusual", in that it possessed "the largest anti-unionist majority" in Northern Ireland.[98]

Subsequent articles during the second phase of the contest concentrated on the rather different atmosphere which prevailed in inner-city constituencies which had been sharply defined by years of violence. In North Belfast, "where the tears cut deepest", 18 candidates were contesting 6 seats in "peace-line country". In a district where there were "corrugated tin walls at the ends of the streets, keeping neighbour from neighbour's throat", it was "harder to love thy neighbour through a hail of bullets and gelignite" than it might have been in "the comparative security of a bar at the golf club".[99] A few miles away in west Belfast, home to the city's two largest cemeteries, "redevelopment and social problems" were the more important practical issues in people's lives. Voters there had been heavily "politicised by what they have come through", and were consequently "more likely than some other people to vote for policies instead of personalities".[100]

Another constituency report concentrated upon south Antrim, an area which had warranted considerable pre-election media attention on account of the opposition of several unionist candidates to party leader Brian Faulkner.

The *Belfast Telegraph*'s report, "Chameleon still showing colour", observed the extent of unionist in-fighting in the constituency, where nominees ranged from Austin Ardill, who had "once held high rank in Vanguard but has since changed his colour", and Anne Dickson who had, the paper suggested, been in a "dalliance" with the Alliance Party. The report concluded that the "big question" in South Antrim was "which colour of the chameleon will come out on top".[101]

Other constituency reports attempted to provide colourful, humorous accounts of local campaigns. From the border constituency of Fermanagh & South Tyrone, *Belfast Telegraph* reporter David Sloan observed "a touch of show business in the air". Here, an independent candidate, David Brien, was entertaining large crowds with his singing and guitar-playing style of electioneering. One of the jingles he performed contained his message to voters: "No clique, no clan – Vote for Brien, the wee fella's man!" In the same edition journalist Alf McCreary, who was following Alliance's push in North Down, focused on its candidate, Cecilia Linehan's, "neat gimmick" of playing Simon and Garfunkel's hit song, "Cecilia" at her election meetings. With its lyrics, "Oh Cecilia, you're breakin' my heart, you're shakin' my confidence daily!", this was a far from subtle attempt at undermining Faulkner and other unionist opponents. McCreary however dismissed its significance, suggesting it would "not put the Unionists out of tune in this area".[102]

June 1973 had been another bloody month in Northern Ireland's escalating conflict, with at least 29 people losing their lives. This violence took a number of forms, including IRA terror bombs and an acceleration of loyalist attacks on both Catholics and the security forces, as well as the grisly murder of prominent Catholic politician, Paddy Wilson. However, the heavy security presence provided at meeting halls and other political venues meant that electioneering activities proceeded more or less as usual.

Yet there were several major security incidents which would have shocked campaigners and voters alike. These included explosions in County Londonderry and County Tyrone. On 12 June, a bomb placed in a car close to Coleraine's railway station killed 6 people and injured several others (3 seriously).[103] The *Belfast Telegraph* described the incident in terms of "slaughter in an Ulster town". The *Irish News* also led with the story, however, although it had all the hallmarks of a Provisional IRA attack, the paper rather coyly suggested that, "until the truth emerges, everyone who addresses himself to the tragedy, will have his own answer to the culprits".[104] Although its editorial referred to "yesterday's holocaust of death in Coleraine", the paper's main story concerned loyalist paramilitaries who had been "shooting it out" with the army in Belfast.[105] Another large explosion occurred near Omagh on 25 June, when three IRA volunteers were killed in the act of transporting the device to another target.

If anything, tension had been growing on the streets of Belfast, with the emergence of another loyalist paramilitary group, the Ulster Freedom Fighters (UFF). This group was believed to have been involved in the murders of two young Catholic men in the city on 16 and 17 June and a few days later, two further attacks, this time of a tit-for-tat nature, also occurred in Belfast. This more pronounced engagement of loyalist paramilitary forces had also resulted in the death in east Belfast of a bus driver, when the vehicle he had been driving crashed following an exchange of gunfire between the UDA and the army; as well as prolonged shooting with the security forces across the Lagan, in west Belfast. In its report of the incident, the *Irish News* headline was "Shankill guns turn on Paras".[106] The newspaper believed that this "large scale" occurrence of loyalist violence had "a nightmare equality" about it, and maintained that the origins of such attacks on the law and order agencies of the British state were "grounded in the creation of this statelet".[107]

News broke a couple of days before polling of the brutal murder of Paddy Wilson, Gerry Fitt's election agent and a former Stormont Senator. Wilson and a female friend had been intercepted by a UFF gang outside Belfast and were subjected to a frenzied knife attack. The news genuinely shocked politicians as the campaign neared its climax, and quickly earned denunciations from numerous political spokesmen on both sides of the community (these included Brian Faulkner). The *Irish News* believed it was "providential" that the attack had occurred at "the end of the political protestations to the electors" and warned that "inflammatory words" from either side would "merely add to the public unease created by these two killings".[108]

"Ulster seeks her place in the sun …"

Election Day, on 28 June, fell on a day of glorious summer weather, which resulted in voters streaming to the polling stations. The *Belfast Telegraph*'s headline that day was "Ulster seeks her place in the sun", describing the contest as "the sunshine election".[109] Both the *Belfast Telegraph* and the *Irish News* were clearly fully aware of the election's significance, which the former described as Northern Ireland's "Day of Destiny", while the latter also judged it to be of "crucial" significance.[110] Party leaders were out and about throughout the day. Brian Faulkner braved hecklers once again on Belfast's Shankill Road, before motoring to South Down to cast his personal vote, whilst Gerry Fitt attended the funeral of his friend, Paddy Wilson, before heading off to vote in his North Belfast constituency.

The electorate totalled some 1,022,820 voters, and 219 candidates representing 15 parties were contesting the 78 Assembly seats. Of these candidates, 44 were from the UUP, 42 from the Loyalist Coalition (25 Vanguard and 17 DUP), 35 from the Alliance Party, 28 from the SDLP, 18 from the NILP and 10 Republican Club candidates. Over 120,000 postal votes, constituting around 12 per cent of those entitled to vote, had already sent in their preferences, and voting on the day was "expected to be very heavy and in some constituencies, it is believed, will reach 80 per cent of the electorate".[111] External interest in the election was considerable, with over 100 "global" media representatives applying for official accreditation. As well as this, on the eve of the election, an all-party Westminster working group of 16 MPs (8 Labour, 7 Conservative and 1 Liberal) had arrived in the Province, to observe procedures at a range of polling stations across Northern Ireland.

Local newspapers were of course keen to report the early declaration of results, as well as any other initial features or incidents which were election-related. One headline referred to the high number of electors – some 3,000 – who had destroyed their votes in West Belfast, and overall this figure was around 2 per cent of those opting to vote (approximately 14,000 in total, significantly higher than for British parliamentary elections).

The first successful candidates appear to have been Paddy Devlin and John Laird, both in Belfast constituencies, and the *Belfast Telegraph* also noted the impact of republican bomb attacks the previous day (these included explosions at Aldergrove airport, where ten people had to receive hospital treatment, as well as at a polling station in West Belfast).[112] The early analyses of the rival newspapers inevitably reflected their political leanings. In its first post-election edition, the *Irish News* reported that, "both the SDLP and the Craig–Paisley Coalition were confident late last night that they had given a good account of themselves".[113] The paper's headline on the following day was, "SDLP riding high for new Assembly", and the paper confirmed that the party were "on the way to yesterday's forecast of 18 seats". Many of these anticipated successes involved party stalwarts such as Gerry Fitt, John

Hume, Paddy Devlin, Austin Currie, Ivan Cooper and Paddy O'Hanlon. With the defeat of Eddie McAteer in Derry, the election had "spelled the death-knell of the once powerful Nationalist Party".[114] Once the majority of seats were confirmed, the mood of the *Belfast Telegraph* was considerably more downbeat than that of its nationalist rival. The paper suggested that a "shadow" had fallen over the new Assembly, and that the likely emergence of a "powerful block" of triumphant coalition candidates had cast "fresh doubts on whether the new Northern Ireland Assembly will work".[115]

Almost three-quarters (72.3 per cent) of those entitled to vote actually did so, with some constituencies registering close to 90 per cent turnouts. Although disappointed by the relatively weak performance of middle-of-the-road groups, the British government was cheered by the fact that no single party had been returned in sufficient strength to dominate the Assembly. The parties most pleased with their electoral fortunes were the SDLP and the Loyalist Coalition, with the Faulkner wing of unionism and the Alliance Party experiencing mixed fortunes.

Two-thirds of the candidates elected to the Assembly were, nominally at least, backers of the White Paper. The largest party supporting the government's recent initiative was the Unionist Party, which saw 23 candidates being returned to the Assembly, out of 41, who had pledged to back the party leader. Pro-Faulkner candidates won 191,729 votes, and gained in the process some 26.5 per cent of all votes cast. Eleven Unionist dissidents opposed to the White Paper were also successful (there had been an estimated 15 such candidates in total), winning 89,759 votes, which represented nearly one-eighth (12.4 per cent) of those who had cast their votes.

Over 35 per cent of all votes cast were for unionist or loyalist candidates opposed to the White Paper, with over 21 per cent backing the Loyalist Coalition of Vanguard and the DUP. Paisley's group fared slightly better than Craig's Vanguard, with nearly half of its 17 candidates (8) proving successful in a poll of 78,228 (some 10.8 per cent of the overall vote), compared to Vanguard's 7 electoral successes out of 25 nominees and share of the poll (75,759 votes or 10.5 per cent of the poll).[116] The SDLP were the other main "winners" in the election, and now formally assumed the mantle of voicing the opinions and concerns of the Catholic minority. The party won 159,773 votes, or 22.1 per cent of the poll, and managed to have 19 of its 28 candidates elected.

Although it managed to gain a sizeable number of seats (8) in the Assembly, as well as polling a respectable number of votes (over 66,000 which represented 9.2 per cent of those cast), the Alliance Party's performance was – considering its high hopes, large number of candidates (35) and expensive, high-profile campaign – somewhat disappointing, especially for Edward Heath and William Whitelaw, who had been anticipating a larger body of middle-ground opinion within the new chamber. Alliance had perhaps underestimated the threat posed to their electoral chances by the small number of remaining "liberal" unionists within the ranks of the Unionist Party – men like Roy Bradford, standing in East Belfast – who were known and respected in their communities, and whose basic appeal differed little from that of Alliance.

Yet the Alliance party's showing was substantially better than the poor performances of the Nationalist Party, Republican Clubs, NILP and the extreme loyalist groups. This motley combination of parties and groups only managed to return a single representative between them (David Bleakley in East Belfast), and despite fielding 10 candidates, the Republican Clubs won barely 13,000 votes overall. The party, which had been synonymous with the cause of Anti-Partition for decades, had failed to return a representative for the first time in half a century, and there would be no political voice for those responsible for the various paramilitary campaigns.[117]

There were several notable individual successes, including the large mandates enjoyed by SDLP leader, Gerry Fitt, in North Belfast, and by Unionist Party chief, Brian Faulkner in South Down – Faulkner won over 16,000 first-preference votes, more than double the number required to be returned at the first stage of the count. There was, notably, a surprising breadth of party representation in constituencies like East Belfast, where successful candidates included the DUP's Eileen Paisley, Oliver Napier of the Alliance Party and the NILP's David Bleakley.

Politicians did not underestimate the importance of their respective parties' degree of success in the contest which had just concluded, or of the other ramifications of the contest's outcome. An obviously jubilant Gerry Fitt pointed out that his party was now "clearly established as a major political force", and dedicated the SDLP to the task of "bring[ing] reconciliation and reform, and establish[ing] some sort of sanity in Northern political life".[118] In a later analysis, Faulkner's assessment of his own party's progress and that of other groups was, not surprisingly, a reflective and sanguine one. Conceding that the election of "a substantial minority" of Loyalist Coalition candidates represented "mixed results" for Ulster Unionism, Faulkner maintained that the "fear and suspicion [that] still existed" amongst loyalists meant that, in the aftermath of the contest, the Unionist Party realised that it "would have to tread cautiously, and reassure" disaffected loyalists.[119] However, despite his reservations over the results for his party, Faulkner celebrated the "decisive defeat" for "the men of violence". He wrote that "clearly the IRA of either wing did not represent the democratic voice of Catholic Ulster, and the SDLP was established as the party with which anyone wishing to accommodate the Catholic community would have to do business".[120]

The *Belfast Telegraph* gave a cautious welcome to the unfolding election results, observing that "no faction" could claim "a decisive mandate". The paper's editorial concluded that the Unionist Party could feel "satisfied" with its performance at the polls, though it also acknowledged the "strong appeal" represented by the Loyalist Coalition. The paper considered that the results constituted an "almost unqualified success" for the SDLP, which had shown that they represented "the vast majority of the minority". The party's successful "elimination" of extreme republicanism, as well as the "eclipse" of extreme loyalist candidates had proved to be "one of the most satisfying and hopeful outcomes of the poll". The paper did, however, stress the considerable "question mark hanging over the Assembly", and posed the conundrum: "How determined are the workers to work the Assembly and the wreckers to wreck it?"[121]

The following day's edition of the *Belfast Telegraph* concentrated on the dilemmas which lay ahead for the Unionist Party leader. Asking whether Faulkner would be able to "reach an accommodation with the waverers in his ranks", the paper also queried whether he would "project his sights towards the SDLP". The latter option would be far from easy, it suggested, and depended on the SDLP's willingness to "bargain", rather than "sticking by their almost impossible demands at the Northern conference table".[122]

As mentioned earlier, the clear overall mandate for the pro-White Paper groups and the apparent "victory of sorts" for Faulkner's Unionist Party were not quite what they seemed, and this became more obvious in the weeks and months following the election count. By the time the Assembly had its initial meeting, on 31 July, Faulkner could only rely on the votes of 20 colleagues.[123] Facing the Ulster Unionists were 27 members of the Loyalist Coalition, and so, in effect, Faulkner's party failed to represent a majority in the Assembly.

Brian Faulkner's leadership of his party became increasingly difficult and contentious, and he resigned in early January 1974, following the UUC's rejection of his stance on the controversial Council of Ireland proposal, which had been discussed at the Sunningdale Conference the previous month. This conference in Berkshire, involving both the British and Irish premiers, Edward Heath and Liam Cosgrave as well as the pro-White Paper parties in Northern Ireland, had also reached a determination on the composition of the proposed power-sharing Executive. Unionists would hold 6 of the 11 main Executive posts, with the SDLP and Alliance Party sharing the rest of the spoils (4 and 1 posts respectively). This new administration commenced its duties on 1 January 1974, when there was a radical shake-up in the nature of Belfast-based government. In the Executive headed by Brian Faulkner (his deputy was Gerry Fitt), significant posts of responsibility were now in the hands of unionism's fiercest opponents, including John Hume as minister of commerce and Paddy Devlin as minister for social security.

The practical setting-up of this Executive had an immediate impact upon the increasingly vociferous loyalist opposition parties in the new Assembly. Dissident Ulster Unionist, Harry West had formed an Ulster Unionist Assembly Party (UUAP) in early December and within days, nearly half of the Unionist MPs at Westminster had indicated they would back West rather than Faulkner as party leader. There was also tension within the Assembly itself, with verbal insults being hurled at pro-Unionist members of the Sunningdale delegation on 5 December and, in a more serious incident on 22 January, members being assaulted, when the parliamentary mace was seized and passed around the loyalist benches. That same day, Harry West replaced Brian Faulkner as Unionist Party leader, and another unionist coalition group, the United Ulster Unionist Council (UUUC) contested the February general election, when it took advantage of pro-White Paper and Sunningdale-backing parties failing to forge an effective election pact, and managed to win 11 of the 12 available seats (51.1 per cent of voters in a relatively low turnout would back their candidates).

Within a few months, another Northern Irish crisis was to consume the time and attention of another British administration, on this occasion, the third Labour Government under the leadership of Harold Wilson. The Ulster Workers' Council (UWC), a group representing loyalist workers and heavily backed by Vanguard leaders and other unionist politicians, called a general strike in Northern Ireland, resulting in factory and work closures, power cuts and the withdrawal of many public services. The province was brought to a standstill before Faulkner and his Executive resigned on 30 May 1974.[124]

Just as unionism would swing to the extremes in the period following the Assembly elections, so too would the SDLP – a party which had been formed to accommodate those with socialist and nationalist leanings – gravitate to the margins. Bad feeling and political disagreement between those representing the left, or "red" wing of the party (men such as Gerry Fitt and Paddy Devlin, representing urban constituencies) and those from a more conventional nationalist background (including Austin Currie, Paddy O'Hanlon and John Hume), would lead to splits in the party before the end of the decade, when the SDLP would advocate more stridently for Irish unity.

The 1973 Assembly election occurred during a period of intense civil disturbances, and indeed, there were several violent incidents during the month-long campaign. Hopes that the contest would herald the onset of a "new" and more "enlightened" political age for Northern Ireland had been high, and several indicators of change were certainly in place. A new type of legislature had been elected under a voting system of proportional representation not employed for nearly half a century, and many of the successful candidates in this election to a new Assembly came from new political parties which had evolved during the early phase of the conflict. In addition, there was little support for those representing the political wings of paramilitary groups, either at the ballot box or in any widespread adoption of the abstentionist tactics advocated by the leadership of the Provisional IRA. The election also saw the final demise of the North's old Nationalist Party and its replacement by the SDLP as the main voice of Catholic opinion, and witnessed further difficulties for the Unionist Party, which had dominated Northern political life for so long.

However, this "new" brand of politics had also been reflected in the considerable success enjoyed by the forces of more extreme unionism, as represented by the Loyalist Coalition of Vanguard and the DUP. Indeed, hopes held by the British government that the political voices of moderation – whether they came from Brian Faulkner's pro-White Paper wing of the Unionist Party, or from the SDLP, Alliance Party or NILP – would come out on top at the election, were to be dashed. Indeed, the early disillusionment of political moderates in the immediate aftermath of the Assembly election would swiftly turn into a more pronounced dismay, as violence continued to cause the implosion of Northern Ireland society, and there was a further hardening of tribal attitudes.

Endnotes

1. A. Parkinson, *1972 and the Ulster Troubles: A Very Bad Year* (Four Courts Press, Dublin, 2010), p. 88

2. *Ibid.*, p. 91

3. *Ibid.*, p. 102

4. *Ibid.*, p. 101

5. P. Bew and G. Gillespie, *Northern Ireland: A Chronology of the Troubles, 1968–93* (Gill & Macmillan, Dublin, 1993), pp. 60–1

6. P. Buckland, *A History of Northern Ireland* (Irish Books & Media, Dublin,1981), p. 166

7. The Vanguard movement announced that a new political party, the VUPP, would contest the elections.

8. J. Bardon, *A History of Ulster* (Blackstaff Press, Belfast, 1992), pp. 701–2

9. The small Northern Ireland Liberal Party was only fielding two candidates, but expressed its encouragement at the "ending of the one-party monopoly era". *Belfast Telegraph*, 12 June 1973

10. Linen Hall Library, Northern Ireland Political Collection, P3075

11. *Belfast Telegraph*, 5 June 1973

12. Unionist Party, "Peace, Order and Good Government": author's collection

13. *Ibid.*

14. *Ibid.*

15. *Ibid.*

16. *Belfast Telegraph*, 6 June 1973

17. *Belfast Telegraph*, 8 June 1973

18. *Ibid.*

19. Linen Hall Library, Northern Ireland Political Collection, P3716

20. *Ibid.*

21. *Belfast Telegraph*, 13 June 1973

22. *Irish News*, 15 June 1973

23. *Ibid.*

24. *Ibid.*

25. *Belfast Telegraph*, 18 June 1973

26. *Belfast Telegraph*, 13 June 1973

27. *Ibid.*

28. *Irish News*, 6 June 1973. Another editorial, over a week later, also urged the SDLP and indeed nationalist voters, to recognise the new Assembly as "a basis for power-sharing", which it believed "could develop into an enterprise of real success". *Irish News*, 14 June 1973

29. *Ibid.*

30. *Irish News*, 19 June 1973

31. *Ibid.*

32. *Belfast Telegraph*, 21 June 1973

33. *Ibid.*

34. *Belfast Telegraph*, 27 June 1973

35. *Irish News*, 6 June 1973

36. *Irish News*, 20 June 1973. The paper also triumphantly noted that, "the day of the share-out is coming".

37. *Irish News*, 5 June 1973. Glengall Street was the party's headquarters at the time.

38. *Ibid.*

39. *Irish News*, 8 June 1973

40. *Irish News*, 28 June 1973

41. *Belfast Telegraph*, 14 June 1973

42. *Belfast Telegraph*, 21 June 1973

43. *Belfast Telegraph*, 27 June 1973

44. *Irish News*, 28 June 1973

45. *Irish News*, 29 June 1973

46. *Irish News*, 28 June 1973

47. *Belfast Telegraph*, 25 June 1973

48. *Irish News*, 25 June 1973

49. *Irish News*, 2 June 1973. That day's edition of the *Belfast Telegraph* reported the claim of the major parties that the local council results had been "a massive rejection of the men of violence".

50. *Irish News*, 27 June 1973. One interesting exception was the Unionist Party, which had for so long been firmly backed by the *Belfast Telegraph*. There were few examples of Unionist Party advertisements in editions of the *Belfast Telegraph* during this contest.

51. *Irish News*, 6 June 1973

52. *Belfast Telegraph*, 25 June 1973

53. *Irish News*, 8 June 1973

54. *Belfast Telegraph*, 8 June 1973

55. B. Faulkner, *Memoirs of a Statesman* (Littlehampton Book Services Ltd, London, 1978), p. 196

56. *Belfast Telegraph*, 7 June 1973

57. *Belfast Telegraph*, 14 June 1973

58. Brian Faulkner, *Irish News*, 26 June 1973

59. Brian Faulkner, *Belfast Telegraph*, 8 June 1973. Faulkner also accused Vanguard of being engaged in talks with republicans about a potentially independent Ulster, and dismissed the chances of the DUP convincing the wider British public to "accept its peculiar vision of 'British Ulster' [in]to full fellowship with them".

60. *Belfast Telegraph*, 25 June 1973

61. *Belfast Telegraph*, 27 June 1973. Over a week before, another pro-Faulkner candidate, Maureen McClure (standing in North Down), had also insisted that the "driving of terrorism and fear from our streets" and the aim of "working constructively in the Assembly" should be accepted as the main priorities of elected unionist representatives.

62. *Belfast Telegraph*, 9 June 1973

63. *Belfast Telegraph*, 12 June 1973

64. *Belfast Telegraph*, 15 June 1973

65. *Belfast Telegraph*, 26 June 1973

66. *Belfast Telegraph*, 21 June 1973
67. *Belfast Telegraph*, 18 June 1973
68. *Belfast Telegraph*, 8 June 1973
69. Jim Rodgers, Vanguard candidate in East Belfast, *Belfast Telegraph*, 9 June 1973
70. *Belfast Telegraph*, 13 June 1973
71. *Belfast Telegraph*, 15 June 1973
72. *Irish News*, 4 June 1973
73. *Belfast Telegraph*, 16 June 1973
74. *Belfast Telegraph*, 15 June 1973
75. *Irish News*, 23 June 1973
76. *Belfast Telegraph*, 27 June 1973
77. Austin Currie, *Irish News*, 21 June 1973
78. *Irish News*, 12 June 1973
79. John Turnly, *Irish News*, 23 June 1973. Turnly, a former British Army officer, was later elected to the Northern Ireland Convention before defecting to the Irish Independence Party. He was shot dead by loyalist paramilitaries in County Antrim in June 1980.
80. *Irish News*, 15 June 1973; 25 June 1973. Various SDLP speakers also counselled against abstaining from voting. Mid-Ulster candidate, Stephen McKenna told his Omagh audience that "you cannot afford to abstain", as this strategy would only "hand seats to the unionists". *Irish News*, 23 June 1973
81. *Belfast Telegraph*, 4 June 1973
82. *Belfast Telegraph*, 9 June 1973
83. *Belfast Telegraph*, 25 June 1973
84. *Belfast Telegraph*, 20 June 1973
85. *Belfast Telegraph*, 16 June 1973
86. *Irish News*, 27 June 1973
87. *Belfast Telegraph*, 13 June 1973
88. *Belfast Telegraph*, 11 June 1973. The Alliance Party ambitiously set out to deliver 340,000 copies of their manifesto to households across Northern Ireland.
89. Liam McCollum, the Alliance Party's candidate in South Belfast, *Belfast Telegraph*, 8 June 1973
90. *Belfast Telegraph*, 26 June 1973
91. *Belfast Telegraph*, 18 June 1973
92. *Belfast Telegraph*, 8 June 1973
93. *Belfast Telegraph*, 18 June 1973
94. *Irish News*, 26 June 1973
95. *Irish News*, 22 June 1973
96. *Irish News*, 26 June 1973
97. *Belfast Telegraph*, 13 June 1973
98. *Belfast Telegraph*, 15 June 1973; 16 June 1973
99. *Belfast Telegraph*, 20 June 1973
100. *Belfast Telegraph*, 22 June 1973
101. *Belfast Telegraph*, 21 June 1973
102. *Belfast Telegraph*, 25 June 1973
103. Three of the fatalities came from the same family.
104. *Irish News*, 13 June 1973; *Belfast Telegraph*, 13 June 1973

105. *Ibid.*
106. *Irish News*, 12 June 1973
107. *Irish News*, 13 June 1973. On 18 June, the paper resumed its denunciation of loyalist extremists, who were "only helping the Provisionals in their campaign to destroy Northern Ireland".
108. *Irish News*, 27 June 1973
109. *Belfast Telegraph*, 28 June 1973
110. *Ibid.*, and *Irish News*, 28 June 1973
111. *Irish News*, 28 June 1973
112. *Belfast Telegraph*, 29 June 1973
113. *Irish News*, 29 June 1973
114. *Irish News*, 30 June 1973
115. *Belfast Telegraph*, 30 June 1973
116. A vital source of reference for those researching modern elections in Northern Ireland is the CAIN website: www.cain.ulst.ac.uk/issues/politics
117. Sinn Féin had opposed the calling of the election, and the handful of loyalists associated with the UDA polled badly.
118. *Irish News*, 30 June 1973
119. Faulkner, *op. cit.*, p. 197
120. *Ibid.*, p. 198
121. *Belfast Telegraph*, 29 June 1973
122. *Belfast Telegraph*, 30 June 1973
123. This was a combination of tragedy, parliamentary procedure and internal feuding. One pro-Faulkner Assemblyman, David McCarthy, was killed in a motor accident shortly after the election and Nathaniel Minford was appointed Assembly Speaker, therefore forfeiting his right to vote on parliamentary business. Additionally, other "official" unionists, including James Kilfedder and Austin Ardill, were fervently anti-White Paper.
124. Faulkner, who had formed the Unionist Party of Northern Ireland (UPNI) in 1974, was disillusioned with Northern Ireland's prospects and had accepted the offer of a peerage shortly before his death in a riding accident in 1977.

CHAPTER SIX

Election of a Hunger Striker
The Fermanagh & South Tyrone By-election, 1981

"A casualty of a perennial war"

The April 1981 Westminster by-election in Fermanagh & South Tyrone arguably generated more external media interest and debate than any other political contest which took place in the north of Ireland, and also produced one of Irish republican politics' most sensational victories, that of dying IRA hunger striker, Bobby Sands. Set against the backdrop of a society which was being torn apart by terrorism and sectarian murder, the involvement of a convicted republican paramilitary – campaigning on behalf of the rights of "political" prisoners – gained considerable media attention, and his election just over two weeks later would shock an increasingly fascinated national and international audience. On another, more local level, the by-election, and particularly its outcome, came to exemplify the depth of division within Northern Irish society at the time. Worn out by a decade or more of bitter conflict and frustration at the continuing political stalemate in the region's governance, the outcome of the vote illustrated that, even in the prevailing exceptional circumstances – when a convicted terrorist was the only political alternative to the Unionist Party's candidate – Catholic electors were reluctant to change the voting habits of a lifetime by voting for a representative of the unionist regime. Likewise, the election of unionism's sole opponent, a republican prisoner, showed the sterility of the Unionist Party's politics, and their inability to elicit meaningful electoral support from a Catholic minority increasingly alienated from the Northern Irish Ireland state.

Although the circumstances behind this contest were unusual, it would not be the first time that the North had experienced a hunger strike campaign, and indeed the constituency in question had its own history of returning "political" prisoners as Westminster representatives. Cahir Healy had been elected to represent Fermanagh & South Tyrone on two occasions during the 1920s, and another Sinn Féin prisoner, Phil Clarke, had been successful in an election in 1955. The hunger strike strategy had also been adopted by the IRA in the past, most notably by Terence McSwiney, Mayor of Cork, who had fasted to death in Brixton Prison in 1920. In addition, there had been two abortive attempts at "political fasting" in the decade preceding this 1981 contest.

The model for subsequent fasts in Northern prisons had been the hunger strike in Belfast's Crumlin Road Jail in 1972. At this relatively early stage of the Troubles, whilst those internees who had not been charged or convicted of acts of political terrorism were segregated from criminal inmates and allowed to wear their own clothing in Long Kesh Prison, those who had been convicted of "political" crimes were treated like ordinary criminals, made to wear prison uniform and to mix with other prisoners. Billy McKee, the leader of convicted IRA prisoners at Crumlin Road jail, led 40 of his comrades on a hunger strike which started in June 1972. They demanded the granting of special category status and, after a period of refusing to co-operate, the Northern Ireland Secretary, William Whitelaw eventually acceded to their request, resulting in the fast ending after 37 days. Whitelaw was concerned about the likely backlash which the deaths of hunger strikers would provoke, and he had also been hopeful that an IRA ceasefire was in the offing. However, continuing high levels of violence and the authorities' central focus on "criminalising" those responsible for "political" violence, which in turn led to the predominant role of the RUC in dealing with paramilitary forces, led within a few years to a different scenario. Following the establishment of the "no jury" Diplock courts in 1973, legal acknowledgement of special category status was removed, and by March 1976 all inmates of Northern Ireland's prisons were treated as "criminals".

The IRA's response to this policy of criminalisation and Britain's phased withdrawal of special category status was immediate. By the end of 1976 over 200 republicans were refusing to wear uniforms, and their comrades outside prison had started to target the prison officers, who were implementing the changes within the H-Blocks at the Maze Prison. Eighteen prison officers were killed between 1976 and 1980. This refusal to wear prison uniform was followed by the start of the "blanket protest" in 1977, which led in turn to the "no wash" and "dirty" protests of the late 1970s.

By 1980, an estimated 450 republicans were on the "blanket protest", and on 27 October that year, another hunger strike commenced, involving seven prisoners from different parts of the North, including the prison's IRA commanding officer, Brendan Hughes. The strikers had five specific demands, focusing around the rights to wear their own clothes, to receive regular visits, enjoy free association, the right to refuse to do prison work, and finally, the restoration of remission rights. The prisoners' early determination to see the strike through was apparent, as they pledged to, "put our lives in the hands of the Irish nation and [our] souls to the most high God".[1] The strike was expected to reach its conclusion around Christmas, and the potent symbolism of this timing was not lost on Hughes and his colleagues.

Negotiations between the prison authorities and the republican strikers had reached an advanced stage when Hughes, convinced that the British were on the verge of conceding to their demands, called off the strike on 18 December, when one of those on the fast, Sean McKenna, was given the Last Rites. It later transpired that the prisoners' demands had not been met by the British, and that the prisoners had been hoodwinked by the prison authorities. This strike ultimately failed because the prisoners were not prepared to be "the instruments of one another's deaths". When the "burden of the decision to allow one another to die became theirs", the republican strikers were unable to "bear [that] burden, and group cohesion collapsed".[2] Those who witnessed the confusion and unsatisfactory end to the fast – they included Bobby Sands, who had replaced Hughes as commanding officer in the Maze – would quickly learn from these organisational mistakes, including the strategy of adopting simultaneous fasts.

Within a day of the suspension of this hunger strike, an angry and frustrated Bobby Sands raised the question of sanctioning another fast, early in the New Year. Sands and a number of colleagues, both in the Provisional IRA (PIRA) and Irish National Liberation Army (INLA), were determined to proceed with a renewed fast, which would not backfire in the manner of Hughes' strike, and which would be more tightly organised and uncompromising in its tone. Although republicans remained wary of a second strike so soon after an aborted one, Sands and his associates reassured them that they would not expect the military campaign to be suspended – as it had been during the previous fast – and that there would be no embarrassing and potentially damaging retreat during its final stages.

On 5 February 1981, the prisoners announced their intentions of starting another hunger strike the following month, this time adopting the strategy of a string of selected volunteer prisoners joining the fast at fixed intervals. Again, the timing of the hunger strike was significant, as 1 March was the fifth anniversary of the beginning of the phasing out of special category status, and the strike's anticipated climax at Easter would evoke clear parallels with previous Irish revolutionaries and, of course, Jesus Christ. In a statement, the prisoners warned off well-meaning representatives of their own community, insisting that on this occasion, the outcome of the fast would, unless the authorities agreed to their demands, prove to be very different. They maintained:

> It needs to be asked openly of the Irish Bishops, Cardinal O'Fiaich, and of politicians like John Hume: what did your recommended ending of the last hunger strike gain for us? Where is the peace in the prisons which, like a promise, was held before dying men's eyes? And who but the British are responsible for our state, which is worse now than it ever was?[3]

Bobby Sands would soon lead his comrades on this new fast and in a diary entry, he admitted that he was "standing on the threshold of another trembling world", and asked God to "have mercy on my soul".[4] The hunger strike commenced on the first day of the new month, though its profile, especially in the national and international media, would remain low-key until the calling of a by-election in Fermanagh & South Tyrone.

Bobby Sands' background was far from being the conventional, inter-generational one of many republican figures. The eldest of four children, he was born in 1954 to parents who had not shown any interest in politics, and was brought up in a mainly Protestant area, Rathcoole, to the north of Belfast. As a youngster, Sands played in a religiously mixed soccer team and, rather bizarrely, participated in cross-country events with the Willowfield Temperance Harriers in loyalist east Belfast. He was not considered by his teachers to be academically gifted and, on leaving school in 1969, worked for short spells as a barman and apprentice coach-builder. Early in the Troubles, his family was intimidated out of the predominantly loyalist district in Rathcoole, and subsequently moved to the nationalist Twinbrook estate in west Belfast.

Sands is believed to have joined the Provisional IRA in 1972, and the following year, was charged for possessing handguns. He served a three-year sentence in Long Kesh where he struck up a friendship with another young republican, Gerry Adams. On his release from prison in 1976, Sands resumed his paramilitary activities, taking over the leadership of an IRA active service unit in his estate. Such activity resulted in his capture later that year for his involvement in a bomb attack at Dunmurry. This time, he was jailed for 14 years, which would mean that, by the time of his death at the age of 27, he had spent over a third of his life in prison.

In the H-Blocks, Sands soon became involved in the "blanket protest", and would eventually become the IRA's officer commanding within the prison. He was an avid reader – he was especially influenced by the writing of revolutionaries like Che Guevara and Camilo Torres – and, amongst other contributions to sustaining republican morale within the H-Blocks, he conducted impromptu Gaelic language classes and wrote poetry and articles for a republican magazine. A leading advocate of the renewed prison fast, Sands commenced his hunger strike on 1 March, with the next prisoner, Francis Hughes, due to follow him two weeks later.

Conscious of its potentially immense propaganda value, senior republicans encouraged Bobby Sands to keep a prison diary of his feelings and progress (inevitably, this was discontinued after 17 days). In some of his early, pre-hunger strike writings, Sands focused more on articulating the grievances of republicans within the prison. Arguing that it was his "political ideology and principles" which his captors sought to change, by "suppressing" his body and attacking his "dignity", he maintained that, "to accept the status of 'criminal' would be to degrade myself, and to admit the cause I believe in and cherish is wrong".[5] On the first day of his hunger strike, Sands described himself as "a political prisoner", who was "a casualty of a perennial war" which was being fought between "the oppressed Irish people and an alien, oppressive and unwanted regime that refuses to withdraw from our land".[6]

Much of Bobby Sands' prison writing was representative of the idealistic, moral-high-ground-seeking outpourings associated with many "political" prisoners. However, one piece of writing suggests that, for him at least, the hunger strike represented much more than merely a protest against prison rights and status, as this passage reveals:

> I am dying, not just to attempt to end the barbarity of H-Block
> or to gain the rightful recognition of a political prisoner but
> primarily because what is lost in here is lost for the Republic and

those wretched oppressed whom I am deeply proud to know as the risen people.[7]

The Fermanagh & South Tyrone seat had been held by Frank Maguire, an independent Nationalist, since the October 1974 general election, when he had successfully defeated the challenge of Unionist, Harry West, with a majority of just under 5,000. Maguire had been conspicuous by his extremely low profile at Westminster and rare visits to the Commons. His sudden death on 5 March 1981 precipitated the calling of an early by-election. Community engagement in local politics had traditionally been intense in this constituency, which often boasted of the highest electoral turnouts in the United Kingdom. More significantly, with a built-in Catholic, or nationalist, majority of around 5,000, it was a constituency which had always voted along sectarian lines.

The decision on 26 March to put the name of the leader of the hunger strikers on the ballot paper – as an "Anti-H-Block/Armagh Political Prisoner" – was however not without its dangers. Apart from being an outsider in an area where candidates tended to be known locally, Sands' candidature was "a dangerous high-wire act", with the "potential … for political embarrassment" if there was a setback at the forthcoming polls. It was also virgin territory for nationalists, at least in the modern Troubles, to "vote en masse for somebody who was associated with the armed struggle", and it was far from certain how moderate Catholics would decide to vote.[8] Although some writers have suggested that this by-election represented a conscious attempt by Sinn Féin to add a further political dimension to its military campaign, it is more likely that, in allowing Bobby Sands to stand under an "Anti-H-Block", and not a Sinn Féin, ticket, the chief aim was to maximise a ready opportunity to "dramatically publicise the hunger strike, and put severe pressure on the British government".[9] However, in the putting forward of Sands' name, and more particularly, in the light of his subsequent success, republicans had "[made] it possible, much sooner than anyone had imagined, for Sinn Féin to fully embrace electoral politics".[10]

To stand or not to stand …
A statement from Bernadette McAliskey (née Devlin), confirming that she would postpone her plans to stand in the Fermanagh & South Tyrone constituency for the forthcoming by-election and instead back a republican

prisoner, was followed by the "surprise announcement", that Bobby Sands was allowing his name to be put forward as an "Anti-H-Block/Armagh Political Prisoner" candidate.[11] Sinn Féin's support of Sands was unequivocal. A party spokesman said that Sands' participation in the contest provided the electorate with, "the opportunity of quantifying their support for the political prisoners in Armagh Prison and the H-Blocks of Long Kesh", as well as offering the chance of clearly rejecting, "British attempts to criminalise opposition to their presence in this country".[12]

Announcing the candidature of a hunger striker (Bernadette McAliskey was Bobby Sands' proposer), who was destined to be 40 days into his fast by the time of Election Day, was by no means a risk-free strategy on the part of republicans. Writing some time later, journalist Kevin Rafter pointed out that, "should Sands be nominated but fail to win, there was no telling the damage the result would do, not only to the prison campaign but also to morale in the wider republican movement".[13] Despite the small Catholic majority in the constituency, there was no certainty that things would fall into place for Bobby Sands. Abstentionism by less hard-line Catholics, wary of being associated with a representative of republican paramilitary violence, as well as local antagonism against outsiders, who had been responsible for persuading a respected local person, Noel Maguire to stand aside for Sands, were genuine obstacles in the way of harnessing support for him across the local Catholic community.

This "persuasion" of the local candidate not to run was the subject of much rumour and allegation. Republican determination to strive for a political mandate was strong and as Nomination Day drew closer, hard-line republican resentment towards Noel Maguire's candidature grew in its intensity. The degree and nature of such "pressure" – and especially whether physical intimidation was employed – is uncertain. However, one particularly strong rumour was that emotional pressure was applied on Nomination Day itself, when Noel Maguire was reported to have made his mind up not to proceed, following a telephone conversation with the mother of Bobby Sands.

Much of the justification for Sands being put forward for the by-election, as well as the rationale given for voting in favour of the H-Blocks prisoner, centred round the argument that to do so undoubtedly would help to save his life. The premise behind this claim was insufficiently challenged by Catholic opinion-makers, who apparently refrained from pointing out that such claims might be regarded by many external observers as naïve and irrational. For a hunger striker almost six weeks into his fast, time was not on the side of Bobby Sands, or indeed, of the British authorities. It was also highly unlikely that an uncompromising administration like that led by Margaret Thatcher would concede the legitimacy of the hunger strikers' claims, in the event of a Sands victory.

Both the *Belfast Telegraph* and the *Irish News* speculated on the likely response at Westminster if Sands were to emerge victorious on 9 April. The *Belfast Telegraph* asked the question, "if Sands did win a seat, can a prisoner become a MP?", and retraced the history of political involvement by previous IRA prisoners, as well as discussing the mood at Westminster on the issue.[14] Several days later, the *Irish News* pointed out that Bobby Sands' eligibility could "only be challenged if a motion was passed by a majority of MPs".[15] The *Belfast Telegraph*, in a later edition, suggested that the forthcoming election would prove to be "a bizarre affair", which would probably focus on "dealing in realities as far removed from the Westminster forum as the constituency itself is".[16] In this leading article, entitled, "What choice?", the paper reminded its readers of the eccentric electoral practices in this seat in previous contests, including the most recent one in 1979. It explained that, "such absurdities are nothing new, in a place where voters have previously elected a MP, whose chief claim to fame was that he never uttered a word in Parliament on their behalf".[17] Despite its apparently cynical tone, the *Belfast Telegraph* conceded the likelihood of an "emotive republican campaign", regretting the position that many Catholic electors would soon find themselves in. The editorial went on:

> It must be deeply offensive to many anti-unionists, that their only choice is a candidate who is serving a prison sentence for firearm offences, and who purports to be commanding officer of the IRA inmates of the Maze, whose objectives have been shown repeatedly as having no political support in the community at large.[18]

The temporary and provisional nature of republican prisoners' involvement in the North's political process was highlighted, not only in the uncertain nature of Sands' entry into the election, but also by the ambiguity surrounding his actual participation in the contest, which persisted until the close of nominations on 30 March. Sands' friend and political advisor,

Gerry Adams, and his election agent and eventual successor as MP for the constituency, Owen Carron, were sitting in a car outside Dungannon electoral offices, anxiously awaiting the arrival of Noel Maguire who was about to withdraw his nomination. So close was the call on this, that Adams had actually put already together a statement anticipating Maguire's failure to comply with their request to stand down, and was instead prepared to announce Sands' own withdrawal from the contest.

Once the uncertainty over his participation had been sorted, Sands expressed his determination to continue with his political quest. In a note smuggled out to "Brownie" (Gerry Adams) on 2 April, Sands wrote:

> Seems like we've well and truly entered new realms. Hopefully we'll be successful, if only for the Movement's sake. Feel myself getting naturally and gradually weaker. I will be very sick in a week or two, but my mind will see me through.[19]

The previous day Sands had, through Carron and the rest of his election team, issued a statement, thanking Noel Maguire and the SDLP for withdrawing from the contest, and, "allowing the focus of national and world media to spotlight the present hunger strike and general plight of Britain's political prisoners".[20] In another part of the same statement, he stressed that there was "but one issue at stake" in the contest, and that was "the right of human dignity for Irishmen and women, who are imprisoned for taking part in this period of the historic struggle for Irish independence".[21] Sands also expressed his "abhorrence" at the region's sectarian divisions and promised that the Protestant community had "nothing to fear from me as a republican".[22] Although he was directly addressing Northern Ireland's Protestants in this press release, there can be no doubt that Sands' advisers were more concerned about the impact of these apparently mild and conciliatory words on wavering Catholic voters. This non-confrontational approach encapsulated the message of the H-Blocks candidate and his electoral appeal, and it eventually persuaded many middle-of-the-road Catholics to make a departure from their normal patterns of voting, and to vote in this case with their hearts. There would be no call to back the armed struggle, and the simplicity of Bobby Sands' message – support the prisoners and help to save their lives – appeared to strike a chord right across the Catholic community.

A major feature of interest for the media was the speculation in both political camps over not only the actual candidates, but also over those who would not be standing for election. Parties, which might have had largely shared views on the constitutional issue but which were experiencing in their ranks considerable political infighting and personal hostility, were frantically endeavouring to ascertain whether "Unity" candidates were a feasible option for this contest. One *Belfast Telegraph* journalist observed that, "as wheeling and dealing no doubt continues over the weekend, parties from both sides of the political trenches are querying if there is really such a thing as a unity candidate". That Monday afternoon was the last chance for candidates to withdraw their nomination papers, and it was anticipated that, "some parties would have their spies on the electoral office doorway, in case of tail-end switches".[23]

Most of this last moment political manoeuvring occurred within nationalist-leaning parties. The SDLP's active participation in the contest was widely anticipated, and one *Belfast Telegraph* report had speculated that the party was ready to "enter the fray" and would be "selecting a candidate tomorrow night".[24] The experienced politician, Austin Currie, was expected to contest the seat, but rumours of his imminent withdrawal circulated a couple of days later, when the paper's headline read, "Currie denies deal on vacant seat", with much speculation that he would "stand down if Noel Maguire contests the seat".[25] The following day, it was confirmed that not only was the SDLP declining to field a candidate but that Noel Maguire, the brother of recently-deceased Westminster representative, Frank Maguire, had withdrawn his candidature minutes before the deadline. Noel Maguire explained that his last-minute decision to withdraw from the contest had been "a matter of conscience", maintaining it had been "the only way of saving Sands' life".[26]

Clearly the withdrawal of Austin Currie was bound to lead to accusations of political cowardice and skulduggery on the SDLP's part, with claims that the party was "selling out" to pressure from other nationalist groups. This issue also had exposed considerable differences of opinion within the SDLP, as well as touching the party's ultra-sensitive "green" nerve-ends. Currie himself admitted that he felt "unhappy" about his party's decision, while former, now estranged, party leader, Gerry Fitt, was more outspoken in his criticism.[27] Fitt described it as, "a shame, an outrage and a gross betrayal of non-unionist voters in this constituency", and concluded that these electors had been "denied the opportunity of voting for an anti-unionist candidate".[28] Ivan Cooper joined Fitt, Paddy Devlin and Austin Currie, in querying the party's decision not to stand in the constituency. Cooper, a founder member of the party, dismissed its central body's decision as "a betrayal of a lot of decent people", who had "supported our policies of non-sectarianism".[29] Nor would this internal storm quickly die down. Seamus Mallon was quick to defend his party leader and to castigate his internal critics, maintaining that their interventions had "clearly portrayed them as political poodles snapping at the head of a mastiff".[30] What, then, had motivated the SDLP to make such a controversial move? Some suggested it was a matter of the party's executive bowing to pressure at local level, though the interpretation of others was that the party had simply gone for the least confrontational option by withdrawing from the contest.

Unionist reaction to this turnaround in SDLP thinking was mixed. Austin Currie's long-standing political sparring partner, John Taylor, was unambiguous in his condemnation of the SDLP's instruction to Currie to stand down, describing this as "a surrender to republican extremism", which only illustrated that the party was "controlled by green republicans".[31] The *Belfast Telegraph* however was more circumspect in expressing its opinions.[32] The paper articulated its "regret" that the SDLP would not be challenging Bobby Sands in the forthcoming by-election, but believed this was "consistent" with their approach at the previous general election, when Austin Currie (standing as an independent) had been defeated by Frank Maguire. Implicit criticism was, however, evident in the article's concluding remarks concerning the SDLP's degree of culpability for the eleventh-hour drama on Nomination Day. The newspaper suggested that "the best that can be said for the SDLP is that their decision was taken before Mr Maguire's brother, Noel, dramatically withdrew his nomination at the last minute".[33]

For several days, the headlines in the *Irish News* had focused on the speculation surrounding the potential withdrawals of nominations by nationalist-leaning candidates. As late as 28 March, the paper led on the news that, despite "a day of rumours", the by-election field was "unchanged". The previous day, Noel Maguire had told the press that he was "still in the field, and I am there to stay". The *Irish News* conceded the "divergence of opinions within the leadership" of the party, and would return to its non-engagement in the contest several times during the following week's coverage.[34] Its headline on 6 April was, "Fight every seat – Currie", when the over-ruled senior party member appeared satisfied after a meeting of the party's executive. Austin Currie insisted that, "all recriminations over the absence of an SDLP candidate would now cease".[35] Although the SDLP was undoubtedly doing its belated best to patch up these internal differences, there remained the thorny issue of who the party's faithful in Fermanagh & South Tyrone should vote for on 9 April. John Hume's characteristically tetchy and slightly ambiguous response to this dilemma failed to provide traditional nationalists with clear advice for polling day. Hume explained in an interview that, "if one isn't in the field, one should not be giving advice from the sidelines". He tried to reassure party supporters that they would not find themselves in such a tricky predicament again, pledging that, "never again will there be any pressure on the SDLP to agree to such a [Unity] candidate", and declaring that the removal of such an "albatross" had been the "one positive outcome of the last week".[36]

"An unusual election"
Bobby Sands' publicity officer was the well-known figure of Bernadette McAliskey, a former Westminster MP, who was also at the time recovering from an assassination attack by loyalist paramilitaries. In the physical absence of their named candidate, the public soon came to regard McAliskey as the face of the republican prisoner's short campaign. McAliskey who, a decade earlier, had been a leading figure within the People's Democracy movement, had re-emerged from a lengthy period on the political sidelines. In a revealing interview at the time, she expressed her ongoing antipathy to the RUC for stopping her on "election business", and also stressed that the "one single issue" in the election was that of prisoners' rights and political status, rather than that of the armed struggle. As McAliskey put it, the electorate had to "declare to the Government that they are not prepared to let Sands die in prison for five just demands".[37] Described as "the driving force behind the campaign", the former civil rights agitator cut "a striking figure, as she hobbles her way around on crutches". Indeed, it was suggested that it was "like old times for Mrs McAliskey, who is the obvious focal point for media attention in the run-up to this unusual election".[38]

The uncertain circumstances which had accompanied Sands' confirmation of his candidature, along with the dearth of existing political machinery at the behest of his new, temporary group, and the brevity of the election contest, combined to produce an inevitably frenetic campaign. Despite these disadvantages, the enthusiasm and hard work of a large group of election volunteers – many of them were republicans, who had flocked in to Enniskillen and Dungannon from across Ireland – soon had the effect of concentrating, and even galvanising, republican fervour in the border constituency. Opposition was to come from both nationalists and unionists in Enniskillen. The circumstances which had led to the hasty withdrawal of local candidate Noel Maguire had irked many nationalists, including one Enniskillen shop owner, who declined to offer his premises as an election headquarters for Sands' campaign. Political opponents and members of the security forces reacted with some hostility to the campaign, and were suspected of removing many of the "Vote Sands" posters erected around the towns and villages of the constituency. Gerry Adams, the Sinn Féin vice president, pronounced himself shocked by the virulent response by loyalists to his participation on Sands' account. Despite all of this, there was a growing belief amongst the Sands' election team that they were making significant progress.

An early decision in the campaign had been to appoint a relative unknown, Owen Carron, as Sands' election agent. Carron, who barely knew Sands before meeting him in prison, would be the crucial conduit between the "hidden" candidate and the electorate, making several journeys between the Maze Prison, outside Belfast, and his election nerve-centre in Enniskillen. Carron would provide updates to journalists on Sands' worsening condition, as well as passing on his candidate's appeals to voters. Following a visit to the Maze on 7 April, Owen Carron told reporters that Bobby Sands weighed barely eight stone and was growing weaker, but had asked voters to "ignore Unionist calls for Nationalists to boycott the election".[39]

Central to the Sands' campaign were the claims, from both the candidate and his election team, of alleged harassment and intimidation, which had apparently taken place just before and during the campaign. Such was their concern that they would not receive fair treatment in the closing stages of the contest, that McAliskey and her colleagues contacted several Labour peers, Amnesty International and a group of European lawyers, inviting them to Enniskillen to inspect the conduct of the security forces.[40] Sands' election team had also been thwarted in their requests for prison permits for election workers (the Northern Ireland Office turned down 23 of these, allowing only 1 for Owen Carron as Sands' election agent).[41] Towards the end of March, complaints were made that Sands had been moved from his prison cell to the hospital at the Maze to "isolate him from his comrades", rather than on medical grounds, but it was the refusal to provide the imprisoned candidate with the usual media access during an election which provoked most republican fury. Sands' election team clearly realised that the sight of a deteriorating hunger striker speaking from his hospital bed in the Maze Prison would have a dramatic impact upon a television audience, especially on those Catholics reluctant to vote for paramilitaries, but liable to be moved by the sight of a dying Catholic prisoner. McAliskey, Carron and their colleagues had considered making an application to the High Court in an attempt to give their candidate broadcasting access, but hopes were dashed due to the shortage of available time and the government's rejection of such a request on the eve of the election.[42]

Given the unavailability of their parliamentary candidate, the Anti-H-Block group's campaign relied heavily upon advertisements in the local press, and on the staging of a handful of political rallies in towns and villages, including at Enniskillen, Lisnaskea and Coalisland. At a meeting at the last location, on the eve of polling day on 8 April, Bernadette McAliskey and another former MP, Frank McManus were the chief speakers.[43] Election literature was crucially important for Sands' election team. This tended to play down the paramilitary status of the candidate and his prison comrades, and there were no direct references to the IRA's ongoing campaign. The spontaneous and one-off nature of the intervention in this contest of the "Anti-H-Block/Armagh Political Prisoner" candidate was highlighted in this extract from a campaign leaflet:

> The blanket men and the women prisoners are *borrowing* this election in an attempt to illustrate your support for the prisoners and your opposition to the British government. Bobby Sands' intervention in this election permits the basis of the broadest possible platform for unity among those people who oppose unionism and British rule. His life and his comrades' lives can be saved if you elect him.[44]

Another advert, composed by the Republican Press Centre working in conjunction with Sands' campaign team, was most likely designed to stress that Sands' initiative, both in being the first hunger striker this time and in his decision to stand for Parliament, had the unqualified support of his fellow republican prisoners in the Maze. In this advert, the latter gave their "warm welcome" to Sands' participation in the political contest, which would give them the chance to "show that the Republican movement commands support". This statement on behalf of republican prisoners also emphasised that the contest provided the electorate with an "excellent opportunity" to display their "revulsion at the callous, immoveable British attitude", which, they maintained, was the cause of the prison protest, and which "could lead to the death of the hunger strikers".[45]

Few well-known, mainstream politicians were prepared at the time to openly back Sands at rallies or in press conferences. One exception was the quixotic figure of Neil Blaney, an independent TD for Donegal, who had long been an outspoken critic of British policy in the North, dating back to his alleged involvement (with Charles Haughey) in gunrunning to the North in 1970. Blaney had spoken at a press conference in Enniskillen on 3 April, when Bobby Sands' manifesto was launched. His participation prompted an subsequent intervention by Sands' election opponent, Harry West, who condemned Blaney's "unwarranted intrusion" into Northern Ireland's constitutional affairs. Blaney responded to such criticism the following day, when he argued that a vote for Sands was "a vote against the institutionalised violence" of the Maze Prison. He also pointed out, correctly as it transpired, that a victory in the by-election would have "an immense effect internationally and would do more for the H-Blocks issue than ten years of discussion at the European Parliament".[46] In a further contribution, this time at an Anti-H-Block rally in Lisnaskea on 5 April, Neil Blaney dismissed Gerry Fitt's advice to wavering nationalist voters to abstain during the forthcoming contest. Blaney somewhat obliquely suggested that, "a vote for Bobby Sands is a vote against violence".[47]

Official Unionist leader, James Molyneaux was criticised for his "indecent haste" in demanding a swift by-election following Frank Maguire's death, and the unionist's call for a speedy electoral contest appeared to have ultimately backfired on him. Official Unionists were also accused of "a calculated attempt" to "regain lost ground amid the hysteria surrounding the Paisley rallies".[48] Molyneaux believed that Ian Paisley's strategy of copying the historical precedent of Sir Edward Carson, in holding rallies across Ulster – in this instance as a protest against the British government meeting its Irish counterparts a few months before – held the potential for street violence, and would prove to be unpopular with unionist voters. The Official Unionist leader felt that the early selection of a well-known candidate in Fermanagh & South Tyrone would boost his party's chances of electoral success. However, Molyneaux's intervention ultimately "opened the door for the politicisation of the republican movement, and for the eventual entry of Sinn Féin into electoral politics".[49]

The importance of agreeing on a widely acceptable candidate in this constituency was as crucial for unionists as it had been for nationalists. The selection of Harry West, a former Unionist Party leader and Westminster MP for the constituency, and a vastly experienced politician, deterred the entry into the contest of the DUP's Roy Kells, a former UDR officer, who pulled out of the field on hearing of West's intentions. Press speculation was rife that, despite the fact that only one unionist candidate was actually standing, divisions amongst the various factions of unionism would result in a split and possible abstentions on the part of some Protestant voters. The *Belfast Telegraph* reported that both the DUP and UUP were "keeping tight-lipped about their plans" as, "neither party offered any immediate support" to Harry West.[50] Indeed, there were rumours that Paisley had been endeavouring to establish behind-the-scenes discussions which would result in an alternative unionist candidate with broader appeal than the Official Unionist choice, and just a few days later, the DUP were claiming that the Northern Ireland Office had "pressed Harry West into running".[51] Although there would be no further nominations of unionist candidates, all was not well in the relations between loyalist groups in the constituency, and an "uproar" was reported in Fermanagh District Council on 7 April, when Unionist Party councillor, Raymond Ferguson refused to distinguish between the tactics of Bobby Sands and the DUP, which he lambasted for organising "hillside demonstrations", which would have the effect of deterring foreign investment in the region.[52]

Despite his considerable experience – he had been contesting elections in the province since 1954, and had represented the constituency briefly at Westminster before losing to Frank Maguire in October 1974 – West admitted that this campaign was, by some distance, the "oddest" one he had fought. West had identified attitudes to security and the prison system as being the dominant issues in the by-election, and it was probably the combination of a scarcity of actual policy issues and the absence of the normal cut-and-thrust debate engendered by the respective campaigns of election rivals (inevitable, given that the only other candidate was literally dying in prison), which resulted in West's rather tired, low-key campaign.[53]

A number of the Unionist Party candidate's statements centred on the fact that he was advocating a policy of non-violence. Unusually, for a candidate accustomed to participating in the rough-and-tumble of party accusations and counter-accusations in a border constituency, West appealed not just to his party's traditional supporters but also to the wider electorate, to "all the people, Catholic and Protestant, Unionist and non-Unionist, to come out as responsible Christian people and show that they are absolutely opposed to violence of all forms".[54] Two days earlier, he had also appealed to electors' "common sense" in ensuring that "we don't get the reputation of having an IRA man as our MP".[55]

Most of West's relatively few campaign statements and speeches were restricted to attacking his opponent's membership of the IRA and the threat to security which this posed. In asking nationalist voters to "look at their own consciences", West denounced Bobby Sands' candidacy as, "an attempt by the IRA to gain endorsement of their policies of murder and blackmail".[56] He also stressed the "intellectual dishonesty" evident in his opponent's campaign, particularly in its emotional appeal to the nationalist electorate to save Sands' life. West went on:

> In all the statements of Mrs McAliskey and Mr Neil Blaney, there was not one expression of regret for the victims of the terrorist campaign. There are at least 100 families in this constituency who have lost loved ones as a result of vicious attacks by the evil organisation of which Sands is a leader, not to mention the maimings and tremendous destruction of property.[57]

This direct appeal to the Catholic community was, on the whole, new territory for Ulster Unionists in a border constituency like Fermanagh & South Tyrone. On 6 April, the (Official) Unionist Party leader, James Molyneaux called for SDLP voters to back the Unionist candidate, while other leading figures within unionism, as well as unionist-leaning journals like the *Belfast Telegraph*, joined in offering advice. John Taylor, who was campaigning actively for West, bluntly asserted that the result of the forthcoming election would, "reveal what percentage of the Catholic electorate is prepared to identify with the PIRA's campaign".[58] A *Belfast Telegraph* editorial lamented the "stark choice" facing Catholic electors, and returned to the theme of the SDLP's responsibility for the "debacle" which had surrounded the nomination of nationalist candidates and the party's "outmanoeuvring" by Sands' group. The editorial concluded by "heartily endorsing" a response of Catholic abstentionism on polling day, and this option was also approved by Harry West, who predicted "numerous" abstentions by Catholics on 9 April.[59]

The Unionist Party's candidate's final appeal to nationalist electors was an emotional one. He insisted that he could "not see these people [Catholic neighbours of Protestant families who had lost relatives in IRA attacks] going to the polling station and walking past their neighbours, to vote for a man who belongs to an organisation which has committed such atrocities".[60]

Less than seventy-two hours before Election Day, a brutal murder took place in Londonderry, when an enumerator, Joanne Mathers, who had been collecting census returns, was shot by the IRA. It would be a reflection of the apparent success of Bobby Sands' election team, in managing to persuade Catholic voters to distinguish between the issues of the armed struggle and the more immediate one of the fate of individual hunger strikers, that the execution of this female civil servant by their armed colleagues did not result in a reduction of support for the "Anti-H-Block" candidate. The following day in Parliament, there was cross-party consensus both on this latest killing and the candidature of Sands in the imminent election. Shadow Northern Ireland Secretary Don Concannon maintained that a vote for Bobby Sands would prove to be, "a vote of approval for the perpetrators of the La Mon massacre, the murder of Lord Mountbatten and the latest brutal and inhuman killing of Mrs Mathers".[61]

During the penultimate day of their respective campaigns, the two candidates issued their final statements. Bobby Sands had been visited in prison by Owen Carron on 8 April, after which he reported that Sands was feeling "tired and [was] getting weaker". In a swipe at his opponent, Sands expressed his "amusement" at West's appeal for Catholic support as he "personified Unionist sectarianism and 60 years of Partition". He was "very angry" at being denied access to television and radio interviews, claiming he was being "denied my rights as a candidate." Maintaining that Northern Ireland Secretary Humphrey Atkins had been in "collusion" with West "before and since Nomination Day", Sands argued, with some justification, that the British media were "afraid" of allowing "a tortured prisoner the means of revealing the horrors" of life inside the H-Blocks. However he also expressed his "confidence" that the electorate of Fermanagh & South Tyrone would "not let the prisoners down". Sands suggested that he could manage to be their MP for "approximately two weeks", which, he maintained, would be "better than having Harry West for two years".[62]

Meanwhile, West, who spoke to a small audience in Enniskillen town centre, reminded voters that the key issues were "far from the usual party wrangling across the traditional divide", and urged Catholics to "consider how your vote would be used by the ruthless propaganda machine of the PIRA to promote and intensify terrorism, blackmail and killing".[63] The *Belfast Telegraph*, sensing that tides of high emotion were in danger of drowning out clear-headed political reflection, also appealed to nationalist voters during the campaign's final days. Referring to the "emotional appeal of saving a life" in order to "change the British Government's attitude to the H-Block protests", the paper insisted that such a response would be "completely misguided", as the minds of Margaret Thatcher's administration were "irrevocably made up", and concluded by saying that "only Mr Sands and his 'godfathers', regardless of the election result, can save lives".[64]

In the hours before the dawn of Election Day, Bobby Sands' election team and supporters remained busy. A pirate radio station, "H-Block Armagh", was reported to be transmitting in the Fermanagh area; a hunger strike rally was staged in west Belfast; and Bernadette McAliskey would address another rally in Coalisland.

Although the respective parties expressed their optimism on 9 April, most neutral observers conceded that it would be a close-run contest. The 100-mile long constituency stretched from Lough Neagh to the Donegal border, and had a traditional pattern of highly engaged voting: in 1979, for example, albeit under less controversial circumstances, 88.9 per cent of the electorate had turned out to vote. Whilst in purely sectarian terms, there was a Catholic majority of 5,000 in the constituency, this would not necessarily transfer itself into pro-Sands votes, as a large number of electors were expected to abstain.

A heavy security presence was reported at the 47 polling stations across the constituency, where 180 election staff reported for duty. These staff, as well as representatives from both parties, were "watching, eagle-eyed, for dead citizens whose passion for voting from the grave was a byword in

Fermanagh & South Tyrone".[65] The hours of voting had been extended to provide all legitimate electors the opportunity of casting their vote, with the polling stations open from 7.00 a.m. to 10.00 p.m. – three hours longer than in the recently-held local council elections.

The *Belfast Telegraph* confidently anticipated "a high turnout", and its front-page report showed electors casting their votes in the "bright midday sunshine" in Dungannon town centre.[66] Although a few media pundits had put their necks on the line by making clear predictions of the election's outcome, most remained cautious.[67] A report in the *Irish News* the next morning maintained that, "all that could be said with certainty at the close of the polling stations in Fermanagh & South Tyrone last night was that there had been an exceptionally heavy turnout".[68] Reporting that both sides "appeared confident of victory" by the end of polling, the paper concluded that "the result hinges on spoiled poll papers", the extent of which would "decide whether Sands could hold off West's challenge".[69]

"A virus infection of the system"

Once polling had been completed, speculation that Bobby Sands had pulled off a major victory began to spread during a seven-hour count at Enniskillen Technical College. This growing belief, that the IRA prisoner had clinched a remarkable victory, was based on the high turnout of voters and on the fewer than anticipated spoiled votes. The percentage of pollsters casting their vote was only marginally down on the 1979 election, and the high figure – 86.8 per cent – dashed any remaining unionist hopes that significant numbers of uncertain Catholic electors had stayed away from the polling booths. As well as this, the lower than anticipated number of spoiled votes – a total of 3,280, or 5 per cent of the total electorate – suggested that there had not been a large number of uncertain or reluctant voters passing through the constituency's polling stations. Early editions of the *Belfast Telegraph* captured this swing in anticipation over the election's outcome, with one headline forecasting that Bobby Sands was now considered "a hot favourite for the seat". The newspaper explained that the "large turnout yesterday was the first hammer-blow to the Official Unionists' hopes".[70]

During the mid-afternoon of 10 April, in Enniskillen's Technical College, the presiding officer announced the dramatic news that a hunger striker close to death was the new Westminster representative for the Fermanagh & South Tyrone constituency. Although his victory was far from being an overwhelming one, Bobby Sands had obtained a majority of 1,446, polling 30,492 votes to Harry West's 29,046. News of the return of the "Anti-H-Block candidate" quickly filtered from the hall to a small crowd of Sands' supporters in the street outside. It would be the images of his "overjoyed" relatives and jubilant supporters which would dominate the front pages of newspapers around the world the following day.[71] Rosaleen Sands, the victorious candidate's mother, was pictured hugging her daughter shortly after the election announcement, and she told reporters that her son would, "keep on with the fast".[72] The victorious candidate first heard the news on a transistor radio smuggled in to the Maze and, according to a priest who had been visiting him, celebrated by having a bath.

The emotional reaction of the defeated candidate was very different. Newspaper reports described a far-from-confident Harry West looking "ashen-faced, and visibly shaken, when the result was read out".[73] Shortly afterward, a "saddened" West pointed out that the election result had been a "disturbing" one for unionists, who had just "learn[ed] that they lived among 30,000 people who supported an IRA man".[74]

Republican jubilation at Bobby Sands' momentous election victory was unrestrained in both the Maze and in nationalist areas across Northern Ireland.[75] It fell to Sands' election agent to read out his victory speech. Owen Carron told reporters that despite "intimidation" by the security forces, electors had "stood by" the prisoners, and that they demanded "an immediate end to the intolerable situation in the H-Blocks".[65]

For those espousing different shades of nationalism, there was a distinct reluctance to question the electoral judgement of Catholic voters in the Fermanagh & South Tyrone constituency. Rather, John Hume and the nationalist-leaning *Irish News* turned their anger on the Unionist Party. Hume appeared to justify the election of Sands by claiming he had obtained political creditability, and that there was little to choose between leading unionist political figures and the newly-elected republican prisoner. Hume maintained that Sands had, by becoming elected, "achieved political status", which, he asserted, was distinctly "preferable to any status that could be conferred by the British Government". The SDLP leader went on to suggest that there was "no difference between Bobby Sands and Ian Paisley, as both have declared they will stop at nothing in order to achieve their ends".[77] The *Irish News* also attacked unionism and the British government, and attempted to justify the blatant decision of the vast majority of Catholic voters to side with a convicted terrorist rather than a constitutional politician. The paper instead castigated the unionist candidate for quoting from the recent appeal for peace by Pope John Paul II in a pre-election appeal to voters. The editorial fumed:

> When Unionists take the trouble to remove obscenities referring to a revered Catholic figure from walls and buildings, when certain unionists remove vulgar references to Catholics from their own mouths and voices, when unionists agree to meet constitutionally-minded Catholics to discuss legislation with them about the rights of Catholic citizens, they may have the right to make an appeal to Catholic voters.[78]

Contemptuously dismissing the claim in the Commons of Labour's Northern Ireland spokesman, Don Concannon that "a vote for Bobby Sands is a vote for violence" as being "grotesquely wrong", the *Irish News'* leading article conceded that the Catholic voice in Fermanagh & South Tyrone had been a defensive and ultimately negative one. It contended that the result did "not represent a 'for' anything but an 'against' something vote", and that Catholics had been reluctant to "vote directly, or by abstaining, indirectly, for unionism, the system under which [they] had suffered for the duration of Stormont rule".[79] In another editorial, three days later, the *Irish News* returned to the theme of British culpability for the ongoing situation in Northern Ireland, claiming that "a great deal of tragedy would have been avoided" if successive British administrations had reacted more promptly to "the repercussions of Unionist policy" during the half-century of Stormont rule.[80]

The election of a hunger striker so close to death took the British public by surprise, and the *Belfast Telegraph* noted the "deep shock" in Britain when the result was announced.[81] Even the *Guardian* – normally sympathetic to the cause of Irish nationalism – admitted that the likely impact of Sands' election was a "dangerous" one, whilst *The Times* feared that Northern Irish society would prove to be "so far polarised, as to render useless any early revival of an attempt to introduce provincial institutions acceptable to the leaders of both communities".[82]

Much of the early media reaction to the outcome of the election concentrated on subsequent attempts to oust the newly elected representative for Fermanagh & South Tyrone. The *Irish News* informed its readers that "only hours" after Bobby Sands' election, "moves were being made ... to have him expelled from the Westminster House of Commons".[83] The paper explained that the British authorities' plan to cancel the election result was based on the grounds that Sands would be "unable to represent his constituents properly from prison".[84] Although Francis Pym, the leader of the Commons, was investigating the possibility of arranging a Commons vote designed to authorise Sands' expulsion from the lower chamber, this was never a likely scenario. During hastily-convened cross-party discussions, not only did a substantial section of parliamentary opinion express its opposition on principle to such a move, but, as the *Belfast Telegraph* pointed out, such a step would prove to be "an embarrassing propaganda battle".[85] Crucially, it would also be an illogical move, as the British government had allowed Bobby Sands to stand in the first place, and to disqualify him after he had legitimately triumphed would appear to the outside world to represent the antithesis of British fair play.

Within forty-eight hours, such expulsion moves were reported to be "in doubt", as "growing opposition" to the expulsion plan was reported at Westminster.[86] In a leader entitled, "Verdict Stands", the *Belfast Telegraph* made a strong case against parliamentary intervention which would precipitate Sands' expulsion. Conceding that "the voters have done their worst", the paper insisted that, "their verdict should stand". While pointing out that Sands was likely to "never occupy" his Westminster seat, it insisted that a change in the law was required to prevent any further cases:

> The deal has been done, exposing the naked tribalism in Fermanagh and South Tyrone but, to prevent any repetition, Parliament should now consider laying down tighter ground rules for elections to Westminster. Does it make sense, ultimately, to let candidates stand who cannot take their seats? Democratic rights are one thing, but permitting them to be abused for propaganda purposes is another.[87]

Following Sands' election, the mood in the Protestant community was mainly one of delayed shock, as well as anger. Even the normally cautious Alliance Party denounced the "election of a terrorist", and unionist representatives and public alike contemplated with dread the worsening divisions within an already torn and bloody society. The *Belfast Telegraph* did not try to disguise the fact that the result had been a "tragic" one, and a clear "defeat" for "all the moderate voices" in the region. The paper tried however to deflect some of the serious significance of the election's outcome by claiming it had been, "a wholly unusual and, it is to be hoped, never-to-be-repeated by-election", fought out in "real border country", where attitudes tended to be "unreservedly tribal", and also reminded its readers that Sands had not been the first terrorist to be elected to the Westminster Parliament. However, the paper's leading article did not attempt to disguise the potentially fatal blow which this result had delivered. It went on:

> After every allowance has been made for the serial factors in Fermanagh and South Tyrone – the straight fight between two prime symbols of Unionism and Republicanism, the sympathy for a hunger-striker, and the Republicans' skilful avoidance of the connection with violence – it has to be admitted that the result amounts to the biggest fillip to the IRA since the introduction of internment ... This result will act like a virus infection of the system, driving communities even further apart, and building walls of mistrust and fears that will last for years to come.[88]

Unquestionably, the election had a major impact upon the subsequent progress of the republican hunger strike. Historian Padraig O'Malley suggested that the election actually "transformed the context in which his [Sands'] hunger strike was conducted". This was due to the considerable media interest in the contest and, most especially, the election's surprising outcome, which "fixed the issue indelibly in the public mind". As a result of his election, Bobby Sands became "a public figure, the focus of intensive scrutiny and attention".[89] In the three weeks or so between the election announcement and the significant decline in Sands' physical condition, there was a flurry of activity at the Maze. A succession of public representatives from the Irish and European parliaments, as well as Catholic priests and even a papal envoy met up with the weakening MP for Fermanagh & South Tyrone. Irish Prime Minister Charles Haughey, and SDLP leader, John Hume joined Catholic bishops in their demand for an intervention by the European Commission of Human Rights, whilst the Pope, John Paul II, sent his Northern Ireland-born secretary, John Magee to the H-Blocks in an abortive attempt to mediate. However, British premier Margaret Thatcher was not renowned for her willingness to compromise, maintaining that the actions which had resulted in Sands being confined to the Maze Prison did not constitute "politics" but rather added up to a "crime".

After 66 days on hunger strike, Bobby Sands died at the Maze. Not surprisingly, there was a violent response in Belfast's nationalist districts, and two milkmen were shot going about their work. Manifestations of an international condemnation of Britain's perceived intransigence on the hunger strike issue were evident in a variety of responses across the world. The American government issued a statement of "deep regret" at Bobby Sands' passing, and dockers in New York boycotted British ships in dock. Condolences were expressed in several national parliaments, including those in Italy, Portugal and India, and demonstrations supporting those on hunger strike were organised in places as far apart as Brisbane, Chicago, Oslo and Athens. There was a sharp contrast between the responses of most international newspapers and those of the British press. The *New York Times* wrote of "Britain's gift of martyrdom" to Bobby Sands and the IRA, whilst even the more guarded *Washington Post* pointed out that, despite the deceased's "record of violence", he would be "remembered mainly for the manner of his death after a 66-day fast, holding in his hands a golden crucifix presented by a special papal envoy".[90]

The large right-wing contingent of the British press had no such censure for the actions, or more accurately inactivity, of their government. The *Sunday Express* had, in the wake of the election result, denounced those Catholics who had decided to vote for Sands, suggesting that "their attendance at Mass this morning [is] as corrupt as the kiss of Judas", whilst the day after Sands' death, the *Sun* reminded its readers that the Irish hunger striker had stood for "the dark tyranny of terror by the bomb cruelly placed, to maim and kill unsuspecting innocents". The *Daily Mail* criticised the IRA for its attempt to turn Bobby Sands' funeral procession into "a macabre propaganda circus", describing the firing of volleys into the air by the paramilitary funeral party as "a gangsters' parody" of respected military tributes to dead comrades. Sands was, the *Daily Mail* maintained, "the tool of wicked conspirators who, if they ever took control of Ulster, would bring the Province nought but bloodshed, tyranny and desolation".[91]

Bobby Sands was buried in Belfast on 7 May, when an estimated 100,000 people (representing close to 20 per cent of the North's Catholic population) lined the route from the funeral service at St Luke's Church on the Twinbrook estate for the interment in Milltown Cemetery on Belfast's Falls Road. International journalists and television cameramen captured the undisguised paramilitary funeral – the British authorities, fearing a potential propaganda catastrophe if they had attempted to arrest the armed paramilitaries guarding Sands' coffin, kept a discreet distance from the coffin-bearers – which ensured that the prison dispute would remain in the international media spotlight.

After Bobby Sands' death, the efforts to break the hunger-strike deadlock continued, with the Reverend Denis Faul helping to broker a solution to the impasse. Considerable pressure was placed on Gerry Adams and the Sinn Féin leadership by the families of subsequent hunger strikers, and rumours spread that the strike would be called off. On 9 September 1981, five strikers agreed to accept the medical treatment which had been requested by their families and shortly after this, new Northern Ireland Secretary James Prior met with republicans to discuss ways of solving the crisis. On 3 October, the strike was formally called off and three days later, Prior announced that prisoners would now be able to wear their own clothes, that prison visits and correspondence would be improved, and an extension in the remission of sentences granted. Prison work, however, would continue for all inmates for another two years.

The 1981 hunger strike had lasted 217 days and directly resulted in the deaths of 10 republican prisoners, as well as 61 other, indirect, deaths (including 30 members of the security forces). More crucially, the effects of the election result and the wider hunger strike would culminate in a distinct hardening of the polarisation between Northern Ireland's two communities. Within the Catholic community, the chasm which had previously existed, between those completely opposed to the armed struggle and those who unreservedly backed it, narrowed substantially, as Catholics discovered an issue which united them, in their opposition to what they regarded as the "intransigence" of the British authorities. Although these differences in approach and political preferences would soon re-emerge, especially as the republican paramilitary campaign intensified during the following year, the political legacy of both the Sands' election victory and the 1981 hunger strike would be the emergence, over the next 25 years, of Sinn Féin as a genuine political force and the undoubted voice of the North's Catholic community.

Later in 1981, Owen Carron, Bobby Sands' agent, would beat Official Unionist, Ken Maginnis by over 1,000 votes, and in the 1982 Assembly elections, Sinn Féin would make inroads into SDLP support, gaining 10 per cent of the overall vote and 5 of the new Assembly's seats. Bobby Sands' victory in April 1981 heralded a change in the approach of republicans, whereby they would make a conscious step to becoming more closely involved in the electoral process. For Protestants, on the other hand, the election of an IRA leader to Parliament, and the growing support within the Catholic community for the hunger strike, would be perceived as a confirmation of their deep suspicions that most Catholics actually sympathised with the IRA, and that the periodical condemnations by SDLP-leaning Catholic voters were rather meaningless and tokenistic.

The 1981 by-election in Fermanagh & South Tyrone was one like no other in the North of Ireland. Rarely had an electoral contest been staged in such a surreal atmosphere. The physical absence of one of the two candidates contesting the seat meant that the normal cut-and-thrust of a political campaign – the exchange of political accusations and personal rebukes between the rival candidates – was strangely low-key, despite the valiant attempts by the respective camps to drum up support for their men. Although many elections in the region have been dismissed as being contested on fundamentally constitutional, rather than party-political issues involving social and economic policies, this contest stands out as being about something else.

Bobby Sands' election team frequently referred to the "moral" choice facing voters as their candidate lay on his death-bed, and Harry West's campaign also highlighted the hypocrisy of his opponent's associates who, on the one hand, were campaigning for saving the lives of political prisoners, whilst on the other were actively endeavouring to take away the lives of many others, both in Northern Ireland and Great Britain. For Catholics, this "moral" dimension was about whether they should desist from voting for a Catholic candidate whose rights as a prisoner had allegedly been abused, and allow him to die as a partial outcome of their ambivalence in backing a once-active republican paramilitary. For Protestants, the "moral" challenge lay in whether they should allow internecine disagreements between the UUP and DUP to deflect them as voters from their broader "duty" to return a notable local unionist who would raise a different type of "moral" question at Westminster – the right of his election opponent's associates to take away the lives of his constituents by the use of political terror. This election was also different on account of the fact that as much of the early political speculation and debate had centred round those who would not be standing, as on those who had actually been nominated. Indeed, the "ghosts" of Austin Currie, Noel Maguire and Roy Kells would hover over the rest of the short campaign and fuel continued infighting, long after its results were known.

It would be the long-term political legacy of this contest, rather than its short-term impact, which would prove to be most significant. Bobby Sands' tenure as constituency representative would be inevitably short-lived, but the success of his prison-based political pressure group soon convinced Sinn Féin to strive for a major breakthrough in Northern politics. Within a year, Danny Morrison and Gerry Adams had announced their party's commitment to an "Armalite and ballot box strategy", and at the next general election, in June 1983, Adams would oust the long-serving republican socialist, Gerry Fitt, from his West Belfast seat. The 1981 election's outcome also had an impact upon British political policy in Northern Ireland, especially in terms of its public justification of its role there. In particular, the contention of the authorities that the Provisionals did not enjoy substantial support from the minority community appeared to have been a misjudgement.

However, despite these ultimate whole-scale political changes, the impact of this by-election and the interrelated hunger strike would not result in major political change for the region for many years to come. Divisions between the two communities were rarely as bitterly exposed as they had been by this contest and its aftermath, when the republican fighting-machine was boosted by a sharp influx of new, eager recruits who threw themselves into an intensified paramilitary campaign. Indeed, in the wake of Bobby Sands' election victory, hopes of political compromise and cross-community governance seemed to be light years away.

Endnotes

1. P.J. O'Malley, *Biting at the Grave – the Irish Hunger Strikes and the Politics of Despair* (Blackstaff Press, Belfast, 1990), p. 29
2. *Ibid.*, p. 34
3. *Irish News*, 5 February 1981
4. O'Malley, *op. cit.*, p. 36
5. *Ibid.*, p. 50
6. *Ibid.*
7. *Ibid.*

8. B. Flynn, *Pawns in the Game: Irish Hunger Strikes, 1912–81* (Collins Press, Cork, 2011), p. 206

9. C. Ryder, *Inside the Maze – the Untold Story of the Northern Ireland Prison Service* (Methuen, London, 2000), p. 235

10. E. Moloney, *A Secret History of the IRA* (Penguin, London, 2007), p. 210

11. *Belfast Telegraph*, 26 March 1981

12. *Irish News*, 25 March 1981

13. K. Rafter, *Sinn Féin 1905–2005: In the Shadow of Gunmen* (Gill & Macmillan, Dublin, 2005), p. 109

14. *Belfast Telegraph*, 28 March 1981

15. *Irish News*, 3 April 1981

16. *Belfast Telegraph*, 1 April 1981

17. *Ibid.*

18. *Ibid.*

19. D. Beresford, *Ten Men Dead: The Story of the 1981 Irish Hunger Strike* (Harper Collins, London, 1987), p. 108

20. *Irish News*, 2 April 1981

21. *Ibid.*

22. *Ibid.*

23. *Belfast Telegraph*, 27 March 1981

24. *Belfast Telegraph*, 25 March 1981

25. *Belfast Telegraph*, 28 March 1981

26. *Belfast Telegraph*, 31 March 1981

27. *Belfast Telegraph*, 30 March 1981

28. *Belfast Telegraph*, 31 March 1981

29. *Belfast Telegraph*, 1 April 1981

30. *Ibid.*

31. *Belfast Telegraph*, 1 April 1981

32. *Belfast Telegraph*, 30 March 1981

33. *Belfast Telegraph*, 1 April 1981

34. *Irish News*, 28 March 1981; 27 March 1981, 1 April 1981

35. *Irish News*, 6 April 1981

36. *Irish News*, 7 April 1981

37. *Belfast Telegraph*, 6 April 1981

38. *Ibid.*

39. *Irish News*, 8 April 1981

40. *Irish News*, 4 April 1981

41. *Belfast Telegraph*, 4 April 1981

42. *Belfast Telegraph*, 7 April 1981

43. *Irish News*, 8 April 1981

44. L. Clarke, *Broadening the Battlefield: The H-Blocks and the rise of Sinn Féin* (Gill & Macmillan, Dublin, 1987), p. 143

45. *Irish News*, 2 April 1981

46. *Belfast Telegraph*, 4 April 1981

47. *Irish News*, 6 April 1981

48. *Belfast Telegraph*, 27 March 1981

49. Rafter, *op. cit.*, p. 109
50. *Belfast Telegraph*, 25 March 1981
51. *Belfast Telegraph*, 30 March 1981
52. *Belfast Telegraph*, 8 April 1981
53. The *Irish News* (8 April 1981) noted Harry West's "very low profile" during the short campaign.
54. *Irish News*, 8 April 1981
55. *Belfast Telegraph*, 6 April 1981
56. *Irish News*, 7 April 1981
57. *Belfast Telegraph*, 4 April 1981
58. *Belfast Telegraph*, 6 April 1981
59. *Ibid.*
60. *Ibid.*
61. Beresford, *op. cit.*, p. 112. Twelve people died following an IRA blast at the La Mon Hotel, County Down on 17 February 1978, and the Queen's cousin, Earl Louis Mountbatten, was one of four people who died aboard his boat in County Sligo after another IRA bomb in August 1979.
62. *Irish News*, 9 April 1981
63. *Ibid.*
64. *Belfast Telegraph*, 6 April 1981
65. Beresford, *op. cit.*, p. 112
66. *Belfast Telegraph*, 9 April 1981
67. The *Belfast Telegraph's* political correspondent, Barry White, "confidently predicted victory" for Harry West: *Belfast Telegraph*, 9 April 1981.
68. *Irish News*, 10 April 1981
69. *Ibid.*
70. *Belfast Telegraph*, 10 April 1981
71. News of Sands' electoral success had to compete for front-page coverage with reports of racial riots in London.
72. *Irish News*, 11 April 1981
73. *Ibid.*
74. *Ibid.*
75. There was little immediate violence, though some stone-throwing occurred when a nationalist victory parade was halted in Lurgan on 12 April.
76. *Irish News*, 11 April 1981
77. *Ibid.*
78. *Irish News*, 13 April 1981
79. *Ibid.*
80. *Irish News*, 16 April 1981
81. *Belfast Telegraph*, 11 April 1981
82. *Guardian* and *The Times*, 11 April 1981
83. *Irish News*, 11 April 1981
84. *Ibid.*
85. *Belfast Telegraph*, 11 April 1981
86. *Belfast Telegraph*, 13 April 1981; *Irish News*, 13 April 1981
87. *Belfast Telegraph*, 13 April 1981

88. *Ibid.*

89. O'Malley, *op. cit.*, p. 60

90. *New York Times*, 6 May 1981 and *Washington Post* (undated): as quoted in *H-Blocks: What the Papers Say*, Northern Ireland Office publication, July 1981 (in author's collection).

91. *Sunday Express*, *Sun* and *Daily Mail*, 13 April 1981: as quoted in *H-Blocks: What the Papers Say, op. cit.*

CHAPTER SEVEN

Election for the Never-Never Land
The Westminster By-elections, 1986

Accord at Hillsborough

The Westminster by-elections in January 1986 were precipitated by the mass resignation of the total complement of sitting unionist members (14 from the Official Unionist and Democratic Unionist parties, as well as Independent Unionist, James Kilfedder), in protest at the signing of the Anglo-Irish Agreement in Hillsborough two months earlier. This remains the only instance of a series of simultaneously contested Westminster by-elections – covering the vast majority of parliamentary constituencies in Northern Ireland – being fought on one central issue, namely the constitutional and political changes proposed by the Hillsborough Agreement. It also represents a rare example of unionists setting the political agenda during the modern conflict – even if the outcome of these elections would prove to be far from the resounding success which some loyalists had anticipated. These by-elections also constitute an occasion when the vast majority of candidates and much of the fervour around the short election campaign were largely restricted to the Protestant section of the community.

On the surface at least, the shift in Margaret Thatcher's thinking on the Irish question, between the 1984 publication of the New Ireland Forum report (with its central emphasis on a key role for the Irish government in the governance of Northern Ireland) and her signing of the 1985 Anglo-Irish Agreement, is startling. Thatcher, who had been deeply influenced on her Northern Ireland policy by staunch unionist, Airey Neave, had been vehemently opposed to the undisguised unitary Irish state dimension of the John Hume-inspired Forum report, and her relations with Charles Haughey's Fianna Fáil administration deteriorated after this. However, she forged better working relationships with Haughey's successor as Irish prime minister, Fine Gael's Garret FitzGerald, and was persuaded by a combination of behind-the-scenes advice from prominent civil servants (in particular, Sir Robert Armstrong) and the worsening security situation in the North, that the need for a new Irish initiative was urgent. The death and destruction she witnessed first-hand at her party's annual conference at Brighton in October 1984 – 5 died and over 30 were injured, including several of Thatcher's party colleagues – convinced her that immediate security improvements directly involving the Dublin government were a prerequisite for defeating the increasingly out-of-control IRA. Thatcher was also aware of the political threat posed by an ever more politically aware Sinn Féin to constitutional nationalism in the North. Several years later, she acknowledged the time was right for a reassessment of her Irish policy. In her memoirs, she would write of the "imperative need for greater security" and that, despite a reluctance to "making limited political concessions to the South", she felt obliged to "contemplate" it.[1]

Secrecy was crucial if such a joint governmental initiative was to materialise and it was accepted that, in terms of the groundwork required for such a complicated constitutional arrangement to see the light of day, discretion would be of paramount importance. Thus, only an "inner" cabinet was fully briefed regarding these preparations, and Ulster Unionists were conspicuously kept in the dark.[2]

On 15 November 1985, in the presence of full political, diplomatic and legal teams representing both British and Irish Governments, the Anglo-Irish Agreement was signed at Hillsborough Castle. Described as "a brave attempt to bury an ancient conflict", the formal signing of the accord by Thatcher and her Irish counterpart, Dr Garret FitzGerald, was followed by a press conference.[3] At this, Thatcher "persistently rejected claims of a sell-out" of the loyalist community in Northern Ireland. Instead, she "continually emphasised that for the first time, Eire [sic] had formally recognised the legitimate rights and aspirations of the unionist majority". She maintained that the document was "not one of interference" in Northern affairs by the Irish Republic's government, but was rather a matter of "both sides working together", in a joint endeavour to "defeat the men of violence".[4]

The twelve-clause document would be probed and dissected by a range of constitutional experts in the days and weeks that followed its historic signing in the small County Down town, situated ten miles to the south of Belfast. What was fundamentally different about this agreement was the direct involvement of the southern government in Northern Ireland affairs. The

Dublin administration was now entitled to "put forward views or proposals for major legislation and on major policy issues, which are under the purview of all Northern Ireland Departments and which remain the responsibility of the Secretary of State for Northern Ireland".[5] Also radically different was the acceptance by the Irish government of the North's existing constitutional status. The south's refusal to acknowledge this had been a long-time source of discontent for unionists. However FitzGerald's acceptance, that any constitutional change would "only come about with the consent of a majority of the people of Northern Ireland", earned few plaudits from irate unionists. The chief target of their anger was the newly-created Anglo-Irish Conference, established to provide a discussion forum on the North's internal affairs for representatives from the two governments. Though this was purely a forum for discussing relevant issues and contained no executive powers, Northern loyalists disputed British government's "acknowledgement" of the right of the Irish government to "put forward views and proposals on matters relating to Northern Ireland"[6] Beyond this, although a range of issues were mentioned in the Agreement – including devolution (Article 4), Dublin's role (Articles 5–8), and the need to improve cross-border security (Article 9) – critics of the Agreement were also furious at the lack of concrete proposals for dealing with the immediate threat of terrorism, as well as its failure to offer any olive branches to marginalised unionists.

A few days later, the British House of Commons was virtually unanimous in its support for the Agreement. Margaret Thatcher insisted that Hillsborough constituted the "only lasting way to put an end to the violence and achieve peace and stability" in Northern Ireland, and stressed that the "goal" of the Agreement was "reconciliation" between the two sections of the region's society. Appealing directly to both the unionist representatives listening to her speech and to the wider community they represented, the prime minister suggested that they now had "a right to feel secure about Northern Ireland's position as part of the United Kingdom". The agreement had, by "reinforcing the principle of consent", ensured that loyalists would "feel more secure, not only today but in the future".[7] Thatcher's Labour counterpart, Neil Kinnock, whilst reiterating his party's commitment to "a united Ireland by consent", more significantly recognised the "priority" issue in the Agreement, namely "the reconciliation of the communities" in the province.[8] Nationalist spokesmen also stressed the opportunity for reconciliation presented by the Accord. John Hume appealed to unionists sitting across the Commons chamber to respond more positively to the Agreement, pointing out that his "quarrel" with them had been that they "sought to protect their own heritage, by holding all the power in their own hands and by basing that on sectarian solidarity".[9]

Despite a greater-than-usual tolerance of unionist dissent, only a small number of Conservative diehards joined with the 15 unionist representatives in voting against the Agreement, which gained the Commons' general assent, by 473 to 47 votes. Ian Gow, a junior minister who would be a target for IRA assassination in 1990, was also highly critical of his government's actions at Hillsborough, and resigned from Thatcher's administration as a consequence of these objections. He told his parliamentary colleagues that Hillsborough would be "perceived as having been won as a result of violence".[10]

Not surprisingly, the most vituperative condemnation of the Anglo-Irish Agreement came from unionist politicians, both in Parliament and back in the province. James Molyneaux, the Official Unionist leader, described "a universal cold fury" in the Protestant community, which "none of us have thus far managed to contain".[11] Molyneaux also dismissed the idea that somehow the Accord would produce peace, suggesting instead that it would act as a "sword".[12] Much of the denunciation of the recent historic meeting had a personal edge to it. Enoch Powell used parliamentary privilege in his stinging rebuke aimed at the prime minister, reminding her that "the penalty for treachery" was to "fall into public contempt".[13] Ian Paisley's pulpit condemnation of Margaret Thatcher was unparalleled in its ferocity. In a sermon, which provoked much condemnation in Great Britain, Ian Paisley urged God to "take vengeance upon this wicked, treacherous, lying woman".[14]

Undoubtedly however, the most emotive speech from a unionist politician on the Agreement came from Armagh's Westminster representative, Harold McCusker. Speaking in Parliament a few days after the signing of the Accord, McCusker told a hushed Commons about his experience outside the gates of Hillsborough Castle the previous Friday. Standing "like a dog" in the street, he described his feeling of "desolation", as "everything that I held dear turned to ashes in my mouth".[15] Addressing the prime minister directly, the impassioned Official Unionist MP informed the signatory of the new Agreement that she had "sold my birthright". He went on:

Does the prime minister realise that, when she carries the Agreement through the House, she will have ensured that I shall carry to my grave with ignominy the sense of injustice that I have done to my constituents down the years – when, in their darkest hours, I exhorted them to put their trust in the British House of Commons, which one day would honour its fundamental obligation to treat them as equal British citizens?[16]

Initial reaction from the unionist press to the momentous events at Hillsborough Castle was also far from complimentary about the actions of the British premier. Although the *Belfast Telegraph*'s main headline highlighted Northern Ireland Secretary of State, Tom King's claim that unionist leaders were "betraying the people of the Province by dismissing the Anglo-Irish Agreement out of hand", its "Viewpoint" editorial column was significantly entitled, "Agreement signed – but consent does not exist". The paper pointed at apparent inequities at the heart of the new accord:

The formal recognition of Northern Ireland's status … is no advance on the present situation, though that is how it is being presented. Consent is a recurring theme, but is there consent to the right to say "no" if it fails an electoral test? The sentiments are fine – peace and reconciliation – but insufficient attention has been paid to the mistrust engendered by 16 years of conflict. If this is the price for nationalist consent to participation in Northern Ireland, it has been fixed at an unrealistically high level. The nationalist minority would have input into government while unionists would be excluded. That will not work.[17]

Unsurprisingly, the *Irish News*' interpretation of the ramifications of the breaking news from Hillsborough was rather different. The paper's headline the following morning read, "Dublin gets greater say in the North"; its leading article, "Now it begins" – which pointedly ignored the marginalisation of unionists – claimed there was "consensus" in a shared recognition that the Agreement marked, "a historic step in the involvement of Ireland in the affairs of this country". The paper, whilst resisting the temptation to describe the accord as a "solution" to the North's political problems, did claim it was "a brave and commendable attempt to begin the healing process".[18]

Unionist leaders had decided at an early stage that their Agreement protests would not be confined to Westminster. Barely a week after its signing in Hillsborough, a massive loyalist demonstration opposing its contents took place outside Belfast City Hall. The city's municipal headquarters had been an iconic venue for Ulster protest in the past, most notably on "Covenant Day" in September 1912, and the huge exhibition of rank-and-file loyalist fury at recent events would be followed by the announcement of the mass resignation of all unionist Westminster representatives.

The rally, attended by a crowd estimated to be in the region of 200,000, was peaceful and illustrated the unity of resolve of the respective leaders of the unionist parties, James Molyneaux and Ian Paisley. It was an occasion better suited to the oratorical skills of the latter, rather than the mild-natured, quintessentially parliamentarian approach of Molyneaux. In his "Triple Never" speech, the DUP leader claimed that, "the heart of Ulster has been shattered by betrayal", and reminded his huge audience that they should be "prepared to lay down their lives for Ulster".[19] Ian Paisley also pointed out that resistance would not be confined to the "unionist family", and that what lay ahead constituted "the battle of the loyal people of the whole of Ulster".[20]

The rival daily newspapers reacted predictably to the massive demonstration. The *Irish News* only featured the meeting on its fifth page, downplaying the scale of opposition to the Hillsborough pact. The paper claimed that, "a great majority say 'yes'" (to the Agreement), which "must not be forgotten in Dublin or London". Conceding that the meeting had "demonstrated the size of the task facing the two sovereign governments who must implement it", the paper urged opponents of the pact – "those who see darkness when only light exists" – not to "fear such a new beginning".[21]

The *Belfast Telegraph*'s response combined an acknowledgement of the strength of loyalist feeling about the Accord with a plea for alternative, constructive proposals to be put forward. In its leading article, "Democracy discord", the paper conceded that the unionist leadership could "speak with strength" after the "quiet determination" expressed at the large gathering two days earlier. However, it warned that loyalists "must also realise that saying 'no' is not enough to convince a House of Commons, which is overwhelmingly in favour of Mrs Thatcher's efforts at what is regarded by the British as bridge-building". Urging the unionist leaders to come up with "constructive and positive alternatives", which would "accommodate the minority in the running of the Province", the paper also appealed to both loyalists and the British premier to avoid the inevitable confrontation which would follow in the wake of "simply meeting determination with determination".[22]

The unionist leadership and wider loyalist community, despite being aware of ominous-sounding reports of an imminent political initiative, appeared to be caught off guard by the Agreement. Responses of shock, horror and betrayal were much to the fore in the unionist press, and in the statements of a range of unionist representatives.[23] The morning after the signing of the Agreement, the *Belfast News Letter* argued that "the ghosts of Cromwell and Lundy had walked hand-in-hand" at Hillsborough the previous day, and that what had just been announced represented "a recipe for bloodshed and conflict which has few parallels in modern history".[24]

Unionists' political isolation at this juncture contrasted sharply with a previous period of political crisis before World War I, when Ulster Unionists knew they could rely upon the support both of the Conservative Party and a large body of public opinion in Great Britain. Now, after the shock and anger had subsided, they would be replaced by a prevailing sense of impotence and sullenness within the loyalist community. The way forward was obviously going to be a difficult one to navigate, and unionists' natural instinct, to be wary of compromise and to adopt a confrontational position with the agencies of government, was always going to be problematic and potentially self-defeating. As political scientist Paul Dixon has pointed out, the dilemma for constitutional unionists was that, "by threatening violence [they] could encourage and legitimise the position of those who actually used violence".[25]

Yet the Hillsborough crisis ironically provided unionists with a chance of re-evaluating their own position and future tactics. In his study of unionist resistance to the Hillsborough Agreement, policital scientist Arthur Aughey posited that "for too long, unionism had remained spectacularly passive and inarticulate" and that the shock of the Agreement had "stimulated an exciting and acrimonious reconsideration of what, after 15 November 1985, unionism actually meant".[26] It certainly led to the implementation of a range of campaign strategies to counter specific proposals outlined by the two governments at Hillsborough. Apart from the demonstrations against the meetings of British and Irish civil servants at Mayfield, just outside Belfast, and street demonstrations (including a one-day strike staged in March 1986), there was an organised withdrawal of unionist councillors from local councils across the province, the drawing up and signing of a petition (this attracted an estimated 400,000 signatures, and was handed in to Buckingham Palace in February 1986), and, later in the campaign, the emergence of a quasi-paramilitary group, the Ulster Clubs.[27]

Key amongst unionist strategists' most immediate plans was a determination to have the political and constitutional changes tested at the ballot box. With the chances of the government conceding a referendum on the Accord remote, Paisley, Molyneaux and their advisers decided that a mass resignation of Westminster parliamentary seats by all 15 Unionist MPs (11 of these were from the Official Unionist Party, 3 were DUP representatives, and Kilfedder was representing the Progressive Unionist Party) would give rise to the opportunity of ascertaining the popularity or otherwise of the recently-signed Agreement in most parliamentary seats across Northern Ireland. This was a bold and unprecedented move by the unionist leaders, who were conscious of a natural reluctance on the part of their grass-roots supporters to be seen to be avoiding the British parliamentary process, especially by boycotting Westminster altogether – abstentionism had been long regarded by unionists as a nationalist strategy.

The resignation of all 15 MPs was confirmed on 17 December 1985, creating the prospect of a bitter New Year electoral contest. What unionists were unable to plan for was the likely response of their political opponents. In the short period just after the declaration of the election and the start of the actual campaign, it became apparent that, apart from 2 seats – West Belfast, which had been won by Sinn Féin's Gerry Adams in 1983, and Foyle, the seat of SDLP leader, John Hume – only 4 other seats, which were considered to be marginal (Mid-Ulster, Fermanagh & South Tyrone, South Down, and Newry and Armagh) would be actually contested by unionism's main opponents, the SDLP. In addition, as detailed below, unionists would be obliged to field token candidates in four other constituencies, in order to avoid any "unopposed" returns.

The Battle for the "Never Never Land"

The long Christmas holiday and the decision to call the election during the third week of January meant that the campaign, centred round the single issue of the Agreement, was confined to a period of just over two weeks. It also witnessed a slow, rather sluggish start, with opposition parties undecided about whether they would actually stand in a few marginal seats.

By Nomination Day on 7 January 1986, there were 41 candidates (including 4 "dummy", or token, candidates) standing in the 15 constituencies being contested. Photographs of smiling unionist candidates, including Enoch Powell and Official Unionist Party leader, James Molyneaux, were featured in the *Belfast Telegraph*, which announced that "the starting flag went up today on Ulster's mini general election".[28] The *Irish News* noted that the nationalist community would be "looking at the four marginals and the performance of the SDLP and Sinn Féin", which, the paper suggested, would form "a fairly accurate barometer of how the Anglo-Irish Agreement rated within the nationalist community".[29]

On the eve of electioneering, there was considerable speculation about whether the contest would be accompanied by street protest and violence. Just days before the nomination of candidates was completed, a loyalist crowd's protest against a Mayfield meeting ended in violent attacks on the RUC. The *Belfast Telegraph* condemned unionist leaders for choosing street demonstrations as an anti-Agreement protest strategy, arguing that there was an "inevitability" about such violence, and suggesting that, "whenever people are taken on to the streets, in a march or rally, there are bound to be uncontrollable elements among them". The paper concluded that "the days for such mass meetings are long gone".[30]

It was not just the local political parties which commented on the debate surrounding the Agreement that January. Dick Spring, an Irish cabinet minister, claimed at a meeting in Oxford on 11 January that unionist fears over the Accord were "unfounded", whilst Northern Ireland Secretary of State, Tom King insisted that the by-elections, no matter what their outcome, "would not overturn the Anglo-Irish Agreement".[31] King reminded unionist dissenters that the "sovereign" parliament "had voted" and pointed out there was "no way in any part of the United Kingdom [that] a number of by-elections can overturn the will of Parliament".[32] During the campaign itself, community leaders who normally avoided taking sides on political issues during such contests, joined together and wrote an open letter to the local press, expressing their support of the Hillsborough Agreement. In this letter, local business, education, medical and church sectors urged people to consider the opportunities afforded by the Anglo-Irish Agreement, and warned of the dilemma between rejecting the "chains of conflict" and accepting the "progress of partnership".[33]

Unionists had been irritated by the slow responses of opposition groups to the calling of the election. As it became clear that nationalists would only be interested in contesting a handful of marginal constituencies, this irritation swiftly turned to anger. On 10 January, the *Belfast Telegraph*'s headline, "Stand and Fight", reported on the "angry Unionist spokesmen's challenge" to nationalists, who had refused to nominate candidates in all 15 seats.[34] Unionist strategists had clearly anticipated their position in the eventuality of nationalists not contesting safe unionist seats. Keen to avoid a situation where a majority of unionist candidates would be returned unopposed, they decided to field token or "dummy" candidates. On 6 January, the *Belfast Telegraph* reported the joint unionist "promise" that there would be contests in every constituency and that unionists were "hoping [that] the intervention of other parties would save them the trouble of fielding 'dummy' candidates".[35]

Around this time, both the SDLP and Sinn Féin announced their intentions to contest four marginal constituencies, but it soon became apparent that there would be no rival candidates in another four constituencies with clear unionist majorities, Strangford, East Londonderry, North Antrim and South Antrim. Ian Paisley challenged supporters of the Agreement to "come out of their foxholes" and contest every seat, and James Molyneaux stressed the importance of politicians ensuring that there was a proper "exercise of democracy".[36] Token candidates, bearing the name of Peter Barry (the Irish foreign minister), were nominated by unionist supporters in each of these four seats. Although admitting their "regret" at taking this action, unionists insisted that this was due to the "cowardice" of their opponents.[37] Their rivals wasted no time in mocking such an unusual election strategy. Seamus Mallon described such a move as "crazy", claiming that unionist leaders had their "heads firmly in the sand", and were only offering "irresponsible leadership" to their followers.[38] A few days later, the SDLP candidate in Newry and Armagh poured further scorn on James Molyneaux in particular, claiming that "the real dummy candidates in the coming elections are the 11 Official Unionists now totally in the grip of Paisley, who is leading them towards UDI". Addressing an SDLP meeting in Newtownhamilton, Mallon wryly remarked the unionist leaders were, "telling their people that they were on the good ship *Lollipop*, and the next minute, warning they were all on the *Titanic*".[39]

Unusually, the Official and Democratic Unionists put aside their party differences, and presented a joint manifesto at a press conference in Stormont on 14 January. Dismissing Northern Ireland Secretary of State Tom King as "a parrot of Dublin", Paisley and Molyneaux insisted they were "not just saying 'no' to everything", as their detractors were suggesting, and warned King that he would be "treading the road of dictatorship" if he ignored the results of the pending election.[40] Hoping to gain advantage from the emotional capital recently gained by the Polish Miners' Solidarity movement around this time, the authors of the manifesto, the Unionist Joint Working Party (UJWP), adopted for the document's cover a "Solidarity" style motif, with a strand of barbed wire and the Union Jack. The manifesto's title was, "1986, the Year of Decision – Ulster Says No!", and its authors explained their choice of image early in its text. The Anglo-Irish Agreement, they argued, had been "born of secrecy and deceit", and the forthcoming Anglo-Irish Conference would be held "behind closed doors and barriers of barbed wire". Notions of contractual loyalty and equality of citizenship were central in the unionist rationale. Referring to the recently-signed Accord, the manifesto argued:

> This is not the Union. This is not democracy. This is not justice. This is not the law of the land. And British citizens in Northern Ireland are under no moral or legal obligation to conform to it ... Ulster's historic legal demand has been for equality of citizenship within the United Kingdom. But we insist that where Parliament proposes to govern by way of arrangements which separate and distinguish us from the rest of the kingdom, it must first seek to enlist the support and consent of the people.[41]

In a reference to the British government's offer of referenda to the Scottish and Welsh electorates over recent devolution proposals, unionists maintained that the forthcoming election would be "Ulster's Referendum". At the heart of unionists' decision to call the election had been their desire to "invite the people to deny the government the moral authority to implement this Agreement".[42]

The joint unionist campaign stirred up more interest in the British media than most previous Northern Ireland elections, and several newspapers, including the *Guardian*, covered it in some detail. The *Guardian* noted the "amazing contrast" between the respective leaders of unionism, who were now advocating the "same message". One election report described the election as the "battle for the Never Never Land."[43] Although the sidelining of the unionists had prompted a modicum of sympathy for Ulster Protestants in the immediate post-Hillsborough days – the *Sunday Times* had pronounced that MPs would, "do well to reflect on Britain's indifferent record in Ireland, before they rush to condemn them [unionists]" – most serious newspapers preferred to focus on the disquieting, nihilistic characteristics of the unionist campaign than on the rationale behind it.[44] The *Observer*, for instance, dismissed the unionist position by pointing out that "the bull-horn oratory of Dr Ian Paisley and the pedantic constitutionalism of Mr Enoch Powell are not calculated to win friends or influence people this side of the Irish Sea".[45]

It was however the united campaign of unionist candidates and their leaders that would impress Protestant voters, who had been more accustomed to the inter-party bickering which had caused the haemorrhaging of wider unionism during the twenty-year period since the collapse of the long-standing unionist hegemony. Ian Paisley and James Molyneaux spoke together at several meetings and rallies, including one in Ballymena, and were photographed canvassing together in the blustery streets of seaside towns like Bangor. At the Ballymena meeting on 18 January, the town centre "came to a standstill around noon, with shops and pubs closing for the protest which attracted support from all over north Antrim". At this meeting, Ian Paisley claimed the Hillsborough pact was "crumbling" and that, due to the scale of loyalist opposition, the Northern Ireland Office was "on the rush" whilst "in London corridors, people were saying the deal was doomed".[46] Other unionist candidates spoke together at joint rallies that day, including Harold McCusker and Peter Robinson in Tandragee, and in a Ballynahinch demonstration that afternoon, Enoch Powell claimed the Agreement had been procured by "American bribery and blackmail".[47] The presence of loyalist paramilitaries at the latter rally provoked considerable criticism from opponents, with John Hume claiming unionists were "running with thugs".[48]

The unionist candidates were, unsurprisingly, strongest in their condemnation of the architects of the Accord, as well as those parties lending their support to it. At a meeting in Rathfriland early in the campaign, the DUP's deputy leader, Peter Robinson denounced the British premier for "running scared of the IRA", and suggested that the deal was "a surrender to the murder campaign". Robinson mocked the recently-devised moniker for

Margaret Thatcher, sneering that "the Iron Lady has shown that she is made only of the flimsiest tinfoil, and cannot stand the heat of a sustained terrorist campaign".[49] The following week, Robinson turned his anger on Agreement backers, the SDLP. He maintained:

> On the one hand, they condemn the terrorists and weep crocodile tears for their victims, while on the other hand, they are happy to fuel the flames of anger so that they can sit back and reap the benefits.[50]

Seeking to drum up passionate resistance at constituency level, many unionist candidates drew attention to the imminent centenary of a previous attempt by British ministers to implement political change against the will of Ulster's unionists – Gladstone's first Home Rule Bill of 1886. The Reverend Martin Smyth, defending a sizeable majority in South Belfast, argued in his election pamphlet, "South Belfast Says No", that, "one hundred years on, the conspiracy continues to deny the Ulster people the right to self-determination". Smyth also emphasised the inequitable nature of an agreement between two separate countries, which in the case of one of them, "puts a minority in a place of domination over a majority".[51] Like many of his colleagues, Smyth attempted to present the crucial choice at the election as a moral rather than a political or constitutional one. He implored his electors to, "deny government the moral authority to implement this Agreement", and promised that if the electorate's verdict was "ignored", the unionist leadership would conduct "a continuing campaign of opposition, embracing every form of legitimate political protest".[52]

The *Irish News*, with its full- and half-page election advertisements for the SDLP and its strong advocacy of the Agreement, made no secret which party it was backing.[53] The SDLP had serious chances of electoral gain in a couple of constituencies, Newry and Armagh, and South Down. Aware of a tangible post-Hillsborough "feel good" factor amongst Catholics and some moderate Protestants, the party poured its energies and resources into the Newry and Armagh contest in particular. Here, Seamus Mallon was endeavouring to win the seat at the fourth attempt from a low-profile unionist representative, Jim Nicholson. An *Irish News* report on this contest started with the headline "Mallon pulls out all stops in crucial fight", and the paper's assessment was that the seat represented, "a real knife-edge job with the outcome having not only deep implications for the SDLP but also the Anglo-Irish Agreement".[54] According to a purely sectarian headcount – around 60 per cent of the constituency's 65,465 electors were believed to be Catholic – the seat should have been a safe one for a nationalist candidate, but the presence of Sinn Féin in recent contests, as well as significant voting apathy, had resulted in unionist electoral success. The *Irish News* political correspondent, William Graham, observed that "a great deal of effort" was being expended in the SDLP's campaign, which was being "fought out in atrocious weather conditions". Judging that "only a few hundred votes are in it either way", Graham postulated that a unionist defeat in Newry and Armagh would tarnish the effect of their likely victories in the other seats. He claimed that it would be "a severe psychological blow" for the Unionists to return to Westminster with reduced representation, since they had precipitated the contests as "a type of informal referendum against the Hillsborough Accord".[55]

Eddie McGrady was another SDLP candidate attempting to win a Westminster seat after previous setbacks in the constituency. Contesting South Down for the third time, McGrady expressed confidence at the prospect of unseating the Official Unionist MP, Enoch Powell, whose majority was a mere 548. An *Irish News* report noted how, "the party election machine was in top gear in a bid to bring out every possible SDLP vote", and emphasised McGrady's optimism as regards increasing the overall electoral turnout by up to 10 per cent, on account of the fervour generated by the Agreement. It was believed that "moderate unionists and 'soft-core' Sinn Féin voters" were being directly targeted by the SDLP's canvassing team.[56] McGrady concentrated on discrediting the unionist case for opposing the Hillsborough pact and in particular, the creditability of his chief opponent Powell, whom he accused of "hypocrisy", on account of his recent alliance with the DUP, whose leader Powell had once dismissed as being "worse than the IRA".[57] In the same speech, McGrady slammed the "sham" unionist unity which, he maintained, amounted to "nothing more than a desperate attempt by Mr Enoch Powell to conceal the fact that he has nothing to offer the people of South Down".[58]

SDLP leader John Hume, free from the stress of personal campaigning, also attacked both unionist parties, for whom he suggested there were three stark choices: "UDI, talking to the SDLP or talking to Dublin". Hume also confirmed that successful SDLP candidates would take up their seats at Westminster and in the proposed Anglo-Irish parliamentary tier, "so that constituents would have a strong voice in the implementation and development of the Agreement".[59] Hume also castigated the presence of paramilitaries at a number of political rallies, suggesting this was "a very serious blunder", which would "destroy unionists'" credibility in Britain and abroad.[60]

Another quarry for SDLP attack was Sinn Féin, and one of the most outspoken candidates was Austin Currie, contesting the Fermanagh & South Tyrone seat.[61] Currie argued that Sinn Féin had, "nothing to offer but more bombing and killing, more tragedy, unemployment, more division and no progress towards the unity they solemnly boast of".[62] The following day, Currie renewed his attack on Sinn Féin, claiming it had "its back to the wall in all four constituencies", following the upsurge in support for his party in the previous May's local council elections, and also on account of changing opinion within the nationalist community precipitated by the Hillsborough Agreement.[63]

As noted in Chapter Six, Sinn Féin had become politicised in the early 1980s, with Bobby Sands gaining its first major political success in April 1981. Its leading personality, Gerry Adams, had won the West Belfast seat from Gerry Fitt in the 1983 general election, and the party was committed to an "Armalite and ballot box" strategy. However, in the wake of the Forum Report in 1984, constitutional nationalism had been revitalised, with the SDLP making significant gains in the local elections of May that year. When it came to the question of contesting these by-elections at the start of 1986, the SDLP was clearly attempting to avoid repeating its huge mistake in not standing in the Fermanagh & South Tyrone by-election five years earlier, and were determined to maintain a presence in the marginal seats to provide the electorate with an alternative to "physical force" nationalism. Sinn Féin had to counter the growing confidence and ebullience of a party which had been rejuvenated by the Hillsborough Accord. Meanwhile, Gerry Adams condemned the Agreement because he believed it "institutionalised" the British presence in Northern Ireland and he described the Accord as "a carrot-and-stick agreement, a mixture of repression and appeasement".[64]

Although Sinn Féin did not put forward high-profile candidates for the four seats which it contested, its nominees included Owen Carron, (who had succeeded Sands as MP in Fermanagh & South Tyrone before losing his seat to Ken Maginnis in 1983), and Danny Morrison, the party's publicity officer, who was standing in Mid-Ulster. Carron had been released on bail from

Belfast's Crumlin Road jail to commence his constituency campaign, and soon denounced the offer of post-Agreement financial aid from America as being "hyped up", to boost the SDLP's election prospects.[65]

The Mid-Ulster contest was a lively affair, involving rancorous exchanges between Belfast-born Morrison and his colourful DUP opponent, William McCrea, who was defending a seat he had won by only 78 votes in 1983.[66] Sinn Féin had unsuccessfully appealed in the High Court in order to postpone the contest in this constituency after its electoral officer's refusal to accept 50 postal votes handed in just after its deadline of noon on 8 January. The party had claimed that these votes were late due to Morrison's election agent being detained by the RUC.[67] Morrison spent much of his time attacking his SDLP opponent on a number of issues, including the detail of the Hillsborough Agreement and the question of flying the Irish tricolour in the North, but the main beneficiary of this nationalist in-fighting would prove to be the idiosyncratic William McCrea. An *Irish News* report described the DUP candidate's electioneering style during a visit to Sion Mills. McCrea started his electoral invective in "a narrow country lane" outside the village, before eventually realising that "the sheep grazing at the side of the road were the only potential voters within earshot".[68] Describing the gospel-singing McCrea's campaign as one of "political negativity", the *Irish News* maintained that the DUP representative was "happy to depict the SDLP and Sinn Féin as being one and the same on the one hand, and FitzGerald and Thatcher as one and the same on the other – traitors all!"[69]

Other parties that contested several seats afforded support – though in at least one case, somewhat reluctantly – for the recently-signed Agreement. The Workers' Party, which was contesting nine seats, backed the Accord primarily because it "offered a chance of peace". In its twelve-page election manifesto, the party described Hillsborough as an "important first step in creating a democratic ambience in Northern Ireland, within which we can build democratic political institutions and tackle the critical economic and social problems which face all our people".[70] Although the document appeared to express a degree of sympathy for unionists on account of their "anti-democratic" sidelining during the lead-up to Hillsborough, it was also critical of unionist leaders and their previous record, both in terms of the party's manifesto and in the statements and speeches of their candidates. The "hypocrisy" of the main unionist parties, in hurling abuse at a British prime minister whose economic and social policies they had previously backed, was condemned in the manifesto, whilst John Lowry, the party's Lagan Valley candidate (the constituency of James Molyneaux), dismissed all 15 unionist candidates as "duds".[71] Mr Lowry poured scorn on unionists' record at Westminster. Judging them on this basis, Lowry suggested that "all 15 candidates may as well cast themselves as Hopalong Cassidy, and ride off into the sunset as soon as the poll is over".[72] Other Workers' Party candidates condemned the "Orange" and "Green" parties for their "naked sectarian headcount philosophies", and Gerard Carr, the party's South Belfast candidate, suggested that younger voters in particular deserved "a radical alternative to the tired old policies of sectarianism".[73]

The Alliance Party, which was fielding 5 candidates, was more effusive in its praise for the Anglo-Irish Agreement, and predictably, it was the unionist critics of the Accord who formed the chief target for Alliance rebuke. In the party's manifesto, "Say no to UDI", the party leader, John Cushnahan (who was standing in North Down) claimed that the loyalist tactics amounted to, "defiance of the authority and will of the sovereign Parliament", a strategy which "could have catastrophic consequences for Northern Ireland's constitutional future".[74] Another Alliance candidate, Paul Maguire in North Belfast, claimed that "the Ulster Says No brigade had sought to misrepresent the Agreement largely as a cover for their own parliamentary bankruptcy". A week later, the same candidate despaired of the unionist campaign's "anti-Irish element".[75] However, the Alliance Party also warned that other parties had to shift their positions to accommodate unionists, as a result of the terms of the Agreement. Speaking at a conference in Galway, an Assembly representative, William Glendenning suggested that nationalist leaders had an obligation to clearly illustrate that the Accord had "changed attitudes on their side, if they expected unionists to move".[76]

Both the *Irish News* and *Belfast Telegraph* churned out a series of hard-hitting editorials in the days and weeks before the election. The *Irish News* was unambiguous in its support for the party of constitutional nationalism. Apart from the advertisements promoting the SDLP and detailed reports charting its candidates' progress and chances, the paper was critical of the party's chief opponents within the nationalist community. Advising caution to readers, a leading article reminded them they were "not likely to hear a candidate calling for their vote of approval to murder a fellow human being, but that is precisely what it is like in certain cases". The paper advised that voters "should be sure in their conscience of what they are giving approval to, when they finally enter the silent privacy of the polling booth".[77] At the end of the campaign, the paper insisted that Sinn Féin had "adopted an ambivalent and inconsistent attitude towards the Agreement", and there were other adverse references to the party's position from the paper throughout the campaign.[78] However, it was the unionists who received the full brunt of journalistic vitriol from the *Irish News*. Although the paper conceded that unionists were likely to be triumphant in most of the by-elections, the paper castigated the "ugly rhetoric" of loyalists' electioneering, maintaining that the region's economic future was "bleak almost to despair", and imploring John Hume and the SDLP to stress to the electorate "the economic advantages that will flow from the growing implementation of the Anglo-Irish Agreement".[79]

The *Irish News* endeavoured throughout to slice through the political dogma of the main parties, and instead highlight the "cardinal issue" involved in the contest. Addressing those readers who were more sympathetic to physical force nationalism, the paper pointed out that the Accord did "not copper-fasten Partition", but rather marked "a fundamental and irreversible change in the nature of the six-county state", including "an expanding role for Dublin in the governing of the North".[80] Denunciation of unionist candidates was contained in the same editorial. Molyneaux and Paisley's supporters were described as being "isolated, as the most intransigent element in West European democracy", whose "sheer negativity over the decades has starved them of sympathy in Britain and abroad". The editorial painted a frightening picture of the Armageddon-type scenario facing unionists if they followed their political leaders along an anti-Hillsborough path:

> They are now plunging aimlessly into the whirlpool which their founding-father, Craigavon, once warned them to avoid – a confrontation with the sovereign Parliament at Westminster.[81]

The paper's final editorial before polling day predicted that the results of the contest would show that it had proved to be "a futile exercise". It also suggested that the unambiguous statements of the unionist leaders, in addition to their "shotgun marriage with the sinister forces of the loyalist underworld", revealed the "unveiled fist inside the apparently veiled glove".[82] The leading article ended with a plea to nationalists to back a settlement which had "outmanoeuvred 'Not an Inch' unionism for the first time since

Partition". The proposed Anglo-Irish framework provided "a rightful place for northern Catholics who, in the four constituencies they were contesting, had it in their power to oust sitting unionists, thereby inflicting considerable psychological damage [on unionism] and robbing it of a propaganda advantage".[83]

The *Belfast Telegraph*'s analysis of the election was arguably less partisan and more insightful. In a leader entitled "Election Choices", the paper concluded that issues in the contest were "becoming clearer" during its final stage, and forecast that "a massive 'no' vote can be expected". The paper acknowledged how differences between the rival unionist parties had been "successfully suppressed in the interests of anti-Agreement solidarity", and argued that this combination of "a united unionist vote and a divided nationalist vote should bring its rewards" later that week.[84] The paper's assessment of the "split" between Sinn Féin and the SDLP was also an accurate one. Maintaining that there was "much less certainty about voting intentions" within the Catholic community, the paper concluded that nationalists were now "divided" between "optimists who believe that opportunities have been created, and pessimists who say that nothing has changed".[85]

Two days later, the *Belfast Telegraph*'s "Facing Realities" editorial accepted that the contest's outcome was "not in doubt", though there remained "a chance of SDLP success in Newry and Armagh". The paper's leading article contained a mixture of sympathetic and qualified support for the unionist case, as well as critical suggestions on its future political positioning. Warning the British government that the Agreement "cannot work" unless it received majority consent in the North, the paper argued that this principle of consent, "should be accepted by all democrats, whether they are for or against the principle of the accord".[86] Distinguishing between loyalists' rejection of the Agreement and their willingness to consider broader Anglo-Irish cooperation, the *Belfast Telegraph* suggested that Thatcher's administration would be "greatly ill-advised to ignore the results of the poll and [to] carry on as if nothing had happened". This approach, which many believed was clear in the responses of Tom King in particular, had been an ignominious failure just over a decade before, when British prime minister Harold Wilson had ignored loyalist protests over power-sharing, and "within a few months, Sunningdale was dead". Yet the paper also counselled unionists about the necessity of developing a more coherent and rational political strategy, and argued:

There can be no resting on laurels, waiting for others to react. Regardless of what the two governments do, or do not do, in response to the by-election results, unionists must get down to the urgent business of winning friends, and influencing people at Westminster by putting up their own political alternative to Hillsborough. The whole world knows what unionists are against but what are they for?[87]

Public responses to the popularity or otherwise of the Anglo-Irish Agreement and the likely outcome of the by-elections featured prominently in newspaper coverage and, indeed, the *Belfast Telegraph* carried out an opinion poll on the popularity of the Hillsborough initiative.[88] In this, the paper reported its chief finding, that "half the [Ulster] population believes that over the next six months, either the Anglo-Irish Agreement will not work, or will lead to increased confrontation between unionists and the British Government".[89] Worryingly for security ministers, an estimated 42.9 per cent of likely unionist pollsters, as well as over 50 per cent of Catholics, believed the Agreement would have "no effect on the level of support for Sinn Féin".[90]

Commenting on these findings the following day, the *Irish News* concluded that unionists "should have the reddest faces, for their claim that 'Ulster Says No!' has again been exposed as the lie, which anyone with half an ounce of wit knew it to be." The paper's editorial went on to argue that there was "ample room for compromise" in the province, "as long as people on either side are not asked to do so at the point of a gun".[91] Within a couple of days, the *Irish News* had returned to the implications of the *Belfast Telegraph*'s poll. Now taking the stance that these findings, although sympathetic to their own position – 61 per cent of Protestants had expressed support for the principle of power-sharing – were unlikely to materialise into meaningful backing from pollsters, the paper's analysis of the poll findings was more reasoned than its initial one. The *Irish News* informed readers that it would be "highly unlikely" for such voters to vote for parties like the SDLP or Alliance, which "would have to be partners in such a principle". Additionally, the paper noted that those Sinn Féin sympathisers who had expressed their support for the Agreement in the *Belfast Telegraph* poll were also "unlikely to vote for pro-Hillsborough parties".[92]

The last day of the contest saw the respective party leaders "firing [their] final shots", as Northern Ireland's electorate of nearly one million prepared to go to the polls.[93] Ian Paisley declared that the forthcoming poll constituted, "the acid test of whether the Agreement can stick", and warned that Margaret Thatcher's administration would "not be able to sidestep the results of an election" which had been organised "according to British electoral law and procedure".[94] John Hume was at pains to defend his party's decision to field candidates against Sinn Féin, which inevitably improved the chances of unionist candidates in marginal constituencies. He maintained that his party would "not sacrifice the respect and support" which they had built up internationally by "compromising our stand on violence for electoral gain".[95]

Whilst the *Belfast Telegraph* was debating the chances of unionists reaching their targeted half a million votes, the central focus of the *Irish News* was the likelihood of Seamus Mallon defeating his unionist opponent, Jim Nicholson in Newry and Armagh. The latter newspaper described the "last-dash" nature of the SDLP's campaign in the constituency, with a photograph of Mallon canvassing in Armagh. Noting the high turnout of nationalists at polling stations across these marginal seats, the paper revealed that up to 250 SDLP workers had been engaged on Mallon's campaign. One area where rival newspapers and politicians did agree was the effect which the inclement weather might have upon voter participation. A day before polling, the *Belfast Telegraph* forecast "a cold, windy and showery trek to the polls". Twenty-four hours later, its Election Day headline read, "Cold snap fails to deter voters".[96]

In a poll costing around £1 million to stage, 529 polling stations across the province opened their doors, as 41 candidates – 15 unionists, 4 SDLP, 5 Alliance, 4 Sinn Féin, 9 Workers' Party and 4 "Peter Barry" candidates – contested the 15 seats. The usual photos, of smiling, optimistic and warmly-clad candidates arriving at polling stations to cast their votes appeared in the respective newspapers.[97] Yet the combination of election overload – this was the sixteenth contest to be staged in Northern Ireland in as many years – and unfavourable weather, as well as the dearth of "bread-and-butter" economic and social issues, and the new identification requirements for voters, resulted in a reduced overall electoral turnout. Nevertheless, many did display considerable tenacity and determination to exercise their democratic right, with one person sadly paying the ultimate price.[98]

"Two separate elections"

The disappointing turnout at the January 1986 by-elections reflected a significant degree of election "fatigue", considering the normally higher-than-average polls at Northern Ireland elections. Barely 62 per cent of the electorate voted, which was over 10 per cent down on the figure for the same constituencies during the 1983 general election. Unionists managed to increase their share of the total votes cast from the 1983 figure of 62.3 per cent to 71.5 per cent, with the Official Unionists gaining considerably more votes than Ian Paisley's DUP. (The Unionist Party's share was 51.7 per cent of the total votes cast, compared with the DUP's 14.6 per cent.) In a significant boost for the Agreement's architects, the party representing constitutional nationalism fared considerably better than the party associated with physical force nationalism. Provisional Sinn Féin's comparatively low vote – 38,821 across the four seats it contested – represented less than 7 per cent of the votes cast, and constituted just over a third of the nationalist vote (down by over 6 per cent to 35.4 per cent). The chief beneficiary of this post-Hillsborough "feel good" factor amongst Catholics was the SDLP, which netted close to 71,000 votes across the 4 constituencies, which represented a 6 per cent rise in its share of the vote in these marginals.[99]

Unionists of one hue or another won 14 of the 15 seats they were defending, though there was one casualty – Jim Nicholson in Newry and Armagh (see below). In terms of the total number of votes cast, there were mixed messages for those unionist strategists responsible for orchestrating the election campaign. Although there was a clear majority in terms of those who had voted for the parties opposed to the Agreement, compared to those who had backed the Accord (127,937 in total), the total number of those electors rejecting the Agreement (418,230) fell some way below the half million "no" vote coveted by unionist leaders, and represented barely 44 per cent of the total electorate.

Otherwise, the contest produced contrasting fortunes for Unionist candidates. Some, like Peter Robinson in East Belfast, had benefited from the non-participation of the Official Unionists. Robinson actually increased his majority to 21,690 (compared with 7,989 in 1983), and a similar result was gained by James Molyneaux in Lagan Valley, where the Ulster Unionist leader gained ground on account of the DUP absence (Molyneaux's majority rose by nearly 12,000 to 29,186).[100] In three of the four marginal constituencies, unionists gained from the engagement of both nationalist groups, which inevitably resulted in a split in the nationalist vote. The DUP's William McCrea, who had scraped home in the previous election with a majority of 78, now boasted one of nearly 10,000 over Sinn Féin's Danny Morrison, whilst Ken Maginnis, who had previously been vulnerable in Fermanagh & South Tyrone, increased his majority over Sinn Féin to nearly 5,000. Though it was much closer in South Down, Enoch Powell held off the SDLP challenge of Eddie McGrady, increasing his majority in the process (by 1,842, which compared with 548 in 1983). Whilst other pro-Agreement groups such as Alliance and the Workers' Party were far from decimated, there would be no major breakthrough and Oliver Napier's normally strong showing for Alliance in East Belfast did not occur. Napier's personal vote was nearly 3,000 down on his 1983 election campaign.

The rival newspapers interpreted the results in very different ways. The *Irish News* acknowledged "a predictable overall Unionist turnout", but pointed out that barely 2,000 additional votes had been gained by unionists across the 15 contested seats, and that "the number of votes against the Accord fell well short of the half million mark".[101] The paper claimed that the unionist campaign, which had been planned as a "referendum", had "paradoxically illustrated that less than half the voters [had] said 'no' to the Anglo-Irish Accord", and had therefore "backfired".[102]

Its rival unionist paper saw things in a different light. The *Belfast Telegraph*'s headline the following day was, "Unionists hold vote on low poll", and the paper claimed the election showed the "massive rejection of the Anglo-Irish Agreement, in spite of a sizeable section of the community staying at home".[103] The following day's *Belfast Telegraph* editorial argued that the results, now confirmed, had illustrated that "two separate elections, one for unionists and the other for nationalists" had been contested. Suggesting that the "mini election" had "posed as many problems as it had solved", the paper went on:

> The stark truth is that Unionist Ulster voted an emphatic 'no' to the Anglo-Irish Agreement, while constitutional nationalist Ulster registered an equally emphatic 'yes'. There is still no consensus in how Northern Ireland can be made to function politically, and that is the sobering lesson from Thursday's poll.[104]

The *Irish News* was effusive in its praise for the electoral response from the nationalist minority. It concluded that the Anglo-Irish Agreement had "appeared to receive a broad endorsement from a large part of the nationalist community".[105] The paper also believed that the "essential winners" of the contest had been the SDLP. Dismissing the clear parliamentary returns of all but one unionist, the paper focused most of its attention on the "significant shift in the nationalist vote", which reflected "a vital change in nationalist thinking". Citing a trend which indicated that "thousands of Sinn Féin voters [had] switched their votes to the SDLP", the paper's interpretation of this shift was that nationalist voters now believed that "the constitutional politics so long and patiently advocated by Mr John Hume and his party is the way forward".[106] The *Belfast Telegraph* agreed with its nationalist rival that constitutional nationalism had "proved it can push back the tide towards violence", though its sombre qualification was that "without some compromise, confrontation is inevitable".[107]

Otherwise, a revealing report in the *Irish News*, "What happened to the City Hall faithful?", highlighted the apathetic response of various party officials and followers at the election count in Belfast City Hall on 24 January. Journalist Mary Kelly described the "lack of interest" and "low turnout" at the official count, which had often proved to be an enthusiastic and lively affair in the past. She accurately pointed out that it had been "hard to whip up much excitement from the party faithful, for what was clearly a foregone conclusion", and that, unlike previous election counts in Belfast's municipal headquarters, there had been, "no Union Jacks or Ulster flags in evidence and there were no crowds singing hymns or party tunes".[108]

The major news story emerging from the otherwise predictable set of results came from the marginal seat of Newry and Armagh. Here, Seamus Mallon won the seat at the fourth attempt with a majority of 2,500 over sitting member, Jim Nicholson (although defeated, Nicholson's personal vote in fact increased by over 1,000). The *Irish News* front-page headline was, "Nationalists steal limelight from unionist camp – Mallon wins Yes for Pact", and a photo of the successful SDLP man being hugged by his happy daughter appeared below. Describing the border constituency result as being "a poll boost for the deal", and "a severe psychological and embarrassing blow for the 'Ulster Says No' campaign", the *Irish News* described Mallon's success as "a practical and symbolic dent in the unionist protest".[109] The paper's analysis of the election's impact upon the balance of power between nationalist groups was also illuminating. Claiming the swing in the nationalist vote towards John Hume's party was of "considerable significance", the *Irish News* pronounced that SDLP's "more vigorous and energetic, well-oiled election machine" had succeeded in enticing a combination of reticent voters and less hard-line Sinn Féin sympathisers to vote for Seamus Mallon.[110] However, the paper was probably guilty of reading too much into the SDLP's triumph in Newry and Armagh. It claimed that nationalists, after this "strange" election, were now "unarguably more solid and politically adhesive than for many years", and that their future progress could "now be faced with increased hope".[111] Mallon's victory, the paper insisted, should be regarded "as almost the perfect end to a very good day for [the SDLP]", and declared that, "the good guy, for once, has won".[112]

Unionists' hopes that British politicians would quickly reassess their decision to go ahead with the Anglo-Irish Agreement were soon proven to be misguided. The secretary of state for Northern Ireland was careful not to entirely dismiss the importance of the response of the vast majority of unionists in the election. Tom King acknowledged the "concerns" unionists had about the Agreement, and insisted he wanted to talk to them further about it. However, in a press interview just after the election results, King stressed that "the most significant thing" about the recent contest was "what happened on the nationalist side".[113] Margaret Thatcher, embroiled in the Westlands helicopter crisis at the time, was reported in the *Belfast Telegraph* as offering "a courteous but firm rejection of their [the unionists'] demand to retreat from the Anglo-Irish Pact".[114]

Yet the British premier would ultimately change her mind about the relative merits of the Hillsborough Agreement. When it became clear that Hillsborough had not led to a reduction in the level of violence, nor resulted in the permanent sidelining of Sinn Féin, her enthusiasm for the Agreement started to diminish. Indeed, in her autobiography Thatcher made a rare admission of having made a wrong decision, in relation to signing the pact in November 1985:

> In dealing with Northern Ireland, successive governments have studiously refrained from security policies that might alienate the Irish Government and Irish nationalist opinion in Ulster, in the hope of winning their support against the IRA. The Anglo-Irish Agreement was squarely in this tradition. But I discovered the results of this approach to be disappointing. Our concessions

alienated the Unionists without gaining the level of security cooperation we had a right to expect.[115]

The importance of Anglo-Irish relations and co-operation between the two governments remained central to the thinking of British administrations for most of the next decade. It was reflected in the Downing Street Declaration (1993), but with the IRA ceasefire the following year and the need to bring a resurgent Sinn Féin back into the political process, attention returned to the chances of establishing a power-sharing administration in Belfast. Although the concept of Dublin engagement in political initiatives within the region had been first raised at Sunningdale, this proposal was different, in that the role of the south's government as a "defender" of the Catholic position in the North was acknowledged at Hillsborough for the first time. One of the fundamental weaknesses of the Accord was its failure to directly address the security situation in Northern Ireland which was, on account of its intensity at this time, overshadowing the need for political change. Therefore, the main rationale behind the Agreement – the need to make political concessions to the party representing the voice of constitutional nationalism, and thereby ostracise those representatives of republican paramilitarism – was proven to be flawed in the months and years which followed Hillsborough. In the two-year period between 1983 and 1985, 195 people lost their lives in violent incidents in the province, which compared with 247 in a similar period between 1986 and 1988 (several of these died in some of the Troubles' most graphic terrorist incidents).

As mentioned above, unionist resistance to the Anglo-Irish Agreement was sustained throughout 1986, with the ongoing boycott of local councils by unionist representatives, strike action, and the convening of sinister groups such as the Ulster Clubs. The impact of the Agreement on the loyalist psyche was real, and whilst it would not prove to be calamitous for Protestants, it had sent "a deep shudder of horror" through their ranks, "ushering in an era of direct rule with a green tinge".[116] The virulence of unionists' anti-Hillsborough stance, highlighted in their representatives' decision to resign their parliamentary seats and to come out on the streets in protest, would win few friends in Great Britain, where their perceived belligerence resulted in a lessening of public sympathy, unlike the response which followed unionists' low-key reactions to the Downing Street Declaration in 1993, and to the first IRA ceasefire of 1994. In the period following Hillsborough, unionists were forced to reassess their political options, and mainstream unionism opted to pursue a more integrationist approach. As the passage of time revealed that the Agreement had not resulted in the nightmare entrapment loyalists had dreaded, unionists' almost obsessional focus on Hillsborough gradually faded. Their anger would soon turn in the direction of British security chiefs for their failure to cope with a renewed IRA terror onslaught which followed in the slipstream of Hillsborough. Two years down the line, many loyalists would have gained a perverse satisfaction in the wearied response of Catholics to the Anglo-Irish Agreement.[117]

The "mini General Election" of January 1986 did not produce the much-heralded community denunciation of an externally-devised constitutional arrangement. Therefore, despite the relative unanimity of the Protestant community's political response to Hillsborough – the safe return of 14 MPs and a "No" poll in excess of 400,000 – the contest had not produced the hoped-for support of a majority of the region's electorate, and it had in fact precipitated the loss of one seat to the nationalists.

Despite the brief spell of cross-party unity of January 1986, divisions between the Ulster Unionists and the DUP soon re-emerged. The fortunes of the Unionist Party would take a further knock in the 1987 general election, when Enoch Powell lost his South Down seat. Otherwise, despite this 1986 upsurge in support for the SDLP, the party was ultimately unable to offset the growing challenge of Sinn Féin which, following the calling of the 1994 ceasefire, would emerge as the main political choice of nationalists. The political chasm between the two communities had been illustrated by their very different reactions to Hillsborough, but in just over a decade, a process of political conciliation between the parties representing unionism and nationalism would commence, which would ultimately transform Northern Ireland's political landscape.

Endnotes

1. M. Thatcher, *Downing Street Years* (Harper Collins, London, 1993), p. 385
2. Ulster Unionists were once again the victims of a Westminster "sucker-punch" (as they had been during the run-up to the introduction of direct rule in 1972).
3. *Daily Mail*, 16 November 1985
4. *Belfast News Letter*, 16 November 1985
5. Article 1, Anglo-Irish Agreement: quoted in T. Hadden and K. Boyle, *The Anglo-Irish Agreement: Commentary, Text and Official Review* (Sweet & Maxwell, London, 1989).

6. *Ibid.*, Article 2(a)

7. *Belfast Telegraph*, 28 November 1985

8. *Ibid.*

9. P. Bew and G. Gillespie, *Northern Ireland: A Chronology of the Troubles, 1968–93* (Gill & Macmillan, Dublin, 1993) p. 192

10. A. Kenny, *The Road to Hillsborough* (Pergamon, Oxford, 1986), p. 113

11. Bew and Gillespie, *op. cit.*, p. 192

12. *Ibid.*

13. *The Times*, 16 November 1985

14. Bew and Gillespie, *op. cit.*, p. 189

15. *Belfast News Letter*, 28 November 1985

16. Quoted in R. Bourke, *Peace in Ireland: the War of Ideas* (Pimlico, London, 2003), p. 277

17. *Belfast Telegraph*, 15 November 1985

18. *Irish News*, 16 November 1985

19. A.F. Parkinson, "Loyal Rebels without a Cause" (PhD thesis, University of Swansea, 1996).

20. J. Bardon, *A History of Ulster* (Blackstaff Press, Belfast, 1992), p. 758

21. *Irish News*, 25 November 1985

22. *Belfast Telegraph*, 25 November 1985

23. A *Sunday Times* opinion poll conducted shortly after the signing of the Agreement showed that 83 per cent of loyalists interviewed remained unconvinced by the pact, claiming that it would not lead to peace.

24. *Belfast News Letter*, 16 November 1985

25. P. Dixon, *Northern Ireland: The Politics of War and Peace* (Palgrave Macmillan, 2008), p. 207. Historian David Hume agrees that the unionist leadership had to be cautious in planning their protest campaign to "avoid further alienation, and the prospect of Ulster pulling itself out of the United Kingdom through loss of sympathetic support". D. Hume, *The Ulster Unionist Party 1972–92: A Political Movement in an Era of Conflict and Change* (Ulster Society Publications, 1996), p. 108

26. A. Aughey, *Under Siege: Ulster Unionism and the Anglo-Irish Agreement* (Palgrave Macmillan, 1989), p. 60

27. Extending this campaign to Great Britain proved to be a distinct failure as interest here was pitiably low. In the Fulham by-election of April 1986, an anti-Agreement candidate polled fewer votes than Screaming Lord Sutch of the Monster Raving Loony Party.

28. *Belfast Telegraph*, 7 January 1986

29. *Irish News*, 10 January 1986

30. *Belfast Telegraph*, 6 January 1986

31. *Belfast Telegraph*, 13 January 1986; 14 January 1986

32. *Belfast Telegraph*, 14 January 1986

33. *Belfast Telegraph*, 21 January 1986

34. *Belfast Telegraph*, 10 January 1986

35. *Belfast Telegraph*, 6 January 1986

36. *Belfast Telegraph*, 10 January 1986; 13 January 1986.

37. *Belfast Telegraph*, 13 January 1986

38. *Belfast Telegraph*, 10 January 1986

39. *Irish News*, 16 January 1986

40. *Belfast Telegraph*, 14 January 1986

41. Unionist Joint Working Party, "1986, the Year of Decision – Ulster Says No!": in author's collection)

42. *Ibid.*

43. *Guardian*, 13 January 1986

44. *Sunday Times*, 24 November 1985

45. *Observer*, 5 January 1986

46. *Belfast Telegraph*, 18 January 1986

47. *Ibid.*

48. *Irish News*, 21 January 1986

49. *Belfast Telegraph*, 13 January 1986

50. *Belfast Telegraph*, 20 January 1986

51. M. Smyth election leaflet, "1986: the Year of Decision" (Unionist Joint Working Party, 1986): in author's collection.

52. *Ibid.*

53. One slogan beside the photos of the four SDLP candidates read, "Vote SDLP – a vote for anyone else changes nothing": *Irish News*, 17 January 1986.

54. *Irish News*, 21 January 1986

55. *Ibid.*

56. *Irish News*, 20 January 1986

57. *Irish News*, 16 January 1986

58. *Belfast Telegraph*, 16 January 1986

59. *Belfast Telegraph*, 20 January 1986

60. *Ibid.*

61. As noted in Chapter Six, his party had forced him to withdraw from the April 1981 by-election, which resulted in the victory of Bobby Sands.

62. *Irish News*, 16 January 1986

63. *Irish News*, 17 January 1986

64. *Belfast Telegraph*, 17 January 1986

65. *Ibid.*

66. William McCrea was one of a number of sitting unionists defending relatively small majorities.

67. *Belfast Telegraph*, 16 January 1986

68. *Irish News*, 21 January 1986

69. *Ibid.*

70. *Belfast Telegraph*, 17 January 1986

71. *Ibid.*

72. *Belfast Telegraph*, 16 January 1986

73. *Irish News*, 15 January 1986; *Belfast Telegraph*, 13 January 1986

74. *Belfast Telegraph*, 16 January 1986

75. *Belfast Telegraph*, 14 January 1986; 20 January 1986

76. *Belfast Telegraph*, 14 January 1986

77. *Irish News*, 11 January 1986

78. *Irish News*, 22 January 1986

79. *Irish News*, 21 January 1986

80. *Irish News*, 22 January 1986

81. *Ibid.*

82. *Irish News*, 23 January 1986

83. *Ibid.*

84. *Belfast Telegraph*, 20 January 1986

85. *Ibid.*

86. *Belfast Telegraph*, 22 January 1986

87. *Ibid.*

88. Another poll, this time conducted by the BBC's *Spotlight* programme, concluded that one half of those interviewed had, "already accepted that the results of next week's elections and continuing demonstrations will do little to change the Government's stance on the Anglo-Irish Agreement": *Belfast Telegraph*, 15 January 1986.

89. *Belfast Telegraph*, 15 January 1986

90. *Ibid.*

91. *Irish News*, 16 January 1986

92. *Irish News*, 18 January 1986

93. The electorate was 953,494 strong. A record number of postal votes – 35,817 – had been cast.

94. *Belfast Telegraph*, 22 January 1986

95. *Ibid.*

96. *Belfast Telegraph*, 22 January 1986; 23 January 1986

97. Ian Paisley was photographed sporting a large "Ulster Says No!" scarf.

98. An elderly Shankill Road woman, who had struggled through a blizzard to vote at Woodvale, collapsed and died in the polling station.

99. W.D. Flackes and S. Elliott, *Northern Ireland: A Political Directory, 1969–88* (Blackstaff Press, Belfast, 1989).

100. *Ibid.*

101. *Irish News*, 25 January 1986

102. *Ibid.*

103. *Belfast Telegraph*, 24 January 1986

104. *Belfast Telegraph*, 25 January 1986

105. *Irish News*, 25 January 1986

106. *Ibid.*

107. *Belfast Telegraph*, 25 January 1986

108. *Irish News*, 25 January 1986

109. *Ibid.* That day's *Belfast Telegraph* also described the Mallon result as, "a symbolic blow to unionists".

110. *Irish News*, 25 January 1986

111. *Ibid.*

112. *Ibid.*

113. *Belfast Telegraph*, 25 January 1986

114. *Ibid.*

115. Thatcher, *op. cit.*, p. 415

116. Bew and Gillespie, *op. cit.*, pp. 188–9

117. In the political magazine *Fortnight's* survey in the spring of 1988, 94 per cent of Protestants and 81 per cent of Catholics rejected the Anglo-Irish Agreement, which had "done nothing to benefit the community"; Aughey, *op. cit.*, p. 204.

CHAPTER EIGHT

A Drift to the Margins
The 2003 Assembly Election

One Election or Two?

The Assembly elections of November 2003 constitute the first convincing evidence of a clear breakthrough on the part of politicians representing the extreme sections of both unionist and nationalist opinion at the same contest. Shocking as it might have seemed for many external observers, this success was by no means an overnight phenomenon. Sinn Féin had been a political force in the North for over 20 years, since the successes of republicans Bobby Sands and Owen Carron in Fermanagh & South Tyrone in 1981. The following year, the party gained over 10 per cent first-preference votes and five seats in the Assembly election, and whilst the party's political momentum was not sustained in several areas where potential voters were deterred by republicans' ongoing paramilitary campaign, Sinn Féin was quick to firmly establish itself in the post-conflict era. In the 1998 Assembly contest, the party gained 17.7 per cent of the vote and 18 representatives (6 fewer than the SDLP, which enjoyed 22.1 per cent of the vote), and within three years, Sinn Féin would represent even stronger opposition for the SDLP. At the 2001 Westminster general election, the party's share of the vote had risen to 21.7 per cent, and the election of four of its candidates was one more than its nationalist rivals, who also garnered a slightly smaller proportion of the overall vote.[1]

Similar, potentially seismic changes were apparent in the fortunes of the province's unionist parties. The future of unionism's original political party was even more perilous than the predicament of the party representing constitutional nationalism. The Ulster Unionist Party, despite internal feuds first evident during the latter stages of Terence O'Neill's tenure as a party leader, had managed to retain its "top dog" status within unionism, due in no small part to the perception of the main alternative to the Unionist Party, the DUP – and particularly its leader, the Reverend Ian Paisley – as being beyond the pale. The DUP, founded in 1971, had been very much Paisley's creation, but it had gradually altered its image of a crudely sectarian, hard-line political group and had, especially from the 1990s, started to widen its political appeal. Indeed, in 2003, the DUP was regarded by many as being on the verge of a political breakthrough.

Much had changed since the previous Assembly contest, five years earlier. The outcome of the 2003 Assembly election was anticipated by some commentators as being likely to be different from that of 1998, when the parties representing political moderation had come out on top of the polls. Although the clear overall majority (over 71 per cent), who came out in support of the 1998 Good Friday Agreement in the referendum which followed its signing, actually disguised a much sharper division in opinion than was first apparent within the Protestant community, unionists still gave their backing – narrow and qualified as this might have been – to those groups advocating compromise and change. In the June 1998 Assembly election, David Trimble's Unionist Party had retained its position as the main loyalist party at Stormont, both in terms of its share of the vote (21.3 per cent first-preference votes and 28 elected representatives, though 2 of these, Peter Weir and Pauline Armitage, would soon defect to the DUP), but its lead over its chief unionist rivals continued to diminish, with the DUP securing 18 per cent first-preference votes and 20 elected candidates. Despite the UUP's record of being more successful at the traditional "first past the post" electoral system employed for Westminster elections, the party fared little better at the Westminster general election, three years later. At this, Unionist Party candidates gained just over a quarter of the vote (26.8 per cent), and 6 of its candidates were successful, compared to the DUP's haul of 5 seats and 22.5 per cent of the poll (2 of the 3 seats lost by David Trimble's party fell into the hands of the DUP).

The circumstances which had led to the collapse of the previous Assembly and the prevailing political tension made for a rather bleak backdrop to the 2003 election. The contest had been originally scheduled for May of that year, but was postponed due to the Assembly's malfunctioning in October 2002, following allegations of political espionage involving Sinn Féin officials at Stormont. Ongoing negotiations led by British Prime Minister Tony Blair and Irish premier Bertie Ahern resulted in a joint declaration being announced at Hillsborough Castle a few months later. This set out a clear timetable for specific stages of the IRA's disarmament process, with an unambiguous emphasis that total disarmament was required before the representatives of the former republican paramilitary groupings were allowed to take their places in government.

Local journalists had an important electoral task in briefing their readers on how to maximise the power of their individual votes. Like previous Assembly elections (as well as European and local council contests), this election was to be conducted under the STV system of proportional representation. The full complement of Assembly representatives – some 108 MLAs – would be elected in batches of 6 in each of the region's designated 18 Westminster constituencies. Such a system required all political parties to negotiate a more sophisticated election choice which would potentially appeal to a much wider range of electors, many of whom would not be part of parties' normal support bases. On paper at least, this system of voting for several candidates, on the basis of preference and the eventual transfer of votes, worked better for smaller political parties, especially those possessing a modicum of cross-community appeal.

However, although there was, to a degree at least, a coming together of parties committed to a full implementation of the Good Friday Agreement, petty personal dislikes and long-simmering rows meant that such cross-party cooperation in pursuit of a "nobler cause" was doomed from the start.[2] The large number of candidates contesting the 108 Assembly seats – 257 in total – also reflected the parties' relative strength and confidence. Sinn Féin, with 38 nominees, had put forward 2 more candidates than the SDLP, which was going through a rebuilding process, with John Hume and Seamus Mallon, its leading lights for so many years, not contesting the election. On the other side of the political divide, a similar pattern was evident, with the DUP fielding only 3 fewer candidates than the once mighty UUP (40 to 43 respectively).

The *Belfast Telegraph* realistically dismissed notions of a parallel between the Assembly contest in 1998 and the likely fortunes of parties in the forthcoming contest. The newspaper reminded its readers that the earlier contest had "come in the wake of a positive referendum result" – namely, that concerning the Good Friday Agreement. The editorial proceeded to argue as follows:

> Then, there was an air of anticipation, as voters had their first chance for decades to restore an inclusive form of devolution.

Today, much of the optimism has drained away, because of the Agreement's failure to deal with the link between paramilitarism and politics. As long as it exists – and the UUP in its charter is pledged to resist power-sharing until the transition to peace and democracy is brought to a conclusion – devolution will remain a dream … The reality is that two elections are being fought for the unionist and nationalist vote, with little thought of compromise.[3]

The nationalist press were equally frank with their readers about the likelihood of further republican success at the forthcoming election. The *Irish News* commented that Sinn Féin was, "now hopeful of breakthrough in several constituencies".[4] This could be attributed to the changing political climate in post-conflict Northern Ireland as well, as the major changes in the policy and leadership of the two major parties representing nationalism. Sinn Féin's belated and unequivocal acceptance of the Good Friday Agreement in its entirety now afforded it more potential leeway with nationalist voters, since the SDLP could no longer claim to be holding the moral high ground over a party previously associated with violence. This increased respectability of republican politicians, no longer directly tainted by current association with paramilitary baggage, meant that the party's expectations of political success were high. In addition, Sinn Féin benefited from its ever-widening appeal as a party of "peace", especially with younger Catholic voters and female electors. Sinn Féin's endeavours to develop a brand of community-orientated politics, which would resonate strongly with these important voting groups, were crucial in terms of its growing popularity.

Party positions
The main parties compiled detailed, attractively-presented, election literature and other party material to entice voters to cast votes for their political group. The UUP's election booklet and manifesto ran to 21 pages. In this, the party claimed that devolution had been successful primarily on account of the party's direct engagement in the process, and listed their practical achievements in government, including "developing a rural energy policy, replacing all mobile classrooms with permanent accommodation, reducing bureaucracy and improving efficiency in public administration".[5] The UUP policy document also identified key targets for the new Assembly, including the establishment of "an integrated primary healthcare centre

in every major population area", and the "creation of a radical, proactive Community Relations policy to focus on where the need is greatest, such as sectarian interfaces".[6] In an accompanying charter, endorsed by all 43 UUP candidates, the party pledged to continue in their mission to bring about the end of all paramilitary activity, by not budging on their previously stated insistence over "acts of completion" relating to the Good Friday Agreement (such as decommissioning), and on their declared opposition to an "amnesty for fugitives from justice". On the last page of the document, entitled "The Future and the Past", party leader David Trimble described his party's transformation over a relatively short period, from being in a position of "political marginalisation" to occupying their current place "at the centre of politics". Trimble reiterated his desire to "see the Assembly restored", but only after republicans had "dealt conclusively with issues of decommissioning, as well as the effective winding-up of their private army".[7] The party leader also lamented the fact that the overall unionist majority in the previous Assembly had not been reflected in the composition of the Executive on account of divisions within unionism, and suggested that this played into the hands of those directly opposed to Northern Ireland's constitutional position.

The DUP's combined policy brochure and "Fair Deal" party manifesto – which ran to 40 pages in total, with several colour illustrations – contained a series of "mini" documents, which argued for a new political agreement, a senior citizens' charter, a bill of rights and even included a charter for motorcyclists! Ian Paisley's personal message to the electorate was that the contest was "Ulster's date with destiny", which represented the "chance to put things right, to give a mandate to a strong and united Democratic Unionist team and to negotiate a new agreement".[8] Under a picture of young children, the question was put to potential voters: "How long are you prepared to wait for benefits for our community?" The manifesto also outlined pivotal policy areas which DUP representatives in the new Assembly and its Executive would endeavour to promote, including the return of meaningful devolved powers, a refusal to negotiate with representatives of terrorist organisations and a ban on Executive positions for those not totally committed to the peace process. This DUP manifesto dismissed David Trimble's record in charge of the previous administration, listing his perceived failures in office. These included "the destruction of the RUC, the withdrawal of the army, the release of terrorist prisoners, the elevation of Sinn Féin/IRA members to government office without evidence of the destruction of weaponry, the creation of ever-expanding, all-Ireland institutions", as well as the tolerance of an "ever-growing list of breaches of IRA and loyalist so-called ceasefires". The party also maintained that a direct consequence of UUP policy was that Northern Ireland was "closer to a united Ireland than we have ever been".[9]

For the SDLP, the 2003 Assembly elections constituted the first major test of the party's strength in the wake of the retirement of key party figures, such as John Hume (who was not defending his Foyle seat) and Seamus Mallon, the former deputy first minister and representative for Newry and Armagh. The absence of Hume, the party's leader since 1979 and one of the architects of the peace process, would constitute a considerable test of faith for nationalist-minded electors across the North. It would be especially pertinent within Hume's power-base in Derry, where a recent redrawing of electoral boundaries had reduced the electorate of Foyle by some 5,000. The *Belfast Telegraph* forecast that Hume's absence from his usual stomping-ground would have "a massive impact on who is elected", and went on to point out that, with the removal of the SDLP's "big hitter", the "chief topic of debate" in the constituency" was "whether Sinn Féin can cash in on his absence and win an extra seat in Foyle".[10] The party's new leader was another Derry native, Mark Durkan, who was optimistic about the prospects of his party's 36 candidates (2 fewer than the number fielded by Sinn Féin). There was no fundamental policy difference between Durkan's SDLP election campaign and that of his predecessor, though some of his promotional strategies were a little different from those favoured by the veteran SDLP leader. New initiatives included the release of 500 balloons with the message, "Stop the DUP!", from Belfast's City Hall on 24 November, and the recruitment of celebrity backers to publicly support the SDLP's cause, with singer Brian Kennedy speaking at a news conference in Belfast the previous day. Durkan would have been fully aware of the closely-fought nature of the imminent contest. This was confirmed in an opinion poll conducted by the *Belfast Telegraph* halfway through the campaign. The paper's findings suggested that the UUP and SDLP remained ahead of their nearest rivals, but that the DUP and Sinn Féin were now "within striking distance" of them, in a "neck-and-neck contest".[11] Durkan would have been buoyed by the views of many Protestant voters who had "rated highly" his chances of being offered a senior post in the Executive (such as deputy first minister). This opinion poll also suggested that the SDLP was maintaining its levels of support, with a figure of 22 per cent of the total electorate being similar to that polled in the previous Assembly election, and one point up on their showing at the 2001 Westminster election.

The SDLP's manifesto, "Equality, Justice and Prosperity", was launched on 13 November. The document was 34 pages long and contained several photographs of the party's new leader. In it, Durkan maintained that the "real battleground" in the election was one "between those who want to protect the Good Friday Agreement, and those who want to wreck it".[12] The manifesto's main message was the need for "continuing progress" in order to "build peace, equality and justice". Durkan argued that his party had already "delivered real change" in the Assembly, but stressed that the job was far from being finished. The SDLP was, he maintained, "determined to secure the full implementation" of the Good Friday Agreement, which "could not be renegotiated".[13] The party's commitment to both the recent major political changes in the North and to its ultimate, long- political goal were blended together in the manifesto, which claimed that the SDLP was "100 per cent committed to the [Good Friday] Agreement, and 100 per cent committed to an all-Ireland". Aware of the shift in the electorate's mood in 1998, when a desire for change had been expressed, Mark Durkan appealed directly to voters to help "change the face of politics" in Northern Ireland.[14]

The SDLP's chief target in their election campaign was the DUP, the main voice of opposition to the Good Friday Agreement. The party was especially keen to make inroads in a number of areas which had been previously favourable territory for the DUP, but about which there were now more audible moans of dissent. The new leader identified East Antrim, South Antrim, Lagan Valley, Strangford and West Belfast as constituencies where his party had chances of picking up Assembly seats – mainly through the transfer of votes – and Durkan urged supporters that, "now more than ever, the time has come to stop the 'No' men!"[15] As well as this, a range of party figures dismissed the nihilistic nature of DUP policy. Standing in North Belfast, Alban Maginness suggested the DUP offered "nothing beyond hot air and bluster", and urged voters to give serious thought to "stopping the DUP".[16] The analogy of road traffic posing danger and the "hazardous" nature of association with a political party like the DUP, was much to the fore in SDLP party material, which adorned lampposts as well as the news pages of the local press. Large advertisements in the *Irish News* during the last week of the campaign included one hexagonal traffic warning sign bearing the words, "Stop the DUP – posing safety hazard!"[17]

The SDLP leader maintained his assault on the opponents of the Belfast Agreement throughout the campaign. Dismissing the DUP's "Vision for Devolution" proposals as a "half-baked 'blueprint' – out, out, out!", Durkan suggested that what the DUP really desired was "majority rule", which he suggested was also "out" for the majority of voters. He also condemned the DUP's proposal that the whole assembly should take decisions which had been made up until then by nominated ministers, since this would prove to be "a recipe for total chaos".[18] Writing in the *Irish News* towards the end of the campaign, Durkan identified a number of "crucial choices" which would "decide our future". He argued that the main choices were "between those who want to save the future, and those who want to turn back the clock", as well as between "shared prosperity" and "shared poverty", and "between developing partnerships and deepening old divisions".[19]

SDLP attacks were not restricted to the DUP. Its chief nationalist opponents, Sinn Féin, as well as the Unionist Party, were also subject to the party's venom, albeit to a lesser extent. Republicans had claimed that they had been approached by the SDLP to agree to an electoral "pact", but the latter strenuously denied this. However, some of the party's official literature and advertising material directly blamed Sinn Féin for its refusal to sit on the Police Board, which had resulted in the appointments of perceived hard-line unionists like John Taylor and Ian Paisley, Junior. The SDLP were also furious with Sinn Féin following Gerry Adams' blatant refusal to encourage republicans to cast their transfer votes to SDLP candidate Alex Atwood in West Belfast.[20] Although this appeared to be motivated more by the personalities involved in the contest than by actual policies – Gerry Adams had no such problems with republicans' transfer votes being cast for Attwood's party colleague, Joe Hendron – John Hume entered the election fray at this point to criticise the Sinn Féin leader's political judgement. The former SDLP leader suggested that Adams and Sinn Féin were "jeopardising the Good Friday Agreement over vote transfers".[21]

The SDLP also rebuked those unionists who continued to oppose the Good Friday Agreement from within the ranks of the UUP. Describing them as "DUP-lite" politicians, the SDLP ridiculed the manner in which they dismissed citizens of the Irish Republic as "foreigners".[22] Alex Attwood even claimed that David Trimble, the chief signatory of the Belfast Agreement, was actually opposed to most of its clauses, and also called for the removal of the Union flag from Belfast's City Hall.[23] Despite a clear fear of entering unknown, murky waters, being led by an inexperienced leader and lacking the wise counsel of respected former leaders – not to mention the threat also being posed by an increasingly confident political foe – the SDLP's position, as reflected in its manifesto and subsequent campaign, was both transparent and optimistic. In an eve of election report entitled, "Mark Durkan's first real test as party leader", the *Irish News* noted that a bullish Durkan was insisting that his party would, "prove the pundits, who have begun to write our obituaries, wrong".[24]

Sinn Féin's rising public profile, largely as a result of its major role in the peace process and its gradual improvement in terms of electoral performance, meant that the party entered this 2003 Assembly contest with high hopes of a major political breakthrough. The party had gained 17.7 per cent of the vote in the previous Assembly contest, five years before, and had increased this to 21.7 per cent in the 2001 Westminster election, and one opinion poll now put its likely share of the vote at around 20 per cent.[25] Party leader, Gerry Adams – described in the same opinion poll as "the most secure party leader" – was hopeful of Sinn Féin taking at least an extra four seats in the forthcoming contest, and the party fielded 38 candidates across the province (this was 2 more than the SDLP, which Sinn Féin hoped it would replace as the largest nationalist party).

Sinn Féin's manifesto and accompanying election booklet, "Agenda for Government", was, at 92 pages in total, nearly three times as long as the SDLP's policy document, and proudly declared itself to be "the most comprehensive manifesto ever produced by our party". The main theme of the document was "building an Ireland of equals", with an emphasis upon its vision of "a peaceful, prosperous and united Ireland".[26] Sinn Féin claimed that it had "made a difference" in a variety of ways during its spell in government. The "transformation" of local government had evolved "largely on account of the involvement of Sinn Féin councillors", and the peace process had been "initiated" and "continually energised" by the party.[27] As was the case in the election documentation of the SDLP, "equality" was a "buzz" word in the Sinn Féin manifesto. Despite the recent "crashing" of political institutions – the role of republicans in creating this situation was conspicuously ignored in the document – the party claimed it had "never given up" on moving the political process forward, but had been constantly negotiating with the London and Dublin governments and with unionist leaders. Proclaiming that Sinn Féin remained "firm" on the 1998 deal, the party pledged itself to implementing the Good Friday Agreement and to "further all-Ireland progress". The manifesto boasted of the party's "success" over the five years which had passed since the signing of the agreement, during which time it had "consistently delivered in government, in our communities and in negotiating on the Peace Process".[28]

The manifesto was launched by the party's deputy leader, Martin McGuinness in the absence of Sinn Féin President Gerry Adams. At a press conference in Belfast, McGuinness directly appealed to unionists to consider voting for his party, arguing that the political situation in the North had been "transformed", and that its citizens would never again witness the "inequality, discrimination, injustice, domination and violence that has happened over the course of many decades".[29] The "comprehensive" coverage of a host of issues in the party's bulging document ranged from an appeal for the full implementation of the Good Friday Agreement and eventual Irish unity (the party specifically called on the Irish government to establish a commission to draw up plans for a unified Ireland), to the abolition of academic selection at the age of 11, as well as police disarmament and the question of introducing water charges in the region.

Like the DUP on the other political extreme, Sinn Féin was therefore entering this contest in a confident vein. As observed above, its political star was very much in the ascendancy, with increasing support displayed in recent elections. In some ways, this appears to be a remarkable trend. Most of the party's key spokespersons at the time reflected the party's paramilitary origins and were, in the main, men who had not experienced higher education or held professional positions of responsibility, as is the trend for most parliamentarians in other western European societies. Yet this close association and involvement in a rather murky, sectarian "war" in the recent past did not appear to have had an overly negative impact on a party, whose candidates uniformly presented themselves as sharp-suited and articulate (if liable to indulge in excessive use of political cliché and obfuscation), as potential representatives who appealed particularly to younger Catholic voters. The latter were impressed by Sinn Féin's focus on dealing with issues at local level in a manner which other political parties had not consistently addressed in the past. Party strategists excelled at political presentation and knew exactly what its wider core support desired – a sense that Catholic politicians were making genuine inroads in a way which did not jeopardise the security of its community, or risk its younger members becoming embroiled in a never-ending war against the British. The party realised that if its bid to present itself as a bona fide, respectable party was to be successful, it had to speak to sections of the growing Catholic middle class, by playing down the militaristic language it had employed during earlier political campaigns. This rationale was also largely behind its move to urge the electorate at large to consider voting Sinn Féin, despite its strategists' undoubted realisation that the party's past association with men and women regarded by many voters as "terrorists" mitigated against any chance of them winning over most of these electors.

Sinn Féin managed to cope well during the election's earliest phase with an unwelcome situation, whereby its two chief personalities were otherwise engaged. Martin McGuinness had been called to give evidence at the ongoing Bloody Sunday inquiry, where he refused to answer questions relating to his alleged involvement with the PIRA during the early 1970s.[30] Gerry Adams, who had been in New York at the start of the campaign, returned to attend his father's funeral in Belfast. However, whilst he was in America, Adams had selected the DUP as his party's chief electoral target. He stressed that the latter would quickly have to "face up to the reality that the Good Friday Agreement is an international treaty between two governments that cannot be renegotiated".[31] This rejection of any suggestion of the possible "renegotiation" of the Belfast Agreement was repeated by party spokesmen at various stages during the campaign, with Sinn Féin promising close to Election Day that it would be "up to the challenge of putting manners on the DUP after the election".[32]

Gerry Adams' own seemingly impregnable position in West Belfast – which, according to the *Belfast Telegraph*, was "the most lop-sided constituency in Northern Ireland", and where he had won two-thirds of the vote at the Westminster election two years previously – was, paradoxically, a weakness for his party. With 4 other Sinn Féin members among the 14 candidates in the division, Adams' popularity, it was argued, might pose its "biggest problem" in the complicated system of transferring first preference votes.[33] Towards the end of the campaign, Adams reminded electors that his party had "taken real risks for peace" over a period of many years. He also pointed to the existence of considerable voter "dissatisfaction" at the perceived weaknesses of the other main parties. This included annoyance at the SDLP's "carping and begrudging" campaign, the "semi-detached" position of the DUP and the "here today, gone tomorrow" stance of the UUP.[34]

The minor parties had performed creditably at the previous Assembly election, and were confident of picking up some seats – especially since the transfer of votes system favoured smaller parties. Enjoying the support of Liberal Democrat leader, Charles Kennedy, who addressed election meetings, the Alliance Party (which had won 6 seats in 1998) launched its manifesto, "Alliance Works", on 14 November. In this, its leader, David Ford maintained that elections should be about "bread-and-butter campaigns", rather than "infighting between rival unionist factions", and nationalists "trying to outgreen each other". Ford argued that Alliance's emphasis was on "building a united community and an inclusive, integrated, open, free and fair society".[35] In his introduction to the manifesto, the Alliance leader described his party as, "the political voice of those who work to create a united community, one characterised by sharing, not separating". His party, he insisted, offered an invitation to all to join "something different, something better than tribal politics", which aspired to a "shared and non-sectarian future". The Alliance Party was the "only political group that rejected the notion that we must all be pigeon-holed into 'two communities', instead respecting personal choice over identity".[36]

The Progressive Unionist Party (PUP), a group which represented the political views of the former paramilitary force, the UVF, had also performed relatively well at the previous Assembly election, and was fielding 11 candidates this time round. Like the Alliance Party, the PUP maintained that it was offering a package of social and economic policies, although it was closer to the DUP in its condemnation of the Belfast Agreement. Reminding his audience that the Protestant community was being "left behind" politically, economically and socially, party leader Billy Hutchinson told journalists that the electorate needed to "realise that if the split between pro-Agreement and anti-Agreement camps continues, and unionist parties don't transfer to each other, it will allow Sinn Féin to pick up seats in places like North Belfast".[37]

The Women's Coalition Party had also experienced a successful election in 1998, winning 2 seats, including the victory of leader Monica McWilliams in South Belfast. This time, the party was mounting a challenge involving 7 candidates, who were campaigning on a range of practical issues, such as the need to reduce hospital waiting lists and discovering ways of tackling child poverty in the province. Other parties fielding candidates in the Assembly election included the Green Party, the Conservatives and the Socialist Party (which was also focusing on cutting poverty and tackling the problem of low wages in Northern Ireland).

"More D-Days than a World War Two matinee"

In the early phase of the contest, the media focused on reminding the general public about the results of the previous Assembly election and the prospects for the various parties this time around. In 1998, as we have seen, both the UUP and the SDLP had retained clear, if not huge, leads over their main opponents, the DUP and Sinn Féin respectively.[38] The *Irish News* reminded its readers that the SDLP had, for the first time in its history, enjoyed the highest number of first-preference votes cast in a Northern election, and that the party anticipated achieving similar success under what the paper described as a "radical" voting system.[39] However, in its first two-page election special of the campaign, the *Irish News* also noted that republicans were "hopeful of breakthroughs in several constituencies". On the other side, the UUP's all-time low share of the vote in 1998, and current strains within the party meant that it would be "a big task" for them to "rally round on an agreed manifesto". Their main unionist opponents, the DUP, were "desperate to close the gap" between the two parties, and "finally declare [themselves] the major voice of unionism".[40]

Most observers agreed about the close nature of the forthcoming contest, with the *Irish News* predicting the "tightest election ever". However, the paper also acknowledged that the province had witnessed several nail-biting contests in the past, maintaining that the North had "seen more D-Days than a World War Two matinee".[41] The *Belfast Telegraph*'s own opinion poll, published on 12 November, confirmed the "neck-and-neck" race between the main parties within their respective communities. The paper agreed with other commentators who believed that the region was "facing its toughest and tightest electoral test for many years", and that both Sinn Féin and the DUP were "within striking range of their rivals".[42]

Later in the contest, both the *Irish News* and *Belfast Telegraph* turned their readers' attention to the danger of voting apathy. In an *Irish News* article, journalist Darran McCann pointed out that the region regularly recorded "a higher turnout than most parts of Britain". However, this trend was less evident in recent contests, with the numbers voting in the 2001 Westminster election believed to have been the lowest recorded since 1918.[43] McCann argued that the North's "good name for voting" was "at risk", and queried if the region's "traditionally diligent" voters would "catch the virulent bug of political apathy".[44] The following week, the *Belfast Telegraph* bluntly asked its readers, "Election Fears – will you vote?" The paper pointed out that "rival attractions" on voting day, as well as that electoral imponderable, the possibility of inclement weather, meant that party strategists were "today raising concerns about voter apathy in the campaign's final phase".[45]

Those newspapers reflecting unionist and nationalist opinion also discussed a range of other features of this election. At an early stage in the contest, the *Irish News* drew the attention of its readers to the impact which an unofficial postal strike might have upon those casting their votes indirectly. The *Belfast Telegraph* also took up this story, suggesting that the large number of Northern Irish university students living in Great Britain would especially be affected by the mail dispute, particularly with its 6 November deadline for the receipt of votes, which was some three weeks before polling day.[46] Another aspect of the contest highlighted by the *Belfast Telegraph* was the large number of dissidents within several of the larger parties, which the paper heralded under the headline, "Rebels tackle big parties in bid for seats at Stormont", pointing out that "at least 17 rebels [were] standing for election".[47] The gender imbalance of parliamentary representatives was the theme of Sharon O'Neill's intriguing *Irish News* article. Only 14 of the 108 MLAs in 1998 were women – this constituted 13 per cent of the Assembly's total, and compared unfavourably with the Welsh Assembly, where women made up half of the representatives, and also the Scottish Assembly, where 40 per cent of the members were female. O'Neill's headline ran: "Politics still male-dominated in the North".[48]

The modern nature of electioneering, especially in terms of the techniques employed in voter persuasion and the breadth of media technology now available for transmitting party messages, was evident in press coverage of this contest. Most of the parties deployed specialist workers, not only to write and design party manifestos and literature, but also to produce election videos. Sinn Féin appeared to be ahead of the game in this respect, and, as the *Belfast Telegraph* reported, its "party-piece ... with its split-screen production, owed much to TV thriller, *24*". Other parties were, according to the paper, less successful in their use of the latest technology. For instance, the "ill-advised" UUP film which accompanied the party's election message showed David Trimble and his wife walking in a deserted park with the

UUP leader "gesticulating wildly", with his audience "not privy to what he was saying". On the other hand, the SDLP, eager to "sell" their relatively new leader to the wider public, opted for a "leader-only piece", which the *Belfast Telegraph* claimed was "quite reminiscent of its last effort".[49] Gone were the days when candidates addressed voters from the back of lorries, charabancs, horse and carts, or Ford Cortinas bedecked with election posters and assorted literature. For this election, the UUP's leader and senior politicians toured the province in a helicopter, while the DUP used a "battle bus" to tour those constituencies which its candidates were contesting. The Alliance Party appeared to be more frugal with its election expenditure, although one candidate – Seamus Close in South Antrim – was pictured campaigning in his "sexy Hyundai coupé" sports car.[50] Even the likely post-election scenario, and its potentially depressing nature, was picked up on by local journalists early in the campaign. One report in the *Belfast Telegraph* noted that Paul Murphy, Labour's Northern Ireland secretary, had confirmed that "the new Assembly may not be formed until after the election" and that, even with the composition of the chamber divided, the Assembly would "probably remain in suspension" until renewed talks had resulted in the creation of another power-sharing executive.[51]

Both the *Belfast Telegraph* and *Irish News* featured a daily constituency focus slot in their election coverage. These features would inform readers, not only about the relative strengths of the various parties in specific constituencies – as well as providing fascinating descriptions of the various political personalities involved in the fight for seats – but would also outline the changing demographic trends within the constituencies in question. Assessing the chances of parties in key seats remained central to both newspapers' coverage. For instance, the fortunes of Sinn Féin in seats like Newry and Armagh, and Fermanagh & South Tyrone (where the nationalist majority had increased following boundary changes in the mid-1990s) were highlighted in the *Belfast Telegraph*.[52] The *Irish News* also put the spotlight on the border constituency of Fermanagh & South Tyrone which had produced several close and exciting contests in the past, as we have seen. This sprawling district, with a total electorate of 64,355, had returned 4 unionists in the 1998 Assembly election, but this time nationalist candidates outnumbered unionist ones: Sinn Féin had 3, with 2 candidates being nominated by each of the SDLP, UUP and DUP groups. The *Irish News* maintained that "the west will be won over" by "devolution, roads and health" issues.[53] The *Belfast Telegraph* also positively assessed republicans' chances of success in North Belfast, where 17 candidates were endeavouring to garner the votes of the 51,335-strong electorate, in what amounted to a "crowded" field. The paper's report observed that Sinn Féin was "looking to shine" and that its two candidates were "leaving little to chance" in the "jigsaw" constituency, where the outcome would be "tight", and where tactical voting seemed "certain to play a significant part in the outcome".[54] Unusually, the *Irish News* agreed with the *Belfast Telegraph* in its analysis of the struggle in this constituency. In an earlier article, the former noted the seat's "highly politicised" nature, in which there was "more chance of winning the lottery than finding a floating voter".[55] This once predominantly loyalist constituency had witnessed major demographic change during the modern conflict, and the percentage of Protestant voters was only slightly greater than Catholic ones, at 51 per cent and 45 per cent respectively. Despite the area's chronic housing shortage and long-term unemployment, the electorate were expected to vote along "orange and green lines".[56]

As mentioned earlier, a large number of candidates (257) were standing for election to the Assembly, with two predominantly loyalist constituencies, East Antrim and North Down, tying for the highest number of candidates in the field (19 in each). The *Belfast Telegraph* reported that, in the latter constituency, the "battle-lines were drawn for the unionist vote", but, as in many constituencies, it would be the battle for the sixth and last seat which would hold most interest. The paper surmised that, in the case of North Down, "any one of six parties have a chance of grabbing the final position".[57] Whilst being considered a "safe" unionist seat, East Antrim was also anticipating "hard-fought battles for the last two seats".[58]

Two of the safest seats in Northern Ireland were in East and West Belfast. Not a single nationalist candidate had been returned in East Belfast at the 1998 Assembly election, and hopes were not high in a seat where the population was over 90 per cent Protestant. Fifteen candidates were contesting the 6 seats in a constituency consisting of 51,582 electors, and incidentally, they included George Rainbow Weiss of the "Vote for Yourself" Party. The constituency had been the domain of DUP deputy leader, Peter Robinson for close to a quarter of a century, and the *Belfast Telegraph* reckoned that he was "likely to top the poll again" in "the most overwhelmingly Protestant constituency in Northern Ireland".[59] A few days earlier, the *Irish News* had also sent a reporter to the old shipyard constituency, where the DUP remained "confident of victory". *Irish News* journalist John Manley visited the Union Jack Shop on the arterial Newtownards Road in east Belfast, which he described as representing "a one-stop shop for a British identity" and which sold products ranging from Parachute Regiment towels and Gibraltar flags to Red Hand of Ulster mouse-mats.[60] Manley concluded that "asserting unionist identity with flags and bunting" appeared to be, "one of the few things left to bind this once proud and united community". His assessment of the election's likely outcome was also interesting, since he contended that East Belfast was, "not a one-party constituency" but rather one, where "all shades of unionism enjoy a degree of popular support across 11 wards".[61]

The constituency across Belfast's River Lagan, West Belfast, was similarly one-sided in its religious composition and political leanings. Gerry Adams, the elected Westminster MP for West Belfast, had gained over two-thirds of the votes cast in the 2001 Westminster election, and Sinn Féin were this time "bidding to take five seats", in a constituency which represented "a city within a city".[62] The *Irish News* returned to West Belfast on the eve of the election, and its reporter Dan McGinn visited the Falls Road to watch Gerry Adams on the campaign trail. He described the scene at the Twin Spires Complex as "like something out of a Western", with two "solitary security guards waiting for their leader and his posse to arrive". Soon the Sinn Féin president and his election team "swept into the lower Falls like Comanches raiding a frontier outpost". McGinn's assessment of the contest was that the party would "stretch its lead over Mark Durkan's SDLP in the battle for the nationalist vote".[63]

In a political environment unaccustomed to rapid major change, there were signs that a number of shifts in the region's political landscape were taking place. Prominent among these were the considerable demographic changes which were gradually redefining Northern Irish society, and had resulted in a higher proportion of Catholics living there and voting in the elections. Even a long-standing unionist constituency like South Belfast was changing rapidly. The *Irish News* aptly described it as "a leafy, tree-lined study in demographics", where the sectarian divide amongst its population was nearly 50–50, and where "nobody can rest easy" as far as the result of the election was concerned.[64] The *Belfast Telegraph* also noted the changes in a largely middle-class constituency, where "the boulevards show up a state of flux" and where there were "likely to be changes" in the constituency's return of candidates.[65] At the last Assembly contest, both the UUP and SDLP had returned two members, with the DUP and Women's Coalition returning a single member each.

South Antrim, "once deemed the safest Westminster seat in the North", was also witnessing a change in its political direction, albeit as part of a trend solely within unionism. The *Irish News* described the "one step forward, one step back" progress of both the UUP and DUP in the constituency as "political pinball". At a by-election in 2000, following the death of Ulster Unionist MP Clifford Forsythe, the DUP's William McCrea had won the Westminster seat from the Ulster Unionists, but the Ulster Unionists had regained it in 2001 when David Burnside defeated McCrea. Describing it as a contest where "the two shades of unionism [were] battling for power", the *Irish News* concluded that Burnside was "regarded as the front-runner in this contest".[66]

Political and demographic change were also providing hope to nationalist-leaning politicians in other constituencies. Strangford was considered a safe unionist seat, but with "a bump in the Catholic population in parts of the constituency [such as Carryduff], the SDLP is talking loudly about picking up a seat here".[67] Political infighting amongst republicans and the resignation from the party of one of their MLAs meant that Sinn Féin's normally strong performance in Mid-Ulster was under some threat. The *Belfast Telegraph* suggested that the constituency might "not be all plain sailing" for the party, and observed that "how the Sinn Féin vote holds up ... will be one of the most interesting aspects of this election".[68] Twelve candidates, including four from Sinn Féin, were contesting this seat, which had an electorate of 56,202 and had produced some intriguing, close-fought contests in the past. The *Irish News*, in its constituency focus, maintained that "the two biggest profile candidates remain Martin McGuinness and William McCrea", and sardonically observed:

> While the former will be shaking hands outside chapels in the remaining campaign days, the latter, a Free Presbyterian minister, will be shaking fists at the evils of sharing power with republicans.[69]

Another unusual trend in a Northern election was the emergence of local issues in a number of constituencies. North Antrim, a vanguard of unionism in the past, was difficult to assess politically, because of economic factors. A large number of families in this largely agricultural constituency had been disgruntled by a series of trends which had a negative impact upon their source of livelihood. In a report entitled, "Tough times could sway North Antrim", the *Irish News* pointed out the extent to which farmers had been affected by "a dramatic decrease in the number of farms and an uncertain future".[70] In another traditionally loyalist seat, East Londonderry, there was – despite the "certain" reelection of the DUP's Gregory Campbell, who had gained close to a third of all votes at the 2001 Westminster contest – "a genuine anger" in towns like Coleraine and Limavady about the "lack of investment outside of Northern Ireland's major cities". The constituency, a major centre of tourism in the North, had been "hit badly by marching season unrest, foot-and-mouth disease, and a downturn in international travel".[71] A further source of irritation for local voters was the persistence of rumours that the area's vital rail connection with Belfast was going to terminate at Ballymena, thus depriving them of an important travel link.[72] West Tyrone was another constituency where candidates were pleading with voters to consider changing their voting habits, and instead register their support with a campaigner fighting on a single issue – in this case, not the border question. Independent candidate, Kieran Deeny, a doctor at a local hospital, was reported to be amassing considerable cross-community backing for his opposition to the cutting of acute service provision at Omagh Hospital.

⌇

The close-run nature of the campaign, especially between the two main unionist parties, inevitably resulted in an even more bitter election campaign than usual. At an early stage in the contest, the *Belfast Telegraph* warned that "unionist splits could shred the vote", and that there were "more brands of unionism than ever in the election line-up". This "welter of individual unionist candidates", opposed to David Trimble and his party's position on power-sharing with Sinn Féin, had resulted in a "confusing" situation.[73] Later in the campaign, the DUP, obviously conscious that they were on the verge of a major political breakthrough, decided to take their campaigning literally to the UUP's doorstep, at Cunningham House, on the Holywood Road in east Belfast. A group of senior DUP personnel, including Ian Paisley, Peter Robinson and William McCrea, wheeled their mobile billboard to the UUP headquarters' entrance and started to hold a press briefing for those members of the media who had clearly been alerted to their plan. David Trimble and some of his colleagues intercepted the DUP contingent and "a full-scale public confrontation" commenced.[74] The numerous personal insults included those directed at the restrained figure of Ian Paisley for his refusal to participate in television debates, as well as Peter Robinson's description of David Trimble as "yesterday's man".[75] The day after the incident, political correspondent Noel McAdam told his *Belfast Telegraph* readers that the "curtains [had] refused to fall on the UUP and DUP version of 'street theatre' … [as the] boos and catcalls continued long after the improvised performance". His succinct verdict was that it had been "a day for histrionics rather than history", on account of "senior figures in the rival parties shouting each other down".[76] McAdam's report also referred to the collateral damage which had resulted. The Unionist Party dissident representative, David Burnside was one of those to "get in on the act", with his comparison of the unionist leaders' confrontation to that of "fighting between cats and dogs on the street". It was, Burnside added, "disgusting, distasteful and embarrassing", and he called for "bottom-line" talks between the two parties to establish channels for future negotiations.[77] The *Belfast Telegraph*'s editorial that day insisted that "serious political debate" would be "suffocated by [such] electoral stunts" and argued that the incident, whilst "raising interest in a lacklustre election", might also have "acted as a massive turn-off to voters already wondering if they should bother voting at all". The paper did not mince words in terms of allocating blame for the affray at Cunningham House. Denouncing the DUP for its decision to congregate outside its opponent's premises, the paper conceded that the UUP would also be damaged by what had happened, and declared:

> No one wins when politicians are reduced to shouting incoherently … showing in their choice of words what contempt they have for each other … As if Mr Trimble's troubles with the DUP were not enough, he has to cope with internal sniping, encapsulated in yesterday's mini-manifesto published by his three rebel MPs.[78]

The *Irish News* also attached considerable significance to the "gutter row" involving unionists, declaring that the incident had resulted in "a fairly restrained assembly election campaign exploding into life".[79] Stating that the DUP had "effectively set out to taunt David Trimble in his own backyard", the paper focused more on the low-profile stance adopted by the DUP leader, who appeared "lost for words" as he squared up to the UUP leader. This apparent "silence" on the part of a normally highly voluble politician, the *Irish News* maintained, "left the initiative firmly with Mr Trimble".[80]

Such animosity between the two main unionist parties was not restricted to the angry words and verbal taunts of their political leaders. Ulster Unionist Party offices were attacked on a number of occasions during the election campaign. Shortly after the Cunningham House confrontation, paint bombers targeted the UUP headquarters on at least two separate occasions. Additionally, Trimble's constituency office in Lurgan was damaged by similar means, in attacks which were believed to have been "related to the bitter tensions within unionism".[81]

At the start of their campaign, the UUP required its candidates to sign a ten-point charter backing their manifesto and proposed post-election direction. As noted above, this caused problems for a small number of dissident candidates who, whilst signing the charter, subsequently produced their own charter with an additional number of demands. The party's manifesto (outlined in detail earlier) was launched on 12 November, and appealed to voters to "look at the future, and not the past". The party claimed that there was, "no one else in the unionist community who could complete the task of having the Stormont administration restored".[82]

Of key interest to both the public and media alike was the contest in Upper Bann between David Trimble and his gospel-singing DUP opponent, David Simpson. Heckled and jostled at the Banbridge count at the end of his Westminster election victory in 2001 – where he defeated Simpson, but with a reduced majority – some experts postulated that Trimble was under similar pressure to his unionist predecessor, Terence O'Neill, over thirty years before. The *Belfast Telegraph*'s headline for its focus despatch on 19 November, "Forget David and Goliath – Upper Bann is the clash of the Two Davids", reflected its belief that the DUP had a reasonable chance of causing the UUP leader considerable embarrassment. Suggesting that a win for Simpson the following week would "produce the kind of headline the DUP dreams of", the paper contended that the Upper Bann contest was "perhaps the key election contest between the forces of pro- and anti-Agreement unionism, partly because it is Trimble's power base, and even though it will most likely end in a draw".[83] The *Irish News* concurred with the *Belfast Telegraph*'s assessment of this contest's significance, especially for the DUP. Pointing out that the widening chasm between two parties which had enjoyed a temporary rapprochement over the Drumcree stand-offs a few years earlier, the *Irish News* noted how it was "now a far cry" from the Orange Order protests when David Trimble and Ian Paisley had "skipped hand-in-hand". The paper stressed that the DUP were "determined to embarrass the Ulster Unionists here more than in any other constituency".[84]

David Trimble's electioneering style also received unfavourable comment in the *Irish News*. Whilst canvassing with his UUP colleague on the traditionally hard-line loyalist Shankill Road in west Belfast, the party leader was heckled as he distributed leaflets – bearing the message, "McGimpsey is best for the West!" – by a woman who accused him of being "a traitor to the Shankill". The *Irish News* reporter, comparing Trimble's stiff style of electioneering with the more relaxed manner of Ian Paisley or Sammy Wilson, suggested he was "not happy on the election trail", where he cut "a quieter, more urbane figure, who is more at home reading a Booker Prize-nominated novel or enjoying an opera at Covent Garden".[85] Towards the end of the contest, Trimble's final appeal to voters was granted considerable space in the pro-Agreement *Irish News*. In a "platform" column, Trimble proclaimed that "the befudgery [of DUP politicians] and those clinging to the violence of the past must not be allowed to wreck our future".[86] In the following day's edition of the paper, another appeal from Trimble predicted that, rather than losing seats, his party would make gains at the expense of the DUP. He asked electors for a chance to "consolidate the progress by supporting those who have made the progress, and to enable us to finish the job".[87]

In different circumstances, characteristics of the DUP's election campaign might well have proved to have been counterproductive and highly damaging to the electoral chances of its candidates. The party's provocative strategy of campaigning directly outside the UUP headquarters was a considerable gamble, which might well have backfired, and individual party members also utilised electioneering gimmicks which did little to indicate that the DUP was a serious party on the brink of becoming involved in the governance of the region. For instance, a leading member of the party appeared in "a headmaster's attire" at a party press conference. Sammy Wilson, a former teacher, claimed to be the head of "St Anthony's Disintegrated School on the Hill", a satirical jibe at the previous Stormont administration led by Trimble, and, when asked if he had contemplated switching to an acting career, confirmed that he would remain in politics, "although I wouldn't mind starring in something alongside Catherine Zeta-Jones".[88] This campaign was however most unusual because of the low profile adopted by the DUP leader, who had not long returned to active politics after a serious illness. Ian Paisley made relatively few campaign speeches and declined invitations to participate in local and national television panel programmes such as *Question Time*. The subsequent success of his party in the election without the drive normally provided by a once-charismatic leader, would prove to be highly ironical.

Into Paisley's place stepped his long-serving deputy, Peter Robinson, who was awarded the official title of "Director of Elections". Robinson conducted a feisty campaign which clearly targeted the UUP more than their traditional nationalist opponents. Central to many of Robinson's media pronouncements was his party's perception that political negotiation in Northern Ireland was far from finished. His party wanted "a new Agreement put in place, which can bring about stable, accountable and efficient devolution". Any new settlement which would be able to "stick, and last" had to "embrace" the DUP, and Robinson maintained that the 1998 Agreement had failed because it did not "provide for an effective form of devolution".[89] Examples of such breakdown in constructive government had, Robinson declared, included the creation of structures which did "not encourage clear direction", decision-making which was "fragmented" and an overall system which did "not provide collective responsibility nor ... [a promotion of] collective ownership of decisions".[90]

This demand for a "fair deal" Agreement, and belief in the "inevitability" of the renegotiation of the Good Friday Agreement, was repeated at various points in the DUP's campaign.[91] In the week before polling day, Peter Robinson and the DUP maintained that the Assembly's "four suspensions speak for themselves" in terms of any assertion that the Belfast Agreement had provided "stable devolution". The party instead proposed "a voluntary coalition with power in the assembly and not with ministers, and an exclusion mechanism to be used against bad behaviour".[92] As the campaign neared its conclusion, DUP optimism at its likely outcome peaked, with the party boasting of winning at least half of the unionist seats in the Assembly. This sense of optimism was shared not only by its own supporters but also by some political commentators.[93] Peter Robinson vowed that his party would "take control of the post-election political agenda", and, in a remarkably accurate prediction of what would actually occur within three years, he forecast that Tony Blair would "deal" with the DUP after the election because "he has to, if he is serious about a lasting political settlement for Northern Ireland ".[94]

Editorial Positions

Some of the *Belfast Telegraph*'s features and opinion content concentrated on the public's fatigue with the endless squabbling of local politicians and their reluctance to place economic and social issues at the heart of their parties' campaigns. In an article brimming with irony, entitled "Plague on all your houses", the paper's veteran journalist, Barry White, bemoaned the Assembly's failure to compromise on key areas such as cross-border bodies, decommissioning, power-sharing and, most fundamentally of all, the Good Friday Agreement. White suggested that the whole experiment had been "a waste of space" in all of these key issues, "except that it gives 108 members a living, not to mention the army of civil servants and the media people who have to follow all of its idiocies".[95] Designing a mock manifesto for the "Plague Party", White urged electors to, "vote for us and we'll bar unionism, nationalism, murder, flags, slogans and, yes, elections", before whimsically concluding, "on second thoughts, don't bother".[96] A couple of days later, the paper's business correspondent reported on the familiar electoral trend which was apparent in the positioning of the various parties, and which suggested that "economic and social policy [issues] would again have to play second fiddle to the constitutional question".[97]

The *Belfast Telegraph*'s editorial of 4 November set out its assessment of what was at stake for the main parties contesting the election. Noting the "wide variety of candidates" who were touting for votes, the paper suggested that the contest was "shaping up along familiar lines". The editorial observed how the unionist groups were endeavouring to "present themselves as the strongest pro-Union negotiators in the campaign to restore devolution", whilst the SDLP and Sinn Féin were engaged in a battle for the "top spot" amongst nationalist-minded electors. The difference between these two positions was "immense", the paper maintained. Referring to the Good Friday Agreement, the leading article continued:

> For unionists, the division is between those who would complete
> its implementation in a balanced way and those who would scrap

it and start again. For nationalists, the Agreement is a closed book and it is for others to honour their obligations.[98]

The editorial pointed to the danger of division facing the Unionist Party especially, which again faced the possibility of being "split into so many incomprehensible divisions" that they would "fail to pull their weight" in the new Assembly. Interpreting David Trimble's task in "rallying his troops" as being "infinitely more problematic" than it had been at the previous Assembly election, the *Belfast Telegraph* described the Unionist Party's recently-published candidates' charter as "a brave attempt" to bring about unionist unity.[99]

A week later, the *Belfast Telegraph*'s "Opinion" column described how the main parties were "neck-and-neck in the race for seats", and how the second half of the campaign would determine the outcome of an election which was "one of the closest on record."[100] Declaring that there was "little to choose between the contenders on either side of the political divide", the editorial also argued that the contest's final outcome was "unlikely to break the present stalemate". Describing the UUP as "retaining support", the paper also pointed out that some Unionist Party candidates were "less than enthusiastic about David Trimble's leadership". Although the leading article was downbeat about the chances of an executive emerging in the near future without genuine IRA "acts of completion", it drew some comfort from the likelihood that both the UUP and SDLP "should remain major players in the game".[101]

The following week, the *Belfast Telegraph* turned to the wider question of the likely barriers facing the newly-elected Assembly when it met a few weeks later. Drawing on the findings of a *Belfast Telegraph*-commissioned opinion poll, which suggested that twice as many Protestants as Catholics favoured a renegotiation of the Good Friday Agreement, an editorial warned that "the IRA factor [was] at the heart of the problem", and would remain so after the completion of the contest.[102] The paper concluded that "the problem, as ever" was the "failure of the IRA to honour its commitments", and that republican "prevarication" had "inevitably fuelled doubts among both unionists and nationalists", as to whether the "required acts of completion will ever happen".[103] The paper also advised that both the London and Dublin administrations should not ignore "the degree of disenchantment apparent within the unionist community", maintaining that the 1998 Agreement, which had won a narrow majority of unionist backing, was patently "not living up to expectations". The leader piece's assessment of the likely outcome of the election and formation of a new Assembly and Executive was far from being an optimistic one:

> Unless the IRA can deliver, it is difficult to see how an Executive can be formed after the election. In such circumstances, everything would point towards some form of review or renegotiation, a scenario that none of the parties can now afford to discount.[104]

In its early coverage of the contest, the *Irish News* maximised the coincidental timing of the start of the election campaign with the Halloween festival. The paper's headline on 1 November was, "Ghosties and ghoolies took a break from their Halloween celebrations yesterday to enter the scary world of electioneering".[105] The accompanying report made much of the "scary" atmosphere of both the festival and Northern Ireland's reputation for political campaigning. Commenting on the DUP's "spectral slide-show" on the "nightmare scenario" of an UUP victory, the report proceeded to describe the DUP's "spooky" vision of Gerry Adams or Martin McGuinness becoming the deputy first minister, and former IRA prisoner Gerry Kelly being appointed minister for justice, and how the party regarded David Trimble's spell in office as being "a horror story" for Northern Ireland.[106]

Ten days later, a leading article in the *Irish News* noted that the contest had "yet to really get off the ground", with "most of the limited interest to date" focussing on the "separate battles for supremacy within nationalism and unionism". Yet the paper reminded its readers that the election also highlighted the paramount significance of the Good Friday Agreement, and encouraged all voters, on both sides of the sectarian divide, to seriously consider voting for pro-Agreement parties. The paper argued that a "largely tribal approach" – in other words, voting along traditional, sectarian lines – made "little sense, at a time when there should be a consensus in the need for a return to a partnership administration at Stormont".[107]

The following week, the *Irish News* pinpointed the emergence of a major departure from the rather predictable tradition of electioneering in the province. In its editorial, "Hasn't it been quiet of late?", the paper described the "effective withdrawal from the fray of Ian Paisley" as being "one of the most striking" features of the contest to date. The irony between the DUP's claim to be on "the brink of a historic breakthrough" and the "profile of its founding father", which had "never been lower", was stark, the editorial suggested.[108] Noting that the DUP leader had refused to take questions at the launch of his party's manifesto and had been conspicuously absent from television broadcasts and discussion programmes, including *Question Time* and *Insight*, the *Irish News* suggested that such an uncharacteristically low profile might owe more to "political considerations" than it did to the "inevitable physical decline on the part of a man in his late 70s". In an uncanny, prophetic portrayal of the emerging political scene in Nothern Ireland, the paper postulated:

> If the DUP emerges as the largest unionist grouping in the incoming Northern Ireland Assembly ... it is inevitable that it will eventually seek to revive a coalition with the Ulster Unionists, the SDLP and Sinn Féin within any new executive. There would be a savage irony if Mr Paisley's brand of politics was finally relegated to the history books, not by his perceived opposition to nationalism, or his actual targets in the UUP, but by the emergence of a pragmatic element within the DUP itself.[109]

In its 18 November edition, the *Irish News* devoted considerable space to denouncing the alleged misdeeds of republicans. Its front-page story featured the case of a young man, Gareth O'Connor, believed to have been abducted or murdered by IRA personnel, and his father's plea to voters to, "think about all the deeds Sinn Féin/IRA have done in the past, and possibly to their own family". That morning's leading article also criticised the harassment meted out by republican dissidents opposed to the peace process to Derry's Mayor Shaun Gallagher (SDLP), who had recently laid a wreath at the city's war memorial on Remembrance Sunday. Apart from sustained verbal abuse, armed men turned up close to his home a few days later and a suspect – albeit hoax – device was also found. The *Irish News* praised Mr Gallagher's "strong and positive contribution to the reconciliation process", and insisted he deserved "the support of the entire community", in standing up to a small "fascist" group. The paper maintained that if dissident republicans had "a case to put forward, they should stand " in the forthcoming elections.[110]

Like its unionist counterpart, the *Irish News* perceived the contest to be too close to call. The paper's political correspondent, William Graham, wrote during the contest's final phase that "nerves are jangling", as it became clear that candidates were participating in "one of the tightest contests ever" in Northern Ireland, and voters fully aware that "just a few votes in the last seats could determine the future of the Good Friday Agreement".[111] Narrow victories for both Sinn Féin and the DUP would, Graham argued, "change quite dramatically the political landscape". With very little between these parties in terms of their anticipated levels of support, he suggested that, "a great deal will depend on the closely-fought nature of the sixth seat in several constituencies, and just how tactically their supporters use transfers". One further interesting observation made by Graham was that this contest had been "less destructive and less about old-style border politics" than previous elections, and that this might "give some hope for the future." However, despite this less tribal electoral atmosphere, the campaigns of the various parties had not followed the conventional pattern of political contests elsewhere in the United Kingdom, where attention was generally focused on the central issue of the state of the economy. Graham concluded his article by reminding readers that the contest was, "all about the Good Friday Agreement, and whether the voter is for or against".[112]

Given the importance of electoral transfers in the complex STV system of proportional representation, the *Irish News* clearly thought it essential to advise its readers on "using transfer votes wisely". An editorial on the eve of the election declared that the following day's contest was "among the most crucial we have faced for many years", with the key issue "beyond doubt" being "the future of the Good Friday Agreement".[113] The paper's main message to pro-Agreement supporters was to "use their transfers wisely" and to "cross over traditional rivalries" in their use of lower-preference votes. Anticipating "likely gains" for the DUP on account of the "fragmented condition of unionism", the paper warned pro-Agreement backers considering plumping for a single party, that such actions would amount to "handing seats to the DUP on a plate".[114]

"Initial deadlock"?

As Election Day dawned, media pundits speculated upon the likely outcome of the contest. The *Irish News* reminded its readers that support for the Good Friday Agreement was "facing its toughest test since 1998" and in a leading article entitled, "Democracy needs you", the paper rounded on dissident republicans for their "redundant campaign of violence", suggesting there "could not be a starker contrast between those who seek to persuade through force", and those groups which had opted for the ballot-box route. "Initial deadlock" would, the paper maintained, be the "likely result" of the election.[115] Meanwhile, the *Belfast Telegraph*, urging readers to "resist the temptation to stay at home and [to] have your say", again condemned the timing of the election. The paper argued that there could not be, under any circumstances, any "renegotiation" of the Belfast Agreement and maintained:

> The worst scenario would be that the arch-enemies on either side of the political divide – the DUP and Sinn Féin – could end up as the leading unionist and nationalist parties ... Whatever happens, the opinion poll evidence shows that the anti-Agreement vote will increase because of disillusionment, and that only a high turnout can minimise the effect. The bookmakers have backed the worst-case scenario, but the voters can and should prove them wrong.[116]

In the following day's edition, the *Belfast Telegraph* despaired that the future of the Assembly was "hanging in the balance", and that the forthcoming declaration of the election result was unlikely in itself to move the stabilisation process forward and was "not expected to deliver an immediate end to direct rule from London".[117] As the votes were still being counted, the paper turned its attention once again to the size of the likely turnout. It suggested that if this was to fall below the 60 per cent mark, many politicians would question the poll's validity, and this would probably lead to demands for the staging of another election in the New Year. Even the likely result of narrow victories for the UUP and SDLP would not lead to the creation of an "as-you-were Assembly", with the likely presence of several unionist dissidents who had the potential of "deep-freezing the deadlock".[118] The *Belfast Telegraph*'s perception that the contest had been a particularly close one was reinforced by the results of a RTÉ exit poll, which showed that the UUP had "a slight lead" over its unionist rivals, whilst the SDLP and Sinn Féin were running neck-and-neck".[119]

On 26 November 2003, electors across Northern Ireland went to the polls. The total electorate had risen to 1,097,526 and they were being asked to elect 108 MLAs from a field of 256 candidates, across the 18 Westminster constituencies. Ballot boxes had been distributed to the polling stations the previous night, and media coverage reminded electors about the idiosyncrasies of the STV voting system and the need to bring photographic identification to the voting centres.

However, electoral participation would be adversely influenced by a range of factors. Firstly, the days preceding the count as well as polling day witnessed a renewal of dissident republican violence, with bomb and shooting attacks reported in Dungannon and Armagh on 24 November, as well as petrol-bomb attacks on several polling stations in Derry, two days later. A large-scale police operation involving over 2,000 officers, was mounted to deal with such threats of terrorist disruption. Secondly, a trade union dispute affecting the punctual delivery of postal votes, and a delay in electors completing voting registration forms, meant that a considerable number of people would be effectively left without a say in the contest. Over and above all of this, that bugbear of all aspiring political representatives – inclement weather on polling day – also conspired to restrict voter participation. In the first November election staged in Northern Ireland for close to 40 years, "cruel November weather conditions" resulted in a "patchy" turnout.[120] Newspaper reports were accompanied by photographs of drenched voters turning up at polling stations which remained open for fifteen hours.[121] In North Belfast, one, presumably bedraggled, reporter bravely stood guard outside a polling station where "high noon was met by high gales, but voters, umbrellas inside out, were still turning up". An Ulster Unionist election worker confided in him: "You feel like you want to hug them!"

The *Belfast Telegraph* repeated its conviction that such a "significantly reduced voter turnout" would inevitably "heighten concerns that the new Assembly will remain in suspension for a considerable period".[122] Perhaps most importantly of all, in terms of limiting voter participation, was a sense of confusion and uncertainty over their political future which created a mood of apathy for many. Political historian Feargal Cochrane described the atmosphere at the polls as "surreal" , suggesting it was caused by the fact that, "voters didn't know when and if the people they were electing would have anything to do".[123] Other news reports on the count concentrated on Sinn Féin's official complaint regarding the banning of international observers from polling stations, the collection of votes from Rathlin Island by helicopter (and not by rowing boat, as in the comparatively recent past), and the entertainment provided by buskers campaigning for the Green Party outside several polling stations.

Fears regarding the likely scale of the electorate's participation were confirmed the day following polling, when it was reported that only 692,028 votes had been cast (just over 63 per cent of the total). Both the DUP and Sinn Féin had managed to secure more first-preference votes (177,944 and 162,758 respectively) than the once dominant UUP, which polled a disappointing total of 156,931. In percentage terms of the votes cast, the UUP had claimed 22.68 per cent – still a slight rise of 1.43 per cent on the 1998 election – whilst the DUP's share of the vote had increased by 7.7 per cent, to 25.7 per cent) and Sinn Féin's gain was of similar proportions – up 5.8 per cent to 23.5 per cent. The SDLP's vote, at 117,547, was considerably less than that of Sinn Féin, and its vote share of 16.99 per cent was down by some 4.77 per cent.[124]

Despite this decline in the number of voters backing the UUP, the party still managed to return 27 MLAs (1 more than in 1998), compared to the DUP's total of 30 (an increase of 10 on their 1998 figure). On the nationalist side, Sinn Féin welcomed an additional 6 MLAs, meaning that their parliamentary group was now 24-strong, whilst the SDLP lost 5 representatives, and now had a total of 18 MLAs. Most of the remaining seats – 6, the same as in 1998, although secured with a smaller number of votes – were claimed by the Alliance Party, with 2 other representatives from loyalist parties and the independent, Dr Kieran Deeny in West Tyrone.[125]

As political leaders (especially David Trimble and Mark Durkan) tried to explain their parties' below-par performances, opinion-makers instead focused on how the contest had "utterly transformed the political landscape on both sides of the political divide".[126] The election had resulted in "a quantum leap forward in seat gains" for both Sinn Féin and the DUP but, it was argued, had also produced greater confusion over practical issues, such as the establishment in the near future of governmental institutions. The *Belfast Telegraph* maintained that there was now "a big question mark over how and when the Executive and Assembly can be restored", and that the political process was clearly "deadlocked".[127] Press comment highlighted the demise of the SDLP as a political force and Brid Rodgers, who had directed their campaign, conceded it had "not been a good election for the party", lamenting that they had "taken a hit". The SDLP had not been the only losers in this election, but the UUP leader David Trimble dismissed the background grumbles of dissidents like Jeffrey Donaldson, that the leader's position was now "untenable", by pointing instead at the UUP's slight increase in its share of the vote and seats gained, simply putting down the success of the DUP to that party's "hoovering-up of other small unionist groups".[128]

Like any election, the results of the 2003 Assembly contest produced a fascinating collection of victorious newcomers and notable casualties. Into the former category fell Diane Dodds (wife of the DUP's North Belfast MP and future party deputy leader, Nigel Dodds) in West Belfast, and independent Dr Kevin Deeny in West Tyrone. Experienced politicians who were defeated included the SDLP's Joe Hendron (West Belfast) and Denis Haughey (Mid-Ulster); Ulster Unionists, Fraser Agnew (North Belfast) and Pauline Armitage (East Londonderry); former Tory MP Andrew Hunter (standing on a DUP ticket in Lagan Valley); and the PUP's Billy Hutchinson (North Belfast). Well-known, established politicians who topped the poll in their constituencies included: the DUP's Ian Paisley (North Antrim), Willie McCrea (Mid-Ulster), Peter Robinson (East Belfast), Iris Robinson (Strangford) and Gregory Campbell (East Londonderry); the SDLP leader Mark Durkan (Foyle); the UUP's David Trimble (Upper Bann), Jeffrey Donaldson (Lagan Valley) and David Burnside (South Antrim); and Sinn Féin's Gerry Adams in West Belfast (a constituency in which as many as four Sinn Féin candidates were returned).

Press comment on the election's outcome, both in Northern Ireland and in Great Britain, reflected widespread belief that the parties representing political extremes had come out on top and that genuine progress in the region was, as a consequence, under serious threat. The *Irish News'* front-page headline on the day after the results were declared – "DUP and Sinn Féin gains cause devolution deadlock" – and a pertinent cartoon, "Tribal Tide", later in its edition were replicated in the pages of its unionist counterpart.[129] The *Belfast Telegraph's* headline was, "Polls Apart – winds of change blast through Ulster politics", and smaller headings confirmed its belief that the DUP was "poised to become the biggest unionist party", and that Sinn Féin were "surging ahead of [the] SDLP". Like many of the British dailies, the paper interpreted the election outcome as "a setback for the political process".[130]

The *Daily Mirror* agreed with the *Belfast Telegraph's* perception that there had been a "squeezing out of the middle ground", and that the two parties furtherest apart in their aspirations would have to "strike an agreement", which was "not likely in the future".[131] The general interpretation of the British print media was that something rarely associated with politics in Northern Ireland had just occurred. Focusing on the "huge strides" in the voting strength for the party representing Irish republicanism, the *Daily Telegraph's* headline was, "Dramatic change in Northern Ireland's political landscape".[132]

The *Belfast Telegraph* again cast its critical eye on the rationale behind the calling of such a contest. Maintaining that the low turnout of voters and the undesired election outcome (on the part of the British and Irish administrations, at least) had justified its unease over the initial declaration of the election, the paper insisted that the results were "unlikely to stimulate the political process". The contest had proved to be, "the wrong election held for the wrong reason at the wrong time of the year", and might well also prove to be "a millstone around the necks of government and people for years to come".[133]

Both the unionist and nationalist press agreed that the contest had proved to be a major setback for "moderate" unionism. The *Irish News* wrote of "victory at a price for Trimble", and both the *Irish News* and the *Belfast Telegraph* noted that, despite its relative success in terms of the number of candidates returned, the UUP, for so long at the centre of political success in the region, had fallen into third place in terms of votes polled.[134] The following day, the *Irish News* reported that "questions [were] arising about David Trimble's leadership of unionism".[135] The *Belfast Telegraph* also conceded that Trimble's leadership was "again under pressure", especially due to the presence of several dissidents within the new UUP Assembly group.[136] The paper then turned its readers' attention to the newly emerging scenario of a political scene dominated by extreme unionists. Its leading article on 28 November described the result as "a setback for the political process", and pondered whether the Good Friday Agreement was "now doomed", considering the DUP's "ascendancy". The likely stance of Ian Paisley's party, now it had asserted its dominant position within Ulster politics, was another topic of discussion for the newspaper. Its editorial speculated on whether the DUP would "in a dominant unionist position, prove to be as intransigent as it was in the days of saying 'no' to virtually everything".[137] The paper also focused on the result's likely impact upon the policy of the British administration. The paper's political correspondent, Chris Thornton, pointed to the "headache" likely to strike both British and Irish governments as they tried to determine how they would "reconcile unionist desire for devolution with their distaste for Sinn Féin".[138]

Press analysis of drifts in the balance of power between the two nationalist groups also revealed a shared recognition that monumental political change had just been experienced. According to the *Belfast Telegraph*, Sinn Féin had "exceeded" the predictions of election pundits and the party had "eclipsed" the SDLP. The paper concluded that the "well-oiled republican machine" had "severely dented mainstream nationalism", and it declared that the crucial question raised by the election's outcome was whether Sinn Féin would, "interpret its mandate as further encouragement to move fully into the democratic process and [to] break its connection with paramilitary activity once and for all".[139] The explanation for such a radical shift of opinion within the Catholic community probably lay an amalgam of different factors. Certainly, Mark Durkan's "painful" first election result as SDLP leader (the party's vote went down by 4.98 per cent from its 1998 figure) was influenced by the "absence of trusty vote-deliverers" like John Hume and Seamus Mallon, and the party's failure to "produce an impressive second-tier of younger politicians capable of taking their place".[140] However, Sinn Féin's electoral surge owed much more to the party's own development and increasing popularity than to any weaknesses experienced by its chief opponents. The party's capacity to attract younger Catholic voters, many of them recent additions to the electoral register, and its leaders' image as the "authors" of a Peace Process which they appeared to be steering, were vital contributory factors to its electoral success. Sinn Féin also displayed an ever-increasing degree of political savvy and professionalism which some of its opponents appeared to lack. The party "understood the single transferable vote system as well as any political scientist and it ran its election campaigns with military precision, to ensure that as many of its candidates as possible were elected with the smallest majorities and thus the fewest 'wasted' votes".[141]

A significant contrast in the analysis of the repercussions of the election results for the province's future governance was evident in the respective editorial columns of the *Belfast Telegraph* and the *Irish News*. The tone of the former's leading articles was somewhat downbeat about imminent political prospects, reflecting its belief that the Assembly was "not likely to meet or have power for many months".[142] The paper described the Good Friday Agreement as being in "jeopardy", and asserted that Northern Ireland had a massive "political mountain" to climb. Turning its attention to the changes in the political balance of power, it wrote about the "new challenges for the Peace Process", of which the main challenge in the near future would be, "finding sufficient ground between the victorious DUP and a triumphant Sinn Féin". The editorial went on:

> The result of the election would undoubtedly have been very different, had the IRA responded to the pleading of the two

governments and dispensed with all paramilitary activity some time ago. In face of republican intransigence, unionist patience has worn thin ... Much will hinge on how pragmatic the DUP can be ... Can it go the extra mile to negotiations? ... The major question now is whether the gulf between the DUP and Sinn Féin can be bridged. On the basis of the evidence to date, it is difficult to be optimistic.[143]

The *Irish News*, on the other hand, saw "a future full of promises" and pointed out that despite the party's success, events had "hardly worked out as Sinn Féin had initially envisaged, after the party moved away from its previous policy of abstention in the early 1980s".[144] "Central" to current republican thinking was "a return to devolved government at Stormont", and leading party figures intended to "play a key role within any new Executive". The newspaper suggested that "most attention will focus on attempts to develop some form of relationship between the DUP and Sinn Féin", although it also noted the "confusing signals" emanating from the DUP on such an "rapprochement".[145] In contrast with the pessimism displayed in the columns of the *Belfast Telegraph*, the *Irish News* embraced the prospects generated by the new, emerging political landscape, and painted a positive picture of what lay ahead for Northern Ireland's citizens. The *Irish News* argued that if republicans took "decisive steps" to destroy their entire arsenal, "some intriguing political manoeuvres could follow over the coming months".[146]

Hopes for a reenergising of the mood of compromise exhibited in 1998 were however dashed by the outcome of the election. Those close to the heart of government later expressed their feelings of deflation. Jonathan Powell, (British Prime Minister Tony Blair's chief of staff, and a key figure at the talks which had led to the Good Friday Agreement), wrote several years later:

> All our hopes about building agreement out from the centre in Northern Ireland were dashed by the election ... The DUP and Sinn Féin came out of it decisively the largest parties on either side and we now had to make peace between the two extremes.[147]

Other observers have also considered that the position regarding the peace process and the possible return of devolved government was "disastrous" in the wake of such a result. What had occurred, Feargal Cochrane argues, was a "radicalisation" of the electorate, a "widening sectarian gulf" between the two sections of the community, and perhaps most crucially, "a narrowing of the centre ground of politics", which was now occupied by wounded political leaders and a considerably reduced number of their supporters.[148] Initially at least, one of the successful parties, Sinn Féin, adapted a more accommodating role, largely at the expense of the DUP, which they constantly derided as being oblivious to political compromise.

Yet the fortunes and bargaining positions of both of the victorious parties would be altered during the course of the next three years. Sinn Féin's attempts to impress the wider electorate that it was sincere about rejecting its violent past were hampered by the IRA's alleged involvement in a number of major incidents (including the 2004 Northern Bank robbery and the central Belfast pub murder of Catholic Robert McCartney in 2005), which angered a community starting to enjoy the benefits of living in an orderly, peaceful society. Despite these setbacks, both Sinn Féin and the DUP continued to make further progress at the ballot box. This was the case at the 2005 Westminster General Election. In its centenary year, the UUP was virtually decimated, winning a single parliamentary seat (Lady Sylvia Hermon, in the largely middle-class North Down constituency), and finishing in fourth place overall (its share of the vote was a paltry 17.7 per cent). In contrast, the DUP won close to twice the UUP's total number of votes, gained 33.7 per cent of all votes cast and taking 9 seats in the process. Although Sinn Féin continued to pick up votes won in the recent past by the SDLP – the party won 5 seats and nearly a quarter of cast votes (24.3 per cent) – these were not on the same scale as the strides made by the DUP at the expense of the UUP, and the SDLP still managed to return 3 representatives, as well as win 17.5 per cent of the poll.[149] The UUP, which had been derailed by the whole question of the Good Friday Agreement as well as personal animosity between senior figures in the party, continued to lose ground to the DUP. This latter group increased its electoral appeal by adopting a policy of renegotiation and ditching its previous rejectionist position towards the Belfast Agreement.

Following the announcement of IRA decommissioning in the summer of 2005, and the agreement at St Andrews in 2006 to restore devolution to the Northern Ireland Assembly, the dominance of these parties of the extremes was further cemented by the results of the next Assembly election in 2007.

At this, both the DUP and Sinn Féin enjoyed clear leads over their rivals. Sinn Féin won 28 seats and 26 per cent of the vote, compared to the SDLP's 16 seats and 15.2 per cent share of the poll. The DUP gained 6 seats to make a total of 30, as well as 30.1 per cent of the poll, compared to the UUP's 18 seats and 14.9 per cent of the votes cast. Within weeks, the unimaginable had happened, with the DUP leader, Ian Paisley and Sinn Féin's deputy leader, Martin McGuinness heading the Assembly's new power-sharing Executive.

The overall significance of the 2003 Assembly election was, therefore, considerable. Indeed, few elections have come close to having a similar impact upon both sections of the North's political divide. Both the campaign and the results fully illustrated the disarray and division within the Unionist Party, whilst nationalist politics also witnessed major change, with sizeable numbers of traditional SDLP voters being prepared to transfer their votes to a now more "respectable" Sinn Féin. A more hard-line approach to casting lower preference votes was adopted by both sections of the community, with a discernible reluctance on the part of many to transfer votes to smaller, cross-community groups (such parties had won 9 seats in the previous Assembly election).[150]

A mixture of demographic and political change had produced this gradual alteration in Northern Ireland's political culture. The electorate was very different in 2001 to that of half a century earlier. In 2001 41 per cent of voters were Catholic (up 3 per cent since the previous census in 1991), whilst back in 1951, they had barely constituted a third of the electorate. The centre ground in Ulster politics, which had never been particularly significant, contracted even further from the early 1980s, with the emergence of a strong republican party and the ongoing decline of Ulster unionism from the late 1960s. The terminal decline of the Unionist Party, which for many decades had dominated the political scene in Northern Ireland, was accelerated by the party's weak performance in the 2003 Assembly election. This clearly paved the way for those parties representing the political extremes which, unlike in the Republic of Ireland, had not previously performed consistently well at the ballot box. The Assembly election of 2003 witnessed substantial change in the progress of all the major parties, as well as heralding a genuine breakthrough for newer parties on either side of the sectarian divide.

Endnotes

1. One of these successful Sinn Féin candidates, Michelle Gildernew, narrowly defeated her UUP opponent, James Cooper by 53 votes in Fermanagh & South Tyrone.

2. For instance, Gerry Adams counselled his supporters not to back the SDLP's Alex Atwood in West Belfast.

3. *Belfast Telegraph*, 5 November 2003

4. *Irish News*, 3 November 2003

5. Linen Hall Library, Northern Ireland Political Collection, P12859

6. This was a reference to the Ardoyne interface which had experienced violence and intimidation of Catholic schoolchildren and their parents in 2001.

7. Linen Hall Library, Northern Ireland Political Collection, P12859.

8. DUP manifesto, Linen Hall Library, Northern Ireland Political Collection, P12905

9. *Ibid.*

10. *Belfast Telegraph*, 7 November 2003. In the 1998 contest, the SDLP had won three seats, compared to Sinn Féin's two.

11. *Belfast Telegraph*, 12 November 2003

12. SDLP manifesto, Linen Hall Library, Northern Ireland Political Collection, P12904

13. *Ibid.*

14. *Ibid.*

15. *Irish News*, 8 November 2003

16. *Belfast Telegraph*, 3 November 2003

17. *Irish News*, 19 November 2003

18. *Irish News*, 21 November 2003

19. *Irish News*, 22 November 2003. Although not standing for election, senior party figure Seamus Mallon lent his weight to the SDLP's cause, requesting "progressive" voters to back the SDLP and other parties supporting the Good Friday Agreement: *Irish News*, 13 November 2003.

20. It was anticipated that four Sinn Féin candidates and the SDLP's Joe Hendron would be elected, with the final seat dependent on transfer votes going either to Alex Atwood or the DUP.

21. *Belfast Telegraph*, 17 November 2003. The bad feeling which existed between the two parties representing the majority of Catholic opinion boiled over during a debate involving Gerry Adams and Mark Durkan on the BBC's *Politics Show* (16 November).

22. *Belfast Telegraph*, 6 November 2003

23. *Irish News*, 5 November 2003

24. *Irish News*, 25 November 2003

25. *Belfast Telegraph*, 12 November 2003

26. Sinn Féin manifesto, Linen Hall Library, Northern Ireland Political Collection, P12895

27. *Ibid.*

28. *Ibid.*

29. *Irish News*, 18 November 2003

30. This story dominated the front page of the *Belfast Telegraph* on 4 November, pushing election coverage back to the middle of the paper.

31. *Belfast Telegraph*, 3 November 2003

32. *Irish News*, 22 November 2003

33. *Belfast Telegraph*, 6 November 2003

34. *Irish News*, 25 November 2003

35. Alliance Party manifesto, Linen Hall Library, Northern Ireland Political Collection, P12899

36. *Ibid.*

37. Hutchinson insisted that this would constitute "a real danger": *Irish News*, 6 November 2003.

38. In 1998, the UUP had 28 of their candidates elected, compared to the DUP's 20, whilst the SDLP had 24 MLAs, compared to Sinn Féin's 18.

39. *Irish News*, 3 November 2003

40. *Ibid.*

41. *Irish News*, 4 November 2003. This article traced the "high drama" of close-run northern elections in the past, including Liberal Home Ruler, Redmond Barry's win over Unionist Drew Henry (by 7 votes) in North Tyrone in a 1907 Westminster by-election, Labour candidate Jack Beattie's 25-vote victory over Unionist Thomas Teevan in West Belfast in 1945, and Sinn Féin's Michelle Gildernew's win in Fermanagh & South Tyrone in 2001 (see earlier).

42. *Belfast Telegraph*, 12 November 2003

43. *Irish News*, 19 November 2003. The lowest poll for any major election was the Stormont contest in 1965, with a vote of only 57 per cent.

44. *Ibid.*

45. *Belfast Telegraph*, 25 November 2003. The "rival attractions" included televised soccer matches involving Glasgow Rangers and Manchester United (both of whom enjoyed huge support in Northern Ireland), and a special edition of *Coronation Street*.

46. *Belfast Telegraph*, 1 November 2003

47. *Belfast Telegraph*, 5 November, 2003. 256 candidates had been nominated to contest 108 seats, with the UUP (44) fielding 4 more candidates than the DUP, and Sinn Féin (38) having 2 more than the SDLP.

48. *Irish News*, 22 November 2003

49. *Belfast Telegraph*, 11 November 2003

50. *Irish News*, 17 November 2003

51. *Belfast Telegraph*, 7 November 2003

52. *Belfast Telegraph*, 22 November 2003; 11 November 2003

53. *Irish News*, 12 November 2003

54. *Belfast Telegraph*, 14 November 2003

55. *Irish News*, 3 November 2003

56. *Ibid.* Three Dáil Éireann representatives were photographed canvassing for local Sinn Féin candidate, Gerry Kelly in the constituency: *Irish News*, 4 November, 2003.

57. *Belfast Telegraph*, 7 November 2003

58. *Belfast Telegraph*, 12 November 2003

59. *Belfast Telegraph*, 8 November 2003

60. *Irish News*, 4 November 2003

61. *Ibid.*

62. *Irish News*, 5 November 2003

63. *Irish News*, 25 November 2003

64. *Irish News*, 6 November 2003

65. *Belfast Telegraph*, 20 November 2003

66. *Irish News*, 20 November 2003

67. *Belfast Telegraph*, 17 November 2003
68. *Belfast Telegraph*, 13 November 2003
69. *Irish News*, 14 November 2003
70. *Irish News*, 19 November 2003
71. *Belfast Telegraph*, 11 November 2003
72. Another interesting feature of the contest in East Londonderry was the failure of nearly one in eight electors to register their votes in time.
73. *Belfast Telegraph*, 5 November 2003
74. *Irish News*, 19 November 2003
75. *Belfast Telegraph*, 18 November 2003
76. *Belfast Telegraph*, 19 November 2003
77. *Ibid.*
78. *Ibid.* This added five statements to the party's official manifesto, including the rejection of the Joint Declaration, the call for improved cooperation between various groups and their opposition of power-sharing with "unreconstructed terrorists".
79. *Irish News*, 19 November 2003
80. *Ibid.*
81. *Belfast Telegraph*, 19 November 2003
82. Linen Hall Library, Northern Ireland Political Collection, P12859
83. *Belfast Telegraph*, 19 November 2003
84. *Irish News*, 18 November 2003
85. *Irish News*, 11 November 2003
86. David Trimble, *Irish News*, 24 November 2003
87. David Trimble, *Irish News*, 25 November 2003
88. *Irish News*, 19 November 2003
89. Peter Robinson, *Belfast Telegraph*, 21 November 2003
90. *Ibid.*
91. *Irish News*, 12 November 2003; *Belfast Telegraph*, 3 November 2003
92. *Irish News*, 21 November 2003
93. On the eve of the election, the DUP received favourable odds from local bookmakers (4–9) to get the highest number of seats and the post of first minister: *Belfast Telegraph*, 24 November 2003.
94. *Irish News*, 25 November 2003
95. *Belfast Telegraph*, 1 November 2003
96. *Ibid.*
97. *Belfast Telegraph*, 3 November 2003
98. *Belfast Telegraph*, 4 November 2003
99. *Ibid.*
100. *Belfast Telegraph*, 12 November 2003
101. *Ibid.*
102. Another interesting finding of the poll was the different response to the full implementation of the Good Friday Agreement in the event of IRA decommissioning. Over 20 per cent more SDLP voters than DUP backers (95 per cent and 73 per cent respectively) were prepared to see the Agreement fully implemented in such an eventuality.
103. *Belfast Telegraph*, 13 November 2003

104. *Ibid.*

105. *Irish News*, 1 November 2003

106. *Ibid.*

107. *Irish News*, 11 November 2003

108. *Irish News*, 17 November 2003

109. *Ibid.*

110. *Irish News*, 18 November 2003

111. *Irish News*, 24 November 2003

112. *Ibid.*

113. *Irish News*, 25 November 2003

114. *Ibid.*

115. *Irish News*, 26 November 2003

116. *Belfast Telegraph*, 25 November 2003

117. *Belfast Telegraph*, 26 November 2003

118. *Belfast Telegraph*, 27 November 2003

119. *Irish News*, 27 November 2003

120. *Irish News*, 27 November 2003

121. Doors opened at stations at 7.00 a.m. and closed at 10.00 p.m. This longer and more flexible provision for voting was in sharp contrast to the considerably shorter times of opening at other contests featured in this book.

122. *Belfast Telegraph*, 27 November 2003

123. F. Cochrane, *Northern Ireland: The Reluctant Peace* (Yale University Press, 2013), p. 234

124. See CAIN website: www.cain.ulst.ac.uk/issues/politics

125. These election results did not portray the complete picture, as 2 UUP MPs, Jeffrey Donaldson and Arlene Foster, defected to the DUP in 2004.

126. Eamon Phoenix, *Irish News*, 28 November 2003

127. *Belfast Telegraph*, 27 November 2003

128. *Ibid.*

129. *Irish News*, 28 November 2003

130. *Belfast Telegraph*, 28 November 2003

131. *Daily Mirror*, 28 November. The paper's headline, "Winners", was placed beside photographs of Ian Paisley and Gerry Adams.

132. *Daily Telegraph*, 28 November 2003

133. *Belfast Telegraph*, 27 November 2003

134. *Irish News*, 29 November 2003

135. *Irish News*, 30 November 2003

136. *Belfast Telegraph*, 28 November 2003

137. *Ibid.*

138. *Ibid.*

139. *Ibid.*

140. *Irish News*, 29 November 2003; *Independent*, 28 November 2003.

141. Cochrane, *op. cit.*, p. 235

142. *Belfast Telegraph*, 29 November 2003

143. *Ibid.*

144. *Irish News*, 29 November 2003

145. The report contrasted the relative openness of some senior DUP figures to such an alliance with the continuing reluctance of its party leader, who had seized the lapels of a journalist attempting to quiz him on such a possibility. A cartoon depicting Ian Paisley "cuffing" Tony Blair was featured on page 12 of this edition.

146. *Ibid.*

147. J. Powell, *Great Hatred, Little Room: Making Peace in Northern Ireland* (Vintage, 2008), p. 236

148. Cochrane, *op. cit.*, p. 236

149. SDLP leader, Mark Durkan, enjoyed a majority of 6,000 in the Foyle constituency.

150. J. Tonge, *Northern Ireland: Conflict and Change* (Routledge, 2006), p. 175

Postscript

A central theme which has emerged from each of the case studies analysed in this book has been the distinctly "different" nature of elections in Northern Ireland. This contrast in political experience with the rest of the United Kingdom is especially striking when one remembers that the region participates in the same Westminster contests every five years as the other constituent parts of Britain. The impression, that electioneering in the North of Ireland is fundamentally different from the rest of the country, is shared by both the region's electorate and observers in Great Britain. They concur that there are significant disparities between the political landscape of Great Britain and Northern Ireland, most notably in the range and types of parties operating on either side of the Irish Sea, as well as in the nature of the key issues which form the channels for electoral debate.

For the vast majority of contests fought between the creation of Northern Ireland in 1921 and well into the modern period, "normal" issues which have tended to dominate the agenda for debate at elections in Britain, the Irish Republic and most other democratic societies – most obviously, arguments over the relative state of the economy – have tended to be sidelined during most local campaigns. Elections in Northern Ireland have tended to focus on the question of the constitutional status quo, although the contests which have taken place since the abolition of Stormont in 1973 have been mainly confined to discussion of the various parties' attitudes to the latest British, or Anglo-Irish, initiative in the North (these included the 1973 Assembly elections and the Westminster by-elections of 1986, examined in Chapters Five and Seven respectively). Fears of intrusion by southern Irish politicians into the affairs of the North preempted the staging of elections by the Belfast administration both in 1938 and 1949, and the dreaded spectre – at least from the unionist perspective – of a Dublin-based administration interfering in Northern political affairs was such a threat to the loyalist psyche that these contests were dominated by the single question of Partition (which had also been central in the debate during the first election to the Belfast Parliament in 1921, as discussed in Chapter Two).

Another fundamental difference between the nature of elections contested in Northern Ireland and the other regions of the United Kingdom is that, on account of the failure of the main British political parties either to organise in Northern Ireland or to put up strong teams of candidates at Westminster elections, the one-million-strong Northern Irish electorate understandably find it hard to empathise with the key battles of the wider campaign, given their exclusion, in practice at least, from active participation in the election of both a national administration and a prime minister.

For many years, a key characteristic of Northern Irish elections was the sheer predictability, both in the nature of the campaigns mounted by the main parties and the uniformity of their outcomes. Constitutional nationalist and unionist groups monopolised the favours of their respective communities, and carved up most of the political cake at Stormont and Westminster elections. Whilst the lion's share of political representation was snapped up by the Unionist Party, various nationalist groups (ranging from the UIL and APL, to the Nationalist Party and the SDLP) also received guaranteed backing from the minority community in the local parliament. The consequence of this seemingly obligatory backing along religious grounds at elections was often landslide successes for the Unionist Party in contests such as those in 1921 and 1949 (described in detail in Chapters Two and Three). Related to this, another regular electoral feature was therefore the domination of the opposition benches at Stormont by nationalist politicians. This political predictability might have produced a modicum of stability for the unionist majority, but the resulting imbalance between the fortunes of the rival groups and the exclusivity in terms of the formation of local administrations meant that there was a hardening of attitudes and a distancing between the two sections of the community, as well as an incapacity on the part of non-sectarian parties to make a significant political breakthrough. Not that there were no opportunities for such a breaking of the political mould. The promise of a left-wing alternative to the conservative ideologies of unionism and nationalism occasionally shone brightly in Northern Irish politics. However, as witnessed in the North Belfast Westminster by-election of 1905 and at the

Stormont general election of 1958, such prospects of political change soon vanished and there was a speedy return to the political status quo.

As the modern conflict deepened in its intensity, external observers diverted their hopes for political moderation in the region to new, alternative parties which had evolved during the early phase of the Troubles. British (and indeed Irish) administrations, whilst resisting the temptation to become embroiled in a deepening political whirlpool in Northern Ireland, forlornly wished for groups like the Alliance Party, Brian Faulkner's Unionist Party of Northern Ireland (UPNI) and the SDLP to assume the role of political leadership in the region (as noted in Chapter Five, this was best illustrated in the mixed results of the election to the first Assembly in 1973).

Although the political pendulum in Northern Ireland was uniquely slow in its movement, a swing in fortunes did eventually occur – though when it did, the result was not the victory for the voices of moderation desired by Westminster. Whilst the Good Friday Agreement (1998) had elicited considerable support amongst minority voters, unionists were divided in their responses to the initiative. Indeed, the cautious backing afforded to David Trimble and his UUP colleagues in their power-sharing arrangement with the SDLP gradually melted away, as the perceived prevarication of Sinn Féin/IRA appeared to prevent the full implementation of the Belfast Agreement. The subsequent fall in popularity for the main parties of constitutional unionism and nationalism (the UUP and the SDLP respectively), and the early signs of their being replaced by more extreme representatives within their respective communities (in the form of the DUP and Sinn Féin) became evident in the 2003 Assembly elections (as observed in Chapter Eight). Indeed, the DUP and Sinn Féin were to consolidate their positions in subsequent contests, with the nadir for traditional unionism occurring at the Westminster elections of 2005, also the party's centenary year, when the UUP, which had for so long enjoyed a virtual monopoly of success at such contests, failed to return a single representative. Such a trend was even more apparent in subsequent contests, including the 2007 Assembly election and the 2010 Westminster contest.

However, although not on the scale of these shifts in control of political power, the results of recent elections have exhibited a small degree of electoral fluctuation for so long not closely associated with elections in the region. Whilst still emerging top of the "voting tables" within their respective communities, both the DUP and Sinn Féin lost seats at the 2015

Westminster election. On top of this, the UUP gained 2 seats, and the SDLP held on to their vulnerable South Belfast seat.

However, despite the occasional surprise, the results of the 2016 Assembly contest were remarkably similar to the 2011 election. Coming as it did, 18 years after the signing of the Good Friday Agreement, it presented first-time voters with the chance of expressing their political hopes for the future. On the surface at least, much had changed since the days when their parents had also been fledgling voters. In this election, the sharper focus employed by most parties on economic, educational, health and moral questions (such as gay marriage) suggested that Northern Ireland was exhibiting a more mature brand of politics, even if there were still strong undercurrents of community and political division, which meant that orange and green issues still dominated local political debate. Following the shift in political power towards the extremes which had been a major consequence of the Good Friday Agreement and the claiming of the middle ground by the DUP and Sinn Féin in a new post-conflict world, as well as the uneasy alliance forged between leaders of these parties at Executive level, this 2016 election provided those groups which had so recently enjoyed the lion's share of political power in the North – namely the UUP and the SDLP – with a chance to reduce the considerable gap between themselves and their chief rivals. However, the election's outcome was broadly similar to the contest five years before. The Ulster Unionists again returned 16 Assembly representatives (fewer than a half of the seats won by the DUP), whilst the SDLP, with 12 Assembly representatives, again failed to challenge the electoral domination of Sinn Féin's 28 seats.

Despite their predictable outcomes and more frequent staging, Northern Ireland elections have often exhibited uniquely dramatic characteristics, as well as being obviously different to those elsewhere in the United Kingdom or in the Irish Republic. Many more elections in the region have been allocated a "special" status than other counterpart contests in Great Britain, and this has been largely due to their specific context, occurring as they generally did in the midst of proposed major political or constitutional change, or in the middle of sectarian violence. These communal disturbances would frequently impact upon the campaigns of high-profile politicians and there would often be allegations of low-key violence, such as intimidation at polling stations.[1]

Notwithstanding the genuine sense of occasion which was attached to many elections in the province, and the correspondingly high voter turnout for many of them, there was often a clear uncertainty over the actual purpose of several contests (as outlined in Chapter Four, the most notable example of this was the 1969 Stormont general election called by Terence O'Neill), and a marked restriction in the range of issues discussed in numerous contests which generally bypassed proposed economic and social policies, concentrating instead on party positions to the constitutional link with Great Britain.

As is apparent in the case studies detailed above, the distinctive approaches to electioneering were also a notable feature of the region's political contests. The perennial focus in campaign speeches and party manifestos on the border question, the regular deployment of marching bands to add fervour to individual campaigns (mainly, but not exclusively, loyalist ones), the symbolic use of historical venues like Belfast's Ulster Hall in adding passion to key election rallies, and the tendency of candidates on both sides to employ a significant degree of street rhetoric during their personal campaigns: all of these were common characteristics of such contests. Candidates, especially those standing in rural seats, also had to embrace the additional challenges of covering sprawling constituencies, which involved tedious journeys across barren countryside, as well as potentially dangerous meetings in religiously-mixed market towns. The atmosphere on election days themselves was similar in many ways to that in other parts of the United Kingdom, with the various parties providing transport to the polling booths for elderly and disabled voters, and party vehicles reminding electors of the attributes of candidates throughout the hours of polling.

Yet there were also occasional reminders of the sinister differences between the implementation of electoral practices in Northern Ireland compared with those in constituencies across Great Britain. In Northern Ireland, rumour, innuendo and intimidation were all periodically experienced. Personal attacks on candidates – often physical as well as verbal – frequently included allegations of paramilitary involvement or association, and electoral malpractices – particularly significant in Northern Ireland, where over the years there have been several very close-run contests, often requiring a number of recounts – have ranged from the abuse of electoral rolls and personation offences to intimidation in the vicinity of polling stations. Inevitably, there have also been changes in electioneering approaches over the last century. These have ranged from the showing of slide-shows on gable walls (as in the 1905 North Belfast by-election featured in Chapter One) and the use of touring-cars bedecked with patriotic flags and party posters (a common feature of the initial election to the Belfast Parliament in 1921: see Chapter Two), to the prevalence of "good luck" symbols such as the handing-over to favoured candidates of black cats and horseshoes (as illustrated at the 1949 Stormont general election, covered in Chapter Three), and the reliance by most parties on public broadcasting (initially radio and subsequently television, which was so influential in the 1949 and 1969 Stormont elections respectively) or, more recently, party-produced videos and internet propaganda.

Northern Irish politics has, over the course of the last century, certainly unearthed a plethora of fascinating representatives, both at Westminster and in regional parliaments. Few other parliaments have witnessed the wide social array of parliamentarians who sat in the last Stormont Parliament, where members ranged from a docker (John McQuade) and former seaman (Gerry Fitt), to Anglo-Irish landowners (Terence O'Neill and James Chichester-Clark). Stormont also had its own "Winston Churchill" figure – in terms of a road-to-Damascus-style political conversion – in the shape of Belfast labour representative, Harry Midgley, who later joined the Unionist Party, where he quickly gained Cabinet rank. Verbosity has long been associated with many Irish public representatives, and there has been no shortage of eloquent speakers either in Westminster or at Stormont. The official record for the longest speech in the latter institution was accorded to the maverick Independent Unionist MP, Tommy Henderson. Powers of political oratory can also be attributed to many other Northern representatives, ranging from the fiery blend of religious fundamentalism and no-compromise unionism advocated for so long by the Reverend Ian Paisley (who had left a prison cell to canvass during his first parliamentary campaign in 1969), to the strong religio-nationalism promoted by another long-serving MP, Joe Devlin, some forty years earlier. Another leading proponent of a united Ireland, albeit one who also advocated a strong socialist message, was Gerry Fitt (also a West Belfast MP), who personified the personal bravery of many representatives subjected to intimidation by opponents for their political positions – in 1983 Fitt was forced to leave his north Belfast home after a republican fire-bomb attack. Other elected representatives in Northern Irish constituencies have included a dying hunger striker (Bobby Sands), a university student (Bernadette Devlin) and a gospel-singing recording artist

(William McCrea), who frequently sang at election rallies.

Northern Ireland elections have, inevitably perhaps, produced a wide range of ebullient characters, and many dramatic moments, several of which have been described in this book. These moments have included the electoral participation by senior members of a new national party (the Independent Labour Party) at the North Belfast Westminster by-election (1905); the head-to-head battle between the voice of constitutional nationalism, Joe Devlin, and that of Sinn Féin, as articulated by Eamon de Valera, in West Belfast in 1918; the collective feeling on the part of voters of stepping into the unknown, when electing representatives for the first Northern Ireland parliament in the midst of severe sectarian violence in 1921; the sense of an unseen role being played by external forces, namely the southern Irish administrations, at the 1938 and 1949 Stormont general elections; the sense of hope on the part of the electorate for a new, post-conflict political future, which was particularly strong at the Assembly elections of 1973 and 1998. Other contests were unique, because of such factors as the return of a candidate unable to speak on political platforms due to his prison confinement (Bobby Sands, 1981), and the street confrontations between rival unionist candidates during the 2003 Assembly election campaign, which flared up outside the UUP headquarters in east Belfast between members of the UUP and DUP leadership.

At the beginning of this book, I referred to Sam Thompson's play, *Cemented with Love*, transmitted by the BBC in 1965, which remains one of the few dramas focusing primarily on Northern Ireland's political system. Although in some senses not regarded as a classic piece of writing, the play accurately portrayed various aspects of the North's political culture half a century ago, especially the "shallowness of politics", which, once "the flags, party songs and slogans are removed", revealed a society where the people in both "tribes" are "interchangeable".[2] The electoral defeat of the pro-reform William Kerr and the crushing of his hopes of removing Northern Ireland's "Iron Curtain", symbolised Sam Thompson's conviction that the intolerance of the majority of voters in Drumtery, and for that matter Northern Ireland as a whole, meant they were complicit in sustaining a political system which in his view was dominated by intolerance, corruption and a refusal to seek compromise.

Much has changed in the fifty years since Thompson penned his drama. The once unthinkable scenario has occurred. The former mainstays of political life – the all-dominant Unionist Party and the impotent voice of political opposition offered by a variety of nationalist groups – have been replaced by the increasingly popular parties representing the political extremes in the community, with the DUP and Sinn Féin sharing power since 2007. However, despite this radical shift in the political pendulum, Sam Thompson and other critical observers dating back to the earliest post-Partition days, and indeed before, would find striking similarities between the region's modern political culture and that of the past. The tribal nature of the political rhetoric, particularly evident at election time, and the failure of most political parties to present meaningful discussion on "real" election issues, remain major obstacles to genuine compromise and progress. Most fundamentally, the emergence of a flexible electorate, full of potentially "floating" voters, has not happened in Northern Ireland, where most people's electoral decisions are still framed in terms of their religious membership and sense of ethnic identity. Northern Ireland remains, politically at least, a place apart, where elections represent periodic opportunities to manifest tribal loyalties shaped by history and tradition, rather than the expression of pragmatic voter choices relating to the modern world.

Endnotes

1. The long-serving nationalist representative, Gerry Fitt experienced intimidation and violence from both sides of the sectarian divide. As observed in Chapter Five, his election agent, Paddy Wilson was murdered by the UVF during the 1973 Assembly campaign, whist Fitt's North Belfast family home was targeted by republican arsonists in the wake of his defeat in West Belfast at the 1983 general election.

2. M. Megahey, *The Reality of his Fictions – The Dramatic Achievement of Sam Thompson* (Lagan Press, Belfast, 2009), pp. 217-8

APPENDIX ONE

Major Northern Ireland Elections, 1905–2017
Chronological Notes

A number of texts and websites have been useful in my compilation of this chronological summary of the main elections (for Stormont/local assembly and Westminster parliaments) in the North of Ireland during the last century or so. They include the CAIN website, edited by Martin Melaugh (www.cain.ulst.ac.uk/ issues/politics), the Northern Ireland Elections Ark website, edited by Nicholas Whyte, (www.ark.ac.uk/elections), and the following publications: *Parliamentary Election Results in Ireland, 1801–1922,* ed. B.M. Walker, (Royal Irish Academy, 1978); *Northern Ireland Parliamentary Results, 1921–72* by Sydney Elliott, (Political Reference Publications, 1973); and *Northern Ireland: A Political Directory, 1968–88* by W.D. Flackes and S. Elliott (Blackstaff Press, 1989).

1905 Westminster By-election
Following the death of North Belfast's sitting Conservative member, Sir James Haslett, Belfast's Lord Mayor, Sir Daniel Dixon took on local Labour leader, William Walker in the subsequent by-election. Dixon won with a majority of 474 (see Chapter One).

1906 Westminster General Election
This election in January resulted in the return of a Liberal administration, and the temporary demise of Conservatism. In the nine-county province of Ulster, however, unionists continued to form a small unionist majority (17 out of 33).

1910 Westminster General Elections
There were two general elections during this year, both of which resulted in the narrow return of Liberal administrations headed by Herbert Asquith, which were committed to introducing a measure of Home Rule for Ireland. The Irish Nationalist Party held the balance of power at Westminster. There was once again little to choose between the relative strength of unionists and nationalists in Ulster, with the former winning 18 of the 33 seats in the January contest, and 17 in the December election.

1913 Westminster By-election

This seat had been vacated by the Marquis of Abercorn on his elevation to the title, the Duke of Abercorn. David C. Hogg, the pro-Home Rule candidate, defeated the Unionist challenger, Lieutenant-Colonel H. Arthur Pakenham by a narrow margin (57), but he died the following year. In the subsequent by-election, the seat was held by the Liberals. It was a blow for unionists, as it occurred during the period of tension caused by the passage of the Third Home Rule Bill.

1918 Westminster General Election

Eight years had passed since the previous electoral contest and, of course, much had changed both in Ireland and across the world. For this December election, the Irish electorate had more than doubled and there was considerable redrawing of constituency boundaries. In Ireland as a whole, Sinn Féin was dominant, with only 6 of John Redmond's pre-war Nationalist Party winning seats (Sinn Féin won 73 and Unionists 23). There were interesting tussles for a range of urban and rural seats across Ulster. Sinn Féin's Arthur Griffith and Eoin MacNeill were triumphant in N.W. Tyrone and Derry respectively, and Joe Devlin defeated Eamon de Valera in West Belfast. For Unionists, it was also a successful contest, with loyalists of various hues winning 23 seats (5 more than in 1910). Sir Edward Carson won the newly created seat of Duncairn in North Belfast, and three independent unionists were also elected in the city: Samuel McGuffin in Shankill; Thompson Donald in Victoria; and Thomas Burn in St Anne's.

1921 Northern Ireland General Election

This first election for the newly-formed Northern Ireland parliament was also the first contest to be held under the proportional representation system of voting. A remarkably high turnout (89 per cent overall) was recorded for an election staged during a period of sectarian conflict. The issue of Partition, which had been the outcome of the Government of Ireland Act (1920), was really the only political question to be resolved by the electorate. The Unionist Party won a resounding victory, with all 40 of its candidates being elected. Joe Devlin's United Irish League and Sinn Féin shared the remaining 12 seats equally. (See Chapter Two.)

1924 Westminster General Election

Northern Ireland's representation at Westminster was increased to 13 members (this included one university seat). At this contest, which resulted in the election of a minority Labour government, all 13 MPs were from the Unionist Party.

1925 Northern Ireland General Election

This contest saw the Unionist Party receive its lowest number of seats (32) in the half-century of "Stormont" rule. The party lost 8 of the seats it had gained in the initial regional election (to a combination of independent unionists, Labour and other independent candidates), and there were several shocks for a party unaccustomed to defeat, as 2 government ministers lost their seats and not a single unionist headed the poll in the Belfast seats. Unionist and independent unionist candidates still managed to gain nearly two-thirds of the total votes cast, but nationalists won nearly a quarter of the vote (91,452 votes) and 10 seats; there were also 2 republicans elected. Notable personal successes came for Jack Beattie, who won as an independent Labour candidate in East Belfast, Tommy Henderson as an independent unionist in North Belfast, and for Joe Devlin, who once again came out on top in the west of the city.

1929 Northern Ireland General Election

This election took place the week before the Westminster contest, and saw the introduction of 48 single-member constituencies, which replaced multiple seat constituencies (there were also 4 university seats). Unusually, both main unionist and nationalist parties performed well, with the Unionist Party winning over half of the vote (50.6 per cent,146,899 votes cast) and 37 seats. Nationalists won 11 seats (6 of them were unopposed), acquiring 34,069 votes (11.7 per cent of the total) in the process. However, anti-Partition candidates would soon be weakened by the abolition of proportional representation, as well as by party division and frequent spells of abstention from parliament which fostered a degree of voting apathy amongst Catholics.

1929 Westminster General Election

Unionists won 11 seats and nationalists, 3 (Joe Devlin and Thomas Harbison), in this contest which returned a Labour administration at national level.

1933 Stormont General Election

The main feature of this contest – the first to return representatives to the new Stormont buildings in east Belfast – was the sharp fall in support for nationalist groups, which won just over 13 per cent of the total vote (22,269) and 9 seats. Unionist Party candidates gained 43.1 per cent of the votes cast (some 72,133) and 36 seats, with the remaining seats being split between independent unionists, the NILP and republicans.

1935 Westminster General Election

At this November contest, Ulster Unionists won 11 seats and nationalists, 2.

1938 Stormont General Election

This contest was called by Unionist Prime Minister Sir James Craig, in direct response to Eamon de Valera's decision to draft a new constitution for the Irish Free State, which highlighted the special position of the Catholic Church. Playing on Protestant fears of a "sell-out", Craig beat off the challenge of W.J. Stewart's Progressive Unionist Party, which was demanding a huge programme of public works and house-building, and which more directly linked politics in the province to those in the rest of the United Kingdom. Stewart's group failed to win any seats and the Unionist Party, with 56.5 per cent of the poll (some 185,854 votes), increased its representation to 39. A state of division within nationalist ranks contrasted with prevailing unionist unity, and anti-Partitionists won only 4.9 per cent of the poll (16,167 votes) and 8 seats.

1945 Stormont General Election

The two elections in this year were the first tests of political opinion for over seven years, on account of the international war. Ulster Unionists won 33 of the 52 seats in the Stormont Commons (6 fewer than in the previous election), and gained 50.4 per cent of the vote. Nationalists won 10 seats and 9.2 per cent of the vote, though a new nationalist group, the Anti-Partition League, was established by Eddie McAteer and Malachy Conlon towards the end of the year. As in Great Britain, where there was a massive swing to Labour, socialist candidates from various parties did well, with Harry Midgley's Commonwealth Labour Party polling over 28,000 and gaining Midgley's seat in Willowfield, and the NILP winning 66,000 votes and seats in Belfast's Dock and Oldpark constituencies.

1945 Westminster General Election

Nine unionists were successful in this contest, which resulted in a landslide victory for Clement Attlee's Labour Party. Independent Labour candidate, Jack Beattie retained the West Belfast seat he had won in a by-election in 1943, and nationalists won in Fermanagh & South Tyrone and South Armagh.

1949 Stormont General Election

This election was called suddenly by Sir Basil Brooke, who demanded a plebiscite backing the North's constitutional status, following the Irish Free State government's decision to leave the Commonwealth and form a Republic. In probably the most intensely fought contest since the creation of the state, sectarian emotions dominated a campaign which, as in 1938 and 1921, was restricted to a single issue, that of Northern Ireland's links with the United Kingdom. The call for unionist unity made by Brooke was maintained during the campaign, and reflected in an overwhelming vote of support from Protestant electors (in sharp contrast to subsequent calls from Brooke's nephew, Terence O'Neill), and the Unionist Party won 234,000 votes and 37 seats. The main loser in this election was Labour, which lost its 2 seats in Belfast. The new nationalist group, the APL, won 101,000 votes and obtained 9 seats (see Chapter Three).

1950 Westminster General Election

There were boundary changes in several of the 12 Northern Ireland constituencies in this February contest, which saw unionists winning 10 seats. Cahir Healy won Fermanagh & South Tyrone and a second nationalist candidate, Anthony Mulvey, was also triumphant in Mid-Ulster. The election was memorable for the result in West Belfast where the Reverend James Godfrey MacManaway (who represented Londonderry City at Stormont) narrowly defeated Labour's Jack Beattie, who then challenged the winning candidate's eligibility for the seat (at that time, Anglican clergymen were barred from sitting in the Commons). MacManaway resigned early in 1951.

1951 Westminster General Election

This October election saw the defeat of Labour at Westminster, as well as the return of 9 Ulster Unionists and 2 anti-Partition representatives, Michael O'Neill (Mid-Ulster) and the veteran republican representative, Cahir Healy in Fermanagh & South Tyrone. The most controversial and nail-biting contest was in West Belfast, where Labour candidate Jack Beattie defeated sitting Unionist MP, Thomas L. Teevan by a mere 25 votes.

1953 Stormont General Election

The fourth election in as many years resulted in a low turnout and a significant drop in the unionist vote. This was partly due to the furore over the banning of an Orange Order march in County Down the previous summer. The main beneficiaries were Independent Unionists (who polled nearly 33,000 votes and won 1 seat), and the NILP (the party picked up 31,000 votes, or over 12 per cent of the poll, without gaining a seat). Nationalists gained fewer votes than Labour candidates (27,796) but managed to win 7 seats.

1955 Westminster General Election

This May election saw unprecedented support for republican candidates, who polled 152,310 votes. Two of these were elected with small majorities – Phil Clarke in Fermanagh & South Tyrone, and Tom Mitchell in Mid-Ulster. Their respective majorities were 261 and 260 votes. The total unionist vote, at 442,647, was nearly three times that gained by Sinn Féin and the other 10 Westminster seats were claimed by Unionist Party candidates.

1958 Stormont General Election

The most distinctive features of this March election were the disappointing results obtained by the APL, and the success of the NILP in Belfast, where it won 4 seats (Pottinger, Oldpark, Victoria and Woodvale), gaining in the process 37,748 votes, or 16 per cent of the poll. Unionists managed to have 37 candidates returned, 1 down on the previous total, garnering 102,700 votes (43.6 per cent of those who voted). Nationalists actually polled fewer votes than the NILP (36,013 or 15.3 per cent of the poll) but won 7 seats. Lord Brookeborough had tried to make the ongoing battle along the border against the IRA the central issue, but an economic crisis led to changes in the nature of electoral campaigning (especially in Belfast), and following the election, T.W. Boyd assumed the title of leader of the opposition at Stormont, where increasing parliamentary time was taken up with the discussion of economic and social issues.

1959 Westminster General Election

The Unionist Party won all 12 seats in this October contest. There was a marked decline in political backing for Sinn Féin, with the party's total poll (63,415) constituting less than half of its 1955 total.

1962 Stormont General Election

Although clearly dominating this election, the Unionist Party won 3 fewer seats (34) and just under half the total vote (48.6 per cent). The NILP won 4 seats in Belfast and its 76,842 votes represented 26 per cent of the total poll. There were 9 successful nationalist candidates (its total share of the vote was 15.4 per cent). This contest also saw the election of Irish Labour candidate, Gerry Fitt for the first time in a major contest.

1964 Westminster General Election

Once again, the Unionist Party won all 12 Westminster seats. However, the NILP continued to score heavily in the Greater Belfast area (gaining over 103,000 votes), despite not picking up a seat. The most newsworthy contest again occurred in West Belfast, where disputes over the flying of an Irish tricolour sparked street disturbances. Unionist James Kilfedder gained a majority of 6,659, with republican candidate, Liam McMillan receiving only 3,256 votes.

1965 Stormont General Election

For the first time, a Unionist Party manifesto concentrated its attention on job creation and house-building schemes (the aim was to create around 65,000 new jobs and to build some 64,000 new properties), as well as outlining an economic policy which promised to cut unemployment and to forge greater economic cooperation with the Irish Republic. The new-look, reformist Unionist Party of Prime Minister Terence O'Neill won 36 seats (gaining 59.1 per cent of the vote and 191,896 votes), whilst the Nationalist Party won 9 (obtaining 26,748 votes or 8.2 per cent of the poll). The NILP, which had performed well in recent Stormont elections, lost 2 of its 4 representatives and, with 66,323 votes in total, was down on its 1962 figure.

1966 Westminster General Election

This contest was dominated by the Unionist Party, which claimed 368,629 votes (61 per cent of the total vote) and won 11 seats. The other seat was West Belfast, which was won by Republican Labour candidate, Gerry Fitt (the winning candidate's majority was 2,011).

1969 Stormont General Election

Described as the "Crossroads Election", this contest coincided with the start of Northern Ireland's modern conflict. It was unique in its degree of openness – more seats were contested (45 of the 52 at stake) than at any contest since 1925. It was memorable for the political infighting between the "reformist" unionism advocated by Terence O'Neill, and the anti-reformist, right-wing loyalism of his opponents, many of whom were in O'Neill's Unionist Party. Although Unionists slightly improved their overall parliamentary position, the contest was both a shock for O'Neill (who was nearly defeated in his Bannside constituency by the Reverend Ian Paisley), and for his supporters – 27 of the 39 Unionist Party MPs were backers of the prime minister, but at least 10 were opponents. The other key feature of this election was the demise of the Nationalist Party, which lost 3 of its 9 seats to independents who had been prominent in the Civil Rights movement. These included John Hume, who defeated Nationalist Party leader, Eddie McAteer in Foyle. (See Chapter Four.)

1969 Westminster By-election

In this April contest, called after the death of Unionist MP, George Forrest, People's Democracy candidate, Bernadette Devlin defeated the previous representative's widow in a two-way contest (her majority was 4,211). At the age of 21, Devlin became the youngest female MP to be elected to Westminster.

1970 Stormont By-election

In April, the Reverend Ian Paisley won the seat of Bannside, which had been vacated following the resignation of its long-standing representative, Captain Terence O'Neill.

1970 Westminster General Election

This June election, which resulted in Edward Heath's Conservative Party narrowly beating Labour, also witnessed Ulster Unionists obtaining their smallest share of Westminster seats (8 out of 12). Bernadette Devlin retained Mid-Ulster and another independent nationalist, Frank McManus was elected in Fermanagh & South Tyrone. The Reverend Ian Paisley won the North Antrim seat, thus becoming a representative at both Westminster and Stormont parliaments within the space of a few months, and starting a parliamentary career which would span nearly four decades. Gerry Fitt retained West Belfast, this time on an SDLP ticket. The overall poll (76.8 per cent) was an impressive one.

1973 Northern Ireland Assembly Election

The election in June was called for the purpose of electing representatives to a 78-seat assembly (elected by proportional representation), from which a power-sharing administration would be formed. This was a time of intense sectarian conflict and also one in which the citizens of Northern Ireland were experiencing considerable political change. A poll in March on the border question had resulted in a massive boost for retaining the region's constitutional position within the United Kingdom. The Assembly election proved to be a success for the SDLP, which won 159,773 votes (22.1 per cent of first-preference votes), and the party managed to have 19 of its 28 candidates elected. The Alliance Party succeeded in returning 8 of its 35 candidates and gained 66,541 votes (9.2 per cent of the poll). The recently-established Anti-White Paper Coalition of dissident unionists from the Vanguard Ulster Unionist Party, the DUP and dissatisfied members of the Unionist Party, inevitably meant there would be major splits in the loyalist vote, with those unionists backing Unionist Party leader, Brian Faulkner's qualified support of the White Paper gaining 23 seats (the party fielded 41 candidates) and 26.5 per cent of the vote, compared to their unionist opponents' tally of 27 seats and 35.4 per cent of the poll (see Chapter Five).

The 1974 Westminster General Elections

Industrial disputes and economic turmoil resulted in the calling of two elections in 1974. In Northern Ireland, there had been a major revision of the boundaries of seven existing constituencies, mainly in Belfast and County Antrim. The February contest occurred weeks into the start of the shared government which had been set up by the

Sunningdale Agreement, and unionists' slogan for this election was, "Dublin is just a Sunningdale away". The majority of electors rejected the Agreement (422,000 or 50.8 per cent of the poll were against, whilst only 296,000 were in favour); 11 of the 12 representatives returned were Unionists (6 were from the Official Unionist Party, 2 from the DUP and there were 3 Vanguard MPs, including party leader, William Craig, who won East Belfast); the SDLP's Gerry Fitt was the only nationalist. Voters were deterred by a combination of political apathy and ongoing disturbances, and turnout was down by 7 per cent on the previous Westminster contest. Tension in Belfast was particularly high on polling day, and there were several bomb blasts across the city. (The author recalls working as an assistant election officer in an East Belfast polling station and having to carry ballot boxes on to an army jeep which, with election officials on board, sped off to the count at the City Hall!). The election's outcome was very different from that desired by the British government, and pressure was increased on the fledgling Assembly Executive.

The results of the October contest were even more disappointing for the British architects of Sunningdale, with 407,788 voters (57.4 per cent of the total) expressing their rejection of this initiative. Attitudes had hardened since the UWC strike in May, which had brought down Faulkner's Executive). One setback for the UUUC, which returned 10 members (6 Official Unionists, three Vanguard and Ian Paisley from the DUP) was the defeat of party leader, Harry West in Fermanagh & South Tyrone, where Unity candidate, Frank Maguire won. The election also saw Enoch Powell, a former government minister and right-wing Tory, elected as an Official Unionist in South Down. The SDLP's only success was Gerry Fitt's win in West Belfast, but the party did receive 154,193 votes (21.7 per cent of the poll).

1975 Northern Ireland Constitutional Convention

This election was not a parliamentary one as such, but rather one where delegates would be elected to discuss constitutional options. Again using the PR system of voting based on the region's parliamentary constituencies, the contest for the 78-seat Convention attracted a reduced number of candidates (165, which was 54 fewer than the number involved in the Assembly contest two years before), and a significantly lower number of voters turned out for what was the seventh poll in just over two years (at 65.8 per cent, it was 7 per cent below the turnout for the Assembly contest). The Loyalist Coalition, the UUUC, obtained over half of the vote (54.8 per cent), although less than half of this was won by Official Unionists, who got 19 delegates on a 25 per cent vote. The DUP had 12 representatives and Bill Craig's Vanguard Unionist Progressive Party's share was 14. The SDLP, with 23.7 per cent of the vote, secured 17 delegates, and the middle-of-the-road Alliance Party had 8 delegates (9.8 per cent of the poll).

1979 Westminster General Election

This national election resulted in the return of the Conservatives to power, and the poll in Northern Ireland was 68.4 per cent. The DUP gained 2 seats from the Official Unionists in Belfast – Peter Robinson in East Belfast and John McQuade in North Belfast – and, whilst the party now had 3 representatives at Westminster, its share of the vote was less than a third of that enjoyed by Official Unionists (10.2 per cent and 36.6 per cent respectively) – 5 Official Unionists were elected and in addition there were 2 other independent unionists (Robert Bradford in South Belfast and James Kilfedder in North Down). The SDLP's Gerry Fitt and independent republican, Frank Maguire retained West Belfast and Fermanagh & South Tyrone respectively. The total anti-Partitionist vote remained at under half of the pro-British vote (28 per cent and 59 per cent respectively). An interesting feature of this election was that over half of the contenders for seats (33 out of 64) lost their deposits, including 7 Republican Clubs candidates.

1981 Westminster By-election

Following the death of independent nationalist MP, Frank Maguire, republican H-Block prisoner Bobby Sands defeated the former Official Unionist leader in a straight fight in April for the Fermanagh & South Tyrone seat (see Chapter Six). Following Sands' death shortly afterwards, a new by-election took place in August, when his election agent, Owen Carron was also returned, with a slightly larger majority, on an Anti H-Block ticket.

1982 Westminster By-election

Official Unionist candidate, the Reverend Martin Smyth was elected for the South Belfast seat (his majority was 5,397). He succeeded the Reverend Robert Bradford, who was shot dead by the IRA.

1982 Northern Ireland Assembly Election

Elections for a revived Northern Ireland Assembly, which were central to Northern Ireland Secretary James Prior's "rolling devolution" scheme, took place in October. Using the PR system for the election of representatives to the 78-seat Assembly, the election constituted the first real test of Sinn Féin's political creditability since their move towards a joint military and political strategy – that of the "Armalite and ballot box". Polling 64,191 votes (10.1 per cent of all first-preference votes) and winning 5 seats, the party polled over half of the votes secured by the SDLP (118,891 or 18.8 per cent of the poll and 14 seats). The Unionist Party also did well in this election, winning 26 seats and gaining the highest percentage of votes. The DUP, which had enjoyed a recent spell of considerable success (including Ian Paisley's emphatic victory in the first European election three years earlier, and gains in local council elections) fared less well in this election, although the party still won 21 seats. The Assembly would soon witness considerable bickering and infighting between the various parties, especially within the unionist groups. The abstentionist tactic was again employed by nationalists, and the Assembly was dissolved in June 1986.

1983 Westminster General Election

This election in June, which on a national level produced a landslide victory for Margaret Thatcher, was also a momentous one in Northern Irish politics. Redrawing of the electoral boundaries had resulted in the creation of an additional five seats (Foyle, Newry and Armagh, East Antrim, Lagan Valley and Strangford), and there was a high poll (72.8 per cent) in the province. The UUP, with its 11 successful candidates, won a total of 259,952 votes (34 per cent of the total poll), compared to the DUP's 20 per cent share of the vote and its 3 seats, while James Kilfedder returned as an independent unionist in North Down. Although the nationalists' vote held up, only 2 representatives were successful (Gerry Adams in West Belfast for Sinn Féin and John Hume winning the new seat of Foyle). This was on account of nationalist splits in Mid-Ulster and Newry and Armagh, where unionists had unexpected success. The most controversial contest was in West Belfast, where long-serving MP, Gerry Fitt (who had left the SDLP and was standing as an independent Labour candidate) encountered stiff opposition from both Gerry Adams and Joe Hendron (SDLP). Fitt finished in third place, with Adams enjoying a majority of 5,445. There were angry scenes at the count in Belfast's City Hall and within days, the Fitt residence on the city's Antrim Road was destroyed in an arson attack.

1986 Westminster By-elections

In these January by-elections, 15 of the 17 Northern Ireland seats were contested. This was the consequence of the mass resignation by sitting unionist members, in protest at the signing of the Anglo-Irish Agreement towards the end of 1985. Unionists managed to obtain over 400,000 votes in protest at the signing of the Hillsborough Agreement, but in the process, they lost Newry and Armagh to Seamus Mallon of the SDLP (see Chapter Seven).

1987 Westminster General Election

In this June election, a relatively low turnout of voters was recorded (67.4 per cent). There was a slight dip in the vote for the Unionist Party (down from 57.1 per cent in 1983 to 54.8 per cent) on account of middle class unionists' misgivings over the anti-Agreement protest campaign and the boycotting of governmental institutions. The

Unionist Party still obtained 13 seats, though Enoch Powell lost South Down to the SDLP's Eddie McGrady. The SDLP performed well, winning 3 seats and increasing their share of the vote by 3.2 per cent.

1990 Westminster By-election
Following the death of the Unionist Party's Harold McCusker, 11 candidates (including one from the Conservative Party) contested the Upper Bann by-election. David Trimble of the UUP won with a large majority (13,849).

1992 Westminster General Election
This election witnessed a large number of candidates – 100 in total, representing 14 parties – standing across the region's 17 constituencies. The overall poll was 69.7 per cent. The SDLP enjoyed a good result, with their sitting MPs in Foyle (John Hume), Newry and Armagh (Seamus Mallon) and South Down (Eddie McGrady) enjoying increased majorities, and the party's share of the vote (23.5 per cent) up by 2.4 per cent. Winning support for its efforts in initiating secret peace talks, the party also gained West Belfast, where Joe Hendron defeated Gerry Adams at the third attempt (his majority was 589). Sinn Féin's defeat in this constituency was accompanied by a slight decline in its overall percentage of the poll (down from 11.4 per cent to 10 per cent). With Popular Unionist candidate, James Kilfedder retaining North Down, the UUP and the DUP shared the remaining 12 seats (9 and 3 respectively). The DUP's share of the vote increased slightly (from 11.7 per cent to 13.1 per cent), whilst the UUP's share fell by over 3 per cent (down from 37.8 per cent to 34.5 per cent). This probably reflected lasting irritation amongst middle-class Protestant voters over the ongoing mainstream unionist belligerence fuelled by the Anglo-Irish Agreement, over six years before.

1995 Westminster By-election
Following the death of Popular Unionist MP, James Kilfedder, who had held the North Down seat since 1979, Robert McCartney, leader of the United Kingdom Unionist Party (UKUP), won the seat with a majority of 2,892.

1996 Northern Ireland Forum Election
At the May contest for the newly-constituted Forum, the UUP's share of the vote dropped 5 per cent from the local council elections three years before. The DUP's share increased to 18.8 per cent, whilst Sinn Féin's record share of the vote (15.3 per cent) was an unpleasant shock for British premier, John Major. The increase in Sinn Féin's popularity was probably due to the IRA's original ceasefire in 1994, although this had broken down a few months before the election to the Forum. Despite its

success, Sinn Féin's vote was over 6 per cent down on the support given to the SDLP (21.4 per cent of the poll).

1997 Westminster General Election

This landslide victory for Tony Blair's "New Labour" also reflected significant changes in political fortunes in Northern Ireland. Apart from the creation of an additional seat (West Tyrone), there was alteration of existing constituency boundaries. Despite a record number of candidates (125) contesting the 18 seats, the overall turnout of the electorate was down by 2.4 per cent on the previous Westminster election (now 67.3 per cent), although yet again, there were considerable variations between the polls recorded in different constituencies. For instance, Mid-Ulster had a 85.8 per cent poll, compared to the 57.8 per cent turnout in the safe unionist seat of South Antrim. Sinn Féin, now openly engaged in peace negotiations, recorded its highest number of votes since 1955 (126,921 or 16.1 per cent of the poll), with Martin McGuinness winning a second seat for his party (Mid-Ulster). Other new MPs included the UUP's Jeffrey Donaldson and William Thompson, and two seats changed hands in an unusually dramatic election by Northern Ireland standards. These were West Belfast, where Gerry Adams regained his seat from Joe Hendron, and Mid-Ulster, where the DUP's Willie McCrea was defeated by Sinn Féin's Martin McGuinness. The UUP, which gained 32.7 per cent of all votes, won the new seat of West Tyrone and increased its Westminster representation to 10, though the DUP's representation fell to 2 (it had fielded 9 candidates and won 13.6 per cent of the poll). The SDLP, despite losing West Belfast, actually increased its share of the vote (from 23.5 per cent in 1992 to 24.1 per cent) and won 3 seats. The combined nationalist vote of 317,736 (40.2 per cent of the total votes cast) was the highest in Northern Ireland's history.

1998 Northern Ireland Assembly Election

This followed a referendum which supported the implementation of the Good Friday Agreement by 71 per cent to 29 per cent. The new Assembly, elected on the STV system of proportional representation, was to be composed of 108 members or MLAs, divided along the lines of the 18 Westminster constituencies, with 6 members in each.

The election broadly endorsed the verdict of the referendum. Anti-agreement parties only gained 28 seats, a minority even within the loyalist community, though the poll was relatively low (68.7 per cent). The UUP won most seats, 28 with a 21.3 per cent share of the vote, followed by the SDLP with 24 seats and 22 per cent of the total poll. The DUP spearheaded loyalist opposition to the Belfast Agreement, winning 20 seats and 18.1 per cent of the vote, and Sinn Féin obtained 18 seats with

17.6 per cent of the poll. The voting system was kind to the smaller parties, several of which were less focused on the constitutional question, and 18 MLAs from a range of political groups were elected, including representatives from former loyalist paramilitary groups, the Women's Coalition Party and six from the Alliance Party.

2001 Westminster General Election
The Ulster Unionists won the highest number of seats (6) for any party in the contest, though hot on their heels were the DUP with 5 seats and Sinn Féin with 4, whilst the SDLP won 3 (Seamus Mallon's majority over Sinn Féin's Conor Murphy was only 1,011). David Trimble was also returned, albeit with a reduced majority, in Upper Bann (this was down from over 9,000 in 1997 to just 2,058). Other interesting results in this election included: the DUP's Gregory Campbell's victory over long-serving UUP representative, Willie Ross in East Londonderry (the latter's previous majority of 4,000 was overturned by Campbell, who enjoyed a 1,901 majority); Sinn Féin's Michelle Gildernew's narrow win in Fermanagh & South Tyrone (she defeated Unionist James Cooper, who had been hoping to win the seat held by Ken Maginnis for 18 years, by a mere 53 votes); the winning of the Strangford seat by the DUP's Iris Robinson (her majority over the UUP's David McNarry was 1,110); and the UUP's David Burnside's ousting of sitting DUP member, Willie McCrea in South Antrim (Burnside's majority was 1,011).

2003 Northern Ireland Assembly Election
This election constituted a significant shift in the balance of political power in the region and can be seen as evidence of parties on the political extremes beginning to assume the role of mainstream parties. The DUP won 25.7 per cent first-preference votes and 30 seats, and Sinn Féin enjoyed a 23.5 per cent slice of the vote, with 24 of their candidates being elected to the Assembly. On the other hand, the SDLP's share of the vote had dropped to 17 per cent and they won 18 seats, whilst the UUP's representation in the Assembly was down by one to 27, although its share of the poll rose marginally, to 22.7 per cent (see Chapter Eight).

2005 Westminster General Election
The political breakthrough of the parties representing the political extremes in Northern Ireland in 2003 was consolidated at these Westminster elections two years later, when the DUP and Sinn Féin won the bulk (14) of the seats between them. The DUP got the lion's share (9 seats and 33.7 per cent of the votes cast overall), with Sinn Féin winning 5 and gaining 24.3 per cent of the poll. The other 4 seats were shared between the SDLP (3 seats and 17.5 per cent of the vote) and the UUP which, although it won 17.7 per cent of the vote, managed to return only one member, Lady

Sylvia Hermon in North Down. This nadir in the fortunes of the UUP, coming ironically in its centenary year, was encapsulated by party leader, David Trimble's loss to the DUP's David Simpson in Upper Bann; 3 of the UUP's 4 lost seats went to the DUP, with the other, South Belfast, being claimed by the SDLP's Alasdair McDonnell (the first time the constituency had been won by a nationalist).

2007 Northern Ireland Assembly Election
In this contest, the DUP and Sinn Féin asserted their dominance of local politics by making significant gains. The former party won an additional 6 seats (now 36, with a 30.1 per cent share of the vote) and Sinn Féin gained an additional 4 seats (now 28 MLAs, with 26.2 per cent first-preference votes). The UUP returned 18 of its candidates (its share of the vote was 14.9 per cent and its number of representatives in the Assembly was reduced by 9) and the SDLP won 16, with a 15.2 per cent share of the poll (this was 2 down on the 2003 contest). The result of the Alliance Party was interesting as it appeared to reflect a bucking in this trend of a swing to the parties representing the political extremes, with the party's creditable return of 7 MLAs and 5.2 per cent of the poll.

2010 Westminster General Election
Once again, over two-thirds of the seats were won by the DUP and Sinn Féin. The former returned 8 representatives (winning a quarter of all votes cast) and republicans won 5 seats, with a poll of 25.5 per cent. The SDLP won 3 seats and gained 16.5 per cent of the vote, but for the first time in its history, the UUP failed to return a MP to Westminster (its share of the vote was 15.2 per cent). The Alliance Party's Naomi Long defeated DUP party leader Peter Robinson in East Belfast, whilst Michelle Gildernew (Sinn Féin), with a majority of just 4 votes, was again a narrow victor in Fermanagh & South Tyrone.

2011 Northern Ireland Assembly Election
The DUP won 38 of the 108 seats in the Assembly (gaining 30 per cent of the total vote), with Sinn Féin returning 29 candidates and harnessing 26.9 per cent of first-preference votes. More moderate parties claimed just over a third of the seats, with the UUP returning 16 MLAs (on 13.2 per cent of the vote), the SDLP, 14 (on 14.2 per cent of the poll) and Alliance winning 8 seats (7.7 per cent of first-preference votes).

2015 Westminster General Election
Although the DUP and Sinn Féin again gained the lion's share of the Northern Irish seats, this election which saw the Conservative Party win an overall majority, and also witnessed the return of two Ulster Unionists to Parliament. Danny Kinahan

ousted the sitting DUP member, Willie McCrea in South Antrim (he had a majority of 949), and former party leader, Tom Elliott defeated Michelle Gildernew (Sinn Féin) in Fermanagh & South Tyrone (his majority was 530). The DUP won a seat back in East Belfast, where Gavin Robinson enjoyed a 2,597 majority over sitting member, Naomi Long (Alliance). The SDLP retained its seats in Foyle, South Down and Belfast South, where sitting member Alasdair McDonnell confounded critics by retaining his seat, with a 906 victory over the DUP's Jonathan Bell. Sinn Féin retained 4 of its 5 seats, winning in West Belfast, Newry and Armagh, Mid-Ulster and Tyrone West. With the exception of Fermanagh & South Tyrone (where 72.5 per cent turned out to vote), the poll returns were significantly below usual levels, dropping below 60 per cent in most constituencies.

2016 Assembly Election
The party pacts which had been largely responsible for the surprise election of two UUP MPs at the Westminster election the previous year were not in operation for this contest. Here, the DUP and Sinn Féin maintained their domination of their respective sections of the Northern Irish community, with each party obtaining remarkably similar results to 2011. The DUP – fighting the contest under recently-appointed party leader, Arlene Foster – again gained 38 seats, whilst Sinn Féin lost a single representative in the Assembly (now holding 28 sears). The UUP again returned 16 candidates to the Assembly, but the SDLP only managed to return 12 Assembly representatives (a reduction of 2 from the 2011 contest). Alliance again came out on top of the minor parties, returning 8 of its candidates, whilst two other parties managed to have 2 of their candidates elected – the Green Party and the People Before Profit Alliance (PBPA).

Perhaps the most remarkable result was in West Belfast, where Gerry Carroll (PBPA) surprised Sinn Féin by topping the poll. Several sitting MLAs – including independent John McAllister, Sinn Féin's Phil Flanagan, Ian McCrea of the DUP and the SDLP's Dolores Kelly – failed in their quests to be reelected. Once again, there were signs of electoral fatigue, with just over 54 per cent of the electorate (some 703,744 voters) casting their preferences. This, however, camouflaged significant differences in turnout between certain constituencies, which ranged from a higher poll of 64.5 per cent recorded in Fermanagh & South Tyrone, to the relatively low figure of 49.5 per cent recorded in North Down.

2017 Assembly Election
This unscheduled contest was the outcome of the Executive's sudden collapse. Precipitated by the resignation of Sinn Féin's Deputy First Minister Martin McGuinness in protest over Arlene Foster's involvement in a botched green energy

scheme, the election campaign was a bitter one even by Northern Ireland's standards, with the DUP leader expressing her scorn at Sinn Féin's 'crocodile' tendencies. Issues debated during the campaign included the influence of Brexit negotiations on Northern Ireland's border with the Irish Republic, same sex marriage, the legislation of abortion in Northern Ireland, the role of the Irish language and the legacy of the Troubles, but most exchanges were restricted to personal and political insults.

UUP leader Mike Nesbitt's advocacy of cross-community vote transfers backfired, resulting in his party's weak performance (its representation in the Assembly was down to 10 MLAs) and his own subsequent resignation. The rancid nature of the campaign and a fiery leaders' debate on the eve of polling captured the electorate's interest, with close to 10 per cent more electors casting their votes than in the previous year's election (64.8 per cent in 2017). The chief beneficaries of this snap election were Sinn Féin and its new Stormont leader Michelle O'Neill. The party's overall vote increased slightly but the group succeeded in reducing the DUP's majority in the smaller-sized Assembly (now 90 instead of 108 members) from 10 MLAs to one (28 and 27 representatives respectively). Sinn Féin claimed it was a watershed result, on account of the combined republican and nationalist representation pipping that of the unionist parties for the first time in the region's history. Although the Alliance's share of the vote increased (it returned 8 MLAs) and the SDLP secured a respectable return (12 MLAs), the domination of the parties on the political margins continued.

2017 Westminster Election

Following Theresa May's snap decision to call a general election in June 2017, Northern Ireland experienced its fourth election inside a two-year period. The Brexit issue dominated another bitter campaign and despite voters' understandable election fatigue, high turnouts were reported in most constituencies. The relatively strong performances of the UUP and SDLP in the previous Westminster contest were not repeated, with the parties of the extremes continuing their domination of Northern Ireland's political scene. The DUP gained another 2 seats, increasing their Westminster representation to 10 (the party gained 36 per cent of the vote), whilst Sinn Féin gained 3 seats (up to 7 representatives and winning 29 per cent of the vote), with the principal losers being the SDLP (who lost its 3 seats) and the UUP, which lost both seats it had won in 2015.

It soon transpired that a surprisingly close national election result meant that the DUP held the balance of power at Westminster. Relishing its new role as "deal-makers", the party's negotiators won a £1-billion-plus package for the region in return for backing the minority Tory administration in parliament. Derided by journals such as the *Daily Mirror* for accepting "a shady bung" from a desperate

Conservative administration and lampooned for being "a party of crackpots", the DUP's good fortune had produced an economic bonanza for the citizens of Northern Ireland. However, these short-term economic gains had to be balanced alongside the likely long-term fallout in terms of public opinion and political support in Great Britain. Another short-term casualty of the DUP–Conservative alliance was a speedy restoration in the operation of the region's Assembly, where Sinn Féin bitterly resented the new political arrangement at Westminster.

Endnotes

1. *Daily Mirror*, 27 June 2017

APPENDIX TWO

Biographical Notes

Gerry Adams

Born in 1948, Adams was brought up and educated in west Belfast, going on to work as a barman before the start of the modern conflict. A member of a prominent republican family, he was interned in 1971. He is believed to have been commander of the IRA's Belfast Brigade during the early 1970s, though he has always denied IRA membership. Adams participated in the unsuccessful London ceasefire talks (1972), and was released from Long Kesh in 1976. Appointed vice president of Sinn Féin in 1978, he became its president in 1983. He played a prominent role during the "hunger" protest (1980–1) and entered politics, winning a seat in the Belfast Assembly (1982). The following year, he was elected West Belfast MP, but like all elected Sinn Féin representatives, refused to take his seat at Westminster. He successfully defended this seat in the 1987 election, but was defeated by the SDLP's Joe Hendron in 1992. Adams won the seat back in 1997, and was also successful in the 2001 and 2005 Westminster elections. He was a major player in the peace process talks and the negotiations which preceded the signing of the Belfast Agreement (1998). He was elected as an Irish Parliament representative (TD) for Louth in 2011.

Jack Beattie

A north Belfast Presbyterian, Beattie, who was born in 1888, spent his early working life in a textile factory and later trained as a blacksmith, before becoming a trade union official (1918–25). A supporter of Irish unity, he was elected NILP MP for East Belfast in the Northern parliament and served for over twenty years. Expelled from the party in 1934, he was later readmitted and became its leader in 1942 after Harry Midgley's resignation (two years later, he was expelled again). Beattie was elected Westminster MP for West Belfast (1943–50), and later on an Irish Labour ticket (1951–5). He was defeated by a Sinn Féin candidate in the Westminster election of 1955 and subsequently retired from politics. He died in 1960.

Basil Brooke

From an aristocratic County Fermanagh farming family, Brooke was educated at Winchester and Sandhurst. He was decorated for his service during World War I. Brooke entered politics in the late 1920s, becoming MP for Lisnaskea in 1929. He held government posts as minister of agriculture (1933–41), and minister of commerce and production (1941–5). In 1943, at the age of 55, Brooke succeeded John Andrews as prime minister of Northern Ireland. He led his party and government for twenty years, adopting a largely one-dimensional, "not-an-inch" approach to politics (this was most evident in his quick decision to call an election in 1949, in response to John Costello's announcement that he was leading the south of Ireland into a Republic. Brooke was elevated to the title of Viscount Brookeborough in 1952. He resigned his Stormont parliamentary seat in 1967, but continued to make political pronouncements, particularly in criticism of the liberal unionism of his nephew, Terence O'Neill. He died in 1973.

James Craig

Born in Belfast in 1871, Craig was a landowner and businessman, primarily as a director of Dunville's distillery in Belfast. He served as a captain in the Royal Irish Rifles during the South African War. Craig represented County Down as a Unionist MP (1906–18) and, after the war, was Westminster MP for Mid-Down (1918–21). The organiser of many anti-Home Rule meetings in Ireland and Great Britain between 1911 and 1914, he was quarter master general of the 36th Ulster Division (1914–16). He was knighted in 1918, and gained governmental experience as parliamentary secretary to the minister of pensions (1919–20) and financial secretary to the admiralty (1920–1). He succeeded Sir Edward Carson as leader of the Ulster Unionists in February 1921, and went on to represent County Down in the Northern parliament (1921–40). Craig served as Northern Ireland's first prime minister (1921–40) and was in charge of an administration which introduced draconian anti-terrorist legislation (May 1922). He was elevated to the title of Viscount Craigavon in 1927. He died in 1940.

William Craig

Born in Cookstown in 1924, Craig was educated at Dungannon Royal and Larne Grammar Schools, before studying law at Queen's University, Belfast. He served in the RAF (1943–6) and qualified as a solicitor in 1952. He was elected to Stormont as MP for Larne in 1960. He held several ministerial posts, including government chief whip (1962–3), minister for home affairs (1963–4 and 1966–8) and minister for development (1965–6), before being sacked from his Home Affairs post by Terence O'Neill in 1968. Becoming a strident critic of liberal unionism, Craig was defeated by Brian Faulkner for the Unionist Party leadership in 1971. The following year, he founded the Vanguard Unionist Progressive Party, and was elected to Westminster as MP for East Belfast February 1974. Narrowly defeated (by 64 votes) by the DUP's Peter Robinson, Craig left politics in the early 1980s. He died in Belfast in 2011.

Bernadette Devlin

Another native of Cookstown, Devlin was born in 1947. She studied psychology at Queen's University, Belfast, where she soon became a Civil Rights Association member and a leading light in the left-wing group, the People's Democracy. She was elected to Westminster in 1969 as an independent MP for Mid-Ulster, when she became the youngest ever female representative. She was imprisoned for inciting a riot in Derry's Bogside in 1969. Devlin was ejected from the Commons for striking Home Secretary, Reginald Maudling during a debate about Bloody Sunday (1972), and was defeated at the February 1974 election. She founded the Irish Republican Socialist Party (IRSP) in 1974, and became a member of the National H-Block Committee (1980). Bernadette McAliskey (as she was now known) was seriously wounded in an attack at her home by loyalist paramilitaries, but recovered sufficiently to act as a spokesperson for Bobby Sands during his election campaign later in 1981.

Joseph Devlin

Popularly known as "Wee Joe", Devlin was born in west Belfast in 1871 (his family originally came from County Tyrone). Educated at the Christian Brothers' School in Belfast, he began his working life as a barman, before starting work at the *Irish News* (he later became the paper's chairman). Devlin was appointed Secretary of the United Irish League (UIL) in 1901, and its British secretary in 1902. He represented Kilkenny as a Home Rule MP at Westminster (1902–6) and was general secretary of the party (1904–20). He was elected Westminster MP for West Belfast in 1906, where he served until 1918 and then went on to represent the new constituency of Belfast Falls until 1922. Devlin was a MP in the Northern parliament for County Antrim from 1921 to 1925, and for West Belfast from 1925 until 1929. He also served as MP for Belfast Central (1929–34) and was leader of the Nationalist opposition in the Northern parliament from 1922 until 1934. Devlin also represented Fermanagh & South Tyrone at Westminster from 1929 until his death in 1934. He served as president of the Ancient Order of Hibernians from 1905 to 1934.

Patrick Devlin

Born in Belfast, Devlin worked in a mill, before being interned at the age of 17 for IRA membership in 1942. He joined the Irish Labour Party in 1950, and was a Labour councillor (1956) before joining the NILP in 1958. He was elected as a

Stormont MP for Falls (1969–72) and was a founding member of the SDLP in 1970. Devlin represented the SDLP in the Assembly (1973–4), and was minister for health and social security in the Executive. He also sat in the Northern Ireland Convention (1975–6), but was expelled from the party in 1977. He died in 1999.

Brian Faulkner

Born in Helen's Bay, County Down in 1921, Faulkner was educated in Armagh and at St Columba's College, Dublin. He joined his father's textile business and was elected to Stormont as Unionist Party MP for East Down in 1949. He held a number of ministerial posts, including chief whip (1956), minister of home affairs (1959–63), minister of commerce (1964–9) and minister for development (1969–71). He was narrowly defeated by James Chichester-Clark for the party leadership in 1969, but in 1971 succeeded him as party leader, and then prime minister. Faulkner was widely criticised for introducing internment in the summer of 1971. He resigned as prime minister after the announcement of direct rule in March 1972. He angered many in his party by signing the Sunningdale Agreement (1973) and was appointed chief executive of the Northern Ireland Assembly in 1974. After this collapsed in May 1974, he formed the Unionist Party of Northern Ireland (UPNI). Brian Faulkner retired from politics in 1976 and was awarded the title of Lord Faulkner of Downpatrick, shortly before being killed in a riding accident in 1977.

Gerry Fitt

Born in Belfast's Docks district, Fitt was educated at the city's Christian Brothers' School. He joined the Merchant Navy in 1941 at the age of 15, serving there for twelve years, before entering politics. He served in Belfast City Council before being elected Republican Labour MP for Stormont's Dock constituency in 1962. His seventeen-year spell as a colourful, well-known Westminster MP started when he was elected in West Belfast (1966). Fitt spent his early years in Parliament encouraging the Labour Party to take a closer interest in the affairs of Northern Ireland. He was the co-founder of the Social Democratic and Labour Party (SDLP) in 1970, and served in the ill-fated Assembly (1973–4) and Convention (1975–6). He was deputy chief executive in the power-sharing Executive (1974). He resigned from the SDLP in 1979, sitting at Westminster as an independent socialist. Fitt was defeated by Sinn Féin's Gerry Adams in the 1983 general election, and following an arson attack on his north Belfast home shortly afterwards, moved his family permanently to London. In 1983, he was awarded the title of Lord Fitt of Dock. He died in Kent in 2005.

Cahir Healy

Born into a farming family in County Donegal in 1877, Healy worked as a reporter for the *Fermanagh News* and became a Gaelic League activist. He was also involved in early Irish Republican Brotherhood and Sinn Féin activity. Staunchly opposed to Partition in 1921, he was interned on the *Argenta* in 1922. He had been elected as Fermanagh & South Tyrone representative at Westminster, but was subsequently interned. Following his release from prison, he was elected as MP for South Fermanagh in the Northern parliament (a position he maintained for forty years), and along with Joe Devlin, formed the National League. He was later elected on two occasions as the representative for Fermanagh & South Tyrone at Westminster (from 1931–5 and 1950–5). For part of his time as a political representative, he abstained from participation in parliamentary life. Perceived as a threat to national security, he was interned in Brixton Prison in London (1941–2). He joined the APL in 1945. He retired from political life in 1965, spending much of his time spearheading a campaign to establish the Ulster Folk and Transport Museum. He died in 1970 at the age of 93.

Tommy Henderson

A popular independent unionist for Belfast Shankill's constituency in the northern parliament for over twenty years, Henderson had started working life as a house painter. Elected as MP for North Belfast in 1925, he was returned in the Shankill in 1929, serving until 1953. He was unusual in unionist circles, in that he concentrated on the social and economic conditions directly affecting his constituents. He also held the record for the longest speech made at Stormont (some nine-and-a-half hours, delivered in May 1936).

John Hume

Hume was born in Derry in 1937, and educated at St Columb's College, Maynooth and Queen's University, Belfast. His early working life was spent as a languages teacher, and he also forged a reputation locally when he founded a housing association and credit union in Derry. A leading member of the Civil Rights Association (1967–9), he was elected to Stormont as an independent for Foyle (1969). He was a founder member of the SDLP in 1970 and sat in the Assembly (1973–4), where he was also appointed minister of commerce in its Executive. He was elected as a European MEP in 1979, and replaced Gerry Fitt as SDLP leader, also in 1979. Hume was also elected to Westminster as MP for Foyle in 1983. He was the architect of the New Ireland Forum proposals (1984), and acted as a conduit between Sinn Féin and the British government in their quest to secure a lasting republican ceasefire. In 1999 John Hume was, along with David Trimble, awarded the Nobel Prize for his contribution to the Northern Ireland Peace Process. He resigned as SDLP leader in 2003.

Martin McGuinness

Another native of Derry, McGuinness was born in 1950. He worked as a butcher's apprentice, before becoming a senior officer in the Provisional IRA during the early 1970s. He was arrested and imprisoned in the Irish Republic in 1972. He became prominent in Sinn Féin during the 1980s, and was elected Sinn Féin MP for Mid-Ulster in 1997, though like other elected party representatives, he did not take up his seat at Westminster. A keen supporter of the Good Friday Agreement in 1998, he was elected as a MLA for Mid-Ulster. He was appointed deputy first minister in 2007, serving alongside Ian Paisley and later Peter Robinson. In a memorable moment, he met Queen Elizabeth during her visit to Belfast in 2012. McGuinness resigned as deputy first minister in January 2017 in protest at Arlene Foster's involvement in a failed green energy scheme and her subsequent refusal to stand down as first minister. He died two months later.

James McSparran

McSparran was a member of a prominent Catholic family in County Antrim and practised as a barrister. A leading member of the Ancient Order of Hibernians, he entered politics in 1945, becoming Nationalist member for the Mourne constituency (he was to remain in this seat for thirteen years). He was the leader of the APL during the pivotal "Chapel Gate" election of 1949.

Harry Midgley

Born in north Belfast in 1892, Midgley worked as a joiner and served during World War I. A member of the ILP before the war, he became a Labour councillor in 1925 and was elected a Labour MP for Dock at Stormont (1933–8). Chairman of the NILP, he resigned from the party after failing to persuade its members to formally accept the Union. Midgley formed the Commonwealth Labour Party in 1942 and represented the East Belfast constituency of Willowfield at Stormont. He joined the Unionist Party in 1947, serving as minister for labour (1949) and minister for education (1950–7). Harry Midgley died suddenly at the age of 65, after attending a teachers' conference in County Down.

James Molyneaux

Born in County Antrim in 1920, Molyneaux served in the RAF during World War II. He held senior positions in the County Antrim Unionist Association and the Orange Order during the 1960s and early 1970s. He was elected to Westminster as MP for South Antrim (1970–83) and for Lagan Valley (1983–97), and also served as a Unionist representative for South Antrim in the Assembly (1982–6). Molyneaux was defeated by Harry West for the party leadership in 1974, though he became leader of the Ulster Unionist group of MPs at Westminster and subsequently was appointed leader of the Ulster Unionist Party (1979–95). He was joint leader of the unionist protest against the Anglo-Irish Agreement (1985–7). He was knighted in 1996 and elevated to a peerage (Lord Molyneaux of Killead) in 1997. He died in 2014.

Terence O'Neill

Born in London in 1914 and educated at Eton, this Anglo-Irish aristocrat served as an officer in the Irish Guards during World War II. Elected unopposed as Unionist MP for Bannside at a Stormont by-election in 1946, O'Neill held a number of ministerial posts, including minister of home affairs (1956) and finance minister (1956–63). He succeeded Lord Brookeborough as Unionist Party leader and prime minister in 1963. His six years in post were characterised by his "liberal" approach, both to the province's Catholic minority and the administrations of the Irish Republic, and his meeting with Irish premier in 1965 was the first of its kind since the early 1920s. O'Neill's reform programme, allied to the Civil Rights street protests, resulted in serious divisions within mainstream unionism, and these were brought to the fore in the "Crossroads" election (1969), which would ultimately result in his resignation and retirement from politics. He was elevated to the title of Lord O'Neill of the Maine of Ahoghill in 1970, and spent his retirement in Hampshire. He died in 1990.

Ian Paisley

Paisley was born in County Armagh in 1926, but spent most of his formative years in Ballymena, County Antrim. Ordained in Wales in 1946, he was the co-founder and moderator of the Free Presbyterian Church in 1951, and first came to public prominence after leading street protests against ecumenism during the 1960s. He orchestrated several counter-marches in opposition to Civil Rights protesters and was imprisoned in 1968 for obstructing one of these marches. His political career started with a rare defeat against Terence O'Neill in Bannside in 1969, but he won the seat the following year when he was also elected Protestant Unionist MP for the Westminster constituency of North Antrim. Paisley founded the DUP in 1971 and during the early 1970s was committed to a policy of Northern Ireland's integration in the United Kingdom. An initially reluctant supporter of the UWC Strike in 1974, he organised a workers' stoppage which failed to receive sufficient support (1977). He was elected an MEP in the region's first European election in 1979, and led a "Carson trail" protest against British-Irish governmental talks across Ulster two years later. He was the joint leader and main public spokesman of Ulster's resistance to the Anglo-Irish Agreement (1985–7). Paisley and his supporters strongly condemned the Good Friday Agreement (1998). However, he agreed to share power with Sinn Féin and became Northern Ireland's first minister in 2007. He resigned from this post and that of the leadership of the DUP in 2008. He was elevated to the title of Lord Bannside in 2010. He died in 2014.

Peter Robinson

Born in Belfast in 1948, Robinson worked in insurance and as an estate agent before entering politics. A founder member of the DUP and party secretary (1972), he was elected Westminster MP for East Belfast in 1979, beating sitting MP, William Craig by a mere 64 votes. Deputy leader of the DUP for nearly thirty years, he was elected to the Assembly in 1998. Robinson initially earned a reputation for being a hard-liner, an image which was reinforced by his leading a loyalist "invasion" of the County Monaghan town of Clontibret in 1986. He succeeded Ian Paisley as first minister (2008). In 2010, he was sensationally defeated by Naomi Long (Alliance) at the Westminster general election.

John Taylor

Born in Armagh in 1937, Taylor was educated at Royal School Armagh and Queen's University, Belfast. A civil engineer and successful businessman, he was elected Unionist MP for South Tyrone at Stormont in 1965. He served in the last Stormont administration as a minister at the Home Affairs department (1970–2). Seriously wounded in an assassination attempt by the Official IRA in 1972, he soon returned to political life. He was elected Unionist MP for Strangford West at Westminster (1983–2001) and appointed Unionist Party deputy leader in 1995. He also served in Brussels as a MEP (1979–89). He was elevated to the title of Lord Kilclooney in 2001.

David Trimble

Born in 1944, Trimble was educated at Bangor Grammar School and Queen's University, Belfast, where he lectured in law for over twenty years. He was elected as a VUPP Convention member for South Belfast in 1975, and later appointed deputy leader. He joined the UUP in 1978 and was honorary secretary of the UUP Executive. He was elected Unionist MP for Upper Bann at Westminster in 1990, and became his party's leader five years later. He was heavily involved in the stand-offs at Drumcree in County Armagh during the late 1990s, a role which earned him a hard-line reputation. He was elected to serve the Upper Bann constituency in the Northern Ireland Forum (1996) and Assembly (1998). David Trimble was appointed first minister of Northern Ireland (1998–2002). He received the Nobel Prize (along with John Hume) for his contribution to the Northern Ireland Peace Process in 1999. After losing his Westminster seat in 2005, he resigned from the party leadership. The following year, he was elevated to the title of Lord Trimble.

Index